Value-Driven IT

Achieving Agility and Assurance
Without Compromising Either

Cliff Berg

Cliff Berg Imprints, Reston VA, USA

Many of the designations used by manufacturers and sellers to distinguish their products are claimed as trademarks. Where those designations appear in this book, and the publisher was aware of a trademark claim, the designations have been printed with initial capital letters or in all capitals.

The author and publisher have taken care in the preparation of this book, but make no expressed or implied warranty of any kind and assume no responsibility for errors or omissions. No liability is assumed for incidental or consequential damages in connections with or arising out of the use of the information contained herein.

Dilbert cartoons used by permission of United Media. They may not be reproduced (except for "fair use") without permission from United Media.

Other books by Cliff Berg:

High-Assurance Design: Architecting Secure and Reliable Enterprise Applications. Addison-Wesley, 2005.
Advanced Java 2 Development for Enterprise Applications. Sun Microsystems Press, Prentice Hall, 2000.
Advanced Java Development for Enterprise Applications. Prentice Hall, 1998.

Table of Contents

Figures

Tables

Comments From Reviewers

Angela Yochem, SVP Strategic Architecture, Bank of America:

"I was surprised as I read through the book to realize that the intended audience must be folks like me – concerned about organizational effectiveness and strategy, and comfortable with the notion of "agile" as introduced in the technical community years ago… I am thrilled to see such a thoughtfully constructed book. Every C-level technology officer, their staffs and all architects should have this… This is the type of book that folks will read more than once."

Diane R. Murphy, PhD, Chair, Information Technology, Marymount University, Arlington, VA.

"The two-part book is very thought provoking… In Part 2 of the book, Cliff Berg puts the principles developed earlier in the book into practice… He suggests focusing on the increased expected value of the total set of features and accounting for the opportunity that is presented once all features are complete. This is especially important for enterprise architecture elements… This book is recommended reading for everyone in IT leadership, provoking thought about how to improve IT integration into mainstream business processes."

Dianne Houghton, former CEO, Digital Focus.

"The question that must drive every decision, every action in an organization is 'What is the value that this brings to our business, to our customer, to our stakeholders?' Many businesses have learned the merit of bringing what were once dismissed as 'back office' activities – finance and human capital – into a more strategic role with direct responsibility for creating business value. Why, then, does IT continue to escape this mandate? Why, in the midst of many other strategic alignments, does IT remain the group that must be 'connected to', or 'translated from'.

"Cliff Berg presents a compelling argument for the benefit of changing this condition from both the business and IT point of view. Better still, he lays out a thoughtful, detailed approach for doing so, mapping a path to ensuring IT professionals understand and consider the business value of their decisions and actions in their day-to-day work."

Craig Connell, Director of IT, Unistar Nuclear.

"People discuss aligning IT with the business every day, without really understanding what it means or the implications. Cliff not only brings visibility around the types of issues that cause misalignment, but also provides meaningful, applicable, and concrete ways of recognizing the issues, resolving them, and measuring success through business value… Cliff insightfully recognizes some of the issues that cause communication failures between IT and the business… I thoroughly enjoyed this book and the perspective it provided for both people roles thought of as 'traditional' business and IT."

Foreword

By Mark Lutchen

Business Value and IT - For some executives, even placing those words in the same sentence can be considered an oxymoron. Others would argue that you can focus on achieving business value and get it right or you can focus on delivering IT and get it right, but never the twain shall meet. I would argue that the real imperative within organizations today is to ensure that business value and IT are so commingled and intertwined with each other, that to not focus on getting them both right or to not understand how dependent each is upon the other, is to set up your organization for potentially disastrous failure.

The complexity and rapid pace of change in business today is rivalled only by the even more rapid pace of change and the never-ending complexity associated with anything IT. It's a fact of life, and as a former Global CIO of an organization operating in 150 countries with the purpose of servicing a highly mobile and demand user base, I can tell you with all candor that your role is to live with it and make it work. The days of IT people knowing little about the businesses they serve and business people knowing little about the IT services they consume are long gone. In today's world, there are very few strategic business solutions that can be achieved without having some IT component to them. On the other hand, there isn't a single IT activity, effort, asset, or expenditure that should be made without linking it, directly or indirectly, to a business goal or objective in some manner. In today's world, IT is expected to constantly meet an exponentially growing set of business expectations. To meet the challenges ahead successfully will require closing the communication gap between IT and the business.

The subtitle of this book, *Achieving Agility and Assurance without Compromising Either*, actually tells the whole story. The game going forward will no longer be about either/or. Rather, it will be about doing both, it will be about cause and effect, it will be about tight coordination and collaboration, it will be about effective balance, and it will surely be about effective leverage. In this book, Cliff Berg has done an admirable job of pointing out many of the practical reasons *why* this must be done and *how* to make it happen by weaving together a very credible latticework of concepts, approaches, advice, and real examples. This book presents a *call to action* for many different players within the IT organization - CIO's, IT architects, developers, programmers, and implementers, among others.

The combination of agility and substance can be very powerful, indeed. Winning organizations of tomorrow will recognize the need for both and also have the capability to understand that driving value into IT is a continuing journey, rather than an event or a single end-point. Hopefully, as this journey progresses across more and more organizations, so too will the recognition that business value and IT are not just distant cousins, but rather more like inseparable, identical twins.

Mark D. Lutchen

Partner and Practice Leader, IT Business Risk Management Practice, PriceWaterhouse Coopers

Author of *Managing IT as a Business* (John Wiley & Sons, 2004)

March 2008

Foreword

By Scott Ambler

Agile software development methods, techniques, and philosophies have clearly crossed the chasm in North America and I suspect are just about to do so in the rest of the world. Project teams are discovering that agile approaches, when implemented correctly, do in fact improve time to value through a combination of proven development techniques and improved management of project risk. The majority of organizations have discovered that agile approaches can be tailored to meet the needs of their unique situation. Being successful at agile software development is only the first step, now we must learn how to apply agile in a disciplined and assured manner – that's going to be easier said than done.

Cliff Berg shows how to take this next step in the pages of this book. He examines many of the debilitating misconceptions that people have regarding IT, misconceptions often held by IT managers with decades of experience. As an executive coach who specializes in helping senior IT executives to transition their organizations to more effective ways of working I'm often astounded by how rarely these executives have stopped to question and examine the traditional IT strategies of yesteryear. Or worse yet, how every few years they manage to fall for slightly different flavors of traditional strategies which they themselves have seen fail several times before. You need to get off that treadmill and try a new strategy if you're to have any hope of success.

For example, I can safely say that Chapter 4 where Cliff examines control-based governance is worth the cost of the book. When bureaucrats are allowed to define the governance processes we shouldn't be surprised when we wind up with bureaucratic, inefficient governance which is ignored by the people in the trenches. Yet how many times has your organization attempted to put an IT governance program in place, or even something simpler such as a data governance program, only to see it fizzle out a year or two later after having little or no impact on the way that you work? Your governance programs didn't fail for lack of management support, or lack of resources, or lack of sensible policies (okay, that may have been a problem in some cases), instead they likely failed because they didn't reflect basic human nature. IT professionals are intelligent, educated people and as such they rarely like to be told what to do or how to do it. Intellectual works need to be motivated. They need to be enabled. They need to be respected. Effective governance programs have a foundation in these three concepts, they're not based on an outdated command-and-control philosophy from the age of "organization man."

Cliff argues that we need to rethink our concept of IT organizational maturity, and I couldn't agree more. In practice few people are interested in repeatable processes, what they really want are repeatable results. The implication is that to achieve this organizations must be flexible so that they can adapt to the situation, all the while doing so in a disciplined and consistent manner. This level of disciplined agility within IT is difficult to achieve, and over the next few years will prove to be a significant competitive advantage to the first organizations in their respective market sectors until like all advantages is whittled away as the survivors catch up. Will your organization choose to be a leader or a follower?

This book addresses fundamental business issues in a refreshing manner which has been missing for years from the IT discussion. Cliff correctly promotes the concept of tangible business value measurement as being critical, yet this is something that most organizations give lip service to at best. More important, and yet another feature which justifies the investment in this book, is the focus on Total Value of Ownership (TVO) over Total Cost of Ownership (TCO). Both are important, but at the end of the day the primary goal of your IT efforts is to provide value to your organization. Interestingly, agile approaches reduce your time to value while at the same time reduce your TCO through increased quality.

This book exudes common sense based on real-world experience. It doesn't hold out any quick-fix, silver bullets but instead promotes practical strategies for methodically improving your IT organization in a viable manner. Many of the core ideas of the book seem straightforward and obvious, yet time and again not only do I see organizations not following them I see them actively fighting against them. These ideas include: if your governance effort hasn't impacted execution then it's clearly failed; you need to focus on enabling and not controlling people; you should implement passive controls instead of checks/reviews (the equivalent of teaching people to drive in a disciplined manner instead of installing speed bumps); you should address the problems at the root cause instead of putting bands over them; and do not focus on artifacts/documentation but instead on activities of understanding information.

Within IBM we're focused on improving our own productivity, time to value, and quality. As a result we're not just adopting agile strategies, but instead are adopting disciplined agile strategies which can prove to be a very big difference in practice. Disciplined agile is the sweet spot between "out of the box" agile and "out of the box" assurance, a theme that Cliff explores thoughtfully throughout this book. This is a great book, I've learned a few things, and it's definitely been an honor to write this foreword. I've already started talking this book up with key executives within IBM and the customers that I'm working with.

My advice: Read this book and hope that your competitors don't.

Scott W. Ambler
Practice Leader Agile Development, IBM Rational

Author of *Maturing Usability: Quality in Software, Interaction, and Value,* 2007; *Refactoring Databases: Evolutionary Database Design,* 2006; *The Enterprise Unified Process: Extending the Rational Unified Process,* 2005; and many others.

May 2008

Preface

In this book I make the case for connecting business value with IT efforts. This has been tried countless times before, but today only a minority of firms are able to make this connection. It is a hard problem, and the gulf between IT and business is as great as it ever was. I believe that this is because of an excessive focus on project cost over value, as well as a failure of our educational system to provide the necessary business fundamentals to IT graduates. In most cases, senior IT architects do not even know how to create a business model – *and they need to*. In short, financial analysis needs to be a core skill possessed by IT architects, for the purpose of establishing visibility and transparency in IT spending and performance.

Further, the analysis techniques used by IT architects must address the range of ways in which IT business value manifests. Currently, business value analysis and IT technical analysis are disconnected processes. Business value analysis must be integral to proper governance to ensure that the organization's resources are deployed optimally; and conversely, governance is critical to the realization of maximum business value since without proper value-based governance there can be no assurance that priorities are optimally balanced and that policies are consistently implemented.

> ## This book is based on experience across the domains of IT policy and IT execution.

There are many books about IT management, governance, and business agility. Many of these books provide excellent perspectives, and many are referenced herein. Some of those sources are based on thorough research and comparisons of successful and not-so-successful companies. Others are based on the experiences of senior IT managers.

Still others are based on the experiences of consultants who have provided assistance to many organizations of different kinds.

I am not a CIO, nor have I ever been one. I am an IT architect at heart, but one who has had business-level responsibility and who appreciates the business side of things. I have helped to launch and develop "mentor" organizations such as what is described in this book, and I have been fortunate to have done stints in almost every aspect of IT, from security analysis, data architecture, and enterprise architecture to IT policies and planning.

The foundation that has helped me most in these activities is that I had been co-founder and CTO of a respected company, Digital Focus,[1] that has *profitably* built a large number of very sophisticated and large-scale business-to-business systems *for a fixed price*, and so the importance of economy and business relevance were impressed upon me. Digital Focus' fixed price approach is relatively rare in the commercial sector in which the company operated during the period of my involvement. At Digital Focus, the CTO role was essentially a risk management role, and required me to develop a deep understanding of what can go wrong in IT projects in terms of technology and customer relationships, and what the early architectural decisions are (or failure to identify the important decisions) that can impact success later. My recent book, *High-Assurance Design*, attempts to document the lessons that I learned from the perspective of an IT architect.

The projects that Digital Focus undertook for our customers were almost always C-level initiatives within large companies to build strategic processing platforms with substantial business value. Our approach therefore involved protracted involvement with the customer's business side to understand their strategies and goals and the intended new value proposition in the market.

I then went on to consult to large organizations at the SVP, VP, and director level to develop IT risk models, assess process and technology weaknesses, help to establish enterprise architecture and processes, help to develop governance mechanisms to address concerns for these areas and for SOX and other kinds of compliance. After all, the techniques for risk management in an information-oriented enterprise are relatively independent of the type of risk.

---

[1] In 2005 Digital Focus was acquired by Command Information.

The perspective of this book is therefore rooted in what really works at a tactical level when trying to *implement* strategic change. I hope that CIOs read this book, because while the problems manifest at a tactical level, they must be solved at all levels and driven from the top.

The view from the ground is not pretty: ground level IT staff have a deep disrespect for policies, compliance, paper processes, and indeed for the entire mindset that is represented by the parts of the business that promote these. This is due to ignorance and a lack of communication between these two important parts of the business. The view from the middle is not pretty either: mid-level executives in IT and in business units do not know how to change their organizations to address the resistance that they experience when it comes to implementing change. Finally, the view from the top is best characterized as misinformed: executives think that their IT staff have a handle on their technology and the executives do not realize how far their people are from having the skills that are really needed to get the job done.

Who This Book Is For

This book has many intended audiences. Broadly speaking, this book is for anyone who is concerned with strategic and aggressive change management within an IT-intensive organization. To make the changes outlined in this book possible, it is eventually necessary to implement change at all levels, and both IT and lines of business will be impacted. The messages are therefore intended for a broad audience, with certain messages intended for certain roles within an organization, including the CIO, IT managers are various levels, and managers and analysts in parts of the organization that are impacted by IT. The CEO is also an intended reader because CEO-level support is required for any strategic change: chapter 9 in particular is written for the CEO, with a humble but sincere message from an entrenched IT perspective. Chapter 10 is written for the CIO and proposes a blueprint for advocating and implementing the ideas that are outlined in the rest of the book. Most of the remainder of the book is written for IT architects, managers, analysts, and thought leaders at all levels who practice or rely on IT in some way. Hopefully it will be clear whether the material in each section is applicable to the reader's role in his or her own organization.

While the focus is on IT, the principles described herein are general and are by no means limited to IT. In fact, that is one of the main points of this book: that IT now permeates all business processes to such a degree that it no longer makes sense to divide an organization based on the application of IT. However, the book is primarily applicable to environments in which information processing and management is a large component of operation.

Some people who have seen the draft manuscript of this book have asked me if I have actually seen the principles in this book implemented. Indeed I have, but not all in one place. However, in some cases the fit is pretty comprehensive: for example, in one instance I was the lead architect of a new CIO department that had pretty much the same mission as the "mentor group" described in this book, and I was able to institute and nurture most of the practices in this book through that organization and as a result helped to transform the way that IT was done at a fundamental level.

Most organizations implement some of what is recommended here in some form. What I offer is a perspective that emphasizes the elements that I think truly make a difference and that one cannot forego. There is no element in this book that I have not seen tried, and I provide seven case studies that I use repeatedly as examples.

How the Book Is Organized

This book is divided into two parts. The first part makes the argument for what the problems are with current approaches and what needs to be done to remedy those problems. The second part provides plans of action and techniques for putting the remedies into practice.

Some readers who are anxious to get to "the meat" might want to survey what is contained in Part II as they read Part I. In Part II have done my best to refer back to the places where ideas in Part I are first introduced. Each chapter also contains a summary that encapsulates the main themes and ideas. In the first chapter of Part II, I take the presumptuous step of talking to the CEO. It is not that I expect a great many CEOs to read this book; but hopefully that chapter will establish what I think IT needs from the CEO to make this plan successful in the long term, and so those who do talk to the CEO will have some guidance as to what they might say. In the chapter that follows that one, I then address the CIO (or whatever equivalent role applies), and provide guidance as to what things need to occur over time in order to establish a capability-focused IT organization. After that, the subsequent chapters are mainly targeted at the CIO and below, including enterprise architects, initiative and project architects, and analysts who wish to implement this book's ideas within their own work.

Why this Book is Published Under Creative Commons

One of the challenges with an inter-disciplinary book that breaks new ground is that in order for people to become aware of the ideas in the book, people must be able to use, extend, and share the ideas. A Creative Commons license is ideal for this purpose.

I hope that this book provides some useful new ideas and is a catalyst for improving the way that IT currently operates.

Cliff Berg

Acknowledgments

From a professional standpoint, I would like to thank the following individuals (in no particular order) for their valuable feedback and discussion that produced thoughts that found their way into this book:

Mark Lutchen, Partner and Practice Leader, IT Business Risk Management Practice, PWC.

Scott Ambler, Agile Practice Lead, IBM Rational Canada.

Amy Dansky, Business Consultant.

Suvajit Gupta, Enterprise Security Consultant, Cigital.

Diane Murphy, Chair, Information Technology, Marymount University.

Craig Connell, Director of IT, Unistar Nuclear.

Rakesh Mehta, President, Global Technology Partners.

Ron Hulen, CTO, Command Information (Commercial).

Dianne Houghton.

Greg Doench, editor, Pearson Publishing.

Tom Poppendieck.

Paul Preiss, President, International Association of Software Architects.

Angela Yochem, SVP Strategic Architecture, Bank of America.

Eric Hartung.

Michael Benson.

John Wyatt, President and COO, Cigital.

Stephen Cohen, Senior Architect, Microsoft Enterprise Services.

Dave Hoffman, Partner, PWC.

Lloyd DeVaux, COO, BankAtlantic.

Hugo Alvarez, CIO, BankAtlantic.

Dipasis Bhadra, Principal Economist, MITRE Corporation.

Tah Yang, Business Application Officer, US Forest Service.

John King, Business and Information Officer, US Forest Service.

Murray Cantor, IBM Distinguished Engineer and the governance solutions lead on the IBM Rational Software CTO team.

From a personal standpoint, I would like to thank Jackie, for her patience, understanding, and support with my continual intense projects. I would also like to thank my sister Roxanne for always being there for me.

Part I: Ideas

The Core Ideas and Premises

1. Introduction

The Importance of *What* and *Why*

*To understand fully <u>why</u> an algorithmic procedure does what
it is supposed to involves insights.*
— Roger Penrose[1]

The highest-level enterprise strategies that an organization can
have are: (1) assurance that current goals and concerns – whatever
those are – are being addressed, and (2) the ability to change
course quickly without sacrificing the former, as goals and
concerns change over time. In other words, *assurance* and *agility* are
the two dimensions to any enterprise strategy.

Transparency provides a window into these issues. Transparency
has two aspects: *What* is occurring, and *why* it is occurring. The
"what" is what current planning and measurement approaches are
all about. The "why" is what is missing, yet it is key to
transparency: one cannot assess whether enterprise strategies are
being implemented throughout unless the why is explained; and
one then has no framework for ensuring that enterprise strategies
are maintained as plans change.

The classic approach to achieving change is to plan programs and
initiatives to change the organization's capabilities in order to align
the capabilities better with the organization's new goals. The
classic approach to ensuring proper execution is to institute
metrics that check that initiatives are constrained to their budget

---

[1] From *The Emperor's New Mind*, Oxford University Press, 1989, p. 55. The
profoundness of this understated quotation becomes apparent when one
reads the aforementioned seminal book.

3

and schedule, and to a lesser extent that the desired outcomes are produced.

The problem with these approaches is that they do not account for the countless decisions that occur *during execution* and which collectively have a huge impact on alignment and on ultimate success, as well as on future business agility. In short, there is no transparency into how plans are executed, nor is there transparency into why the myriad execution-level decisions were made. There is therefore no basis for assessing internal alignment with business goals and concerns, and there is no basis for assessing the level of agility for further change that remains after initiatives have reached their milestones and spent their budgets. The macro-level strategies of the organization are therefore in jeopardy, even though the initiatives may have completed on time and in budget and the desired new capabilities built. Has the organization painted itself into a corner such that *future* capabilities will be very capital-intensive or time-consuming to add? Have the new capabilities been built in such a way that there are hidden problems lurking that have the potential to threaten the entire organization? With traditional approaches these things cannot be known. In short, there is no transparency into how capabilities are implemented, or why the myriad internal decisions were made, and so there is no way to assess future agility or the level of assurance with respect to all strategic concerns.

The Tension Between Agility and Assurance

In later chapters I will discuss agility and assurance at length, and the fact that there is a tension between these two needs. Just as during the Cold War there was a tension between the need to be able to launch missiles quickly and the need to control those missiles and prevent an accidental launch, today there is a need to be able to react quickly and strategically yet maintain control and prevent accidents that can have far-reaching consequences. These are competing goals and balancing them is a major challenge; and further, the trend is for these two competing goals to become more acute and difficult to balance.

Another trend is for IT to play more and more of a role in business, and conversely for business to be more and more involved in IT. There will always be a role for IT specialists, and there will always be a role for business staff who do not play a part in designing IT-related processes, but the distribution is changing it is somewhat inevitable that business will eventually plan its own capabilities as technology enables this. This is inevitable because it provides the business with the most flexibility and ability to respond to the market, and that will be rewarded. The days of the IT "programmer" are therefore somewhat numbered, or at least that job will become a smaller part of the human resources portfolio of most organizations; and those in IT who understand the business will find themselves more useful to the organization. Similarly, business departments will come to need staff that have sufficiently technical inclination to be able to devise new processes to respond to market changes without having to wait for an external IT group to first learn the department's concerns and then design and build new processes. The market will not reward such rigidity. Yet, if these methodological changes are not implemented with care and in a manner that builds assurance into the process, then the organization will be at great risk as described above. I will support these assertions in chapters that follow.

One of the greatest challenges today in moving to the new model of an IT-aware business and a business-savvy IT is the poor communication between IT and business that predominates in most organizations. Business and IT are often separate camps that view each other with suspicion and grudging respect. IT is seldom invited to the executive table, and senior IT staff are seldom involved in business-level planning at a SVP let alone EVP level. Usually the business decides what it wants and then tells IT to propose a plan for building it. Similarly, IT does not communicate its concerns in business terms, and so it is no wonder that the business does not listen or that its eyes glaze over when it hears IT talk about things such as "extensibility" or "maintainability" because these are not business terms and are too vague to mean anything. The poor track record of IT project success across the industry does not help to add credibility to the profession.

The root cause for this situation is the poor state of affairs of IT education. Computer Science curricula seldom provide instruction in software engineering, and even schools that provide a degree in software engineering do not tend to provide instruction on how to assess the business value of IT concerns, how to write a business plan, or how to integrate an organization's policies and concerns into a software development process. The sad truth is that the IT profession is horribly under-trained for what it is expected to do; and another sad truth is that most IT staff are more interested in learning the latest software development tools than they are in helping the business. I say this not to blame them, for it is also my feeling that business has not done its job to set expectations or to work with academia to change the situation.

Perhaps the root of the root cause is that business value is not addressed as integral to IT. If it were, then IT actions and knowledge would match what is actually needed. However, the IT industry has been talking about business value for years, but the talk is unrealized. Few organizations implement any kind of IT business value measurement system except for intangible measures or scorecards that are completely subjective. This means that it is almost impossible to really put a value on IT and it is difficult to perform tradeoff analysis with respect to IT concerns and business-side concerns.

Current methodologies do not cut it. There are a great many frameworks today for implementing enterprise-scale IT processes, risk management processes, and governance, but they are being adopted in a heavyweight manner, resulting in a new bureaucracy of standards. Risk is being managed by checklist. Agile Software Development Lifecycles (SDLCs) are not trusted and there is currently no framework that reconciles the need for agility with the need for assurance and strategy alignment. Maturity models are seen as a lifecycle rather than as a business process effectiveness scale. Data quality is being approached from the back instead of the front, by adding more control to outputs rather than on improving root causes and the actual processes that produce data. Planning products add more steps rather than simplifying things.

This book provides a new way, based on a very simple premise: business case analysis must be fundamental to all IT decisions. Further, that analysis must account for both opportunity as well as risk, in an integrated manner. And further, planning must be transparent in that both actions and rationale are accounted for. For this to work, large organizations need a champion for change.

6

The Four Main Premises: Agility, Assurance, Accountability, and Amplification

To address the problems outlined above, this book proposes four main premises. These are explained at length throughout the book, but in summary form they are as follows:

1. To achieve business agility within IT, organizations need a potent *champion for change*, and that champion needs to have a *mission to ensure consistency*.

2. To achieve assurance within IT with regard to the organization's many risks, the aforementioned champion for change needs to have a *mission to ensure that all enterprise concerns are addressed in a balanced manner*.

3. To achieve accountability (transparency) for IT decisions, organizations should focus on *quantifying and measuring the business value of IT choices*, as well as *recording the reasoning behind IT decisions*. Further, the key to elevating IT to a business level is to *measure the actual value produced by IT*.

4. To reduce the apparent cost of IT, one must *increase IT's value*. Rather than being more austere, IT must *use its resources to amplify the effectiveness of the rest of the organization* and IT must be *more transparent about its value when it achieves this amplification*. These can be realized by implementing the above strategies.

In the next chapter I will begin the discussion of these by examining the concept of business agility and make the case for why it is increasingly important to many organizations today.

2. Why Agility Is Important

Enabling Rapid Changes in Direction

Each Business Era Brings a Faster Rate Of Change

According to Gordon Moore, co-founder of Intel and originator of the famous "Moore's Law" which is now part of the English Language, "As far as I can see in the future, we will have rapid change," he predicts. "We move along exponential curves. If we didn't, that would be the biggest change." [1] Indeed, Vernor Vinge, Ray Kurzweil, and many others believe that the rate of change is exponential and that in the near future – 30 or 50 years from now – it will bring about a "technological singularity" and outpace our ability to predict one day to the next.[2]

But in the nearer term, and in the context of the business cycle and the competitive issues that exist in our current environment, it is nevertheless apparent to most people that the rate of change is faster than before, and if history is a guide, changes to the business climate will continue to accelerate.

---

[1] See [Cone1997].
[2] The concept of a "technological singularity" is that at some point in the future technological advancement will reach a point beyond which change is so rapid that it will be impossible for humans to predict the state of their world from even one moment to the next. See [Kleffel2006].

Core Idea: Strategic Change Must Be Increasingly Rapid.

Not everyone supports this notion. For example, Richard Templeton, CEO of Texas Instruments, has observed that the information technology industry seems to experience upheavals about every 20 years.[1] This is ironic given that his industry is the origin of Moore's Law. What he is observing is that while technological change has continued to accelerate, business has been able to keep pace until 20 years have gone by, at which point change has been so drastic that a new paradigm emerges and new companies must emerge to meet it.

That does not mean that during each 20-year period that the pace of activities within companies has not continued to accelerate. In fact, it has. The evidence is all around. Companies now manage their assets on a daily basis. Increasingly, businesses operate around the clock, and are driven by events rather than by planning cycles. The increasing rate of communication, availability of information, ubiquity of access to information, global work schedules, and faster-and-faster R&D continues to push downward on the planning cycle. It used to take ten years to map the genome: now it takes weeks. When launching a startup, inventors used to think about building a company: now they immediately think about an exit strategy.

If You Stop Moving, You Die

The need to constantly grow and evolve is one of the few constants in nature. In order to merely survive, any organism needs to continue through its lifecycle, continuously changing. It is a paradox then why so many business models presume an ultimate steady state. This is particularly true when one talks about assurance and governance: the presumption is that if only one can get sufficient controls installed, that all will be safe and secure from that point onward. Unfortunately, this point of view leads one to focus on the wrong thing: the endpoint view, rather than the processes for evolving that endpoint view in such a manner

---

[1]   See [Darlin2006].

that controls are an integral concern. According to a Cognos whitepaper, "you need the ability to realign in real-time by feeding current and expected future results to adapt the next forecast."[1]

Controls are important, but they can potentially kill an organization by creating a quagmire of conformity that squeezes out the spirit and agility of an organization by making things so rigid that innovation is just too much trouble and involves too much bureaucracy. To focus on an endpoint view of controls is to build into your model the death of your organization.

Today's Competitors Are Agile

Regardless whether your strategy involves being first-to-market, business agility is still critical. Competitors today are increasingly agile. Witness the struggle of the telcoms against startup VOIP providers. Witness the extent to which the entertainment industry was caught off-guard by upstart companies. The ability to respond to disruptive change requires agility, and only those who can respond will survive.

It appears that in most cases disruptive elements originate from startup companies that are single-minded and are not burdened by existing mindsets, business models, capital assets that represent prior investments, and complex infrastructure; but disruptive change can come from established players as well: for example, Sun Microsystems developed the Java programming language which over the course of only a few years transformed the way that IT systems are built, and in the process fueled demand for Sun's servers. The willingness of Sun to invest huge sums in Java and commit to it in order to give it a means of riding the Internet wave rather than merely promote its existing products represented an agile response to the current situation.

A failure to adjust strategy in a timely way can result in loss of market share, dis-intermediation of the value and supply chains, and sometimes even an irreversible slide toward irrelevance.

---

[1] From [Cognos7Steps], in the section "Best Practice #5: Real-Time Alignment Supports Rolling Forecasts and Starter Performance", on p. 9.

A lack of agility leads to lost opportunities. Consider the case of a company that invested hundreds of millions over several years in the development of an improved strategic business technology platform. Throughout this book I will refer to this company as the Large Investment Product Provider. The project was conceived for the purpose of replacing many of the company's core processing systems with a more agile system that would allow new products to be implemented quickly.

Unfortunately, the project was conceived as a "big bang" effort, requiring many years and a very large staff. It took years for the development team members to develop the business knowledge they needed to become productive so that the project finally "got rolling". By this time other priorities came along, and the project was literally stopped in its tracks. While some components reached production status, the major goals of the investment were not realized. The window of opportunity was lost because success was not achieved quickly enough. That is, for any IT investment, you only have a limited window of time to make a success happen, and "big bang" efforts take too long because the window is shorter today: investors are more impatient, and the environment changes more frequently.

To this day it still takes nearly a year for this company to introduce a new product, whereas competitors have shown that they can do it in a couple of months. The lost business opportunities are enormous.

Agile Change Management: The Processes That Define And Create Business Processes Must Be Agile

The assembly line revolutionized production and was one of the great innovations of the industrial age. During the eighties manufacturers began to realize that the future demanded increasing customization, and that manufacturing systems would have to be increasingly flexible, so that retooling could be done quickly. This trend has continued. While it is still important for business processes to be efficient, the process of retooling must be efficient as well, and rapid. The business environment can change dramatically from one year to the next, and today's organization needs to be ready to redirect even its core business model from one year to the next. This is especially true in non-manufacturing realms such as financial services, but is increasingly becoming true in manufacturing as well, as product development lead times and ROI timelines shorten.

> **Focus on the process for creating or changing business processes. That transformation process must be agile.**

Most business processes today employ some level of automation. However, the approach to defining new processes is largely manual: new software is hand-coded, guided by manually-collected requirements and hand-crafted designs. Given the manual nature of such a "retooling" process, it is important to make that process as agile and quick as possible, so as not to be beat to market by the competition. In short, you need to establish an agile operating model for changing operational processes.

Design Your Own Capabilities: Enterprise Change Management Should Address How Departments Will Update And Maintain Their Own Process Definitions

Most large organizations invest a lot of thought and energy into change management. Plans for organizational change are usually drafted by external consultants or internal strategic councils. Changes usually encompass new organizational boundaries, changes in responsibility for managers, changes in policy, new directives, and new funding initiatives. Change management plans must also address how existing IT processes will be changed. To leave out IT process change management is to omit a plan for retooling.

> **Without the human dimension, a business capability does not exist.**

Simply changing reporting boundaries and adding policies does not achieve change. An organization must address how staff will acquire the skills they need to conceptualize and internalize new corporate strategies and policies as new IT processes to support the new organization.

In this book I will use the term *business capability* to refer to a function within the business that realizes tangible business value. For a non-profit this might manifest as tangible value toward realizing an organizational goal. For a for-profit entity, business value is ultimately in financial terms. The consideration of what is a business capability and what is not is discussed with more rigor later in this book.

The groupwide understanding and internalization of a business process is the human dimension to a business capability. Non-human resources such as automated systems comprise the technology dimension. Without the human dimension a business capability does not exist. Delegating the conceptualization and formation of plans for automation to a separate IT group is no longer sufficiently agile because it makes the planning for the human and non-human dimensions disjoint, slowing the process and introducing more chances for mis-alignment.

The line between business staff and IT staff is blurring as more and more processes are automated, and business staff are expected to design or maintain their own business processes using business process modeling tools and business intelligence tools. It is therefore time to begin to expect your business staff to be able to model their organization and design the logical outlines of new IT processes. You must provide for their enablement to make this practical.

I am not saying that a line of business should internally master IT system design or technical requirements definition: what I am saying is that they need to take responsibility for modeling their own processes, and for conceptualizing changes and integration approaches as well as how to model the value proposition of alternatives – business or technical. Getting them to a point where they can do this requires a substantial level of assistance. That is the type of change management to which I am referring.

I am also not saying that every business person should know how to do this: within any department there are those who are technically inclined and those who are less so: those who are must be leveraged to reduce the dependence on IT to devise new capabilities. Similarly, those in IT who are inclined toward understanding the business must be leveraged to take a more pro-active role in envisioning new capabilities.

Concurrency: Agility Means You Don't Wait

Traditional methods of constructing business systems rely on phases as the primary means of coordinating communication between interdependent activities. For an example from IT, consider that since a software design depends on the business requirements, the design people are made to wait until the requirements are all written down. In this model there is no backward communication: all communication flows forward. In this approach, only forward communication is possible, because when design begins, the requirements people are done and might have even moved on to other work.

Iterative methods allow *backward* communication – feedback. An iterative methodology allows requirements for successive iterations to be fine-tuned based on the success of prior iterations. Some agile software development methods take this a step further, by

> **Out with time-based "phases" and other temporal concepts. Enable concurrency, for maximum rate of change.**

shortening the iteration cycle to the current practical minimum, currently 2-3 weeks. With such a short cycle, feedback is nearly continuous: while software developers are creating the current build, they are also talking to the requirements "subject matter experts" (SMEs) to plan the next iteration. When viewed over a period of a month or more, it appears as if requirements, design, development, and testing all proceed concurrently. Thus, instead of a development activity such as requirements or design waiting for a prior activity to complete, all such tasks proceed in parallel and all complete at the same time. It is not hard to imagine a day when there will be software creation tools that are so advanced that requirements can be tweaked at will, immediately generating a new software implementation. In the meantime, we have two-week minimum cycles.

Orchestration: Agility Requires A High Level Of Orchestrated And Just-In-Time Communication

The introduction of greater concurrency into a business process raises the possibility of chaos. One can no longer count on the traditional orderly progression of phases. Instead, there must be a well-designed communication and decision-making process to ensure that changes reach the right people in a timely manner and that decision-making includes all affected parties. This facilitation is the role of the *mentor* in agile software projects.[1] A single project manager is not sufficient, because the level of communication and orchestration must be much higher, given the dynamic nature of the environment.

> **Communication paths are processes in themselves, and you need agile process managers – "mentors" – to help you to create and manage them.**

Communication must be accurate and honest. This implies a high level of trust between parties. On agile projects the mentor helps to ensure this honesty, because the mentor is knowledgeable and circulates enough to be able to see through half-truths; and also because the mentor acts as an advocate for the technical concerns and struggles of the developers and therefore they tend to allocate the mentor more trust than a project manager who tends to be most concerned with the interests of the external stakeholders.

Effort only where it matters: Agility Means Conserving Energy, And Applying It Only Where It Matters

Unnecessary complexity is the bane of agility. According to Ray Ozzie, Bill Gates's replacement as head of software strategy, "Complexity kills. It sucks the life out of developers, it makes products difficult to plan, build and test, it introduces security

---

[1] Some agile software methodologies refer to the mentor role as a "coach".

challenges, and it causes end-user and administrator frustration." [1] This is because a little extra complexity adds a lot of communication and coordination. Unnecessary work is also the bane of agility. This is because unnecessary work inserts "impedance" into the process, killing agility. For example, if a small change requires six documents to be updated, then the team will spend its two-week build updating those documents and not have time to make all of the software changes that they had promised. Therefore, agile mentors are trained to watch for unnecessary complexity and for make-work, and pull them out of the project like weeds. In the ideal agile project, you do only what you really have to do in order to achieve your objective, and not a single keystroke more.

This is very much like the use of "Lean" practices in manufacturing, which espouse the deep involvement of workers and line managers in working together to locally optimize their work. In fact, proponents of Lean such as Mary Poppendieck have sought to apply these lessons to IT.

Incremental: Agility Means You Build Processes Incrementally, Verifying Them All The Way

Years ago I was asked to participate as an architecture expert in a project to build a banking loan origination system from scratch. The project had originally been contracted to one of those three-letter-acronym mega-vendors which I will not name. After two years of requirements gathering, and many cost overruns the vendor had been fired and a new team was formed, which is when I become involved. The original vendor had been unable to create a complete, consistent, and usable set of requirements, even though they had ready access to SMEs.

Everyone in software has war stories of large projects that get mired in requirements and design, leading to a "death march" at which point the project collapses because the weakness of the requirements and design finally are revealed in the inability of the team to actually build a system that works.

---

[1] See [WaltersOzzie].

Agile proponents will tell you that it is fool-hearty to even try to build a complete system at once. Instead, one should build a little at a time. They take this a step further and gather only a few requirements at a time, building as they go. On an agile project, there may be a long-term vision, but one does not try to realize that vision in a single up-front design.

And while they build, they verify, from a technical perspective and from a requirements perspective: each build of the system is shown to stakeholders, in order to solicit feedback on whether what has been built is what meets the needs; and each component that is built is accompanied by a comprehensive set of tests, so that when the system is finally done there is a large regression test suite that verifies the system's functional behavior. If one is smart, one also verifies success in capability development against metrics that are meaningful outside the project as well – metrics that plug into a business plan or model that include all corporate goals.

This approach is fast becoming the norm. A 2008 survey found that the vast majority of IT organizations have agile projects, and those projects had incremental feature development cycles between 2 and four weeks.[1] This is in sharp contrast to the way things were done ten years ago.

Measure Capability, Not Tasks: Agility Means Focusing On Building Skills Rather Than On Measuring Tasks

There has been a lot of interest in recent years in forward-looking business metrics. The thought is that in this rapidly-changing world, metrics that tell you how you did are not as valuable as predictive metrics that tell you how you will likely do.

Accounting responsibilities aside, metrics that tell you how you did are only useful for validating a predictive model. After all, business is not about the past: it is about the present and the future. To the extent that you have full transparency about where you are, and where you might go, you can develop a strategy for success.

---

[1] Ref. [AmbAA08].

What this means is that you need to be able to measure what your capabilities are, and what they can become. Toward that end, your metrics should have a heavy emphasis on what your capabilities are, how quickly they are developing, and how effective your processes are for developing them. Powerful metrics for measuring capability development are the key to developing powerful capabilities.

Measuring progress in terms of a pre-ordained plan does not achieve this. Yesterday's plan reflects yesterday's concept of your capabilities. As capabilities are developed, the concepts for those capabilities change. Therefore, the plan becomes obsolete. Trying to keep it up to date locks you in to yesterday's model, and focuses on the wrong thing: the tasks to completing yesterday's concept.

As concepts evolve, the plan needs to evolve, but it can only evolve properly if its underlying capability model is updated, and that means that you must have an accurate view of what capabilities have actually been developed so far. As we see, capability measurement is essential even as an initiative proceeds.

The focus of project metrics therefore needs to shift from schedule item completion, to a focus on capability development. These capabilities need to continually be related to an ongoing business strategy.

Putting emphasis on capability measurement also forces the initiative teams to think in terms of developing capabilities, rather than in terms of tasks. This frees them to act more autonomously and to be creative. It also requires more oversight, to ensure that all corporate concerns are considered.

It also helps to avoid the "last 5%" syndrome, in which a project stays parked at 95% complete, unable to reach 100% because that last 5% requires that deep problems be solved. When one focuses on capabilities, deep problems tend to be found early, because at every stage from the first build the system must be operational and provide tangible value.

Agility Has Risks. There Is Potentially Less Control. Agile Governance Provides That Control Without Sacrificing Agility

When my father taught me to drive, he instructed me that whenever I enter an intersection that I should slow down. This was common sense that is sometimes lost on an impatient teenager who is oblivious to risk. However, the message makes sense in a broader sense: when there is a lot going on around you, things can go wrong and get dangerous very quickly. Slowing down reduces risk.

Agility implies going quickly, so it almost goes without saying that risk will increase unless you take steps to mitigate that risk. Certain practices can reduce your risk, even if you are going a little faster. Wearing seatbelts does not decrease your chance of a car accident, but it does decrease your personal risk. Effective agile methodologies address risk reduction[1], so that speed can be increased while keeping a lid on risk.

So far I have only been discussing basic principles, but not really providing any answers, such as how to reduce risk while increasing agility. In the second part of this book I will endeavor to provide practical answers; but first we must lay the foundation for understanding the problems that exist with current approaches.

Summary

Business agility is the ability of an organization to respond quickly to unforeseen change – and possibly radical change – in the organization's operating environment.

Organizations that are not agile are increasingly at a disadvantage as change in their environments of operation become more frequent. Those organizations that succeed in responding to change have a greater chance to survive and prosper at the expense of others.

---

[1] For example, see [BerAmb2006].

To provide agility, change management processes should enable an organization to continually re-define its operational processes in a manner that is responsive to changes in the operating environment.

Organizations should require its departments to define the changes that are needed for their own operation, rather than defining those processes externallly and then imposing them.

To provide for maximum agility, business process re-design should be approached through prototyping of end-to-end activities, rather than in a "big bang" manner. Do not define phases for design, testing, and deployment. Rather, utilize a continuous process of refinement and expansion of a tractable workable approach that addresses nearly all pertinent concerns from the outset.

Address the need for communication head-on, rather than relying on ad-hoc processes. Establish individuals whose main job it is to accelerate communication about technical and business issues. This is not a project management function: it is a mentoring function. This enhanced focus on communication is necessary to deal with the rapid pace of change and decisions that accompany rapid change and rapid re-design.

Address the need to economize in a just-in-time manner, in which the mentor function determines in real time where effort needs to be expended and where it does not, based on consideration of risk and return on effort. This conservation of effort makes it possible to apply more diligence where it really matters.

While it is important to track expenditures, time, and construction and deployment milestones, do not use these metrics as a substitute for measuring progress. Progress metrics should be in terms of the value that is realized in terms of proven new capabilities.

3. Why Assurance Is Important

Note: This chapter provides some background on governance concepts as they apply to large organizations. Those who are knowledgeable about this topic may wish to skip to the next chapter, or to skim this chapter to obtain the perspective presented here.

What Governance Is

Within IT, when one speaks of "governance", one is often thinking of risk management and assurance of alignment with regard to execution. This usage is a narrow use of the term, as I will explain momentarily. Broadly speaking, *governance* is a set of mechanisms of any form that serve to ensure that an organization's objectives are met. It is normally a collection of people (directors), policies, checks and balances, and processes that together ensure alignment with the organization's actions and its goals and concerns. The goals of the organization are determined by its controlling constituents: shareholders, voters, etc. Its concerns are aspects of risk and opportunity identified by its leadership. Governance serves to reduce the risks of not maximizing or failing to achieve the goals of the constituents.

Relationships Between Corporate Governance and Operational Governance

Corporate governance directly represents the interests of shareholders, and its implementation is through the corporate board of directors and ultimately the voting shareholders. The scope of control of corporate governance includes the corporate executive officers (particularly the CEO, who reports to the board) and the bylaws and charter of the organization. Typical concerns for governance of a public corporation include shareholder value, effective use of capital, corporate audits, executive compensation and human resource concerns, market and growth goals, non-financial goals, risk management, and SEC regulatory compliance.

For a corporation, *operational governance* represents these same interests in the end, but operates at multiple levels down, beginning with the chief executive and other officers or senior executives who report to the CEO. Its scope of control is the corporate operational assets. Operational governance is usually implemented through one or more senior executive committees and supported by special-purpose committees, boards, and organization structures at various levels of the company. In this book, when I speak of governance I will usually mean operational governance.

Operational governance represents the various strategic concerns for the company's operation, including legal, financial, regulatory, security and privacy, profitability, market growth, and so on. Somewhere in there, IT and technology fit, and so many organizations have a CIO or a CTO or both who serve to oversee the governance of those functions.

The primary mechanism of operational governance is a set of organizational structures, and the rules of engagement and processes by which those structures operate: the policies and standards. These organizational structures are chartered to monitor, assess, and control the overall organization from the top by instituting policies and standards, by creating initiatives to implement change as needed, and by providing for the arbitration of bottom-up decisions.

Core Idea: Change Must Ensure Alignment

The purpose of operational governance is to ensure that the organization maintains alignment with the organization's overall goals and priorities. Toward that end, the primary actors of operational governance must be accountable to the CEO and measured based on their success in aligning the various parts of the organization in a timely manner.

A failure to implement effective governance results in greatly increased risk for the organization. Risks can be catastrophic, but more often they are insidious, and symptoms can appear at all levels: from a tendency for initiatives to not achieve their goals, to an inability to point to the root causes of problems that cross

Case In Point

departmental[1] boundaries. For example, I was once called in to research the root causes of chronic failures of a series of independently reliable IT systems that together comprised a strategic, mission critical platform. I will refer to this company as the company with the Responsive IT Department. The problems were confounding because the IT group had a very close relationship with the business and tried to be very responsive. The IT manager was very hands-on and was highly knowledgeable about all of the systems. Yet, problems occurred on an ongoing basis – always from a seemingly different cause. The business felt that IT was not doing its job properly, but IT felt that the business did not spend enough time trying to understand what IT's challenges were. Senior management was not able to determine what the truth was due to a lack of transparency into the problems. What I found was a failure to integrate the planning of short-term goals and long-term goals based on long-term business value, and this caused the large issues to be pushed aside in favor of tangible short-term requirements. Further, the measurement and tracking of the causes of problems was not integrated. In short, mechanisms for alignment with overall company goals were not established. Proper governance at multiple levels would have fixed this.

The Term "IT Governance"

A word about terminology is in order before I go much farther. According to Scott Ambler and Per Kroll, "The goal of an IT governance program is to establish chains of responsibility, authority, and communication to empower people in support of the overall enterprise goals and strategy." In other words, it is not just about control. It is about coordination and enablement as well.[2]

---

[1] In this book I use the term "department" to refer to a sub-section of an organization, and usually a small, non-strategic section. In the government sector the term often represents a very large organization, such as the US Department of Commerce. When I use the term "department" I am implying a relatively small group compared with the overall organization.

[2] Ref. [AmbKroll07].

25

Implicit in any concept of governance is the existence of two roles: (a) the role of management and direction – including business opportunity identification – and (b) the role of oversight and alignment with strategic concerns and risk management strategies – in other words, *assurance*. These can be broken up into separate parts as well, but that is not the point. In IT today there is a tendency to limit the concept of IT governance to (b), namely, the oversight and risk management functions, and to exclude the management and direction-providing functions as an external force to IT. This is a legacy of the history of IT as viewing itself apart from the business, waiting for "requirements" to be delivered so that IT can act. Unfortunately this view of "IT governance" has taken root. I do not use the term in this way because it is not in agreement with one of my main premises: that business value needs to be integral to IT. The reader is forewarned therefore that my use of the word "governance" differs from how the word is used in current IT literature.

Assurance is therefore only one part of governance. It is an important part though. In the sections that follow I will illustrate this with ways that an organization can fail because of inadequate assurance strategies.

> **The term "IT governance" as used by the IT industry is a legacy of the separateness between business and IT.**

Impact Of Initiative Failures

In a survey a few years back, financial services executives were asked what the top barrier was in implementing e-business goals, and 67 percent cited the need to re-engineer processes as the top barrier.[1] The implication is that re-engineering is a very risky or costly undertaking – or both.

A recent Standish Group survey found that in the US more than a third of software projects are eventually abandoned before they are finished; that in large companies only 9% of projects complete

---

[1] See [FinExecInt2001].

on time and on budget; and that even when completed, these projects are usually "no more than a mere shadow of their original specification requirements. Projects completed by the largest American companies have only approximately 42% of the originally proposed features and functions." [1]

On the other hand, another survey found that project success rates are much higher when people were allowed to define "success" in their own terms. [2] For example, 87.3% of respondents believed that meeting the actual needs of stakeholders is more important than building the system to specification.

The obvious implications of this are that initiatives evolve dramatically in the course of their execution; and that success is far from guaranteed, and can even be hard to define. If corporate strategy is counting on success, the organization had better take a measured approach and ensure true transparency – transparency that is meaningful in *business terms*, not merely schedule terms. True transparency is a critical ingredient of organizational assurance, and too often it is missing because organizations measure the wrong things, or use metrics that are based on intangible and subjective criteria.

Impact Of Failures In Financial Transparency

Before the Sarbanes Oxley (SOX) Act of 2002, executive officers could often claim ignorance if their organization did not have accurate and transparent financial reporting. The claim of ignorance is no longer a feasible defense since SOX establishes that executives of public companies are *criminally* liable for inaccurate financial reporting. It is no wonder that SOX compliance has taken on an urgent status in many companies.

There can also be, at some level, indirect impact on those who do business with companies that are found to have questionable reporting. According to Paul Chaney of the Owen Graduate School of Management at Vanderbilt University, *clients* of Arthur Andersen averaged more than a $30M drop in equity value each immediately after it was disclosed that Andersen had shredded

---

[1] Ref. [Standish06].
[2] Ref. [AmbPS07].

27

Enron-related documents.[1] And as everyone knows, Andersen subsequently went out of business (even though they were exonerated later).

Impact Of Failures To Provide For Operational Transparency

Transparency is not limited to financial concerns. A lack of transparency in how a company operates can lead to a lack of confidence, on the part of investors, on the part of regulators, and on the part of customers.

For example, many companies (legally) manipulate shipment schedules to balance earnings across reporting periods.[2] However, do their customers know this? What would be the impact if their customers found out? – especially if a customer experienced financial damage as a result of a deliberately-delayed shipment? Would it damage the reputation of the company? This kind of risk must be properly weighed against the narrower advantages of balancing earnings. Many kinds of risk are therefore eliminated if policies and practices are fully disclosed, but disclosure is not always sufficient.

Impact Of Failures To Be Cognizant Of and Uniformly Respond To Changing Laws and Regulations

International e-commerce is becoming a global minefield of jurisdictional laws related to intellectual property, consumer protection, encryption restrictions, taxes, and content restrictions. US companies that have to file income taxes in all 50 states are familiar with the burden of compliance with laws from multiple jurisdictions. International Internet-based commerce is heading toward becoming exponentially more complex than the 50-state problem, as jurisdictions around the world become aware of the reach of Internet-based commerce.

---

[1] See [Chaney03].
[2] A large network equipment provider is rumored to do this.

For example, something as innocuous as receiving documents from business partners can result in financial liability. In 2006, Campden Publishing of London was found to possess £80,000 worth of unlicensed fonts, primarily in documents received from external sources. From an article [PinsentMasons06] about the situation: "The problem is complicated by the fact that some fonts can arrive as part of other people's documents and can sometimes stay, unlicensed, on a network."

In such an environment, it is foolhearty to not have a legal assurance system in place for identifying jurisdictional business risk, evaluating the risk, and implementing actions to reduce the risk. Since the actions of a single employee can often do great damage to a firm's reputation, it is important that any risk reduction strategy include a governance system for ensuring that the strategy is actually implemented throughout the organization. Policies that sit on a website just don't cut it.

Impact Of Failures To Anticipate and Respond To Changes In Local Market and Operating Environments

In 1997, Jim Breyer, a managing partner of Accel Partners, referring to the pace of investment during the Internet bubble, said "You can't invest well at that pace...Classic business-analysis discipline gets subjugated to emotion and gut-feeling." He also stressed that having good market intelligence and analysis requires focus: "We need to come into a situation already informed." [1]

Some companies approach this by partnering broadly and forming alliances, realizing that their predictive abilities are limited and in effect hedging their bets. Texas Instruments attributes its recent success to its approach of partnering with a broad range of innovators, regardless how large or small. According to Gregory Delagi, TI's Vice President of Digital Signal Processing Systems, "We get very early access to what people are working on...We aren't smart enough to know which of these small guys is going to be big." [2] Their market intelligence strategy is therefore

---

[1]   Ref. [Cone1997].
[2]   Ref. [Darlin2006].

interwoven with their business development strategy, providing a level of breadth and resilience within their market.

Impact Of Failures To Be Aware Of and Respond Uniformly To Usability Or Customer Issues

Not too long ago I changed cellphone service from one wireless carrier to another so that I could have a GSM phone that worked around the world. The US has a law informally called "number portability" that requires that one be able to keep one's phone number when one changes their service provider. I therefore requested to keep my phone number during the change. This caused a great many problems, and I found that I was on the phone a lot to the wireless carrier's customer service. Eventually my issue was elevated to their network operations department, and once there they said something like "oh we are very familiar with that kind of problem." I then asked why Customer Service was not aware of the problem, and the reply was, "Yeah, we should tell them about that."

This is an example of an issue that is very important to a large number of new customers, but has no immediate measurable business impact because most customers will probably persevere until the problem is solved, even if their perception of the carrier is destroyed in the process.

As another example, the same wireless carrier mentioned above provides a WiFi wireless service in a widely known coffeehouse chain. This service worked great until the coffeehouse chain began to deploy a convection oven for heating breakfast offerings. The oven interfered with the WiFi signal. The coffeehouse chain was completely unaware of this problem for a year because when a coffeehouse customer has a problem with the WiFi service there is no one to complain to. The coffeehouse store manager often does not even know where the equipment is or anything else about it.

I could go on and on with examples, because examples of this phenomenon, which I call the *orphan customer* phenomenon, abound. An orphan customer is a customer who has no human advocate assigned to them with the service provider organization or organizations. The phenomenon is a result of today's complex service delivery environment that often involves partners and many different parts of a large organization. For example, if you have a problem with delivery of an order placed through Amazon but fulfilled by an Amazon partner, who do you complain to? Similarly, if you have a problem with service received from an outsourced call center, do you complain to the call center or to the company that has contracted with the call center? And would most people bother, or simply stop buying things from the company?

Everyone knows the power of viral marketing: what many do not realize that it can work for you or against you. Therefore, protecting your reputation is critical to long-term success. The orphan customer phenomenon is a growing kind of risk. To avoid it you must ensure that customer-level success is measured in a comprehensive manner across the customer experience lifecycle, and that special attention is paid to the points at which partner handoffs or service changes are involved. This is an operational effectiveness transparency issue.

Let me connect the dots directly: If it is not clear how the orphan customer phenomenon is related to governance or business assurance, it is perhaps because of the limited roles that governance and assurance play in the minds of IT today. As I have explained, governance is about management, direction, and alignment. The orphan customer is a failure of governance because the organization fails to take responsibility for the overall customer lifecycle experience that is provided by the *many disjoint business functions and partnerships*. Thus, while each business function might be providing a service based on its narrow interactions with the customer or with third party providers, the overall goals of the organization are subverted because of the ways in which the services are deployed and operated and the ways in which they interconnect. Proper governance should ensure that those who design and deploy the services should implement the right kinds of metrics for actual customer satisfaction and ultimately business value rather than focusing on metrics that are narrowly focused on each particular step in the service chain. Governance should ensure measure alignment with overall business goals.

Impact Of Failures To Properly Govern Technical Decisions

Senior management does not always properly evaluate (or even hear about) the level of risk in all of the highly technical operational issues that arise from one day to the next. A case in point is the ill-advised but well-intentioned publishing by AOL in 2006 of research data about user search queries, leading to the resignation of AOL's CTO and several other executives and severely damaging AOL's reputation. Therefore, transparency in terms of what actions are being taken is important, but it is not sufficient to mitigate risk. Risk must be assessed in a manner that integrates the many areas of concern of an organization: that is, the rationale for each decision must be transparent so that one can ensure that all concerns have been considered.

Some technical decisions are made by default, as a result of the lack of a decision. For example, a great many technology choice decisions are made as a result of grass-roots adoption within organizations. As a case in point, this author witnessed the widespread download and usage of Weblogic Server (then known as "Tengah") by programmers within companies for small trial projects. The product was free for limited-scope usage, so it was adopted quickly. A few years passed, and organizations became aware of the need for this class of product, and when they asked their programmers what they recommended, they of course heard "Weblogic Tengah", because that was what everyone was using – not because it was better, but because it was freely available.

But grass-roots decisions are not always the best. Programmers are very quick to jump on new tool bandwagons, and vendors know that they need to produce demand for a new generation of tools every few years as tool markets saturate and need to be re-stimulated. As a result, the industry heavily promotes new generations of tools whether they are truly beneficial or not. This book is not the right forum to argue the merits of various technologies, but it is this author's opinion that many generations of tools have gone by the wayside because of popularity trends rather than technical merits.

Another phenomenon is that certain technologies become entrenched because classes of users evolve who have based their careers on the technology, and therefore they continue to recommend it even after it is obsolete. Relational database technology is a good example of this. Relational technology is extremely powerful for systems that must discover relationships, but it is a *very poor technical choice* for most middle-tier line-of-business applications which repeatedly traverse the same relationships through data; yet it continues to dominate in that domain and be the universal choice, partly because there is a small set of very powerful vendors who invest heavily in marketing, and partly because all of the DBAs who have become certified in these products continue to recommend them as the "only viable enterprise choice". This has long been a fallacy, but it is an entrenched one, and it has had the effect of killing promising non-relational products, resulting in the self-fulfilling reality that today there are few viable non-relational choices left, and very few people will now speak against relational technology because of fear of ridicule. It is as if new kinds of products in the database realm are prohibited even from serious discussion. As a result, enterprises suffer in terms of the huge development costs of building and maintaining relational interfaces to object-oriented applications, and the inability to scale when data relationships are complex.

The relational database conundrum is but one example of how enterprises bear the cost of inappropriate decisions made at lower levels within IT but that have very large aggregate impact on the enterprise in terms of agility and the ability to implement new capabilities in a cost-effective and timely manner. I could give you many more examples.

Proper Criteria For IT Technology and Process Choices

Technology choices should be made based on enterprise criteria, including:

1. The lifecycle cost of the technology for the planned scope of deployment.
2. The availability of sufficient vendor selection within the technology, to prevent vendor lock-in.

3. The ability to find or develop staff in a cost-effective manner who can use the technology, over the expected lifetime of usage.
4. The simplicity or effectiveness with which the technology can be deployed and used.
5. The level of interoperability of the technology with other technologies.

Criteria 1 and 2 are primarily economic considerations, although criteria 2 impacts the ability to find quality products as a result of the presence of adequate competition. Criteria 3 and 4 are people issues in one sense, but also have to do with the ease with which users of the technology (including programmers) can be trained. Criteria 5 is purely a technical consideration and therefore is perhaps the easiest to evaluate.

> **Technology evaluations in actual usage should be performed in an objective manner and include enterprise criteria.**

It is important that these criteria are not evaluated in a grass-roots usage mode. Rather, issues such as ease of development and effectiveness should be evaluated in a setting that utilizes a process for an objective evaluation.

Enterprise concerns such as maintainability pertain to criteria 4 and 5, and asking programmers whether they can maintain something will not give you an answer that reflects the lifecycle of the technology nor will it reflect operational aspects that developers do not experience. Programmers have a very strong bias toward technologies that are the current trend, because it provides them with personal marketability. They also have a bias toward technologies that are fun to use or that allow them to create intricate things – a characteristic that is antithetical to maintainability, security, and reliability.

Summary

Popular notions of IT governance limit the role of governance to risk management. A broader view of governance encompasses value creation. It is necessary to link these because only then can one properly balance their respective elements. Therefore, governance must be more than risk management, and needs to account for all aspects of governing an organization, in the sense of directing, growing, and overseeing the organization in the interests of its constituents.

That said, the risk management functions of governance are increasingly important as the business environment becomes increasingly complex. Inadequate governance can result in failures to realize objectives from initiatives, accounting failures, inadequate transparency into operations, legal problems, market-related errors and missed opportunities, failures in customer service, and technical errors in judgment that have strategic consequences. Governance is about providing transparency into all of these risks and ensuring that balanced choices are made.

4. What Is Missing With Control-Based Governance

"...managers are used to controlling people, but they know they cannot control minds."
- Peter Meyer[1]

"The effect of oversight has been to destroy the ability to do anything rational."

This statement was articulated by the head of the business information systems planning organization, a direct report to the CIO, of a major government agency. He then went on to state, "[Managing business value] is not a command and control problem. You must solve it by enabling money to be attracted most to where it provides the most value.

Whenever there is a problem in anything, there is a tendency in people to try to address the symptom instead of the root cause. For example, if costs are high, then cut costs, rather than investing in making things more efficient. Control-based frameworks originate from this type of philosophy, that problems can be addressed by controlling the symptoms. The theory is that one can identify every kind of problem, and insert a "control" to eliminate the problem. Unfortunately, problems are sometimes the result of complex interactions that cannot be addressed by inserting a single fix at the point at which the symptom emerges.

IT control frameworks such as CMMI suffer from the control mentality, and as a result they are not too well respected at a grass roots level. Here is a quote from a posting to the Northern Virginia Java User's Group on January 31, 2008: "In the one case

---

[1] Ref. [Meyer98].

where I was involved with a company implementing CMM, it had a mainly negative effect on our team... Essentially, CMM makes the assumption that there is one best development process for the entire organization... Most agile methodologies, to the extent that they address process improvement at all, assume that you have to constantly customize the process for your particular project and team."

On the other hand, CMMI has a large following, and it is simply about defining your business processes. The "governance" provided by CMMI is that it defines processes for certifying that your organization follows well-defined and well-controlled processes. What could be wrong with that?

Governance is nothing more than the process of management. However, governance implies a high level of coordination, control, and oversight, including the existence of policies and activities that reflect *all of* the organization's goals and concerns, and mechanisms to enforce and align those policies and activities.

Governance is very much – although not completely – about risk reduction. The recognition that the world has become complex, and that an organization can no longer simply focus on profit, has led to increased interest in ways to ensure that the quest for profit does not lead an organization into areas that put it in peril in other ways. The natural reaction has been to apply accounting-based principles to control the organization's activities so that its profit centers are kept in check with regard to corporate policies. After all, control works for the risk of a cost center spending too much: perhaps it should work for other forms of risk as well. Thus, control-based governance seeks to ensure that controls are in place, analogous to financial controls, to provide assurance with regard to all forms of corporate risk.

> **There are fundamental differences between accounting processes and IT initiative processes.**

Control-based governance is great in theory: focus on putting checkpoints in each process; if you get the checkpoints right, you will forever be assured to follow risk-mitigation policies. However, one problem is that this leads to excessive attention on monitoring the internals of each process, which leads inevitably to an ever-more-microscopic view of processes, and ultimately tracking each task of each empowered individual – which tends to defeat the whole purpose of empowering workers. This kills productivity, innovation, and morale. The impact on morale should not be under-estimated. Indeed, according to Steve Hein, author of *EQ For Everybody*, over-control is considered to be a form of emotional abuse.[1]

There are fundamental differences between accounting processes and IT initiative processes. First of all, accounting processes traditionally occur according to a schedule, and are repeated during each reporting period, usually with only incremental variations. In contrast, IT initiative processes are executed according to unique schedules, and no two IT projects are ever the same. Further, accounting processes can be verified by comparing calculations that are done in different ways but that should produce the same totals. This is known as reconciliation. In contrast, IT initiative processes do not reduce to a numeric result, and proving that business goals have been met is much more challenging.

These differences mean that IT initiative processes cannot be controlled and verified in the same way that financial processes can be. To try to do so is to create a bureaucratic system that will overburden the IT initiative processes and that will not result in the desired control improvements without slowing IT to a near standstill and dramatically increasing the cost of IT initiatives. For

Case In Point

example, the Large Investment Product Provider mentioned earlier discovered that once its many control policies had been implemented it now cost $100K to change the definition of a single field in a database.

> **Let's stop thinking only about IT policy enforcement and start thinking about compliance enablement.**

Among IT policymaker and enterprise architects one often one hears the phrase that "policies must be enforced". This conjures the impression that employees are willfully and cavalierly

---

[1] Ref. [Hein1996].

shirking policy. Assuming that we are talking about professional-level employees, no explanation could be more ridiculous. If policy is not followed on a broad scale, it is because it either competes with other policies, staff are not aware of or do not understand the need for the policy, their day-to-day realities make policy adherence impractical, or the value proposition of adhering to policy is insufficient when compared with the reward from pursuing other concerns. The Large Investment Product Provider had upwards of 200 policies – if one included the policies related to data security and every other area. These were all on the company's internal website and IT staff were expected to be aware of any policies that were "published" on the website. Yet if one asked a typical developer about these policies they did not even know they existed. Similarly, a US government agency that I worked with had more than 300 "directives" (policies) published on their website, and indeed few in IT knew about the existence of these even though a large number pertained to IT (and especially IT security).

In fact, US Federal Government agencies are required to consider overall business value – not just cost or risk. The Clinger-Cohen Act (CCA) of 1996 mandates that government entities be administered using a framework that considers business value, where business value is defined in terms of the success of an agency's mission. The Federal standard known as OMB Circular A-11, Section 300, "PLANNING, BUDGETING, ACQUISITION, AND MANAGEMENT OF CAPITAL ASSETS", according to a process known as Capital Planning and Investment Control (CPIC), provides the framework for executing this mandate. In some ways the Federal Government is therefore ahead of private industry in terms of making decisions based on business value.

What is missing from the controls-based view of governance is the entire role of capability development and insertion.

However, it is the case that the provisions of these laws and frameworks are often addressed in a superficial manner. For some agencies, this might be because Federal CIO performance evaluation and compensation is not as tied to *business performance* (as defined by CPIC) as it should be, and for other agencies it might be because

40

the CIO is not adequately empowered. Perhaps over time agencies will become more adept at implementing these, since as is true with everything, it is not so much what you do but how you do it.

What do the internal controls matter if the output meets objectives? This sounds like heresy, but it is not. Controls *are* important, but one can over-control. If control acts on the end result of each major function, not on each step of a process, there is room for change; but then also there is inadequate measurement for root cause analysis. The problem is therefore complex. In the end, this is the most important point of all: when controls are put in place, they will kill innovation unless they are put in place by the people who must use them. That is, you must not insert them from without; you must insert them from within. Here I am talking about operational controls, not oversight that is intended to be independent. I am talking about controls that are part of your business processes.

Capabilities Are Incomplete Until They Are Integrated

Capabilities are not achieved by acquisition. Any capabilities acquired must be integrated, and that is a long and arduous process. Acquisition of businesses may be a successful way to capture new markets quickly; acquisition of key personnel can be an effective way to bring new ideas to an organization; but hiring of new staff to acquire new capabilities must account for the time and effort to integrate those new capabilities into the organization's overall capabilities. Operational capabilities need to be grown, and that is a complex process that needs a strategic focus. The element of growing capabilities is missing from many governance approaches.

Governance plans invariably address the need to disseminate and educate staff about policies and practices. However, this is usually approached in a very hands-off manner, through curricula, presentations, Q&A sessions, and evangelism. These approaches are not sufficient. To be effective, such "communication" programs need to be far more proactive. In the words of David McDonald, head of Freddie Mac's Finance Program Management Office at the time of this writing, an organization needs to have a "control-based culture", and achieving that is "everyone's job".[1] That is, it is not the job of a communication team. It requires transformation of the entire organization, and that requires aggressive change management. In the words of Andrew McAfee of the Harvard Business School,

"Executives need to stop looking at IT projects as technology installations and start looking at them as periods of organizational change that they have a responsibility to manage."[2]

The Ministry Of Risk

Perhaps the main driver of governance today is risk management. Organizations now invest a great deal in risk management. Many organizations have tackled the problem by creating entire risk departments that develop risk management frameworks encompassing market risk, compliance risk, and every other kind of risk you can think of.

This is actually kind of lopsided. Risks are merely the negative contributors to opportunity. Every opportunity has risks. To single out risks and aggregate them into a department is kind of like consolidating all opportunities into a department – the Opportunity Management department – a department that does not consider the risk side of the equation because the Risk Management department does that. The government equivalent of these would be the Ministry Of Risk and the Ministry Of Opportunity: kind of makes you want to run and hide, doesn't it? Yet if you think abut it, that is the direction that governance is taking as it is implemented in many organizations.

In one organization that I have worked with, management came up with a chart depicting a dozen capabilities needed for enterprise IT architecture governance. Each capability was represented by a box and had a manager's name on it. These boxes included "Risk Registry", "Issue Tracking", Control Registry", "Process Registry", and so on down the list of things that need to be tracked in order to manage the risks and issues associated with the organization's data. While I could not argue

---

[1] Ref. [McDonald06].
[2] Ref. [McAfeeHBR06].

with the functions, the prospect of creating a department for each one made me shiver. The twelve areas were all intertwined operationally but separated in terms of accountability, and separating them to serve accountability needs would be like separating the cooks in a kitchen based on the ingredients. It would be a classic industrial age response to the need to manage issues. Fortunately management realized that the twelve areas needed to be better integrated and not separated, and the identification of these twelve areas enabled the organization to plan that integration.

Today's common approaches to risk management are a monolithic response to the increasing complexity of business and to pressures from auditors. Each opportunity now carries risk, and organizations need to ensure that their approach to reducing risk is economical and comprehensive, hence the consolidated focus. A better approach is that each business undertaking should account for risk through distributed governance processes that ensure that concerns are integrated across the organization with every action that it takes. The only way to achieve this is to elevate the risk management capabilities of *each part* of the organization.

Governance Needs To Plan For Failure

When I was much younger and just out of graduate school I struggled to come up with a personal expense budget that actually worked for me. One day I browsed through my checkbook to see exactly where my money was going, and to my dismay my checks were a series of seemingly one-time purchases: a pair of gloves, a new tire, a birthday present, a parking ticket, an application fee, and so on. There was no apparent pattern unless one looked at a time period spanning years. Finally it hit me: these were not really one-time events; they were recurring categories of events, and to devise an effective budget I had to account for these recurring categories of expenses and put aside money for them.

This lesson in personal finance 101 applies to initiative planning, yet it is seldom followed. In today's complex business environment one cannot assume that failure prevention of any kind will be 100% effective. One needs to assume a failure rate, focus on containment, and build the assumed failure rate into planning.

For example, most organizations experience security failures of various kinds over time. If a failure occurs, what will be its scope? What measures can be taken to ensure that the scope is limited? Methods for making risk mitigation tradeoffs based on business value are presented later in this book.

> **Planning needs to include both prevention and containment, and estimate the frequency that failures can be reasonably expected to occur.**

As another example that might resonate even more, most businesses experience crises that come along and preempt projects that are underway. Such disruptions are very destructive to those projects. Therefore it is advisable when possible to assume a certain level of these crises and build that level into the budget for resources and staff so that when the inevitable crisis comes along the organization has not started things that it will likely not finish.

A plan for success therefore needs to assume some level of failure, and contain built-in buffers and contingencies to ensure that the plan will not be derailed by the myriad of random crises that come along in an almost predictable way. This is fundamental for business assurance.

How Agility Competes With Assurance

To moderate the use of controls seems to be counter to achieving organizational "maturity". That is, how can one achieve complete definition of processes and even optimization of those processes unless every function is rigidly controlled like a Swiss watch? By analogy, the essence of manufacturing process control is to precisely measure every aspect of every process, and thereby determine every last corner where waste can be eliminated. Just-in-time manufacturing attempts to eliminate wasteful inventory.

People are not machines though. The analogy between manufacturing and human intellectual processes is highly flawed. It is an industrial age comparison that views human processes as if they were an assembly line. An assembly line may be very efficient at implementing a process, but if the process needs to radically change, one might have to scrap the entire factory, because the process is hard-wired into the infrastructure. An assembly line is the epitome of rigidity, and is not what is needed for today's agile service corporation.

In an assembly line, each step is highly specialized. Work flows along, with each aspect of the overall work being applied at each step. Each step is highly tuned. The overall time to get through the assembly line from start to finish might be very long, but that doesn't always matter because throughput is often the primary concern. The assumption is that the volume of processing is very high, and that change is very infrequent.

In human processes that require decision-making, there is often interplay between steps, and so an assembly line approach will often result in work being thrown back to prior steps, lots of meetings, and a long time between the start of work on an item and the completion of that work. The work "item" is often an intellectual product, such as an insurance claim, a loan application, or a software component design. Such work requires judgment and often the consideration of many different concerns that are important to the organization.

Let's consider a corporate communications example in which the organization needs a way to ensure that communications with the outside world do

The type of robust maturity that we seek is the ability to change rapidly and have the entire organization remain aligned.

not put the company at risk. In a pure assembly line approach, each intended communication would be passed along for review to the inbox of a "communications department" before it could go out. That is in fact what many organizations do. Certainly any statements about the company's financial condition or intent are subject to corporate communications guidelines, as well as known problems with financial controls, and these concerns are becoming very complex and increasingly apply at lower and lower levels of today's company. Should we restrict all communication, which now occurs not only by email but on text messaging and personal devices as well as websites and customer support message boards? Or, should we filter everything through a communication czar – a corporate equivalent of the bureaucratic Ministry of Communication? Of course the answer to either of these must be no, but what is the ultimate solution, as we are increasingly accountable yet must be increasingly agile in order to compete?

A New Definition Of Maturity

Today's business environment is permeated by diverse and ever-changing risks, and nimbleness is clearly a requirement for survival, especially in a global market where not all competitors have the same set of burdens or concerns. In this environment, maturity is perhaps better measured by *how adept an organization is at responding to change in a cautious and self-regulating but aggressive and innovative manner*. That is, how quickly can it change its core business model, reinvent the organization, and yet do all this in a manner that is methodical and minimizes risk? It is hard to see how the traditional view of organizational maturity characterized by a culture of careful and thorough definition of process, supported by controls at every point, could ever be nimble, and so the traditional form of "maturity" is perhaps more akin to senescence and imminent death.

This is not to say that efficiency and nimbleness are incompatible. In fact, great efficiency is possible if you truly put departments in charge of their own processes and create the right incentives. The challenge then is how to achieve fluidity across departments and across the enterprise.

The Bottleneck Of Concerns

Agile maturity sounds very nice to have but how do we deal with the reality that in today's enterprise there are a multitude of competing concerns, including profitability, accountability, and legal diligence and coverage? These different concerns must be addressed by experts, and it is only possible to organize a company in a single hierarchy. Therefore, one would think that the primary structure would reflect the most important concern, which is usually operational efficiency, and that additional concerns must be addressed through additional control processes layered on top of the hierarchy and driven by officers (CFO, Chief Counsel, CIO, CSO, etc.), policies, and special committees. Officer-level concerns are usually implemented as groups of specialists who report to the officer and who are inserted into the primary workflow at various points. The result is a very complex, interwoven process that is resistant to change because of its complexity.

Consider the case of an initiative to build a new capability to sell a product. Some of the concerns for such a capability might include sales effectiveness, customer relationship management, revenue capture, market goals and strategies by market segment, legal constraints by market region or segment, accounting concerns, regulatory compliance requirements, and security concerns. Clearly it is not practical to merely articulate the functional goals of the project and then leave it to the implementers to figure out the rest. Therefore, in such a situation, the initiative manager must make sure that each enterprise concern is captured as a requirement. Further, as requirements evolve, which is always the case in agile projects, enterprise concerns must be reconsidered. This means that the various parts of the organization must be re-engaged on a continual basis while the new capability is developed.

It is of course possible to fix the initiative's requirements up-front, and capture all the enterprise concerns once; but it has been found that at least for software projects that is not practical. Attempts to capture all requirements up-front tend to fail at a rate of at least 50%, and that is why more and more organizations are moving to more agile approaches, which allow for some level of evolution of requirements throughout a project. Certainly as time goes forward, the trend favors increasing change and therefore the need for increasing agility, and any organization that can achieve agility has a tremendous advantage.

Suppose that each enterprise concern is addressed through a workflow that incorporates an expert at each step who evaluates project or departmental issues from the perspective of that concern and only that concern. The result is a flow such as is shown in Figure 1.

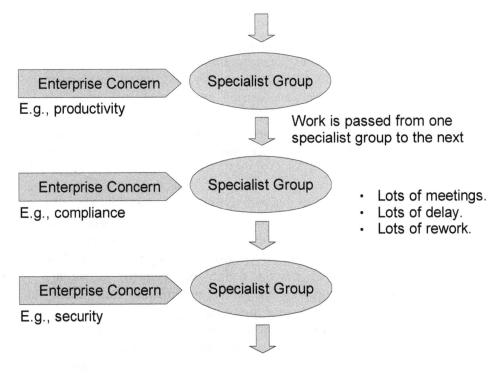

Figure 1: Typical Segregation of Processes By Enterprise Concern

In this kind of flow each specialist group can operate very efficiently, since they are highly specialized. However, what happens if processes need to change? Each specialist has such a narrow view of their focus area that they are not much help in deciding how to re-partition the flow. At a higher level, a single policy change can result in the need to re-evaluate every single process and design guideline from multiple perspectives, and therefore by multiple parties, each specializing in their own narrow area (e.g., architecture, data quality, compliance, etc.).

In addition, every time a work item is rejected by a step, the work item must be modified and then go back to the beginning of the queue of concerns, to make sure that the change did not impact any concerns that it had already passed. Thus, while this layout is very efficient for a static process that involves few exceptions, it is very poor for a process that must be changed from time to time and that experiences many exceptional conditions during normal operation. Human processes tend to be of this kind.

Risk Management as Practiced By Software Developers

In 2007 the Northern Virginia Java User's Group (NovaJUG) took a poll of members to see how many Java software developers practice "risk management". That single question in the poll was, "Does your project manage risk?" and the results of the poll as shown in Figure 2.

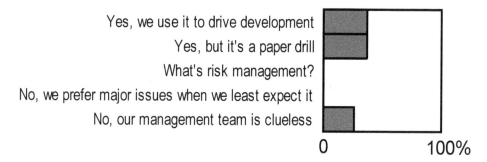

Yes, we use it to drive development
Yes, but it's a paper drill
What's risk management?
No, we prefer major issues when we least expect it
No, our management team is clueless

0   100%

Figure 2: NovaJUG Risk Management Practices Poll

The sample size of this informal poll was quite small – there were only eight respondents – but it does give a flavor for the state of affairs in software development. For example, it appears from the results that risk management is generally practiced in some manner by the majority (75% in the survey) of projects, although in half of those cases it is not effective. The upshot is that according to this survey effective risk management is only practiced 37% of the time.

One of the members of the NovaJUG responded to the survey with the following:[1]

---

[1] I have cleaned up the punctuation and grammar: software developers are notoriously carefree about the way they write on newsgroups. Original posting was made to the NovaJUG Yahoo group by user "jawabean" on 6/18/07.

"Maybe 'risk management' is not the term, which is used in these situations, but implicitly we always evaluate risks and mitigate them. Things like "parallel run," when a new system is run side-by-side with the old system for month or two - it's risk management. The same applies to contingency planning, etc."

It is clear from this posting that the poster is treating risk management as meaning risk related to bugs and catastrophic run-time failure. I am certain that this poster is aware of other kinds of risk, but the implicit assumption that risk management for IT pertains only to run-time errors is built into the profession. Risks related to a failure to address enterprise concerns for regulatory compliance, security, and all the other kinds of risk addressed in the prior chapter are generally not on the radar screen of software developers unless their arms are twisted.

Implications For IT Systems

Today's increasing multiplicity of business concerns has a strategic consequence for IT system development: the designers of these systems can no longer focus on core business functions, but must be cognizant of so many different classes of implied requirements that they have an increasingly hard time planning initiatives.

> **Today's increasing multiplicity of business concerns has a strategic consequence: solution designers have an increasingly hard time planning initiatives.**

For example, consider accounting concerns: any business input can potentially be an accounting or regulatory compliance input. How can an operational IT system be designed if it must also take into account a full range of complex accounting and regulatory reporting needs, representing entirely different categories of users? IT system designers cannot easily decompose the functions that they must build, because the independent accounting (and other) concerns break the natural hierarchy of function: there are now multiple hierarchies of concerns superimposed on the IT system requirements. In the words of Mark Lutchen, "This is the reason there is no such thing as an 'IT project' anymore: there are business projects that have IT components." [1]

For an enterprise operational IT system, this is simply too much complexity to handle using traditional assembly-line approaches for design and implementation, unless you are willing to wait for three years and tolerate many periods of cost overruns and risk not achieving your operational objectives.

Another consideration is that it takes time for knowledge to be transferred, and in fact, as a prominent expert in agile software development recently said, *knowledge transfer is the long pole in the tent, not development.*[2] Therefore, to not efficiently leverage the critical SMEs in some way is to condemn an initiative to being executed serially, even if its projects are operated in parallel. The parallelism is defeated by the fact that people must wait in line for access to SMEs, and so a great many project analysts spend much of their time waiting for meetings.

Figure 3 depicts a solution to speeding up the process of collaboration between solution designers and the various specialists who are knowledgeable about each enterprise concern. In this approach the specialists act as mentors to the solution providers (labeled as the "Implementer Group"). By teaching the implementers about the various specialist concerns, the implementers are gradually able to represent the specialists and make their own decisions about the various concerns, obviating continual review. Of course, the specialists retain their authority over those domains of concern (e.g., legal concerns, financial concerns), but the specialists begin to trust the implementers sufficiently so that oversight is necessary but continual review is not.

---

[1] From a personal conversation, 2007. Mark Lutchen is a partner at PricewaterhouseCoopers and leader of the IT Business Risk Management Practice.

[2] Ref. [Nielsen06].

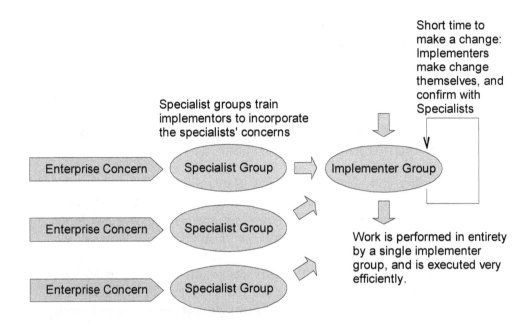

Specialist groups train
implementors to incorporate
the specialists' concerns

Short time to
make a change:
Implementers
make change
themselves, and
confirm with
Specialists

Enterprise Concern   Specialist Group   Implementer Group

Enterprise Concern   Specialist Group

Enterprise Concern   Specialist Group

Work is performed in entirety
by a single implementer
group, and is executed very
efficiently.

Problems: specialists are often poor mentors, and often
don't have time to spare to each and every
implementation group.

Figure 3: Leveraging Specialists (SMEs)

This is in fact what often takes place on an informal basis in
many organizations. The implementers eventually become
knowledgeable and are able to speak on behalf of the SMEs. The
problem is that the SMEs are still a bottleneck because there are
often many implementer groups representing a variety of
initiatives, and the SMEs continue to be pulled in many
directions. Some of the implementers are able to represent the
SMEs, but those implementers too become a bottleneck because
the SMEs have not been able to train enough of them. Thus, the
problem is reduced but not solved. The next chapter takes this
approach a step further to actually solve the problem and ensure
that SMEs are optimally leveraged.

Implications For Initiative Planning

These new realities impact the very process of capability
planning. Let's consider a typical scenario. The traditional process
for planning initiatives is often something like the following:

1. Develop a new enterprise strategy.
2. Issue policies or directives to establish the mandate for the strategy.
3. Perform capability gap analysis to measure what capabilities are needed to implement the strategy.
4. Create initiatives to develop the new capabilities.
5. Measure the progress of the initiatives.
6. Measure the impact of the new strategy for the enterprise (if possible).

One could dissect step one, in which enterprise strategies are developed, but this book is about capability planning, not strategy planning, so we will begin with step 2. The problem with step 2 is that it does nothing to teach the organization what the strategy, new policies, or directives mean, or how to implement them. It is as if management issued a proclamation and then said "make it so". Training programs are inadequate, because traditional forms of training are not effective and the training materials become shelfware. In the words of a manager who had been involved in a security training program, "[the auditor] found that people who had been in training seemed not to remember anything." Training is important for providing a conceptual foundation but it is not effective unless it is coupled with immediate application to force people to internalize what they have learned and convert it into action-based and experience-based knowledge.

In step 3 high-level requirements are developed for enterprise change. Control-based approaches to governance involve adding control requirements during step 3. This tends to dramatically increase the scope, breadth, and complexity of any initiative.

In step 4 initiatives to "develop capabilities" are planned. However, this is usually in the context of new technology. It is common that a plan for developing capabilities in people is omitted, or treated as "training", which I claim to be ineffective. The training aspect is usually an afterthought, much as organizations often treat security as an afterthought: "make it secure". What exactly that means, and how it is to be achieved, is left to the implementer, with predictable results.

In the common approach to step 4, it is really up to staff to create human processes and develop capabilities by trying, failing, and trying again. Perhaps internal or outside consultants are used to help or "facilitate adoption", but consultants will do some of the process design themselves, and then the organization needs to be trained, and classroom training is not effective. Thus, in this approach there is no effective system for creating new capabilities and pushing those through the organization.

Initiatives usually develop software, move people around, or establish classroom-based training programs. None of these actually do much at all to develop true capabilities. True capabilities require that the line of business understand the concerns, are direct drivers of process changes, and generate the artifacts themselves that will need to be maintained.

Step 5 is problematic because the progress of initiatives is measured in terms of the completion of IT elements (project milestones), not in terms of the development of awareness in people and the ability to maintain the documents that describe the new processes, thereby recreating the lack of transparency that plagued the organization before. Progress should really be measured in terms of the creation of business capability, but more on that later.

Step 6 attempts to measure overall success. This measurement is typically in terms of increased efficiency or increased compliance, since IT projects seldom define metrics for true business capability. It is often the case that old systems remain for awhile after new ones are installed, because the "hard cases" can only be handled by the old systems until processes are adjusted and the kinks are worked out. By the time the old systems can be unplugged, new business issues have arisen and the systems must be changed again: i.e., the metrics change. Therefore, it makes no sense to compare such a large-grain before and after picture. Measurement must be ongoing to be meaningful, and in terms of capabilities and business value, not systems. There must be continual improvement, and that means small, incremental initiatives and a continual effort to maintain similar (standard) business processes throughout the organization so that capability measurements can be compared.

A common mistake with step 4 is when a "big bang" approach is used. Creating several initiatives that will result in new business processes might be too much to get right the first time, resulting in tremendous wasted effort and adding a great amount of unnecessary risk. As a case in point, one organization that I worked with launched a program to address a set of risk-related

issues within the company. This program had clear high-level goals for building new capabilities and business results and was funded at an annual rate that represented a good chunk of the overall IT budget. It was not very effective because (a) it was conceived as a big-bang effort (it did not pilot, and there was lots of effort wasted); (b) it did not effectively partner with business units; (c) it was not well-linked with the company's risk management group; (d) it was not well-integrated with accounting improvement efforts; and (e) it was not integrated with business unit capability planning (i.e., not driven by business value). In fact, the group developed a multi-year roadmap that was conceived based on its own goals and then retroactively backed into business priorities when the time came to sell the roadmap. This was unavoidable because of the aforementioned factors. That said, it did eventually manage to alleviate the risk issues that were its main goal – but at enormous cost and after a protracted period that was very disruptive to other IT initiatives.

The bottom line is that the program was conceived as a strategic program, but its implementation was fatally flawed by its approach of operating in a breadth-first big-plan manner and by its failure to adequately build incremental successes and relationships with business units. It would surely have been more successful if it had focused on those relationships and partnered with business units to create a consensus-driven approach for helping business units to address the risk management concerns.

Initiative planning and organization is discussed in more detail in chapter 14.

Portfolio Management Is Not Sufficient

Research shows that organizations achieve higher agility by treating IT projects as investments and prioritizing them based on an analysis of return on investment.[1] However, it is important to remember that IT investments are hands-on: one has the ability to influence the outcome of the investment. Specifically,

[1] Ref. [WeillRoss04].

one can direct the objective of each portfolio project as well as the way in which each project is conducted. Thus, IT investments are not just assets to pick and choose from or discard at will. One can undertake to ensure that the right projects are proposed[1], and one can also undertake to mitigate risk rather than merely discarding risky efforts. Discarded IT investments represent abandoned attempts to solve real problems that will not go away by themselves.

Perhaps it is effective risk mitigation that is behind the success of some firms that seem to be able to undertake risky but high payoff projects and beat the odds by showing consistent returns. One can dramatically increase the effectiveness of IT as a business builder and reduce the risk of high-return initiatives for change if one is careful about the manner in which those initiatives are conceived and executed. As I have said before in this book, with so many things in life it is not just *what* you do, but *how* you do it.

Case In Point

A portfolio approach also sidesteps the important need to provide for integration of concerns across initiatives. Simply picking and choosing does not ensure alignment as different initiative proposals can take different approaches to dealing with issues. The case of the Large Investment Product Provider comes to mind: the company was planning an initiative to revamp a major portion of its collateral servicing infrastructure and alignment with the rest of the business was not considered because it was "out of scope" with respect to the charter of the initiative. The result was a proposal that did not address important enterprise concerns and in fact worked against them by assuming that the "out of scope" processes would not change when in fact those processes needed to be upgraded as well. To accept the initiative proposal then would have had the effect of entrenching the current way of doing things in downstream processes.

---

[1] In the words of Benson, Bugnitz, and Walton in [BenBugWal04],
"Prioritization of projects does not ensure that we will have the *right* projects in the backlog to prioritize. We need better projects, driven from business strategy."

Fallacy: Control Effectiveness and Completeness Can Be Proven Through Documentation

"We have a lot of paper, but what do we have?"
– comment made by a senior manager when discussing the progress of an effort to document the controls within his organization. (The effort – led by a large accounting firm – later failed and was stopped, and the VP in charge was fired.)

Most auditing firms have a methodology for auditing the effectiveness and completeness of controls. The typical method is to request and review documentation of business processes. The documentation is often produced specifically to meet the requirements of the audit, and it is not uncommon that the documentation is produced by an external firm.

> **Documents serve only as a reference, but do not constitute understanding.**

This results in externally-produced documentation that becomes shelfware because it was not written by the owners of the processes and therefore will not be used for actual operation or updated in the normal course of operational evolution. Further, such documentation tends to be of questionable completeness because it is usually produced through interviews and therefore is not materially verified. In fact, true risk areas will likely be omitted on purpose by those who are interviewed.

Remediation efforts often focus on documenting processes as well. However, the creation of process documents does not bring you much farther along in achieving an organization-level capability to maintain and enhance your processes – the very reason for documenting them. That can only be achieved by making the process owners produce and maintain their own documentation. Having someone else do it accomplishes little. It is the act of producing documentation that results in the higher level of understanding. Documenting is for the documenter – the documents themselves serve only as a reference, but do not constitute understanding. Documents contain information; the minds of people contain knowledge and understanding.

The Brick Wall Of Execution

One of the challenges for executive management is the visibility into and control of *how* policies and strategies are actually implemented. Visibility is often difficult because processes are complex and middle management does not have a sufficient understanding of processes in order to be able to distill issues for upper management. Control can be problematic because of key-person dependencies and the same lack of transparency: you cannot control what you do not understand.

> ## Core Idea: If you do not impact *how* execution occurs, you have failed.

The complexity of IT systems and processes make IT a fertile area for these problems. Software applications are nothing more than very complex interwoven sets of algorithms and business rules. A programmer's job is to interpret business process requirements and implement those as automated executable rules and algorithms. In the process of doing so a programmer makes countless decisions and choices. Those choices and decisions are all embedded within the software, and it is very often – perhaps most of the time – the case that those decisions and choices are poorly labeled or identifiable except through line-by-line inspection and reverse engineering of the code. In such a situation, it is no wonder that transparency is non-existent. How then can corporate policies be implemented, if so many decisions are not transparent? As a result of this situation, a programmer is in a position to circumvent almost any policy that they choose, either through ignorance, error, or intent.

> **Programmers are in a position to circumvent almost any policy that they choose.**

Thus, it is very hard to control programmers against their will: if they are not "on board" with a policy, they can easily find a way to get around it.

In the words if Michael Swaine, senior editor of Dr. Dobbs Journal, one of the most respected journals for programmers, "Very often what has been put forth as a solution looks like a whole new set of problems to the programmers who are just trying to get the job done." [1]

Consider an example in which a new IT quality policy requires that all data items should be documented. It is easy to satisfy the letter of this requirement while not satisfying its intent: a programmer could simply document a data item in a very sparse manner. As another example, suppose a corporate policy requires that all data errors should be identified and handled. A programmer can decide to meet this requirement by running checks against data, but handle detected errors by simply rejecting bad values, leaving blank data in its place. Again, depending on how the policy is worded, this might meet the letter of the policy.

It is not that programmers do not want to follow policies: it is that bureaucratic policies have less credibility with programmers today in an environment in which policies and organization structures change frequently, schedules are tight, job changes are frequent, those who deliver new functionality at any cost tend to be rewarded over those who follow policies, and there is little backward traceability between current problems and prior failures by particular programmers to follow quality policies within their code.

One approach to addressing quality is by having adequate accountability for quality as well as performance-based incentives for good quality. This is indeed the solution, but the challenge is that "quality" is often defined in bureaucratic ways that programmers no longer consider to be credible. For example, quality practices often mandate the creation of documentation.

> **Infusing policy into the ranks is an immense challenge that is often oversimplified or overlooked entirely.**

However, the programming community has had such bad experiences with voluminous poor documentation that parts of the community now propose to eliminate documentation altogether, and there is broad ground floor skepticism about the

---

[1]   Ref. [Swaine2006].

value of documentation[1]. Thus, to be credible, quality practices must focus on meaningful value, and not merely a dotting-of-the-i's approach to quality. In this environment, defining "quality" is not a simple matter, and it must be customized for the situation and rooted in actual business value.

It is also not possible to craft completely unambiguous policies that address all of the implementation contingencies: there is always need for interpretation, and the software designer and programmer are the people who make those decisions. They are the "in the field" decisionmakers, and if they do not believe a policy to be credible or implementable, or do not understand it, or if they do not have time to implement it and also meet their project schedule, they are in an excellent position to ignore it with little or no detection and therefore no consequence, and they always have the excuse that they did not understand it. In the words of Michael Swaine, "Developers also have reason to resist burdensome policies when they can see that those policies are poorly conceived and inefficient."

Infusing policy into the ranks is therefore an immense challenge that is often oversimplified as "training" or overlooked entirely. IT organizations therefore cannot be managed from a distance, or treated as if they were commodities or portfolios of commodities. Each organization is different, and the details

> **You must provide an incentive for departments to consider _how_ they implement controls, and not merely focus on whether they have or not.**

of how that organization operates have a large impact on how easy it will be to disseminate new policies, or to integrate the organization with other parts of the organization. Such things cannot be measured in financial terms: they must be measured in operational effectiveness and change management terms.

For these reasons, it is often not appropriate to introduce controls into an organization that will not know how to reliably implement and maintain those controls. If controls are inserted

---

[1] The mantra is that "only the code matters".

by force, and compliance measured, the result will be resentment and the creation of a bureaucracy around the controls. This will have the effect of miring the organization in a control-oriented mentality, and every change will require countless meetings and a long cycle time for every capability change.

It would be far better if controls were integrated into processes, rather than layered on. Often a control is better implemented by preventing problems rather than by detecting them. Only the process owners know how to achieve this: to work smart, rather than working hard. To motivate them to do this, you have to enable them and reward them for increasing the control that they have over their own processes. That is, you must provide an incentive for departments to consider *how* they implement controls, and not merely focus on whether they have or not. The "how" is critical. As I have said earlier in this book, in life it is not only *what* you do, but *how* you do it.

Figure 4 illustrates how to reach and acculturate those who execute: how to circumvent what I call the "brick wall of execution". The key is to have an effective and positive channel for enablement, driven by governance concerns but acting in a mentoring capacity to help execution-level groups to succeed and be rewarded for that success. Without this critical function, execution level groups are left to interpret – and possibly resist – directives and policies on their own.

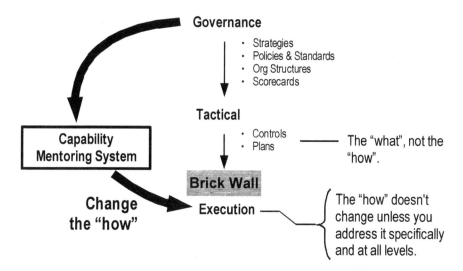

Figure 4: The Brick Wall Of Execution

61

Summary

What is missing from the controls-based view of governance is the entire role of capability development and insertion.

Rather than exclusively trying to guard against tactical failures, organizations should estimate the expected amount of failure and plan for it. That allows them to compare the cost of failure with the investment required to mitigate failure and compare the return with that of other investments.

Current organization maturity models do not account for agility. A high level of process maturity is risky if the organization cannot respond to change and modify its processes. Truly mature organizations can adjust to change while maintaining their maturity level. Those who can perform such transitions routinely and quickly might be said to have agile maturity.

Today's organization has more to worry about than yesterdays, because the world is more complex. T address these concerns, organizations have formed myriad departments to manage the risk associated with each of these concerns. Ideally each of these concerns should have an opportunity to assess each tactical decision that is made by the organization, yet to do this would be to slow down every activity and place a huge burden on the risk management functions. There must be a better way.

IT staff have a very hard time keeping up with the risk management policies of organizations, as these policies become more numerous and more complex.

Knowledge transfer from subject-matter experts to IT staff is the most time-consuming activity in most greenfield IT development projects.

The progress of initiatives is commonly measured in terms of their completion, and does not measure whether the initiatives were executed at all levels with proper consideration of strategic concerns.

Portfolio management must be augmented by introspective examination of each project, to assess what progress is actually being achieved in business terms. Otherwise good investments might be discarded just because root causes of problems have not been identified.

The creation of documentation never represents progress. Documentation is not knowledge: it is only information. Documentation of requirements or business processes does not convey knowledge of those: at best, it is only a starting point. Disbanding a team that assembles requirements as documents squanders the knowledge that the team accumulated.

Software teams are often in a position to ignore and even subvert any policy or standard that they choose, because the code that they create has no transparency to management. Therefore it is imperative to ensure that they have an appreciation and understanding of those policies and standards that matter. Do not expect them to read and learn standards merely because they are published.

If you have not impacted what programmers do each day, then you have not succeeded in ensuring that your policies and standards are incorporated into new automated business processes.

5. Agile Business Power

You Can Have Assurance _and_ Agility

Power is the flow of energy. For an inflow of power, it is the rate at which potential is increased. An organization that is able to react powerfully to change is able to _quickly add new business potential_, in the form of new capabilities to support new strategies. This form of power represents an _inflow_, not an outflow. It is a strengthening of the organization, in response to new demands. From that strengthening, the operational units are then able to project that power outward to the marketplace. To achieve this on a repeatable basis you need a powerful champion for change: an organizational unit that spearheads change to make it happen quickly, faithfully, and consistently.

Your organization runs on power: human brain power. However, when you need to re-tool, when you need to retrain, when you need to change course and develop new

> **Classroom training is costly, and it is not very effective. People need to learn by doing.**

capabilities quickly, do you rely on industrial age methods of training? Or worse, do you leave it to your workers to retrain themselves?

But wait, you say. Training takes people away from their jobs, and its effectiveness is dubious for complex tasks. Classroom training is costly, and it is not very effective. People need to learn by doing.

You are right, _but from now on_ when I talk about training I am not only referring to classroom training. I am referring to the entire process of knowledge transfer and capability development within individuals. A comprehensive system for training that is effective includes a small amount of classroom training to provide a consistent conceptual framework, followed by mentor-based assistance in helping someone to implement what they have learned. This is more cost effective than having someone flounder as they reinvent business methods and they finally learn by making costly mistakes.

It has been proven again and again that people really only learn by doing, and someone has not really acquired a new skill until they have internalized it to a point at which they can use it instinctively. In fact, a recent study proved that people make their best decisions subconsciously, provided that they have sufficient information.[1] A subconscious decision manifests as "gut feeling".

To change direction quickly, you need a powerful means of changing course, just as a large ship needs large engines to change direction. If you want to change your corporate strategy, or make a major adjustment in your business model, you need a highly effective and rapid means of developing new capabilities, and those capabilities reside not in software, but in the minds of the people who work for your organization. If you could put knowledge into their heads, it would take very little time to create any software or system capabilities that you need. Any programmer will tell you: once you know what you need to program, it takes very little to actually write the program; the time consuming part is in figuring out what capabilities need to be created and how they must interact. Your challenge is in developing a system for creating and distributing true knowledge – which includes understanding and self-experience.

IT _Does_ Matter

It is therefore ludicrous to think that in this age of rapidly changing business technologies and opportunities and fickle markets, that new capabilities should be seen as a commodity or not matter at a strategic level. Certainly it is true that new capabilities become old very quickly, and eventually blend into the infrastructure as commodities; but they are quickly _superceded by other new IT technologies_ that must be accounted for strategically, or the organization will surely be bypassed by those who do. It is the inability to envision these continual upheavals that is behind the

---

[1] See [Harris06].

66

recurring idea in some circles that IT does not matter: it is merely a lack of imagination, just as in the early 1900s some people claimed that the automobile had reached its peak and that no other improvements were possible, and that therefore cars would become a commodity.[1]

The challenge today is not only in recognizing the opportunities created by market changes and by new technologies: the challenge is also in being positioned to implement change in short order when it is needed. That positioning is what this book is about.

Directly Tackle the Human Capability Dimension

We go to great pains to program our computers, but we invest comparatively little in training people. While there are some organizations that invest a great deal in training, virtually every large organization has an IT budget that is a significant portion of its operating costs. I have seldom seen organizations invest a comparable amount in training.

> **An organization consists of people and automation systems; for each, you need a means of implementing change and a means of ensuring consistency.**

Yet *people* are the most important "information processors" in a business operation. The assumption is that people can train themselves, by learning on the job. This is the case with some people who are unusually inquisitive. However, it has been my experience that the majority of people learn the skills they need to survive day-to-day and go no further. If the environment does not provide mentors to push people forward, then change will be resisted and the organization will stagnate.

Figure 5 provides a solution to the SME bottleneck problem that was discussed in the previous chapter. In this approach a "Capability Mentor" group – "mentor group" for short – acts as the understudy of the organization's many SMEs. This is the

---

[1] Ref. Scientific American, November 1907.

"champion for change" that I have been talking about. At the same time, this mentor group works closely with implementation teams to devise new solutions that meet enterprise concerns and goals; and if the organization has a "new technology" group that tries out new gizmos, the mentors work with this group as well to infuse appropriate new technology into the organization's operation, thereby *amplifying* the reach of the SMEs

The mentors therefore need to be extremely knowledgeable about SME concerns, and also be knowledgeable about solution design, implementation, and technology adoption. For this reason, these people need to be extremely versatile and have excellent business and technical judgment and acumen. They also need to be natural mentors, to ensure that they are able to infuse their knowledge into the lines of business rather than doing their job for them.

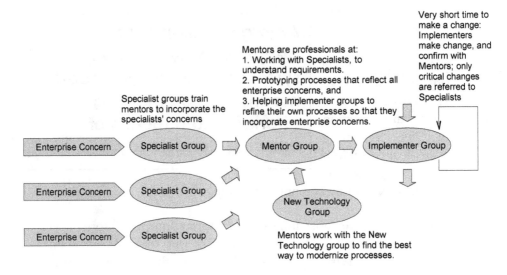

Figure 5: Mentors Leverage SMEs, Providing Scalability of Expertise

The mentors serve another function besides leveraging SMEs. They provide a means of infusing a common approach to addressing enterprise concerns throughout the organization. Even the most ingenious and energetic workers need guidance. Workers who are proactive and who look for improvements in their processes will invent their own ways of doing things. Pretty soon the organization will diverge and become a set of small microcosms, each efficient in isolation, but problematic when efforts to streamline the enterprise from a broader perspective are attempted. This has a profound effect on the ability to share data between groups, because each group has developed its own models of its operation, and to try to integrate the various models is to drown in a quagmire of details. To avoid this quagmire, independent groups need guidance in how to do things. The mentors provide this guidance.

To facilitate this, the mentors should develop a set of blueprints, aka templates, or reference designs. These templates address important decisions so that independent groups do not have to make these decisions independently. Such decisions include things such as standard application components ("stacks"), as well as how data will be exchanged between different groups, who will be involved in designing the interfaces for that exchange, what processes will be used to design and build the interfaces, and how the various data models will be maintained. I have used this approach successfully and it has had a large impact on projects.

Case In Point

As an example, I was once asked to lead an "architecture team" to design and implement architectural improvements based on a deficiency analysis that I had prepared as part of an external assessment. I will refer to this company as the Incubated Product Company. The architecture team prototyped improvements to core the architecture of a system, tried them out in a test version of the actual system, and then deployed them in two ways: (a) by incorporating them as "reference designs" directly into the product on a limited basis and thereby piloting them, and (a) by explaining and evangelizing the reference designs to the development teams so that the new design approaches would find broader use. The result was a drastically more stable and growth-capable underlying platform.

Core Idea: Pilot All Significant New Capabilities

These are all very complex matters and to develop quality blueprints and policies requires professionals who have done it before. Further, to teach groups how to implement and adhere to these templates and policies you need professional teachers – mentors – who can work with the organization's departments until they are able to assume responsibility for new blueprints and policies independently. Mentoring is a refined skill, and cannot be assumed. Professional mentors are the programmers for your staff.

69

The focus therefore needs to be on enabling people, not controlling them. Instead, control the processes, by teaching departments to define their own processes in a proper manner, and monitoring that. This is an agile approach to *governance*, which is the means by which organizations control their processes and ensure accountability. This will become more clear in the discussions that follow.

In chapter 12 I discuss ways that control over IT processes can be achieved without having IT act as a policeman, by enabling and acculturating departmental groups rather than by imposing rules on them.

Use Speed Bumps, Or Improve Driving Skill?

In the section Tracking Progress In Business Terms (page 135) I discussed the problem of how to measure success in the implementation of new capabilities. Then in Chapter 4 I discussed the concept of controls, and how, while an extremely important tool, controls by themselves are inadequate. Here I would like to revisit the subject of controls, and explain how controls operate and how some kinds of controls are much more effective than others.

> **To implement passive controls one must move the attention forward toward business system design and away from real-time checks.**

A control is a mechanism for achieving compliance or alignment with a policy or strategy. A control can take the form of an explicit check, or it can take the form of the integration of those concerns or strategies into operational processes. Explicit checks that are made during or after operation are *active* controls. In-line process measurements that detect and correct errors in real time are active controls. Reconciliation of data or calculations is also a form of active control.

In contrast, checks on the process of designing or deploying the system in question are *passive* because they do not operate as part of the system. Passive controls are more effective because they have the effect of making the *operational* system more robust and less complex. To implement passive controls one must move the attention forward toward the design phase and away from the real-time operation of the system.

As a former nuclear engineer, an example from that industry comes to mind: the types of reactors that have been used by US industry employ a design that is inherently unstable, and so a myriad of redundant active controls are employed to ensure that if something goes wrong that a safe shutdown will be performed. In contrast, there are alternative reactor designs that are inherently stable so that elaborate checks and controls are not necessary.[1] Risk is therefore reduced by changing the very way that the system works, rather than by adding on complex controls. With sufficient diligence, the result is the same, but the approaches are very different. However, one can argue that an inherently stable design is more flexible and secure with respect to modifications and enhancements over time.

It is worth pointing out that the standard taxonomy for controls in the compliance world is (1) preventive, (2) corrective, and (3) detective. This taxonomy is useful, but it is too simplistic in that it represents but one dimension of the problem: where in a process a control is implemented, as opposed to when. Thus, there are actually at least two dimensions worth thinking about when conceiving a control strategy: (A) which lifecycle phase to control (e.g., design, test, runtime), and (B) where in that phase's process (e.g., at process entry, in the middle, or at the output end). The "preventive, corrective, and detective" taxonomy really pertains to dimension B. Dimension A has to do with the important issue of *whether to try to fix the problem at its root cause* – usually by changing the way the system works – *or* by tacking on preventive, corrective, or detective checks in the current system.

Controls should encompass all enterprise concerns and initiative/functional objectives, not

> **Measurement is one form of control: it is not the only form.**

just a single concern such as risk or cost. Thus, we are not just talking about risk-related controls. We are talking about controls

---

[1] This is not an argument for or against nuclear energy. It is merely an example of passive versus active controls.

that implement measurement or some form of active or passive control over *each* enterprise concern.

Substantive measurement on actual operational systems (i.e., during the runtime phase) operates *a-posteriori*. That is, substantive measurement on live data operates after the fact – when it is often too late! It is as far downstream as you can go. Assessment of processes (and their embedded controls) is *a-priori*: it operates ahead of time (the design phase) to *prevent* failure. For a nuclear powerplant, substantive detection measurement is not feasible as a means of ensuring proper control, because an after-the-fact detection of a melt-down provides little assurance to those living downwind: *a-priori* control is therefore necessary by performing great amounts of analysis during the design phase and by applying substantial controls during testing phases, coupled with comprehensive real-time preventive control (to shut down or throttle operation if a serious anomaly is detected) and corrective control (to adjust operational parameters). Thus, as explained above, *a-priori* control can take the form of active controls, or it can take the passive form of enhancing the very system that is being controlled and that it is certified to be inherently stable and aligned with assurance goals so that active monitoring is potentially not even necessary.

If this is confusing do not be concerned. It is indeed a complex area. The point I am trying to make is that control is a problem with several dimensions, and that if one wants to address the root cause, one must try to move control to earlier phases in the overall process of planning, deploying, and running systems. The earliest phase is when a capability is planned, and that is the time to think about controllability and measurement – not later. *More controls are not better: earlier-phase controls are better.* For this reason, capability alignment should be measured in terms of *effectiveness*, not in terms of the number of controls.

> **Capability alignment should be measured in terms of effectiveness, not completeness of process definition or the number of controls.**

Capability alignment should be determined iteratively by growing successful processes and validating those processes through periodic assessment and benchmarking and ultimately certification.

One important difference between a powerplant and a system of human actors is that the machinery of a powerplant has a known behavior and pattern of degradation, whereas people are somewhat less predictable and are certainly more ingenious when it comes to achieving their own personal objectives. Therefore, even a certified process involving people needs to embed some trusted substantive controls, but preferably those controls incorporate enabling components rather than being only punitive. For example, rewarding someone for learning how to produce quality is a control mechanism, whereas punishing them for producing poor quality is also a control mechanism. In the former case, measurement should include measuring the increased skills attained by the staff, as well as the effect on product quality; in the latter case, measurement takes the form of measuring the defects caused by each individual.

Do Not Focus On Artifacts

Executives often hear the message from their staff, "We need good documentation for our systems: then we will know where we are."

This is a hard point to disagree with. It is very logical. Unfortunately, it reflects the obsolete view that business processes must be designed in phases, interconnected by artifacts. The flaws in this way of thinking is that it assumes that artifacts are an effective mode of communication, and that artifacts can be made complete without feedback from downstream phases.

> **"Our departments can't plan IT integration because they don't have a data model". However, the artifact is useless unless it is created by the people who will use it: They must eat their own dog food.**

When a requirements analyst gives an engineer a specification, the first thing the engineer will try to do is to echo the specification back to the requirements analyst, to check their own understanding. The fact is, you cannot be sure that you understand something until you say it yourself, hear yourself say it, and discuss your understanding with those who definitely do understand it. This feedback is crucial.

This is the fundamental weakness of the waterfall approach to development. There is an assumption that information flows in one direction, and that it is possible to complete one "phase" before going on to the next. It is not, unless you either spend an awful lot of money on each phase,

> **Written artifacts go only half way in achieving communication of requirements in a business environment.**

or unless you have done these exact processes so many times before that there is no reason to communicate.

A client of mine had invested a lot of money in documenting business rules. One day a programmer lamented to me: "The business rules are really confusing. They don't really tell you what [database tables] to join. It has been a big problem from the beginning of this project." I replied, "Can you find the people who wrote the rules?" to which he shook his head no.

For one thing, requirements artifacts and design artifacts are usually too informally specified to serve as true requirements: someone using the artifacts must usually go and talk to the author of the artifacts or a SME in order to ask for interpretation, study them, and echo back their meaning – often by rewriting the artifacts in some form, even if it is on a whiteboard. The artifacts provide value in the following ways: (1) they act as the "notes" of the creators of the artifacts, serving to provide durability to the work that was done by those authors; and (2) they serve as a consensus-building device, allowing a team of analysts to communicate among each other and with the SMEs who they are working. Thus, the communication is primarily lateral and upstream, not downstream! The communication takes the form of feedback, not broadcast.

The Fallacy of "People, Process, and Technology"

A common misconception is that business processes hinge on people, processes, and technology. The theory is that people provide the human actors to make things happen, process serves to coordinate the people, and technology serves to leverage what the people can do.

This is wrong. The flaw is in the concept of "process". You cannot have process without people, hence "people" and "process" are redundant, or at least they overlap. To avoid this overlap, managers often assume that "process" means "documents" that define the processes. However, as already explained, documents are not knowledge and are not actionable. Only knowledge is actionable, and knowledge only exists within people. Thus, the phrase "people, process, technology" is somewhat dangerous, because it leads one down a path of creating process documents.

We should focus instead on creating processes that are embodied in people: i.e., knowledge, and knowledge of the kinds that are needed. I therefore propose that business processes are composed of "knowledgeable people, authoritative artifacts, and technology". Here I make it clear that the purpose of artifacts is to define methods, practices, and authoritative information, and these things do not represent knowledge.

Why make a big deal out of this? Because I have seen *too many* projects planned around the concept that you just have to have someone create documents, and then bring in people to execute based on those documents, using some provided technology. It does not work this way, and that type of thinking leads to failure. You need to focus on the knowledge that is created as a result of creating documents, systems, and the other durable elements of your organization. The act of creation creates knowledge, and that knowledge is the core of your business process.

Build Repeatable Processes And Repeatable Models, That Are *Defined By And Maintained By Those Who Use The Processes*

Some organizations employ analysts to document the requirements of the business. Such analyst groups might maintain data models, standards, and process definitions. An entirely separate group might be responsible for maintaining systems and software to support these processes. In this scenario there are three layers of people involved in the definition of software systems that support the business: the actual business staff, the analyst group, and the software implementation group. This means that each of those layers must go through the process of understanding the business requirements, and this must happen in series, introducing a substantial latency into the process. Since most organizations use written artifacts to communicate between these layers of people, this means that three separate classes of artifacts will end up being created, where one would probably do.

It is far better if one or more of these layers can be removed. Say we were to remove all the layers: in that case, the business users would have to program their own systems. Indeed, many small businesses do this, adding great efficiency to their work. It is well-known within the software community that a small team that begins with an intuitive understanding of the requirements can build a system very quickly and at a fraction of the cost of hiring a new team to do the task. However, in most organizations it is not practical to expect that you can train your business staff to learn how to program, because they would not want to. Note that in many professions this is the norm, however: for example, in accounting, it is very typical that a financial analyst will develop their own database queries and spreadsheets. If this is not programming, then what is? However, such end-user created systems are usually hard to maintain by others and represent a substantial aggregate risk and integration problem in many ways.

If we merely remove the analyst team, then the business staff must work directly with the software design team. Programmers and system designers are sometimes thought to have limited interpersonal skills, leading to the assumption that they cannot act as analysts. In my experience, I have observed that programmers are often very excellent analysts. I have rarely seen a programmer try to work with a business user and not succeed.

Still, programmers and system designers are highly-focused on their primary task, which is to create software. They usually work in the context of a project, and so they do not have the luxury to maintain a model of the business. Many programming projects do not have continuity with other programming projects. Programmers are typically moved around as furniture – as commodities. This is a poor use of their skills and knowledge, not to mention the impact on their morale.

The people who are in the best position to maintain a model of the business are the business staff themselves. They do not usually have the data- and process-modeling skills to create and maintain such models. However, one can make a good argument that *they should*: they are the primary operators and maintainers of the business function, and so they should have the best understanding of the business and should be able to create the most accurate models. Further, they would be able to maintain such models in the most timely manner, since as soon as the model needs to change, they are the first to know.

Do not accept an argument that business staff cannot create and maintain process models. It is usually the case that some business staff are inclined in that direction and some are not. Every business operation team must have a mix of people who are detail oriented and can maintain models and others who are fix-it types or decision-makers and who cannot maintain models. You need both types in each area of operation.

One Of the Primary Causes Of Lack Of Business Process Transparency

It has been my observation that one of the main reasons for a lack of transparency in business systems is that programmers design and build systems based on the specific processing needs of a department, rather than based on fundamental business concepts. For example, suppose a department must produce a cash flow analysis and a balance sheet for a particular line of business product. The programmers will likely design a system that combines these needs, and intertwine the functions in the most efficient way from a processing point of view.

How often have you seen "process" diagrams that depict interconnected boxes that are labeled with system names (usually acronyms) with no indication of what functions are being performed? If you were to write down what these boxes actually do, they often perform a combination of functions, making it very difficult to explain them to people who are new to the department.

It would be more transparent if instead each system were designed around fundamental concepts such as cash flow and balance sheet. That way, staff who must plan for changes involving the system would be able to understand what the system really does without having to spend hours with SMEs.

It is a basic problem that IT professionals often do not know core business concepts.

Thus, it is a basic problem that IT professionals often do not know core business concepts. If they did, they would base their design around those concepts, instead of basing them around the detail-level requirements. The result would be a much higher level of transparency which would be invaluable for planning.

It may be unreasonable to expect IT people to have educational training in the line of business (LOB) – or is it? If business tools such as programming tools were more understandable to the LOB, then they would be using the tools themselves. IT people would say that the LOB would misuse the tools, and they would be right, but would you rather have the primary expertise be in knowing the LOB or in knowing the tools? I think you know the answer.

The best solution is to have less of a divide between IT and the business. We are accustomed to providing for knowledge transfer from business to IT, but not the other way around. Provide a mentoring system to elevate the IT skills of the business; and provide sufficient oversight and supervision so that the success of this transfer is ensured. This requires using tools that the LOB is able to become proficient in: high-level tools such as BPM tools, rather than techie tools such as programming languages. Specialized expertise in technology is needed at many points and

IT can provide this service, but the emphasis on IT as the sole wielders of technology is currently imbalanced.

Later on in the section beginning on page 148 I discuss this further in the context of business architects versus technical architects.

The Many Perspectives (Aspects) of Business Processes

In 2006 Verizon Communications settled a class action lawsuit in which it was accused of being overzealous in blocking SPAM such that legitimate emails were being filtered, including e-mails coming from IP addresses in Europe, Asia and elsewhere – and allegedly without notifying customers.[1] One wonders if Verizon's lawyers were consulted when the SPAM-blocking system was originally set up. In your organization, do you consult your legal department whenever technical changes are made to your business systems, especially if those changes affect customers? What about regulatory impacts? What about the impact on your organization's security policies?

Today's business climate is becoming increasingly complicated. Small changes in practices can potentially have a large impact down the road if they are not properly vetted. Yet, involving experts in each small decision is not only unscalable, but it would dramatically slow down your organization's ability to react.

At the highest level, an organization needs to establish strategies for how it plans to ensure that all important (generally officer-level) perspectives are included in each decision at all levels of the organization. Top-level strategies are usually implemented as policies that are published by senior executives. For example, a company might have a policy that its legal group must review each engineering policy, and that its security group must review each software development policy. These policies represent choices for how legal and security will be involved in tactical decision-making that is initiated by other groups.

---

[1]   Ref. [VerizonEmail2005].

A policy framework establishes a baseline set of decisions for building out an overall strategy. To achieve scalability, decision-making must be multi-level, so that it can be distributed across the organization and only reach the top levels when policy needs to be reviewed or assessed.

A hierarchical top-to-bottom, bottom-to-top decision-making process is the default process that is used in industry and is well-known to have deficiencies with regard to lethargy, distortion of policy and inaccurate communication. To inject agility into the process it is necessary to distribute the consideration of all major issues to all parts of the organization, and provide an active and enabling means of ensuring consistency. Think granular: lots of small operating units, but all operating with the same philosophy and knowledge, rather than large bureaus of oversight. I will explore this in more detail later.

However, some things I am ready to say now: a hierarchical system is what is currently used: we must go one notch better. In addition, in today's business environment we can no longer exclude important parallel considerations from even the smallest business decision. The world is too anxious to sue and to exploit the smallest weakness, and it is increasingly true that no weakness remains undiscovered for long.

Mentors: These Are the "People Programmers"

So we see that there are several problems with how things are currently done:

1. There are **too many layers** of people between the business staff and the software systems that they need.
2. Programmers and software system designers are often **used as commodities**, when in reality they represent valuable individual business knowledge assets, each highly unique just as other business staff are unique. Further, once project staff have gone through the pain of learning about a business area's requirements that collective knowledge needs to be treated as an asset, and that means that those staff are no longer a commodity.
3. Business staff are in the **best position to create and maintain** models of their function, but this task is usually delegated to others.

The result of this is that business models are chronically out of date and incomplete. The typical response of business staff is to complain that they cannot plan future requirements because they do not have a good model for what they have. The typical response of management is to bring in an outside team to create the model. However, we have seen that this merely creates a new communication problem: since such models provide for backwards communication – not forwards – and since the creators of the models leave, there is no one to ask what the models mean, and so they are almost useless and become obsolete the day they are published. It is much better instead to bring in a team that focuses on change management, to help the organization to learn how to create and maintain its own business models. Above all, each business function must be accountable for being able to *maintain its own business models*.

The same risk exists with internal teams of analysts. If management instead charges their internal analyst teams with creating the models instead of bringing in an outside firm, then we still have the multiple layers through which communication must occur, and this is not very agile. Such layers of communication create a huge "impedance" against change, multiplying costs and slowing down movement like quick sand.

> **Rather than focus on initiatives to build new systems, focus on initiatives to add capability-building functions that operate continuously and that are self-governing.**

The solution is to invest in elevating the capabilities of your own business staff, so that they can develop and maintain their own business models. In addition, you should treat your programmers and system designers as valuable assets, not commodities. Programmers and system designers *are* analysts. They should be treated as such, and expected to have and maintain analyst skills. In software, there is little difference between designing a data model or designing a software program. Expect your programmers to have all of these skills. And make enterprise-wide analysis and standards development – with assistance from an enterprise team – one of their charters. More on this later.

Mentors help to enhance uniformity in processes. When they help a project team to implement a process, they bring awareness of how others implemented a similar process. This helps to promote conformity in data models, establishment of single points of truth for authoritative information, as well as conformity of how business rules are implemented and managed. A mentor *group* also provides for a continuity of ideas and strategies that ad-hoc committees, grass roots, or short-lived problem-focused initiatives cannot.

The mapping to business need becomes natural, because the line of business is responsible for defining their own models.

Forget The "End State": Design A Capability For Evolving The Current State In The Right Direction

Previously in the section Agile Change Management: The Processes That Define And Create Business Processes Must Be Agile (page 12) I discussed why it is important to focus on agile change management capabilities, and why today these *change management processes are just as important as your actual operational processes*, because if you cannot change quickly, you will not remain competitive. I would like to revisit this theme as it pertains to gap analysis as it is practiced in most organizations.

Nearly all gap analysis and design methodologies espouse the concepts of *current state* and *future state*. The current state is how things are now, and the future state (aka "end state"), or vision, is how you want things to be.

This approach worked once upon a time, but it does not work well anymore if the "future state" is farther out than the current planning cycle. (Some of the problems with gap analysis are discussed in detail in the section Gap Analysis on page 403.) The problem is that *one never arrives at the future state*, so if your ROI is based on achieving a specific future state, you will be disappointed. By the time you get half way there, priorities have changed, or funding has changed. This is more true the larger the scope of the vision.

For this reason, when planning for change, it is important to focus on strategy rather than a specific end state. Your strategy should ensure that you are building value along the way, and continuously positioning yourself to meet the demands of the business as things evolve.

To explain this, let's consider a hypothetical scenario. Suppose you undertake to develop a new business capability, but half way there things change and the capability must be modified to meet new requirements. Is this a setback, or merely a course correction? If it is setback, then your approach to building the capability did not account for the kinds of change that actually occurred. For example, if the capability you were building involved an approach that was not amenable to change, then you might have to rip it all out and start over. Thus, when planning future capabilities, it is important to make then flexible if it is likely that the requirements will change.

This sounds like common sense, but so often I see business processes built that are extremely inflexible. This occurs because the focus is on a concrete need, and the lowest cost path is usually chosen. Management focuses on a particular future state, and does not factor change into the planning.

The core issue is that the future state that people often envision does not include change management or sustainability processes. What will happen after the plans are realized? Too often the answer is that the organization will have created a set of unmaintainable processes. For example, consider an effort to create an enterprise architecture. Once such an architecture is complete, who will maintain it? Maintaining it will be difficult because all of the work processes used to define the architecture have been dismantled. Just asking your architects to maintain it will not work because the scope is too large. There must be an architecture maintenance process. Any system or process that is created requires a plan to keep it current, and to continuously assess if it is delivering the required business performance. This built-in self-assessment is what is usually lacking.

Let's go back to the prior example of building a new business capability. Once that capability has been established how will it be maintained? How long will it take before it starts to take on a life of its own and have alignment problems with the rest of the organization? How long will it be before its systems start to have maintenance issues and are considered to be "legacy"? These are lifecycle patterns that we take for granted, but they are the result of inadequate attention to lifecycle maintenance processes.

Above all, do not try to address alignment issues through a big-bang current state to future state migration effort, unless the effort's goal is to build self-alignment *into* the business processes.

Do not get me wrong: I am not against defining a future state, but I believe that it is *critical that the future state take account for the ongoing processes that ensure that operational processes continue to evolve* and retain alignment with the organization's changing priorities. These self-correction mechanisms must be built into each business process, by measuring performance and by having people whose job it is to work closely with lines of business but retain a holistic view.

Another problem with typical current-state and future-state models is that they usually focus on systems, data flows, and organization structures. Where is the model of the staff's knowledge and capabilities?

Automated Systems By Themselves Are Not Capabilities.

In the section Design Your Own Capabilities: Enterprise Change Management Should Address How Departments Will Update And Maintain Their Own Process Definitions (page 13) I examined the importance of each business unit taking responsibility for a deep and holistic understanding of their own processes that can only be achieved if they have responsibility for maintaining the very design of their own processes, encompassing both the human and automation dimensions. I would now like to stress the need to include human capability assessment in the equation when planning new capabilities.

A capability is not something that you build or buy. It is something that you develop in your staff. It might be supported by "commercial off-the-shelf" (COTS) or custom-built systems once they are integrated. COTS capabilities are not enterprise capabilities until they have been integrated, and until the processes for utilizing, maintaining, and building upon them have been instituted. Until then all you have is a problem and another cost. Thus, any useful end-state model must include a map of the detailed skills and experience of staff, and the achievement of a mature operating model.

But instead of focusing on an end-state, think in terms of what the future state means: what does it give you? What are your goals? That is the real gap: the difference between your current situation and your future goals. What are the strategies for achieving those goals? Forget about the specifics of the future state: allow those to evolve; but retain the goals, and keep them current. Maintain the strategies, and keep them current. And above all, put in place a process for evolving the current state according to the strategies and goals. Focus on creating that process; do not focus on defining the future state. In chapter 10 I will explain how to do this, and then in chapter 14 I will provide a concrete example.

Don't Create "Thin Layers" Of Process

In most projects, work is divided up based on the natural boundaries of the thing that needs to be developed. For example, one might have one group build one component, and another group build a second component. This is very different from a construction project, in which there might be a team that lays the foundation, a second team that comes in to put up the walls, and so on. Dividing up labor based on skill category works fine if the tasks are well-understood and there is little communication required between the different groups of workers. However, if they need to communicate, we have a problem: first of all, they might not even do their work at the same time. Second, if the skills or tasks are not well-understood, they are probably going to end up arguing over who should do what.

It is often the case in large organizations that when software work is divided up based on skill category, such as DBA, architect, programmer, etc., that a lot of time is spent in meetings deciding who will design the logical model, who will design the test cases, who will create database test data, and so on. The problem gets worse the more skill layers you introduce: if you throw in data architect, business architect, assurance architect, test engineer, acceptance tester, and more, then you are probably going to have a lot of confusion about who should do what. You will probably also have a lot of redundancy, as test plans will be written that address similar things, and architectural layers will be created that define similar concepts.

What I have found is that senior data analysts and architects of each specialty must know a lot about all of the other specialties in order to be effective. In fact, when I am in meetings with data architects, business architects, software architects, and enterprise architects, I cannot tell who is from which discipline unless I know beforehand.

I see no value in differentiating between these different types of architect. An architect's job should be to aggregate the various concerns that impact a system or process, make a set of judgments, and select a set of strategies for how to meet the overall goals of the system. It therefore makes no sense to cordon architects by specialty, unless they are early in their career and have not had time to achieve the breadth that they need. Clearly any given individual will have more expertise in some areas than others, but the title "architect" should be hard-won and indicate that the person can understand and speak to any architectural issue, just as any doctor – specialist or otherwise – can intelligently speak to any general medical issue.[1]

This means that if you have separate departments for business architecture, data architecture, and technical architecture, you *can and should consolidate these over time.* Each of these people are usually overworked because they are busy creating finely differentiated views of the enterprise when in reality the various views need to be sufficiently integrated that they are in essence a single layered view that every architect understands. Creating fewer views will reduce the number of meetings required. Expecting architects to be more versatile will also greatly expand the pool of architects.

It should be mentioned that the very profession of "architect" is often questioned as a legitimate role in IT. Many programmers do not trust architects. In many organizations, IT architects have a reputation of creating complex "shelf-ware" that no one uses. It is also often the case that the most important decisions about a

---

[1] Scott Ambler proposes the term "Architecture Owner" to represent the person who is responsible for integrating all architectural concerns, including business architecture, and guiding the team in architectural matters.

system are embedded in the code and are not documented in the architecture, or are not easily located if they are documented.

This is very unfortunate because for large organizations or organizations with complex IT systems, the IT architect role is extremely important. If the role is not effective, the organization suffers. To a large extent, this book is about how to make the IT architect role more effective, by expanding it into a "business architect" role. I therefore do not see the term "business architect" as more specialized than IT architect: I see it as more general, and representing a higher level of maturity and capability.

DILBERT: © Scott Adams / Dist. by United Feature Syndicate, Inc.

Creating Horizontal Slices of Capability Forces the Company's Functions to Operate In Series

A regrettable result of separating the organization into these separate aspects of concern, e.g., financial and IT, is that there might be considerable overlap across their separate initiatives. The problem is not the resulting redundancy and cost; the problem is that these separate initiatives compete for the same SMEs, and whenever the organization needs to changes its processes, each of these initiatives is impacted and therefore must be included in the change process. The result is a very high degree of impedance against change. It is as if the organization were stuck in slippery mud with bald tires. Further, the staff of each of these separate initiatives must meet again and again to divide up what they are doing, because there is so much overlap but perhaps hair-thin subtle distinctions between their objectives. The result is that the initiatives end up carving out very thin layers, and every time there is a change, every layer must be involved. In this situation, you can kiss agility goodbye.

It is therefore important for the CEO to understand the operational impact of each initiative and overlap. Even if each initiative has a very different goal, if there is functional overlap at the ground level, then there will be increased interference and agility will die a slow death.

It is better to have a single team resolve all aspects of a problem, starting small, and then training other teams to replicate that success, than to start large and divide the problem into different aspects to be performed by different teams.

Control Variety In How Things Are Done

Rather than creating departments of specialists, replicate and disperse those processes throughout your organization to achieve economies of integration. Do not consolidate horizontally. This is depicted in Figure 6.

Each department or project should represent a small but complete aggregation of all of the capabilities that it needs. The capabilities should adhere to an enterprise template. This serves to *reduce the variety* in how things are done in different parts of the organization, while allowing each business unit to work relatively independently. The consolidation of variety reduces the effort to plan new processes, and reduces the variety of systems that must be created to support them. It is variety – not replication of function – that increases the cost of subsequent change and kills agility.

To control variety while allowing duplication of function, the part of the organization that prototypes and disseminates new processes – the mentoring group – must be very effective. Otherwise, departments will work around them rather than wait for them, and departments will customize their processes at will. The mentoring group must be the best funded and most strategic element, because they represent the germination of new capabilities and the main agent of change.

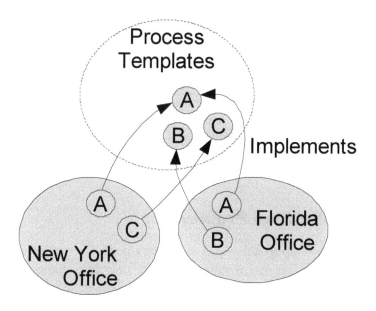

Figure 6: Replicate processes and capabilities to consolidate variety. Do not consolidate functions.

A subtle but important implication is that replicated processes should track each other in terms of their method of operation. That is, if one process is later enhanced, then others should be as well – even if they do not require it. Otherwise, processes will diverge, and variety will creep in.

This tracking of processes is a difficult thing to achieve. I have been in many organizations where I saw nearly identical functions replicated for the use of different departments and later allowed to diverge due to small changes in functional requirements. I have rarely seen organizations ensure that these replicated systems tracked each other, and it always ended up being a big problem and at some point kept the organization from being able to do things that it wanted to do later.

For these reasons the mentoring group must track divergence as a major concern and build the cost of divergence into the business model. This way decisions will account for this cost and balanced decisions can be made.

Avoiding divergence is very easy to achieve technically. Programmers are experts at "refactoring" processes so that shared functionality is separated and unique functions are cordoned off. This allows shared functions to remain identical. The real complexity comes when it is time to release systems and some units are ready to upgrade but others are not; or a few customizations have been slipped in and so now the programmers cannot easily reconcile and retroactively determine what the differences are and what they should be. The problem is therefore a business and management problem – not a technical problem – and like all business problems it needs to be addressed from a risk and value perspective. No one can argue against a solid business case.

The Data Replication Problem

The replication approach does not work well for transaction-oriented or any important enterprise data that can change over time. Keeping replicated data synchronized is a great challenge, but inconsistent data represents a huge cost for business in many ways, including increased risk, increased cost of transactions, and even lost opportunities.

Data represents the state of the business, and so it is important that data be closely tied with the system that generates it. This might in some cases means that multiple databases need to be created, each having a different population according to which users the associated processing system serves. Data for corporate processes then need to be obtained from multiple systems, but always from the appropriate authoritative source. This can be made efficient if the time-sensitivity of processes are examined to see which processes need current data and which need data as of a certain time. Data that is global in nature, e.g., master data describing the organization's products or services, should be consolidated and only replicated if a robust design ensures the required consistency. The consideration of global consistency is often left out of department-initiated efforts as it is an enterprise concern and a very important one.

Even if separate databases are maintained for different subsets – different *populations* – of data, it is very important that the design of each database to be similar if not identical, and that all are designed based on a global information model for the organization. Such a model provides the language for communication and consolidation, and if a common language is not used then systems will be irreconcilable and there will be no

90

agility. Further, such a model must include definition of business events, since events define the meaning of processing steps and changes to the state of the business.

Levels Of Oversight

Mentoring provides a level of oversight that is pro-active and enabling. By requiring the mentor group to *certify* business processes, operating units have a negative incentive to reach out to the mentors for help so that they can ensure certification. However, the mentors add value by helping to inject enterprise concerns into every project and business process, and by helping managers to justify expenses on improvements to their processes. Further, each and every certification is a joint success between the process owner and the mentor team.

This teamwork is a very good thing, but it needs a check to make sure that it stays honest to its goals and does not become incestuous. For this reason there is always a need for independent oversight to verify that certification really means something. For example, the organization can perform periodic "deep dive" assessments on randomly selected certified business processes to see if they really deserve certification. This also helps the process owner to prepare for an external audit. The role of independent oversight is depicted in Figure 7.

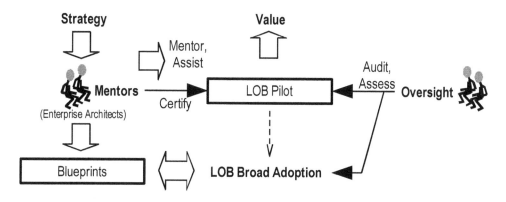

Figure 7: Mentoring with oversight.

In this figure a Mentor team helps a line of business (LOB) to develop a new process as a pilot effort. In the course of this pilot effort the LOB and the mentors learn a lot, and they capture that knowledge in the form of (a) revisions to standards, and (b) blueprints and reference designs. In the end they certify the process as having achieved all enterprise expectations (strategies), after which the process is ready for broad adoption by the rest of the enterprise if that is applicable. Any certified process, such as the pilot, can then be audited by an independent internal oversight group to assess compliance with enterprise standards and strategies.

This approach is better than the hands-off approach of checking enterprise strategies by correlating them with "controls" and then tabulating controls. The problem with the controls-based approach is that it encourages a philosophy that "more controls are better", and shifts attention from the real problems. Data is usually incorrect for a number of flaws in an end-to-end system, from unchecked inputs to errors in processing logic. While explicit controls can enhance input quality, they cannot remediate flaws in logic: they can only detect them. To prevent flaws in logic, one needs to address the root cause, which might trace back to the design process used to create the system. Controls on a design process are usually not on the radar screen of auditors, but these are the kinds of focus that are needed to truly fix problems.

Accreditation

The mentoring role that I have described is at the heart of system conceptualization and design. That role is therefore in the best position to be able to assess which improvements to the design and build process will have an actual impact on the quality of results. It therefore makes sense to give the mentoring role an incentive to accurately assess the quality of the systems and capabilities that they nurture.

> **There is a need to *accredit* the assessment process, to certify that it has the ability to perform an accurate assessment.**

We have discussed the concept that the mentor group should be able to certify that systems are built correctly and in a manner that reflects enterprise concerns. How do we know that they are doing their job properly? There is therefore a need to *accredit* the mentors, to certify that they have the ability to perform an accurate assessment. In this approach, accreditation acts proactively on the certification process instead of waiting to see if that process has failed.

Accreditation can be used as an incentive for the mentors to be comprehensive. It can also provide the means to focus on the right kinds of controls: by certifying – accrediting – the mentors, one can verify that they properly validate controls, while leaving it to them to decide if the controls should be on the system design process or on the actual runtime system. Accreditation leaves it to the mentoring group to figure out what kinds of controls really make sense, rather than encouraging a more-is-better philosophy.

The catch is that the organization's auditing firm will have to buy into this if this approach is used for financial control assessment. But in the meantime, the approach can be used for other areas of concern, e.g., security, legality, and the myriad of worries that organizations have.

Accreditation is a statistically valid approach, and it provides an incentive for the enterprise to standardize controls, since this will make accreditation more efficient and then the cost of assessment can be drastically reduced. There are countless models for it in industry wherever proactive oversight is needed and where third parties must be trusted to properly assess others.

Relationship to "Certification and Accreditation" (C&A)

The term "certification and accreditation" – or simply "C&A" – is widely used by the security industry to refer to the process of assessing and approving a business process or system from a security standpoint. The industry uses the term "certify" to refer to the assessment process, and accreditation to refer to the final approval for use. That is, one performs certification (the process) so that one may obtain accreditation (the goal). This is a little confusing because other industries use these terms differently. For example, in aviation the term "certification" refers to the process of certifying an aircraft design for flight, and once an aircraft completes this process successfully it has been certificated.

Regardless of the terms, the intent is to perform an assessment process, the result of which is a passing (or failing) grade. In IT, C&A almost always refers to security, because it is currently the area that demands such a process. One could also, for example, perform a C&A process with respect to any other objective or criteria, for example GAAP accounting compliance or legal compliance.

The type of certification I have been referring to previously in this book, to be performed by the mentors, is with respect to overall enterprise alignment. Some aspects of enterprise alignment have to do with security, and so for those a security C&A process that already exists (if one exists) can provide the certification with respect to security.

Beware however of C&A processes. I have seen security analysis implemented in many different ways, and security C&A is often done in a bureaucratic check-box manner, with countless forms and standards which all say basically the same thing and are peripheral to the main task of performing the security analysis. For example, I have seen C&A processes that required a great deal of process but that actually performed no threat modeling or penetration testing – elements that are crucial for actual security.

Corporations should be leery of using government C&A processes as a model, since the latter often fall into the paper-heavy and redundant standards category. The best approach for enhancing actual security is to embed security experts within development teams and operation teams and apply security best practices, rather than trying to make the process cookbook through C&A standards. It *cannot be made cookbook*, because security is a complex science and art, requiring a great amount of foresight, experience, and judgment.

Enterprise Architecture and Reference Designs

IT has a habit of appropriating words from older professions and then redefining those words. For example, the term "architect" is widely used in IT, yet the word apparently originates from Greek before computers existed. Applying an old word to a new profession inevitably leads to a period of ambiguity as people weigh in on what the old word should mean in the context of the new profession until eventually some kind of consensus emerges, for better or worse. For "architect", IT is still trying to decide what it means, and there is no shortage of opinions on the matter.

In Table 1 I put a stake in the ground about how I define various design artifact-related terms for the purpose of this book. This is *not to exclude or invalidate other possible definitions*: it is only to clarify my meaning when I use these terms here.

Table 1: Terminology for IT design artifacts.

Term	My Definition
Design	An artifact that expresses a set of decisions about how a system should function, and the rationale for those decisions.
Pattern	A design snippet (usually abstracted in some way) that often recurs.
Template	A pattern that can be reused and extended by adding to rather than by changing it.
Reference Design	A design that includes most of the elements that one usually needs, and that properly solves most of the problems that one usually encounters.
Blueprint	A design, usually implying a level of comprehensiveness appropriate for an entire system. May include reference designs and templates.
Architecture	The highest-level design for a system or set of systems, *focusing only on the most important driving concerns*. Usually includes critical patterns, and decisions as to how important issues should be addressed. May include models of system aspects (e.g., component types and their roles), to facilitate the expression of architecture decisions.

A "template" is similar to a blueprint in that it represents a design, except that historically a template is an actual artifact using in the mass production of something. In the realm of information products, there is no physical mass production, and so the distinction between design of software and production of software is blurred and so the term "template" is easily applied to design-time activities as well as production activities. In software languages, the term has been co-opted to have a very specific meaning, namely a piece of software code that is designed with built-in reusability.[1]

Reference designs are important in the practical trenches of IT. A reference design is a prior design that intentionally incorporates most of the kinds of things that IT designers and programmers have to deal with. A good reference design solves most of these problems in a clear and transparent manner so that the design can be used as a substantial starting point and then customized for the situation at hand. From an enterprise assurance perspective, it is important that reference designs solve problems in the right way, in alignment with enterprise policies and best practices. In that case, those who apply a reference design do not need to learn all about standards and policies, since the reference design already incorporates them.

In this book I will define a *template* as being a baseline design or blueprint that is customizable in predetermined ways. A template is a kind of reference design, that provides space or allowance for customization in a predetermined manner. Now that I have made the distinction clear, in the remainder of this book I will tend to use the term blueprint interchangeably with template, since roughly speaking each is a design that leaves a lot of room for interpretation, extension, and customization, and in computing blueprints should incorporate templates wherever possible for the sake of reusability.[2]

A system design is a set of decisions about how the system should operate. In order to articulate those decisions, it is usually necessary to define system elements or classes of elements. Decisions then often take the form of allowed interactions between those elements. An architecture is merely the highest-level design for a system or set of systems.

---

[1] More technically, "templates" are code snippets that support what are referred to as "parameterized types".

[2] As explained earlier, I concede that there is a technical difference between "blueprints", "templates", and "reference designs", but for the purposes of this book I will include all of these under the umbrella of "blueprints".

The Historical Role Of Blueprints

The term "blueprint" is also often in IT, and it carries a lot of ambiguity. Fundamentally, a blueprint is merely a design. Most people know that the term originates from the 20th century photographic technology used for copying mechanical drawings, now obsolete. However, the term connotes a design of some kind. In usage, it is a very loose term.

In construction, the blueprint is the last word on what needs to be done – until the supervisor on the ground says "ignore that: it's not structural; we're out of 2x6s of that length, so use a 2x4 instead of a 2x6", not knowing that the reason for the 2x6 specification was to accommodate a recent hurricane-related change to the building code. Often the architect does not find out, and as long as an inspector does not find out and the building does not collapse there is usually not a problem.

This highlights one of the fundamental differences between "soft" processes such as computer software design and age-old "hard" processes such as building construction: when creating a building, there are over-arching blueprints known as building codes that consider the range of issues that might be encountered that affect safety. Such codes do not exist in software development unless the organization creates then by specifying policies or standards. There is a *tremendous amount* that is left to the judgment of in-the-field programmers. Further, while the construction of buildings is visible to the eye and intuitively understandable thanks to our brain's built-in circuitry for comprehending spatial things, computer code is relatively obscure and esoteric and small but significant changes can be made without warning.

Accounting for all of the applicable building codes is a difficult task, and that is why architects for commercial and residential construction work under the mentorship of experienced architects until they are familiar enough with prior designs and existing codes so that they can be trusted. When building enterprise business processes, it is extremely helpful to have a mentoring group assist – a group that has done it before *in that organization*, since each organization has its own policies and standards. Further, it is extremely helpful to have a starting point – a blueprint or template – that already can be trusted to incorporate enterprise policies. All that needs to be done then is to customize the template, in such a way that enterprise policies and standards are not compromised. This is where the mentors are extremely helpful.

Architecture Blueprints As a Starting Point

Blueprints are a starting point – a top-level design – and they save a department a tremendous amount of work compared to if they were to start from scratch – and work equals cost.

The cost savings are especially important for soft processes: in hard processes such as building construction, the cost of manufacturing a building is so much greater than the design cost that the cost of detailed blueprints is never questioned. In the design of custom business application software, the cost of programming the code is usually comparable to the design cost, and so an increase in the amount of effort spent on design adds considerably to the total project cost, unless that cost increase can be offset elsewhere such as through fewer errors, a shorter time to code, or lower maintenance costs.

Blueprints need to consider the different perspectives that are important to an organization. The Object Management Group (OMG) has defined five views for enterprise architecture: (a) business, (b) information, (c) conceptual, (d) solutions, and (e) technology.[1] Unfortunately, that vision also describes a traditional purely top-down process that focuses on artifacts. We already know that such a process is not agile, and is very difficult to achieve and maintain.

> **Blueprints should be reference designs that incorporate decisions and strategies for how to address enterprise concerns, and should include the rationale for those decisions and strategies.**

To be effective, blueprints should be *reference designs that incorporate decisions and strategies for how to address enterprise concerns*, and they should also include the *rationale* for those decisions and strategies,

---

[1] Ref. [].

98

as explained earlier. In other works, blueprints should explain why they are laid out the way they are. This is a departure from traditional building construction, where an architect operates in a manner that is fairly independent of the construction team (until the supervisor complains that something will not work the way it is designed!), and where most decisions are known ahead of time, because so many buildings have been built over history.

Blueprints Should Embed Controls And Measures, For All Enterprise Concerns, Including Accountability, Risk, And LOB Concerns

It is a tall order to expect a system developer to locate and digest all applicable enterprise policies, and then devise ways to incorporate those policies into a new system – all while interpreting the system's functional requirements and keeping to a schedule. In fact, it is way too much to expect.

The complexity of today's business environment means that system developers need help. They need a starting point. Blueprints provide this. Blueprints should be developed as an outgrowth of efforts to pilot new policies and standards. They should provide reference designs for how to implement those policies and standards while also implementing important categories of functional requirements. They should provide reference designs for how to measure compliance with policies in a manner that can be used by those who have an interest in such measurements and for rolling those measurements up to management-level metrics. Blueprints should address risk mitigation, for example by providing for data quality definition and monitoring as well as providing for the handling and correction of errors. Such blueprint designs should also lay out a model for the roles and responsibilities of the stakeholders in a system, and provide a security model for defining trust, roles, access rights, and separation of duties.

This is no small undertaking, and that is why blueprints need to grow out of trial efforts so that refinements can be made before there is widespread deployment. Further, the development of such blueprints needs to be led by an experienced and sophisticated team, with cooperation from a line of business alpha partner in order to ensure that real-world business requirements are incorporated and that the pilot system is exercised in the demands of actual usage.

Doesn't SOA Solve all my Problems?

It would be nice if it did. I had some hesitation in mentioning Service-Oriented Architecture (SOA) in this book because it is something that could become dated overnight if something new comes out to replace it; but I decided to go ahead because it can serve to make a point, whether it is dated or not.

SOA collects many age-old concepts in a single package, including the need to publish interfaces for services, to design services to be re-usable, and to govern the design and evolution of those services so that change is managed gracefully. Therefore, SOA is not only a technology: it relies on a set of IT management practices. Therefore, no technology solution can address these issues unless the technology actually does away with IT system development.

SOA systems are just as vulnerable to obsolescence because SOA based systems are typically based on Web services technologies, and these can be replaced as new technologies arrive. Surely a new buzzword will arrive at some point that will replace the SOA mantra, but the concepts in SOA will remain valid.

Summary

An agile organization must have effective mechanisms for driving changes to its capabilities and for ensuring that enterprise strategies are implemented consistently when capabilities in different parts of the organization are upgraded. This applies both the automated systems and to people-based capabilities.

Approaches for ensuring consistency should focus first and foremost on elevating the knowledge, skills, and experience of the people who operate processes, and second on enforcement of policies.

The creation of artifacts such as design or requirements documents should not be a primary objective of any project. Instead, the primary objective of such efforts should be to establish knowledge within the minds of the teams who would use those artifacts.

Operational groups should define their own business processes and maintain their own artifacts that document those processes. Never use outside groups to create artifacts that need to be maintained.

Business processes are often difficult to document and more difficult to explain concisely to those outside of the department. In other words, such processes are not transparent. One of the primary root causes of this situation is that automated systems are typically implemented to address a department's functions rather than to address a set of well-defined processes.

Today's organization has many "cross-cutting concerns" in its operation. This greatly challenges the traditional hierarchical model of organizations.

Mentors are people who have the job of enabling others by helping them to develop new capabilities and to acquire actionable knowledge of the organization's concerns.

When performing gap analysis, do not focus on the gap between current operational capabilities and a desired set of operational capabilities. Instead, focus on the reasons why the organization has not automatically identified the gap in the course of business and migrated toward the required new capabilities. In other words, what is missing from your processes for continuously evolving your organization?

Rather than dividing your architects and analysts into stratified skill categories, demand that they provide generalized skills. This enlarges your pool of skills that can be applied, and reduces communication requirements. However, it also raises expectations for skills and training.

Duplication of data and duplication of functions using different approaches are both the bane of enterprise agility. Reference designs are an important component of enterprise architecture for ensuring that such duplication is minimized.

Independent oversight is needed but it should not be a function of those who mentor.

6. Capability Development Is a Strategic Function

In September 2006 the *International Journal of Accounting Information Systems* published the results of a study of IT spending at 1,000 companies that purports to document a "positive relationship between the level of IT spending and the firm's cost of equity capital". [1]

In other words – according to this study – the cost of capital increases for firms that have a high level of IT spending! The explanation offered is that spending on IT is an investment in something that is intangible and so the long-term benefit is less certain, representing increased risk. The implication is that investors pay attention to IT spending and whether it represents risk. This makes IT investment decisions strategic, from a valuation standpoint. Another implication is that if IT spending is not managed from a risk and value perspective, that Wall Street will notice.

Whether this interpretation is true or not, it is a fact that many firms invest a large percent of their resources on IT, which by itself makes IT a strategic investment. Hopefully all large investments serve a strategic purpose, and therefore deserve a manager who is a true strategic thinker and who can implement change at a strategic level and form strategic relationships within the business and even without when necessary.

> ## Core Idea: Organizations Need a Strategic Capability For Driving Rapid Change

Change is often initiated from the grass roots of an organization. While grass-roots initiated change has been shown to be

---

[1] Ref. [RichDehning06].

strategically important, an organization must have the ability to initiate comprehensive change from the top as well. This is the only way that it can hope to respond in a coordinated way to new opportunities and threats.

In fact, I will go so far as to say that the kinds of changes that are called for require the CIO's active participation as well as the CEO's or COO's buy-in. The reason is that the very role of IT must change. These changes are outlined in this chapter.

Which Kind Of CIO Does Your Organization Have?

The CIO Decisions *2006 Salary And Careers Survey*[1] quotes Mike Easley, the CIO of Home Quality Management, a private long-term care company in Palm Beach Gardens, Fla., with estimated revenue of $184 million: "The role [of the CIO] is transforming every year, and I find my peers are transforming. You're going to see the CIO becoming more of a global business driver and less of an information officer." And according to the survey report, "half of CIO respondents say they report directly to the CEO" and "70% of CIOs hold a seat on their organization's executive committee".

Yet many CIOs are not prepared – or even do not desire – to assume this new strategic role. In the above-cited report, when asked which skill CIOs of the future need most, Easley replied, "Accounting. You already see more CIOs with MBAs. I think you'll see a stronger accounting track in our field." How many CIOs do you know who want to learn accounting?

> **The low compensation of CIOs compared to other officer-level executives indicates that either CIOs as a group are either not delivering substantial measurable business value or are not recognized as delivering that value.**

---

[1] Ref. [CIODecSalSurv06].

As a personal anecdote, I am a member of a business technology council in my geographic region, and CIOs are one group that we have had a hard time getting to participate: CEOs – no problem; CFOs – no problem; CIOs – they won't come out. Here I would like to make the point to all CIOs reading this: we need you! Come out!

Some CIOs are prepared to talk business though; and many business-focused executives might want to accept a CIO role if it is defined appropriately – and compensated accordingly.

There is a considerable variation in CIO salaries depending on the size of the organization and other factors. According to the CIO Decisions 2006 survey, the median total annual compensation for CIOs in 2005 appears to be under 200K. While that would be a healthy income for most professionals, we are talking about a corporate officer who sits at the same table with the CEO and other top-level executives who often earn seven figures or more – and many much, much more. The comparatively low compensation indicates that CIOs as a group are *not delivering substantial measurable business value*: if they were, they would be paid more, since the position is a highly mobile one. Everyone knows the adage that you get what you pay for, but in a free market it is also true that you pay for what you get – and *if you ain't gettin' much, you ain't gonna pay much!* Or as Tony Murphy of Gartner put it, "…there is regrettably little evidence to suggest that [the IT investments made by organizations] has in an overall macro sense generated a satisfactory return." [1]

Indeed, the salary and value problem applies at all levels of the IT hierarchy. Many large organizations today have come to the conclusion that they need to seek staff from additional labor markets in order to lower the cost of IT. The argument is that IT is too expensive. However, large organizations generally have very low IT

> **The expense of IT in large organizations is not due to the cost of resources: it is due to the low productivity and effectiveness of IT staff.**

---

[1] Ref. page xiv of the Preface of [Murphy02].

productivity. *The problem is not the cost: it is the productivity and effectiveness of IT staff.* If the staff were delivering value, the cost would not be a problem, but the value of IT is not accurately or methodically measured. Thus, its value is perceived to be inadequate compared to its cost. IT therefore needs to pay more attention to measuring and demonstrating its own value, rather than cutting labor costs and in so doing killing the wellspring of new capabilities.

In fact, an excessive focus on cost reduction is a prevalent and systemic problem in IT in most organizations. For example, consider the Federal Aviation Administration (FAA), which allocated approximately $1.3 billion for the period 2004-2008 for improvement programs: the bulk of it went to programs for improving operational efficiency – i.e., for reducing cost. Programs for improving safety (an important FAA business value metric) received only $100 million (8%). In fact, the allocation for efficiency improvements was twice as much as for the largest of any other allocation.[1]

Do not get me wrong: improving efficiency is important; but it is a consistent pattern that I see across organizations that the CIOs job is seen first and foremost as a job to reduce cost, as if the CIO were a CFO. The CIO's job should be to advocate the effective use of IT for the mission and goals of the organization. Cost reduction should not be a *primary* goal. The problem is that CIOs typically do not have the informational ammunition they need to make a compelling case for sources of value other than cost reduction, and this is because IT projects are planned and executed in a manner that does not provide this information.

There Is An Urgent Need To Differentiate the CIO's Two Roles

The dichotomy of CIO roles is a real problem. Business-savvy executives are not going to try for a CIO role if they will not be compensated accordingly and if the role is not a growth role; and, such individuals also do not want to be saddled with the old role of keeping track of PCs and worrying about spam filters. But now

---

[1] Ref. [FAA2005]. See also [Bhadra06], p. 9.

we have two vastly different kinds of role, each called "CIO", each providing a very different kind of business value, and yet each sharing a single salary profile. How is one to know what to pay a CIO? If one has a CIO who is a high-performing capability-focused executive and pays that person accordingly, the salary will be out-of-whack with an industry that is currently composed primarily of commodity infrastructure management CIOs.

The previous chapter proposed a process by which new capabilities are proactively infused throughout an organization's operations, in a manner that ensures proper governance while fostering agility. Such a process enables the organization to change direction quickly, to develop new capabilities, and to simultaneously protect itself from the many risks in today's business environment. Such an ability is clearly highly strategic, and any organization that can achieve it has a great advantage in the marketplace. As such, properly governed agility is a strategic feature of an organization and deserves strategic direction in the form of a corporate officer or champion.

Properly governed agility is a strategic feature of an organization.

The management of such a function is a strategic role. It would be workable to refer to this role as an Enterprise CIO. However, such a moniker is potentially ambiguous, because one could argue that a CIO below the enterprise level has the same generic functions but at a lower level of scope within the organization. In contrast, I am arguing for a new role for the CIO. However, for lack of better term I will use the term "Enterprise CIO" or simply CIO/E to emphasize the new role. If I am referring to a traditional CIO role I will refer to that role as a "traditional CIO" or CIO/T. The new CIO/E role therefore is not delineated by information *technology* but focuses on the development of strategic business capabilities.

I also want to emphasize that while the principles in this book might apply equally well to most organizations, my evidence is primarily from organizations for which information processing is a large component of their operations. Today this represents a large percentage of large organizations – perhaps even a majority – but not necessarily all.

I am not saying that there are no organizations that have a CIO who fills the role that I have defined here. In fact, I have known some CIOs of this kind. All I am doing is clarifying what I mean by "CIO" in this book. Also, the fact that most CIOs represent the traditional role is a fact that I have experienced personally and that has been a problem for me in many situations which I will elaborate on later. There is therefore a significant opportunity for change in the industry – although I have also noticed that more and more CIOs are starting to see their role as a CIO/E role.

In order to help define the new kind of CIO position, it is useful to contrast it with other officer-level positions such as CTO, COO, CEO, and the traditional CIO. Of course, *every organization defines these kinds of positions differently*, and to a large extent they are defined by the individuals who hold them. Let's first consider the COO's point of view.[1]

Where to Place the CIO/E In the Organizational Hierarchy

Can the CIO/E role be a VP Under the CIO? Should the CIO/E report to the COO? To the CEO? To the CFO? To an EVP of Ops and Technology?

These are valid questions, and the answer to any of these can be yes for a given organization. As I have explained in the Preface to this book, the domain of my work has been at the interface between technology implementation and business strategy, so I cannot speak to a CEO's issues. However, I can speak to the issues that arise with respect to organizational alignment of solutions and the challenges that a CIO has. From that perspective I believe that it is essential that the CIO/E be treated as a strategic role, with the consequent strategic accountability, business performance focused measures, and authority. However the organization is structured, the CIO/E needs to be on an equal footing with whoever is responsible for the operation of business

---

[1] Some organizations do not have "C-level" positions at all. Still others, especially very large organizations, may have a hierarchy of C-level positions at various levels within the company, to head different business units or subsidiaries.

processes that are the main users of information technology. Otherwise, the CIO/E will not be able to ensure alignment.

In one instance that I am familiar with, the CIO reported to the EVP of Operations, who reported to the equivalent of a CEO, and the mentor group (by another name) was a separate group under the CIO. In that instance they had large challenges implementing change, and had to rely on various mandates to obtain the needed leverage. For example, a mandate for consolidation and cost reduction was issued by the CFO, and that mandate was leveraged by the CIO to drive change and implement the mentor group function. However, over time such a function needs to be elevated, once it proves itself, since the CIO's policies must have authority with respect to all of operations and finance. This can occur after the essential value proposition and method of operation has been proven using an existing mandate to provide the needed clout.

In another instance the mentor group was under an SVP who headed a special "enterprise program" that was a peer of the CIO, who in turn reported to an EVP of Operations and Technology, who reported to the COO. This paradoxical arrangement in which the CIO and SVP of enterprise initiatives were peers led to a great deal of ambiguity, and eventually these ambiguitities had to be reconciled, particularly with regard to the role of enterprise architects, data quality, and IT project accountability. Again, the mentor group (it was not called that) leveraged a mandate, this time having to do with improving data quality based on accounting audit findings.

In the long term, the CIO needs to be accountable for a mentor function, and needs authority at least on a par with routine business operations at an enterprise level.

COO and CIO/E

The role of a COO – indeed, the existence of the position – depends on the organization. In some organizations the COO not only runs the business but also devises internal enterprise strategies, while the CEO focuses externally. In other (usually smaller) organizations the CEO is the primary driver of enterprise strategy and the COO is more of an implementer. Still in very large organizations the COO is usually an operational strategist and has subordinate executives who actually run operations, finance, and marketing. To simplify the discussion, I will refer to the person who is responsible for daily through annual operations as the "COO", even though the actual title and level of the person might be different in a given organization. Similarly, I will refer to the person who is responsible for long-term internal operational and external market strategy as the "CEO", again recognizing that in many organizations the COO position fills this role.

A COO (as I have defined it here for this discussion) is the person who is the primary source of responsibility and direction with regard to the operation of the lines of business. As such, the COO is highly interested in the development of new business capabilities, because those will impact operability and line of business profitability metrics that the COO is responsible for. The COO is concerned with both the near term and the long term. Balancing these timeframes is a significant challenge. The COO also must be able to tell the CEO how business direction will be changed to realize new goals while balancing profitability and other concerns. The COO is therefore interested in change management and agility.

A friend of mine who was the commander of a nuclear submarine once told me that there are only two kinds of people: "spear chuckers" and "spear carriers". Making allowances for his colorful way of expressing things, I asked him who designed the spears, and he didn't know what to say. I guess in his world the spear designers were the military contractors who were not even part of his organization.

This gets to the heart of what a COO should *not* be expected to do: architect new business capabilities. A COO has an operating margin and is generally expected to get it right the first time, so a COO does not have the patience to experiment with new capabilities. The COO has an interest in such capabilities and how they are deployed, but should not bear the burden of inventing them. COOs are fundamentally concerned with operation, not technical invention. These areas of concern are illustrated by the "COO" column of Table 2.

If the COO is a visionary and operational master, the COO and CIO/E should be able to have an envisioning session to conceptualize future capabilities and business models that would make the organization soar. The CIO/E should be able to tell the COO what new capabilities could be developed in the near term if need be, and what it would take to roll them out. This is what makes the CIO/E different from a technical guru: the CIO/E knows how to deploy new capabilities into the organization in a highly effective manner. The COO can then focus on business structures and managing the relationships between marketing, operations, and accounting while the CIO/E takes the ball for creating the new capabilities and getting them into a form in which broad deployment is possible.

Table 2: Functions that are a primary concern of each of four strategic roles.

	Primary Concern For			
Function	COO	CIO/E	CIO/T	CTO
Creating and evaluating strategic technologies.				✓
Incubation of new ideas, prototyping, and refinement.				✓
Operationalization of proven technologies and technology products.	(✓)	✓	(✓)	
Deployment of operational capabilities.	✓	✓	(✓)	
Operation and measurement of business capabilities.	✓			

The CIO/E should assume leadership of any functions pertaining to the piloting or definition of new operational capabilities and advancing them to the threshold of broad rollout. There needs to be a strong partnership between the CIO/E and COO, because the CIO/E will rely on the COO for identifying lines of business to serve as a testbed for new processes, and this contribution requires a level of trust by the COO in the CIO/E. Thus, any success in the development of a new process is a joint success between the CIO/E and the COO, driven by the CIO/E. Similarly, success in the broader rollout of new processes is a joint success between the CIO/E and COO, driven by the COO.

Given this kind of relationship, it is expected that a COO would want to have a say in the selection of a CIO/E. The CIO/E should not report to the COO however. (Again, I am referring to the COO role as I have defined it. If your organization's COO is the person who is responsible for long-term operational strategy, then indeed the CIO/E might report to such a person.) To do so is to weaken the enterprise-level accountability of the CIO/E. The CIO/E must be able to promise the CEO (or whoever leads enterprise operational strategy) that the organization is implementing enterprise concerns with respect to legality, risk, security, and all other enterprise-level concerns – in addition to profitability and innovation.

In Table 2 the checkmarks in the CIO column are parenthesized. The reason is that CIO roles vary, and this book makes the case for having a true CIO/E or enterprise capability-focused CIO – not an old-style IT-only focused CIO – and so whether the CIO has the concerns that are checked depends on the situation.

Infrastructure Components Of IT

In most organizations that have a CIO, the CIO is concerned with the grab bag of *anything* related to IT. Thus, the CIO line of responsibility is defined by a technology boundary – from telephones to workstations to servers to document classification and control as well as software initiatives, regardless of who the user is or what the nature of the initiative is. This does not really make sense anymore in a world in which *virtually every aspect of operations is supported by some level of IT*. Some IT functions are related to a service operation or line of business, while other IT functions are baseline or infrastructure-related. It makes more sense to divide up functionality based on its role in the business.

I would like to distinguish between two classes of IT infrastructure: (1) that which is commodity, and (2) that which is strategic. Granted there are many instances of things that fall inbetween these extremes, but the point is to make a distinction and not treat all infrastructure the same. Commodity infrastructure for a typical organization includes desktop PC, routers, servers, and standard server software such as email, departmental databases, and web servers, among many other things. Strategic infrastructure includes mission critical software applications and systems that serve more than one line of business (unless the company on has a single line of business) directly or indirectly and that represent a significant portion of the market advantage of the organization.

Operation of commodity IT infrastructure should be delegated to an infrastructure-focused VP of IT.

Managing commodity infrastructure is an important and very complex function, but it is an *administration function*, and the person who is most qualified is probably someone with lots of enterprise IT system administration background. The management of commodity IT infrastructure should be moved as a cost center under a technology infrastructure VP-level group under the COO or CFO, because IT infrastructure is now used broadly and operating it is merely one dimension to the people-and-systems operation puzzle. That type of IT manager is essentially what the traditional CIO was: someone focused on defining and operating the IT infrastructure, but not focused on the larger business operation and capability issues that the COO or today's enterprise CIO must deal with.

Managing the creation and operation of *strategic infrastructure* is different from managing commodity infrastructure in these ways:

- Business processes are involved: it is not just about equipment.
- Creation of and changes to the infrastructure often are high-risk.
- The skills needed to conceive and implement change are inter-disciplinary rather than only technical.

The traditional inclination is to put this function under the CIO. However, the challenge is that another manager depends on this infrastructure: the COO and possibly others. Further, such infrastructure tends over time to become a power center that does not need to demonstrate ROI for upgrades because operating it is a "keep the lights on" function. The question of whether it has ROI is not the issue: the issue is what priority upgrades to that infrastructure should have when compared to other IT proposals. In general, keep-the-lights-on infrastructure tends to get whatever it asks for, which can distort the realization of enterprise goals.

If the CIO manages such infrastructure, it then follows that there might be an inclination to give that infrastructure priority compared to IT requests from lines of business. That would subvert the CIO's function of balancing enterprise concerns.

Therefore, it is important that strategic infrastructure have a single primary stakeholder other than the CIO. A VP of strategic infrastructure role might be too broad of a position and would compete with the CIO, and so it is better to create a separate management role for each instance of strategic infrastructure and rely on the partnership between the CIO and COO to ensure alignment and consistency across those.

Another model commonly used is to have the CIO be responsible for developing, operating, and improving strategic IT infrastructure, thereby operating it for the users. This model does not work well because users become too removed from what it takes to actually perform the task of upgrading and operating the systems, and a finger-pointing relationship easily develops in which the business users claim that the systems are not reliable or that changes take too long, and IT claims that the users don't appreciate the challenges or do not articulate their "requirements" properly. This old model is not workable as we move into an era where business takes more responsibility for change as business cycles shorten and agility is increasingly important. The only solution is to make the users have a larger role in actually defining and operating their own business systems. I believe that this is the future model that we are moving toward.

Current CIOs might balk at this thinking: it sounds like I am proposing that one of their main sources of power – the systems that they own – should be given to other managers. However, remember that the CIO/E role that I am proposing is measured by demonstrating success across the enterprise, and over a period of time. It is not a keep-the-lights-on role. Thus, the success of strategic infrastructure is shared by the CIO/E, because that role helps to define and pilot that infrastructure – often at considerable risk. Further, the CIO/E's main skill must be in managing change across the enterprise. This job requires operational experience in order to have the required credibility, and it also requires an adeptness and breadth of viewpoint that is worthy of an officer level position. It is therefore an upwardly mobile role, rather than a role narrowly defined by technology boundaries. CIOs who have moved from that role into the CEO role will attest that the CIO role should no longer be defined by technology.

CTO and CIO/E

In many organizations that have a CTO the CTO is focused on *creating or evaluating strategic technology.* For example, such a CTO would be interested in new technology trends that could lead to new products for the organization, as well as partnerships, technology strategy, and technology investments for the purpose of optimizing the organization's portfolio and market position. Further, the CTO's organization can provide for the incubation of new ideas, providing an opportunity for ideas to be prototyped and refined into business processes before they are operationalized. These areas of concern are illustrated in the "CTO" column of Table 2.

In contrast, a CIO/E (and today's CIO in most companies) should be primarily interested in (a) helping to operationalize new product technology into a line of business as well as helping the COO to develop any new business models that might be possible, (b) developing internal capabilities to make the organization more responsive to change, and (c) deploying and integrating new technology products that the organization could use to make its operation more efficient and productive. Thus, to draw an analogy from manufacturing, the CIO/E is an important actor in the lab-to-factory transition, as well as in factory modernization – except that in today's world this must happen quickly and change is continual.

When it comes to an interest in technology, the line between the CTO and CIO/E/CIO is a thin one, but the primary focus of the CIO/E or CIO is toward lines of business and current or future operations as well as how to scale activities and respond to changing needs, whereas the focus of a CTO should be toward risky new technologies – IT-related or otherwise – that can potentially be productized or leveraged in a strategic way to create market opportunities or reduce cost. A CTO usually has an interest in the organization's IT infrastructure if that infrastructure is an important aspect of the company's strategic advantage, but not otherwise. This allows the CTO to be more effective by focusing exclusively on high-risk high-return strategic technology opportunities and not have to also worry about navigating intricate relationships within the organization or how to operationalize or deploy new capabilities.

Lab-based new technology research and technology policy should remain under the CTO, including the refinement of technology to make it production-ready. However, the trial deployment of new production-ready technologies *in an operational environment*, or the development of new operating processes, should be overseen by a CIO/E position that is highly attuned to operational concerns as well as enterprise risk mitigation. The CIO/E should oversee new IT projects, as well as efforts to define business processes around those new IT systems, with the assistance of the departments that are impacted. Broad-based incorporation into line of business operations should be the responsibility of the lines of business, and achieved in cooperation with the CIO/E.

Lab-based technology and production-ready capabilities are often strongly linked in a strategic way, especially when an organization partners or aligns its interests closely with others. For example, Texas Instruments helps partner companies to understand what capabilities it can develop for those partners to help them reach their goals. According to their CEO Richard Templeton, "When they invent, they grow faster, and that is good for us." [1] Once technologies make it out of the lab and become part of the offering of the organization, they must be integrated with the organization's internal capabilities. Achieving this effectively and in a timely way requires close alignment between the CTO and the CIO/E: the CIO/E must be aware of the CTO's efforts with respect to all new externally-facing capabilities, and must be thinking about how those can be integrated effectively. At a most basic level, new product development requires access to models for how product data is processed, in order to assess if a new product could be handled, and if not, what new capabilities must be developed to handle it.

Empowering the CIO/E

To further encourage cooperation, the COO or CEO should require all business processes to be *certified* by the CIO/E. This certification should not be against a narrow criteria such as risk mitigation, data quality, or security. It should be against an enterprise balanced scorecard for business value, where the term

---

[1] Ref. [Darlin2006].

"value" includes all opportunities, strategies, goals, and risks that the organization has identified.

Certification of processes should be based on all strategic business criteria.

The certification link is important because the CIO/E is the primary point person for actively ensuring that all enterprise concerns are implemented by all of the organization's operational processes. Certification provides the CIO/E's sign-off on the COO's processes, including concerns for operational transparency. The requirement for certification should be an executive-driven mandate. It gives the COO assurance that he or she has cooperated with the broad concerns of the corporation, and it gives the CEO assurance that the board can trust the CEO's reports. In a sense, certification is the business process analog of data attestation.

Core Idea: The CIO/E should not be accountable for LOB system development.

An important ramification of this is that *the CIO/E should not be accountable for LOB system development*. Otherwise, the CIO/E would be certifying the systems that he or she builds. Remember that the CIO/E is a mentor. (When I say "the CIO/E" in this context I am using shorthand for "the CIO/E's organization".) An operational unit needs a capability: this need might be recognized by the unit, by the CIO/E, or by the executive team. Regardless, the CIO/E is the go-to person for planning out how to implement the capability in such a manner that it can be certified. Actual IT system construction can be performed using (a) in-house resources that are owned by the operating unit, (b) resources owned by a resource manager (perhaps under the CIO/E), or (c) obtained from a vendor. An outside vendor can even be used to manage the effort, but regardless the operational unit should be *responsible* for both the construction and the insertion into the unit's operation.

It is therefore best if there is not a separate unit within the company that is *responsible* for IT system development. *Operating units need to be responsible for the successful creation and integration of their own systems,* and *for ensuring that those systems meet enterprise criteria.* I

117

therefore advocate gradually moving most system planning and design resources into the operating units to enable each operating unit to take responsibility for *maintaining its own IT plans and designs.* That said, the units should do their best to elevate system design activities to a business level by using business-focused design tools.

This approach is somewhat of a departure from the traditional concept of having the CIO be accountable for building systems which reflects the obsolete mentality of "if it involves computers, it belongs to the CIO". However, that accountability has not worked well because to build systems requires deep business knowledge and too often the business side holds the CIO to the fire for delivering a system when the business side does not provide the support or sensitivity to non-functional issues that is needed, or even more commonly, changes priorities constantly while holding IT accountable for meeting enterprise criteria. In short, the business side needs to be responsible for its processes – automated or otherwise.

A colleague of mine has provided an excellent example to illustrate the point. Consider a shopping mall: should the mall owner build out and decorate each store? No: it should provide common services and standards; and provide resources that store owners can contract to; but it should not assume responsibility for the stores themselves. This is analogous to the idea that IT should not assume responsibility for providing the IT systems used by the lines of business, unless those platforms are infrastructure services; but there is a definite need to define standards for how higher level services should be built and inter-connect, and since technology is ever-changing and business opportunities are dynamic, the oversight of these standards needs to be highly pro-active and driven by value rather than tradition.

Joint Accountability

To encourage true cooperation and a sense of accountability, the CIO/E function should show the way and be jointly accountable with the COO for IT's aggregate adoption and impact on the enterprise, but not at an individual business system level. The CIO/E function should only be accountable for its impact on the enterprise as a whole.

118

Many organizations attempt to achieve this joint accountability today by putting the CIO under the COO (or equivalent enterprise operations position). This approach has the disadvantage that it does not give the CIO the latitude needed to implement true integrated risk and value management processes.

Achieving a joint accountability model in which new business capabilities are conceived and implemented by functional operating units with oversight and mentoring by a CIO/E will require a very substantial level of IT capability and maturity on the part of the operating units. For this reason it needs to be adopted gradually: that much is probably obvious. However, do not underestimate the ability of operating units to implement this model. Many already have some IT capability that is unrecognized, and there is no reason that they cannot seek outside help as long as they bear responsibility. Further, as with every major change, it is smart to pilot the new model before fully rolling it out. Further, the migration toward more capable operating units is inexorable. Organizations today are beginning to realize that the centralized IT model does not work anymore, and that IT staff who think business are more valuable. The lines are blurring, and we are headed toward an era in which operating units will not be able to wait for IT, but yet they must retain enterprise alignment. The CIO/E is the champion whose mission is to reconcile these competing forces.

Let's Get Right To It: Who Owns What

Here is what I recommend that a CIO/E be responsible for:

1. A strategic capability definition and infusion function, described as a "mentoring" and pro-active change management function.
2. Providing resources to be used for capability development by operating units.

The first function is the mentoring function that I have been talking about, and entails the definition of capabilities, advocacy, assistance with planning, and co-development of pilot projects. In this capacity the CIO/E's team acts as a logical mentor to its operating unit partners. It also provides for certification that operationalized capabilities meet all enterprise concerns.

119

It would be nice to have a more powerful name for the mentor function. After all, this function is the strategic enabler that is the primary value proposition of this book. However, it is important to not over-hype the role and thereby understate the substantial burden that operating units bear for working with the mentor group and for owning final responsibility for their own change.

Let's consider the mentor function first.

The Mentor Function

The mentor function is the core function of the CIO/E unit. It should be core funded, and not derive funding from other efforts. Its purpose is to align and enable the organization in a holistic manner, and so this function represents its own agenda and should have its own funding.

Table 3 lists the functional division that I recommend between the CIO/E's mentor function and the operating units.

Table 3: Responsibilities.

Function	Operating Units (COO)	CIO/E Mentors
Business Unit Operation	✓	
Design and implementation of Controls	✓	
Capability Planning	✓	✓
Enterprise Architecture		✓
LOB Initiatives and Architecture	✓	
Enterprise Infrastructure Initiatives	✓	✓
Control Strategy Piloting	✓	✓
Capability Mentoring		✓
Capability Piloting	✓	✓
Capability Development	✓	
Capability Certification		✓

According to this table, the CIO/E mentoring team is involved in a mentoring capacity but not in a system development capacity unless it pertains to a pilot effort. Mentoring includes advocating approaches that further enterprise strategies, partnering with operating units to conceptualize, fund, and pilot solutions, and eventually certifying any new capabilities that are developed and fielded.

This is very similar to the model that was used by the Large Investment Product Provider discussed earlier to address risk management at a strategic level. However, as already mentioned, in that case there was no piloting, and there was no certification of business processes. Further, there was no linkage between the various functions in terms of a model of business value or risk other than the identification of risk categories. IT therefore had no guidance for making tradeoffs, and did not know how to quantify IT issues in business terms. Risks were often identified, but all risks were treated the same, and were not related to business metrics. Later in this book I will present an operating model that addresses these shortfalls.

The Resource Manager Function

The second function that the CIO/E provides is simple but important. In this role the CIO/E provides resources for operating units to tap for the development of new business capabilities, including IT systems. For the CIO/E this is a simple resource manager role, since the only responsibility that the CIO/E has is to ensure that the resources are trained, effective, and available. The CIO/E is wise to train these staff to think in terms of enterprise concerns, since that will make certification of the systems that they build more successful.

These resources are not mentors: they are matrixed as needed from a resource pool. The CIO/E's share of system development resources should comprise a tactical collection of resources who have broad experience across all business functions, but the CIO/E's view of them is the view of a resource manager and the resource pool should be operated as a profit center with resources billing to projects or departments, as indicated in Table 4. The *responsibility* for capability development should remain with the operating unit that requires the capability. That said, the CIO/E is responsible for achieving *enterprise-scale* change.

Table 4: CIO/E Resources.

Function	Cost Center	Profit Center
Mentor	✓	
Resource Pool		✓

As the staff in the resource pool mature they can be promoted to take on the role of mentor as previously described and participate in efforts to define new capabilities and develop reusable reference designs. The scorecard balance should be such that there is a strong incentive to promote resource staff to the non-profit mentor category if they can be effective there.

Given this division it is natural to consider splitting these functions and making each a separate group under the CIO/E. However, in order to ensure that these two groups work together it is necessary to establish a win-win relationship between them, by requiring the mentor group to train and invest time in helping those in the resource pool, and it is indeed in the best interest of the former, since eventually the best leave the pool to enter the mentor group.

Measuring the CIO/E

The mentor group is a special kind of ongoing program, for addressing the ongoing concern of enterprise-wide value realization and risk management. It performs a pro-active function that helps to define the organization's capability portfolio – not merely approve or dis-approve a portfolio. As such, it requires measurement of its success and effectiveness.

If the call for a new capability originates from the executive team or the CIO/E, the latter takes on the responsibility of finding a business partner to pilot and refine it so that it can be rolled out the all units that need it. In all cases, the CIO/E is measured by the increase in the *entire* organization's capabilities over time, where "capabilities" includes the ability to address all enterprise concerns. Thus, the ability to manage risk is a capability, as is the ability to define and launch new products. The CIO/E is therefore accountable for increasing capabilities, even though that role does not actually build the capabilities, just as an architect does not actually build a house, but uses a contractor to do the actual work.

The CIO/E and each business unit are jointly accountable for the ultimate success of each business capability in business terms. That provides an incentive for them to work together, even though the CIO/E is not specifically accountable for building systems on time or in budget.

The net result is that the CEO or COO can say to the CIO/E, "Can you develop a capability to do ABC, and do it in such a way that we are not put at risk?" and the CIO/E will respond "Of course, but it will take the COO's cooperation." Thus, success requires a strategic level of cooperation and collaboration between the COO and CIO/E: neither can succeed without the other, and each checks the other in terms of relevancy and effectiveness.

The CIO/E's strategy should be linked directly with business strategy. Thus, accountability must be in terms of business objectives for enterprise capability development, not merely in terms of keeping within an IT budget. The CIO/E operation should be run like a business. Its success should be measured based on its effectiveness and its cost: i.e., its return on investment. The CIO/E's customer and business partner is the COO, but the CIO/E's boss is the CEO.

CIO/E must be able to project the cost of new capability development, and the lifecycle costs of those capabilities. This requires very strong financial analysis and the development of relevant capability metrics. Therefore, financial analysis and metric development are a critical competency of the CIO/E office. Some experts even recommend that IT operations include a CFO function.[1]

The CIO/E – today's new enterprise CIO – must decide what capabilities will bring the most benefit first, in consideration of the CEO's goals and the COO's ability to absorb new processes.

Who's Your CIO/E?

A recent survey of CFOs indicated that 50% think that they should be in charge of IT.[2] Ask any CIO about this and they will think it is ludicrous. For example, in a recent interview, Greg Smith, CIO of the International Wildlife Fund and author of Straight to the Top: Becoming a World-Class CIO, asserted that a CIO must be a very savvy IT person: "Would you want a CIO to sign off on corporate financials?" he said as a counter-example.[3] In

---

[1] For example, see [Lutchen2004] on page 104.
[2] See [CFO_ITa05].
[3] Ref. [GSmith06].

fact, an over emphasis on financial control can pervert IT decisions, such as when IT operations are geographically consolidated to save costs without taking into the account of the impact on the mission or effectiveness of remote business units. Running IT as a cost center will result in these kinds of narrowly-focused decisions, as will putting in place cost-focused metrics without meaningful business effectiveness metrics to balance them. Consolidation might be the right choice, but you cannot know unless you consider the holistic impact.

There is likely to be considerable disagreement about what skills a CIO/E needs, and that is why the role of the job and its expectations need to be specified very clearly. If infrastructure management is offloaded to another individual, then the technical acumen becomes less important. The emphasis on capability development, in terms of people, processes, and technology, calls for someone who can easily navigate a broad landscape of issues and form practical and innovative solutions, as well as someone who has shown an ability to incubate and manage the launch of new ways of doing business.

The Function Versus The Position

Regardless what the position is called, or who fills it, the CIO/E function is a critical one for an organization that must manage complex and diverse risks yet also maintain agility. Under the CIO/E position there must be a line organization that can execute according to the CIO/E's objectives of infusing capability and change throughout the enterprise while implementing effective control over risk-related concerns. Since this book proposes a mentoring model for the CIO/E's function, I will often refer to the CIO/E's department as "the mentoring group" for shorthand. When I say "the capability mentoring group", I therefore mean the CIO/E and all of those who report directly to the CIO/E position – or whatever it is called – and who are charged with this integrated risk mitigation and capability infusion role.

Summary

The role of IT must change in order to bring about agility and control at the same time, and this requires the active leadership of the CIO.

The CIO must become business-focused, and delegate infrastructure management to a subordinate.

The CIO must have or develop a partnership with the COO, such that the COO trusts the CIO to prototype processes for transformation that can then be deployed broadly by the COO.

The CIO must develop a partnership with the CTO by working with the CTO to develop processes for lab-to-factory transitions.

The CIO must have a source of authority, and that source should be a requirement for certification. The CIO must also establish their own competence, usefulness, and legitimacy by helping other parts of the organization to perform required transformations with minimum pain.

The CIO should be measured based on the success of enterprise-wide transformation in business terms, and not on the success of individual initiatives.

7.   Business Value Measurement As a Core Strategy

Executive management often has difficulty communicating strategic goals and plans to the organization. Strategic plans often focus on the "what" and not the "how", and are usually expressed in terms of spending levels, initiative portfolios, and organization structural changes. When asked for guidance about mid-level initiatives, executive management often offer a set of easy-to-remember priorities. This is not much help when mid-level managers have to figure out the "how" dimension and decide what to spend their budgets on, nor does it say much about how success will be measured.

> ## Core Idea: Strategic Plans Must Be Actionable At all Levels of the Organization

Case In Point Consider the case of the Large Investment Product Provider mentioned earlier. Strategic goals that were articulated to IT were summarized as a small number of priority catch phrases. This helped to provide an easily understood set of business strategies, but it had the appearance of lacking depth. Executives seemed unable to provide the details behind the catch phrases, leading many to wonder if there was any.

Initiatives were established to address the goals. These initiatives had well-defined charters with clear objectives, and context was provided through presentations that explained how the initiatives related. However, the missing piece was that there was no framework to help make tradeoffs as initiative goals were tweaked or new projects with other goals were fit into the mix. The entire model for how the priorities were developed was not shared, and so managers and senior technical staff were largely left in the dark with respect to the myriad lower-level decisions that needed to be made that crossed initiative boundaries.

In short, there was no published model of business value and how the strategies and initiatives would impact value, and therefore there was no guidance for mid-level managers to trade off the priorities. As a result, the "most important" priority changed with the wind, and the priorities were not actionable in terms of their ability to facilitate analysis of the amount of investment warranted for each priority at an initiative level. There was also no guidance about how success with respect to the various priorities should be measured or rolled up into measures for corporate success.

DILBERT: © Scott Adams / Dist. by United Feature Syndicate, Inc.

Case In Point Consider the case of the Incubated Product Company that I mentioned earlier. The parent company had formed a group of about 100 people to develop a product. The team included a number of executives whose job it was to establish the market strategy and product definition. Unfortunately, this team consisted of former mid-level managers who did not have the required product marketing experience and they did not do their job properly. As a result there was little guidance to the team building the product and requirements were issued by project-level analysts who had a vision of what the product should do based on their own experience. The lack of strategic guidance resulted in inadequate marketing and positioning and by the time the product was market-ready competitors had arisen and circumstances had changed to the extent that the competitive advantage of being early to market had been lost. In short, the strategic goals of the company were not realized because there was inadequate definition of the market-facing goals and business value drivers, and management was not measured accordingly by the parent company.

Value Is Impacted By Implementation Strategy

Anyone who is in business understands the time value of money. It is better to invest sooner rather than later, because then your investment starts working sooner, and if the value of that investment grows exponentially over time, then the benefit of investing early is potentially huge, not to mention first-to-market benefits.

> **Incremental development permits the realization of capabilities earlier.**

Why then are IT projects often organized in such a manner that their benefits are not available until the entire project has completed? Wouldn't it be better if capabilities were developed incrementally, so that some of the investment would be able to bear fruit sooner, while other features are added over time?

Releasing in small increments that individually add business value allows you to realize the value of those increments sooner: that is, you don't have to wait for the entire project to be done before you can start reaping the benefits. To achieve this and foster this way of thinking within your organization, you should expect measurable business value from every capability increment. Consider the time value of money: that way, you can measure the business value of each release, and focus on a business value target, rather than focusing on the completion of a set of tasks.

> **Incremental development results in less wasted effort.**

Another benefit of incrementally developing capabilities is that there is potentially less waste: if each added capability has business value, and is developed with a long view in mind, then nothing without business value should ever be built. My company Digital Focus has estimated that IT projects save up to 40% by building incrementally and avoiding effort on system features that are not needed.

These realizations provide a framework for how to measure the impact that development strategy has on the value of IT investments. IT investments should not be measured only in terms of their cost: they should be measured in operational terms that roll into a business case that accounts for the time value of money, just as for any investment. If you do not have a way to measure business value, then you have not created an adequate business case.

This does not mean that there should be a discernible change to the bottom line for every IT investment. Business value might be somewhat intangible, such as greater security, or better quality data, thereby minimizing risk. However, reduced risk should be quantifiable, and have an expected value to the organization that can be estimated. There needs to be a financial estimation and measurement framework for every kind of risk, and for every kind of capability, that takes into account the interplay and cross-dependencies of capabilities and risks: otherwise there is no way to compare and prioritize initiatives under a limited budget. Such a model should be integrated with the process model for the organization's capabilities, so that the value of process changes can be quantified as changes are planned and later as changes are actually implemented.

Some measurement methodologies attempt to develop forward-looking metrics by modeling supply and demand and their relationship to the current state of the business. The dilemma is that when new capabilities are developed, there is as of yet no supply – at least not from one's own organization. The model is therefore theoretical, perhaps based on industry comparisons and projections rather than on internal experience. Nevertheless, a model is still possible. After all, that is what a business plan is.

A Business Plan Home For Each Initiative

Initiative planning often involves laying out the changes that are envisioned, and also presenting a cost analysis of those changes. The business value for line-of-business changes is usually elaborated in the form of an ROI analysis or some similar financial business plan format – except for IT investments. It is very often the case that IT investments are exempted from a true business plan analysis, with tangible values, and their justification is based on subjective business value criteria such as "improve alignment with strategic priority X", or "refresh technology and retire system Y". The reason is that IT benefits are often hard to quantify, and IT is often viewed as a horizontal cost of operation. However, if we think of IT as the *technical component of a set of enabling business capabilities* then there is no justification for this exemption.

Core Idea: Tangible Business Value *Measurement* Must Be Integral To All Plans

Any IT initiative should define how its success will be measured, and that success criteria should be in the context of an existing or new business plan. If the IT investment is primarily focused on adding a new capability that will have a direct impact on financial metrics, then measurement should be in those terms. However, it is often the case that an IT investment impacts operational effectiveness, which in turn impacts financial metrics in a broad and difficult-to-correlate manner. In that case the applicable IT effectiveness concerns should be modeled in terms of their assumed impact on broader business plans. In this manner the success measures are vertically linked, so that business success explicitly depends on IT success.

For example, suppose it has been determined that the organization's success depends on (1) managing market risk, and (2) managing reputation. IT might have no idea what to do with such concerns. Executive management might conceive programs to enhance these areas, but such programs still do not serve to guide the *many execution-level decisions* that IT must make as initiatives are planned, as new initiatives are added for other purposes, and as major design and integration decisions are made. *Statements of broad strategic goals are completely inadequate for guiding the day-to-day decisions made by IT, and the aggregation of these daily decisions can have a huge impact on strategic goals.*

To address this disconnect, management should develop value models for market risk and reputation risk that IT can use in its own models, employing variables such as market size, opportunity value, the value of the organization's reputation and how that value is impacted by various types of events, and other factors to make planning more meaningful. Without these IT is left with

"Harvey Ball" charts that do not provide any meaningful way to make ad-hoc tradeoffs.

Later in this book I present approaches for modeling the value of IT decisions. These approaches can be used to help articulate the value of IT choices in tangible terms so that they can be integrated with business-developed ROI models.

The ramification is that for measurement to be possible, a plan in business terms must exist. Thus, business value modeling and planning needs to be central to any endeavor – IT-focused or otherwise.

> # Core Idea: Tangible Business Value Must Be Integral To All Planning

Developing and linking business plans is a complex endeavor and most IT staff are not trained in that kind of activity unless they happen to have a business degree. It is therefore necessary for a partnership to be formed between the program management functions that oversee initiatives and the capability development functions that build new capabilities. This partnership can jointly develop high quality plans that link metrics across the different kinds of initiatives in a way that is truly meaningful to the business.

Case In Point
Value-based or risk-based planning can also be integrated at an initiative planning and project planning level, as well as at a project execution level. I have worked with companies to achieve this. In one case, which I will refer to as the Large Financial Services Oversight Group, I helped to build risk evaluation into their IT initiative planning processes to enable the allotment of effort related to risk mitigation. In doing so, we also built success measurement into the framework of standard risk mitigation practices, thereby achieving real-time business value measurement.

While an initiative plan should define concrete measures that link to business value, the initiative should then implement those measures as capabilities. For example, if security is an important driver for an initiative, then the metrics for security should be defined by the initiative and the implementation of the initiative should include the building of measurement systems for those metrics. Such measurement systems are important real-time controls that must be present if there can be any hope of having a management dashboard.

Make Business Case Development One Of The Core Capabilities Of The Capability Mentor Group

Business case development must be one of the core capabilities of the Capability Mentor group for it to be effective. Further, a business case should focus on the impact on the entire enterprise, and not just on a business unit.

> **If business value justification of capabilities is not addressed, then there can be no end to the cancer of expedient IT solutions.**

If business value justification of capabilities is not addressed, then there can be no end to the cancer of expedient and short-sighted IT solutions. *IT architecture must be justified in concrete enterprise value terms, such as dollars, risk, or other concrete and credible criteria.*

> **Should IT architects have MBAs?**

This perspective raises an interesting question: Should IT architects have MBAs? If you expect the business to understand IT concerns, then perhaps you should expect architects to understand business concerns. It will be interesting to see if the trend for IT to focus more on business value leads to any changes in computer science or software engineering curricula, or if one begins to see more enterprise architects with MBAs.

At this point you might legitimately think that the percentage of IT professionals who have MBAs is very small, and so it is not practical to seek that skill combination. However, remember that architects are your most senior non-management IT staff. Further, as a group IT architects are mostly self-taught: computer science curricula generally does not encompass software engineering, and the better members of the profession – those who make it to architect – usually are motivated individuals who are used to learning what they need to know on their own. The point here is to set the expectation that they must know the business dimension and not only the technical dimension. Some strategies for proactively addressing the problem are discussed in the section Working With Human Resources (page 225).

Does the Business Care About Every Kind Of IT Decision?

Peter Weill and Jeanne Ross of MIT's Sloan School have published study results, documented in their book *IT Governance*, showing that successful companies involve the business in IT decisions.[1] However, an important question is whether even those companies involve the business in *IT architecture* or *IT infrastructure strategy* decisions. I maintain that that is because the business does not understand those issues, partly because it feels that it cannot speak the IT language, and equally because *IT has failed to put IT architecture and infrastructure strategy issues in business terms*. It is almost academic: if the business understood these issues, it would want to be consulted. This is because these issues have a large cost impact and often a large business impact, and so to ignore them would be irresponsible.

Business should be interested in any issue that is of a scale or scope at which they deal – technical or otherwise. However, the business can only be expected to evaluate issues from a business perspective: business value, lifecycle cost, risk, opportunity, agility. Every technical issue has these kinds of concerns and therefore is worthy of business involvement. If a significant IT architecture or infrastructure strategy issue is "too techie" for the business to appreciate it, then it means that it *has not been properly interpreted by architects so that meaningful communication is possible.*

> **If a significant IT architecture or infrastructure strategy issue is "too techie" for the business to appreciate it, then it means that it has not been properly interpreted by architects so that meaningful communication is possible.**

IT architecture and infrastructure issues can be important to the business. Decisions on these issues often have major business

---

[1] Ref. [WeillRoss04], pp. 133 ff.

impact. For example, a decision to implement a common messaging infrastructure has major implications for how applications are built, and can have a large impact on business agility. As another example, the decision to utilize a rule-based architecture can have a large impact on the ability to quickly introduce new products, and can enhance financial transparency, but can also change the mix of who is involved in maintaining business logic. One can argue that the real business issue is the degree of flexibility achieved – *but that is my point*: that technical issues must be translated into tangible business terms.

Weighing the tradeoffs between IT architecture choices is not easy, but prioritizing IT choices with respect to other business priorities requires understanding the value in terms of the short- and long-term tradeoffs. This requires a deep understanding of the business value of the types of architectures and infrastructure that are contemplated.

Tracking Progress In Business Terms

In the section Measuring the CIO/E (page 122) I say that the CIO/E should be measured by the increase in the *entire* organization's capabilities over time. How is this increase to be measured? Measurement should not be in terms of the on-time, on-budget completion of projects: it should be in terms of the true goals, whatever they are, and balanced with respect to all enterprise concerns.

In the case of the Incubated Product Company the product technology was being built by a contractor that had claimed that the system was completely on schedule and who filed regular progress reports at a task granularity level. Yet, when the first major pre-operational release was due after a year of work, the contractor suddenly informed their client that three additional months were needed. It turned out that the system was on track with respect to its tasks and established task-completion metrics, but its actual capabilities were not living up to what was promised, and more time was needed. That is when I was brought in to provide an outside assessment.

> # Measures should focus on outcomes, not task completions.

Task-based progress measurement requires prior definition of *all tasks* leading to a goal, and that robs the lines of business of the flexibility to refine as they go. Forcing an initiative to predefine all steps prevents the initiative leaders from employing agile development methods to achieve the initiative's goals.

> # Continuous measurement of actual, tangible progress is a core tenet of agile methods.

Continuous measurement of *actual, tangible* progress is a core tenet of agile methods. Agile software development methodologies stress the use of comprehensive regression testing that is designed to run so quickly that the full test suite is run many times a day during development. Achieving this requires that the test suite be built to run this way from the very beginning. It also often requires that certain features are built into the software, such as an interface that can be called directly by an automated test program rather than having to require a human to sit at a terminal and manually execute tests. The point is: you cannot build a system for anything and then expect to be able to measure its operation unless you build measurability into the design from the outset.

> # Measurability must be a criteria – a requirement – for every initiative and business process.

The same is true of business processes, even at a strategic level. Management dashboards are meaningless if they are based primarily on subjective judgments and obsolete task definitions, and if they do not measure actual capabilities. It is too easy to miss important things, and to be the victim of over optimism when there is pressure to achieve goals.[1] However, to have meaningful dashboards, one must have meaningful metrics that are not subjective. To achieve this, measurability must be a criteria – a requirement – for every initiative and business process.

---

[1] Scott Ambler has coined the term "green shift" to refer to the tendency of dashboards to become more and more optimistic as they are rolled up to the executive level. See [AmbGrShift06].

Shifting to a capability-focused approach will require a change in mindset. Initiatives are traditionally conceived to perform tasks in order to achieve objectives. What I am saying is that an initiative should be conceived instead to achieve an objective, and the plan should be expressed in terms of sub-objectives, not task-focused projects. The same planning tools can be used, but the emphasis is different, because completion is defined by a set of meaningful business criteria. For example, completion of a project should not be that "we built and stood up the ABC system". Rather, it should be something like, "we created a capability to do XYZ and proved that it is effective". One should still assign budgets to each project and sub-objective, but the focus is on achievement of objectives. We need to eliminate the mindset that "we are done if we do ABC", and shift it to "we are only done if we achieve XYZ".

You might think that this is impossible because some capabilities do not have specific business value: their value lies in the fact that they provide an infrastructure that is required for other capabilities to work. However, every capability has value: the challenge is how to express it. Below I will present an approach for modeling the business value of infrastructure in a capability-focused way rather than in a cost-focused accounting centric way.

Measure Future Value At Risk

One of the most important concepts expressed in this book is that one cannot track IT value and therefore IT progress without considering the impact that risk has on value. Rather than being a third decimal point refinement, risk – and its mitigation – is a central component of value in IT as well as in other areas of business. It cannot be ignored. Later in this book in chapter 11 I present a set of techniques for estimating business value, but it is necessary to explain the core concept now so that other concepts can be understood.

It is sometimes difficult to express the value of capabilities in business terms. This is especially true as one dives to more granular levels. For example, how can one express the business value of a single feature of an IT system? One might be able to assign a value to the entire system, by estimating the revenue value of the business that it enables. A single feature, on the other hand, is somewhat inseparable from the rest of the system and so it might not have any value by itself. This is a problem for any methodology that attempts to measure progress strictly based on business value.

There is a way out of the dilemma though. When speaking of business value one must consider opportunity value and investment cost if these are known, but one must also consider and risk.

The Value Of Reducing Risk Related to Capability Realization

Nothing is ever a sure thing. Even an up-and-ready capability does not produce definite revenue, since it might be disrupted any day by technical failure or by changes in the business environment. It is therefore inaccurate and foolhearty to project value without adjusting it based on probability.

A system that is being built and therefore does not even exist yet is highly risky. Studies vary on the probability of IT initiative success – so much so that I will not even bother to quote them – but if you read in the IT domain you surely must be familiar with failure statistics that range from 20% to 80% of large IT initiatives, depending on the study. There is also the risk that the project will be completed but come in greatly over budget, be extremely late, or not realize its true goals. In that case, when projecting investment cost or other variables, one should ideally assume a range and use an expected value based on the organization's historical accuracy in estimating the cost and other metrics of initiatives.

If your organization tracks the success of its projects in terms of business goals (many do not), then you might also have a baseline of data for projecting the likelihood of success in business value terms. This probability should ideally be factored against the projected business value of the initiative.

When a capability is in a pre-operational state, it provides no actual realized business value, but it provides the expectation of business value. Thus, the pre-operational capability has a theoretical value – an *economic* value. That is, an accountant would

138

compute the value to be zero, but an economist would compute it to be positive, based on its expected eventual realized value.

The eventual realized value has risk associated with it, since it is not yet realized, and so it expected value today is reduced by the risk that the system's features will not be completed, as well as by the risk that business needs will change. When a single feature is added to that system during the course of software development, the fact that the feature has been added to the system means that the overall risk of the initiative has been reduced, because the feature's completion is no longer in question. *This decrease in risk is real business value*, and it should be included in any estimation of progress. In addition, while money has been spent in the course of implementing the feature (an investment cost), the cost of completing the entire system is now reduced, and this reduced completion cost means that *the remaining investment is lower* in order to be able to deploy the completed capability. This is true progress, and estimating the combined effect of reduced risk and reduced completion cost is the most realistic way to assess the value added by a single feature.

The method for assessing the true value of a single new feature is therefore to assess the reduction in risk and cost of completing the entire system as a result of having added the feature. The risk reduction is the increased probability of success times the business value of the entire system.

This method works because software project managers are good at estimating the probability of completing a system. They do this routinely without realizing it when they estimate level of effort (LOE), because LOE requires a risk assessment based on complexity and available skills. However, a slight shift in focus to risk instead of LOE can produce feature risk estimates based on the relative risk of each feature and a total risk for the entire system. These risk estimates are inherently well-aligned with LOE estimates. However, they are focused on value instead of cost.

What if there is little risk that a feature can be completed, but that the LOE of the feature is risky – that is, that it might take much longer than projected? That is very often the case. When the feature has been implemented, the risk of completing it is gone, and so while the actual LOE has now been invested, the uncertainty of the feature's *cost* has been removed, thereby removing uncertainty in the cost of the entire system. However, that does not reduce the risk of the system coming into existence: it merely reduces the uncertainty over whether the system will turn out to be a good investment or not. Thus, reduced uncertainty in the cost of the system is not a tangible value, but it should result in a re-evaluation of whether the system should be completed.

Features That Provide Tangible Business Value

Some feature sets provide tangible business value – that is, they represent a true business capability. For example, a feature set that adds a new usable service to a website has a business case in its own right. The value of the feature is evident to the user of the system. Some authors have referred to features with evident tangible value as "Minimum Marketable Features" (MMF).[1]

On the other hand, if a new service feature set depends on the addition of a new core feature set that has no independent business value, then the new service feature set has no demonstrable value until the new core feature has been added. The service feature set depends on the core feature set, and so without the core feature set it is useless from the perspective of the business.

Business value estimation therefore depends on the sequence in which features are implemented. It turns out that the system tends to have the greatest value if the most risky *mission critical* parts are built first and then one starts to add the most high-value components. This is because this approach maximizes the expected Present Value of features that return true value. However, the problem is actually a complex mathematical optimization problem.

Rather than tackle the general problem in a mathematical way, let's consider a simple illustrative case that provides sufficient insight for the typical situation. Please refer to Figure 8.

---

[1] Ref. [Denne04].

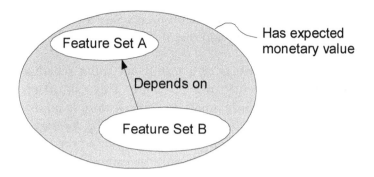

Figure 8: How the completion of feature sets impact the expected monetary value of a capability asset.

In Figure 8 Feature Set A represents a set of core utility features that will enable the operation of Feature Set B. The design is such that Feature Set B cannot function unless Feature Set A has been completed. In fact, Feature Set A has been delineated to represent the minimum set of things that Feature Set B must have to start adding business value; and Feature Set B is delineated such that it only includes features that must all be present in order to start providing a particular kind of business value to the organization. Thus, these feature sets are not arbitrary: they are deliberate partitions of minimum functionality for business value.

This means that when Feature Set B is operational, the organization can start using it; but for Feature Set B to be operational, it must be complete, and Feature Set A must also be complete. Feature Set A provides no business value by itself, but it is needed in order to enable each and every feature in B. Each of the features in B provide direct business value, but the organization would not deploy any of those features unless the entire set of B was complete.

Once A and B are complete, the combination of A and B has an expected monetary value: it represents a tangible asset that the organization believes will provide real business once it is put into usage. All of the risk factors of deployment and ultimate success should be factored into the expected value of the completed combination of A and B. The value of completing A is therefore the reduced risk of deploying B plus the reduced cost remaining.

The point here is that it is possible to use risk reduction as a measure of business value, even for small features, and so the argument that one cannot measure business value for small system features is vacuous. One *can*, and one *should*.

A development plan consists of a feature set and a schedule. At inception, a plan is at a high risk of failure. This risk offsets the value of the initiative. Each time a tangible feature is added, the risk is reduced, thereby *increasing the expected value of the asset that is under development*. Direct costs also offset the value of the asset, but costs are an investment and so you must be careful to put them in the investment column – not in the value column. Costs and reduced risk should offset each other, with reduced risk coming out on top in the long run.

Note that when I use the word "feature", I am not restricting the meaning to automated system features. I am including "features" of the overall capability – human and machine. For example, while the terminology is admittedly not ideal, a "feature" of a capability might be a team's level of experience at using a set of new automated features.

This approach provides an accurate way to model the value of each feature of a capability, using the decreasing risk of realization of the total capability value as the incremental value. This is explained in more detail beginning on page 269 in the section Features That Have No Independent Business Value.

How This Is Different From Total Cost Of Ownership

The Total Cost of Ownership (TCO) approach to modeling the value of IT systems is a wonderful concept. The goal of TCO is to discover the true cost of an IT capability. Unfortunately, the way that TCO is typically used compromises that goal, mainly because the tradition of TCO began before there was a good understanding of how to measure value. It is time to update TCO to reflect more modern ideas about value and cost.

The primary differences are that unpredictability must be accounted for, and one must include business opportunity value rather than merely cost. Measuring the expected value of an asset under development rather than merely its costs – direct and indirect – is the right mindset. A focus on known or estimated

142

costs is inadequate because it does not provide a means of accounting for the interdependence of capabilities on each other, and it does not allow for the value of reducing risk, and it does not differentiate the value of building high-value, high-risk components early to reduce the risk of the investment. TCO is contrasted with an alternative approach, Total Value of Ownership (TVO) on page 283.

Planning and Accountability Horizon

IT decisions impact capabilities, costs, and agility. The last of these is the most problematic because agility is hard to put a price on: to do so, one would have to estimate the expected value of unforeseen future opportunities (or threats) that one might need to react to.

Yet agility is the issue that is first and foremost on the mind of most software architects. Software practitioners are trained to constantly consider the extensibility of the systems that they create. Extensibility translates into agility: if one can extend a system, then one can add extensions that address new requirements as they come along.

If architects think about extensibility all the time, then why are so many corporate IT systems so un-extensible? The reason is that architects are thwarted in their quest for extensibility – thwarted by the very business leaders who demand agility.

The Three Business Reasons Why Corporate IT Loses Agility Over Time

1. Lack of a standard business model that is accepted by both the business executives and the IT architects, and that includes the impacts of IT architecture on agility.
2. Failure to trace the cause-and-effect of actions on agility and lifecycle cost over a period of years, and failure to measure business performance over a period of years.
3. Failure to address the migration of maintenance skills as systems evolve and age.

See also The Three Technical Reasons Why Corporate IT Loses Agility Over Time, on page 250.

143

IT architects are thwarted in their quest for extensibility by the very business leaders who demand agility.

Let us consider an example to illustrate. Suppose a new software application is created. A year goes by, and the designers of that system move on to other projects. This produces the first symptom: the system becomes harder to maintain because the knowledge has moved on. Those who maintain it do not have the benefit of the thoughts and ideas that were behind the design of the system, and so all of the unwritten rationale for design decisions is lost. In the case of the Responsive IT Department this is exactly what happened.

Now suppose a particular department realizes that there is a new opportunity in the market, if they can buy a certain COTS product and connect it directly to the internal database of the application that is now more than a year old in order to read data needed by the COTS product. The original designers of the system hear of this and assert that to do so would compromise the design, because the application was not designed to have other systems connected directly to it. They assert that all systems should exchange data with the application via the application's software interface, and that the right way to achieve this with the COTS product would be to build an adapter from the COTS product to the application's interface. The business claims that this is not cost effective because it would cost more, and the designers have not articulated a good reason why the extra money should be spent. The designers claim that if the architecture is violated in the manner that is contemplated then the system's design will become complex and corrupt and will be less "maintainable". This argument does not win – mainly because there is no historical data for other systems to support this argument – and the COTS system is directly connected to the database.

Now, suppose that a few years go by, and this scenario plays out several more times. The result is that after four or five years, there are many ad-hoc connections to the application in various and sundry ways. The business now asks, "What would be involved in replacing the application with a more flexible system?" The IT group responds that (1) no one is quite sure what data each connection uses are anymore; and (2) the application is so interwoven with various data flows to and from other systems that that nothing can be disconnected and replaced unless everything is replaced at once. The business responds that the IT group has developed an inflexible environment.

The business side is not fully to blame, nor is the IT side. The core root cause of this situation is that there is a huge failure in communication between the business side and the IT side. IT has not articulated in a meaningful way what the long-term costs of ad-hoc design decisions are. On the other hand, the business side has not considered the true lifecycle cost of systems in its measurement of business performance – otherwise it would have asked more questions and demanded that these questions be answered before the ad-hoc connections were made. The sidebar "The Three Business Reasons Why Corporate IT Loses Agility Over Time" summarizes the phenomena.

It might sometimes turn out that an IT architecture must be compromised in order to seize a business opportunity; the point is, one will never know if there is not effective communication between IT and the business. IT must be able to formulate models in terms of business value and risk. The business must extend its planning horizon to five or more years, and must extend accountability for loss of agility and lifecycle cost through that same period. Personnel performance evaluations for management must include these forms of accountability. Otherwise, the calls of IT to keep to the architecture will never have any weight behind them.

The Lost Term: The Value Of IT Architecture Principles

A viable business model must predict the expected value of investment, and also provide metrics that can be used to measure and monitor success. The predictive aspect is often referred to as an "ex-ante" view, and the success measurement aspect is often referred to as an "ex-post" view.

Measuring the value of IT is the subject of much debate and many books. For example, see [Remenyi00], [Devaraj02], [Keen03], [Reifer02], and [Murphy02]. The challenge with IT is principally the intangible nature of many mid-level IT benefits. The traditional cost accounting approach to IT value measurement does not work anymore for major IT decisions because IT impacts the business model of the organization and vice versa.[1] IT spending now accounts for almost 50% of new capital spending for most organizations.[2] The importance of IT now mandates that it simply *must* be integrated into enterprise business models and not treated as a separate line item. The questions is, how?

DILBERT: © Scott Adams / Dist. by United Feature Syndicate, Inc.

A fine point in this issue that is seldom recongized by efforts to measure the value of IT is the measurement of the value of *IT principles*. If you ask a financial advisor about the principle of diversification you will receive a lecture on risk management and you might also receive some instruction on particular techniques such as hedging and portfolio management. Similarly, if you ask an IT architect about the principle of encapsulation you will receive a lecture about the business value of this practice, but the explanastion will be in the language of software architects. Yet as IT becomes more important to the business, IT principles are becoming as important as other business principles and so it behooves business executives to be familiar with those prinicples at a basic level and understand how they translate into recognizable business value terms. As it turns out, the principle of encapslation has important consequences for businss agility and lifecycle cost. Encapsulation of function is an important IT strategy for keeping various subsystems independent of each other, which allows systems to be repurposed and extended more easily to do things such as support new products and services that might come along: i.e., support business agility. The problem is

---

[1]   Reference [Murphy02] has an excellent discussion of the inadequacy of traditional cost accounting methods for measuring the value of IT.

[2]   Ref. the Introduction of [Murphy02].

that the explanation of encapsulation is too far removed from the language and value framework of most lines of business.

Case In Point
It is not that people in business do not want to understand what IT has to offer. In fact, they might be keenly concerned with getting to the root cause of problems and fixing things right, but you cannot expect them to understand problems from an IT perspective since that is not their perspective, and you cannot expect them to make decisions based on rationale that seem technical and far removed from business value. For example, in the case of the Responsive IT Department that I mentioned earlier, the business executive asked IT to propose a solution to fix things once and for all, but when the solution was explained it was based on addressing things such as error handling, integrity of interfaces, and rewrites of code into more robust langauges. These kind of made sense to the business but when calls for new features arose again the root cause work was pushed to the side because it was not rooted in a true cause-and-effect understanding within the minds of the decisionmakers.

The bottom line is that IT architects as a group have no clue how to express the business value let alone integrate the value into a comprehensive project business value model that has true consensus and durability.

The difficulty of this challenge is why it is now increasingly important that IT professionals have some background in financial analysis and experience with techniques such as decision analysis and financial factor analysis[1]. Establishing a model for IT business value requires modeling IT activities in terms of both their internal-facing impact on business processes as well as their external-facing impact on business areas of concern such as customer retention, risk, and the ability to respond to new opportunities in an agile manner.

Despite the challenge, there is a consensus that the business value of IT can be modeled and measured. Sources such as [Keen03]

---

[1] For discussions of decision analysis and factor analysis, refer to [Remenyi00], pages 117 and 173 respectively.

present techniques for modeling intangible IT benefits in terms of tangible metrics.[1]

There are two primary approaches to meausing the value of IT benefits: subjective and objective. A subjective assessment is performed by asking those who are familiar with the business to score (weight) the direct value contributors of an IT function and achieve a believable value through consensus.[2] In contrast, an objective assessment is performed by modeling the value contributors of an IT function in terms of measurable indirect metrics. An objective model still requires subjective judgment because any model is only that and models can be wrong. That is why this activity should not be ad-hoc and the skill of performing this modeling is the primary value that a new generation of business architects can add to their firms.

The Role of the Business Architect

In the section on page 85 I argue that there are too many specialties within IT architecture, leading to silos of understanding of important issues. Here I would like to explore this a little further, and add some precision to the terms that describe different kinds of IT architect.

A *business architect* is someone who specializes in the highest-level design of a set of business capabilities. I claim that an *enterprise architect* is a business architect who works at an enterprise level, i.e., at the highest level within an organization. A business architect needs to be a good mentor, and needs to be versed in both the business and technology in order to be able to interface across the business and technical groups. A business architect also needs to be able to express the business value of architecture in terms that both business managers and IT managers can understand.

In contrast, a *software architect* is someone who specializes in the IT aspects of business architecture. IT architects develop the technical blueprints that define how initiatives should incorporate the various corporate standards and best practices.

---

[1] See for example in [Keen03] the summary of approaches, referred to as "tangibility themes", beginning on page 122.

[2] See [Remenyi00] for a fairly good treatment of subjective methods.

These terms are not standardized.[1] Indeed, that is one of the problems today in IT. There are entire websites devoted to the topic of what an "enterprise architect" and a "software architect" are. This author himself has written articles on the topic. However, I am going to use these terms as defined here, because we need words for these critical roles.

The term "business architect" is especially problematic. The term is the most ill-defined in the industry, and organizations seem to be defining it in an ad-hoc way, which leans toward mere functional definition of processes – much like the role of a "business analyst". However, business architecture needs to be much more than that to be useful.

A business architect first and foremost must have a deep understanding of the business. A business architect also has a broad grasp of applicable technologies, and has *proven astute judgment* with respect to developing approaches to create new and effective capabilities in a cost-efficient and rapid manner – taking account of all relevant technology issues. A business architect is sensitive to all of the needs of the enterprise and is able to integrate all enterprise concerns at his or her decision-making level. Your CIO/E is your most senior business architect, and is the primary conceptualizer of new capabilities for achieving enterprise-level business objectives, and doing so in a manner that integrates all enterprise concerns – i.e., balancing the "how".

This implies that a business architect should have both IT skills and business skills. I have already posed the question of whether IT architects should have MBAs or at least be expected to have a working knowledge – however gained – of financial analysis of IT projects (page 133). In any case, a business architect should have the skills needed to make a business case for an IT solution, and communicate that business case to various parts of the organization.

---

[1] The International Association of Software Architects (IASA) is developing a standard set of definitions for IT architect professional categories, the skills that various types of IT architects should have, and criteria for certification.

Your Business and Technical Architects Ensure Alignment With Your Enterprise Strategies

The job of an architect is not to produce documents, drawings, or rules. It is to ensure that a solution is produced that realizes the intended business value and business concerns. Thus, it is the job of an architect to be sufficiently familiar with project and departmental designs, plans, and processes so that they can not only assess that goals will be met and that risks will be addressed, but also to understand capability weaknesses in the organization so that those weaknesses can be addressed or worked around.

> **A good architect does not stay in his or her office writing documents.**

A good architect therefore does not stay in his or her office writing documents. A good architect stays aware of the organization's concerns and goals, stays aware of each important project and operational function in their domain, and stays aware of the solutions that have been developed. A good architect stays in touch with the technical and non-technical leaders of each of those groups and helps to plan and execute ways of elevating the skills of those groups so that they can address their challenges. A good architect is sufficiently involved with each group so that they can identify risks and ensure that corporate concerns are adequately addressed. The architect should help to interpret corporate policies so that the staff of each department or project does not have to navigate them on their own.

To accomplish these significant responsibilities an architect should develop a toolkit. In this book I refer to such tools as "blueprints". More on this in chapters 12 and 13.

Why Today's IT Architect Is So Ineffective

There is no business value model for IT architecture. That is to say, if a consideration of best practices leads to an architectural decision to "only get data X from system Y", how does one later justify this decision if money can be saved in the short term by siphoning data X from system Y? Most likely the foundation of the architect's case is rooted in subjective judgment with regard to

150

the future lifecycle cost of allowing the architecture to be compromised, and is based on experience from prior systems – not from actual metrics or an actual model of lifecycle cost. Software architects are not trained to do such analysis, nor are many business architects.

Case In Point This kind of analysis must exist. The metrics must have consensus among all officer-level tiers of the organization, so that they can be compared with a common model to trade off pros and cons when weighing various concerns. Too often short-term cash-focused concerns win over long-term concerns, because there is no way to estimate the value of long-term concerns. This was the case with the Responsive IT Department and with the Large Investment Product Provider. It was also the case with a client that contracted with a company that I will call the Guru-Run Technology Provider. In that situation, the client was highly focused on getting all of the requirements specified at a detailed level, at the expense of addressing the major system issues and ways to address them. The client used a feature-based focus rather than business value based focus. Thus, there was no prioritization with respect to major issues, including pressing lifecycle issues related to maintainability and performance, and no understanding of what it would take to address those.

Business architecture is inherently a set of long-term concerns. If there is no way to quantify the value of each element of an architecture, then there will be no way to compare those with cash-focused concerns – and so the architecture concerns will always lose by default. Bad decisions will be made because there is insufficient information to make good decisions.

> **An architect's primary job, first and foremost, should be to establish, maintain, and advocate the business case for each architectural strategy.**

An architect's primary job, first and foremost, should therefore be to establish, maintain, and advocate the business case for each architectural strategy. I cannot stress this enough: it is critical to the entire effectiveness of the organization's ability to implement any strategic policies that impact IT.

I should emphasize that I am not talking about a use case. I am talking about a business case. A use case is a description of usage scenario. A business case explains the value proposition of that scenario, and of the many other scenarios involving the IT system or business process in question – including those that reach beyond the immediate users of the system. It is the creation of the business case that architects do not even attempt. They feel that it is outside of their domain, and that is the problem.

Unfortunately, to create an architectural business case and metric model, one must obtain data from people regarding their costs for various activities and why those activities were undertaken, and those people must be retaining and collecting that data. This is a difficult challenge and is only achievable if there is a mandate to create these kinds of models.

It also means that business processes must be *designed to be measurable*. One of the primary responsibilities of an architect should therefore be to include measurability as an implied but critical requirement for every system.[1]

Summary

Implementation strategies must be aligned with enterprise strategies in order to realize maximum value and to ensure that objectives are met.

In order to make enterprise strategies actionable at all levels of an organization, planning at all levels must be based on business value modeling.

Each initiative and project plan should therefore have a business plan that establishes how enterprise strategies will be implemented and how they will be measured.

To make this feasible, business-level planning must be a core capability for those who spearhead transformation, and eventually of every individual who has a leadership role in initiatives or projects.

---

[1] Some security certification and accreditation frameworks, such as [eMASS], provide standard system requirements for measurability and controls.

Technical decisions should be of interest to the business side if those decisions impact success or alignment. However, it is reasonable for them to expect that such decisions be expressed in business terms.

The progress of any transformation should always be tracked in tangible business terms that measure the actual value received. Tracking progress based on work completed is specious.

Some tasks are difficult to measure the value of because they do not produce tangible value. However, those kinds of tasks can be measured in terms of the degree to which they bring the organization closer to realizing tangible value. An organization moves closer to realizing value by either reducing the risk of failure and by reducing the cost to complete a transformation.

It is extremely important to account for the value of technical choices, so that their rationale can be expressed in business terms. Special techniques for accounting for the value of technical choices must be applied.

Some choices do not manifest their value until late in the lifecycle of a system. Therefore, it is extremely important that value models account for the full lifecycle, and for the impact on the entire organization. This is especially true for decisions that impact technical flexibility and therefore business agility.

The role of a business architect is to define business processes and capabilities, as well as transformations to those. In order to be effective, a business architect must be especially adept at linking business value to the ways in which capabilities can be implemented through automated systems.

Business architects and technical architects must ensure alignment with enterprise strategies.

Today's IT architects tend to be less effective than they could be, because IT architects as a profession are not trained to estimate the business value that is associated with the technical strategies that they employ.

8.   Putting It All Together

Summarizing the Central Ideas

Let's revisit the core strategies that were stated in Chapter 1. They are repeated here, with slightly different wording:

1. To achieve **business agility**, an organization needs a champion for change (which I have called a "mentor group"), and that champion needs to have a mission to ensure consistency across the organization.

2. To achieve **assurance** with respect to the risks that the organization faces, the champion for change needs to have a mission to ensure that all enterprise concerns are addressed in a balanced way.

3. Provide for **accountability** and transparency with respect to the business value of IT choices. This is the key to elevating IT to a level at which it becomes an executive-level player. This accountability must be with respect to (a) the reasons behind IT decisions, and (b) the actual value produced by IT.

4. To reduce the effective cost of IT, while maintaining the IT initiatives that are important, one must *increase IT's delivered value per dollar spent* – i.e., its productivity – by realizing a high level of resuse of its work by others in the organization, and thereby **amplifying** the capabilities of the rest of the organization. Thus, rather than becoming more austere and penny-wise, IT must help others to help themselves, and also become more transparent about its own value (see 3.b).

Figure 9 illustrates how these strategies work together.

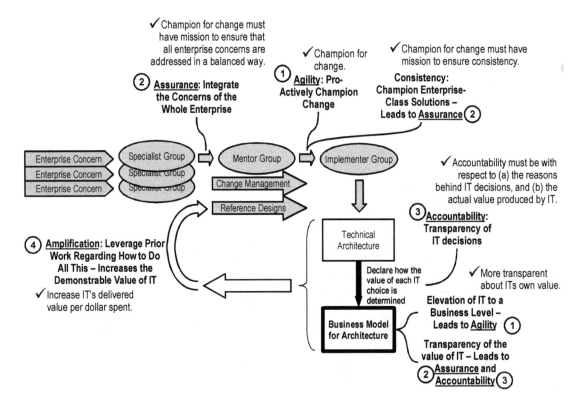

Figure 9: How Agility, Assurance, Accountability, and Amplification result from a mentor-driven organization that focuses on business value.

As we have seen, agility and assurance are competing goals, yet they can be addressed together if one tackles the root cause of problems: poor decision-making processes. The strategy proposed in this book is to establish a special team – the "Mentor Group" at the center of Figure 9 – to serve as the focal point for new initiatives, to "get it right" on a small scale and then to help other units learn how to implement the new initiatives. The Mentor Group is the CIO/E's team that focuses on enterprise change management, and it is a center of activities pertaining to enterprise architecture. The Mentor Group provides the organization with business agility (core strategy 1) by being a proactive agent for change, and it drives the implementation of enterprise policies throughout the organization, using a combination of knowledge transfer and enforcement through certification.

The Mentor Group helps other parts of the organization to enhance organizational assurance (core strategy 2) by integrating the many diverse concerns of the enterprise into every operational capability that is developed or updated. The Mentor Group makes it its business to learn all of the concerns of the enterprise from a holistic perspective, leveraging SMEs so that those same SMEs do not have to spend an inordinate amount of time with each business unit.

The hard work of figuring out how to integrate these concerns into operational capabilities is captured as reusable blueprints by the Mentor Group. More than that, the knowledge represented by those blueprints – the experience of integrating enterprise concerns into actual operational capabilities – exists with the Mentor Group, ready to be leveraged to help other operating units to implement enterprise capabilities of their own. In this way the Mentor Group endows the organization's IT department with increased productivity (core strategy 4). The reference designs encompass both technical architecture and business architecture, including approaches for estimating value and risk. The ability to measure value helps the Mentor Group to demonstrate the value of IT, thereby putting the focus on value and productivity rather than merely on reducing costs.

The mentor group also makes it its business to establish workable methods for estimating the value of IT decisions as well as estimating risk in quantitative terms. This measurement provides the operational transparency that we seek (core strategy 3). To achieve this it must work with other parts of the enterprise to vet these metrics. The methods and metrics for estimating value and risk can then be reused throughout the organization, providing a common basis for making decisions based on actual business value. This common decision framework provides a level of accountability for decision-making that is increasingly necessary for regulatory compliance and is also necessary for being able to balance opportunity and risk in a rational way. Being able to talk credibly in business terms also elevates IT to a true business-level function.

The competing needs of assurance and business agility therefore do not have to work against each other: they can be aligned. The key to that alignment is to succeed in learning how to make decisions in a way that truly addresses business value, and to integrate the way that opportunity and risk are measured so that these opposing concerns can be balanced. To achieve this on a broad scale requires a champion – a center of excellence of sorts – that spearheads the methods for measuring value and that does the heavy lifting of figuring out how to transform business processes in a value-centric way and then pushing that knowledge out through the organization. Figure 10 illustrates conceptually how strategies for Agility and Amplification in IT decision-making can *increase* Assurance and Accountability, rather than having those latter concerns layered on.

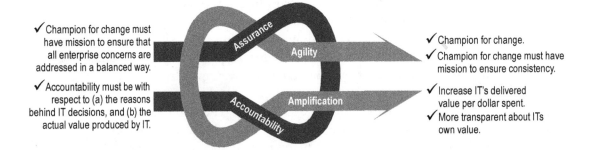

Figure 10: Agility and Amplification can work together to move the organization forward without leaving Assurance and Accountability behind.

These ideas are all well and good, but they are not much use if one does not have a plan for putting them into action. The next part of this book provides guidance for doing just that.

Part II: Transformation

Putting the Principles Into Practice

9. Establishing a Capability Creation Team

A Call to the CEO[1] to Create a Capability-Focused Unit

The Elements Needed At the Outset

In the first part of this book I outlined a vision for how a mentor-based, capability-driven IT operation should work. The rub of course is how to get there: where does one start? In this chapter I present a plan of action for the organization's leadership, because achieving this order of change is only possible with the support of the top tier of the organization, or at least the tier that IT reports into.

Every organization is different of course, and so there is no recipe that can be blindly applied. Each organization has ongoing challenges and priorities, personalities, centers of success and influence, external influences, existing processes and consensus, and existing capabilities. The plan presented here is intended as a guide to the various ingredients of a transition plan for making the vision outlined in Part I a reality.

---

[1] The CEO, or whichever position oversees the functions of business operations, financial operations, and IT.

Be Prepared For Change

Every executive knows that change requires the expenditure of political capital, involves a level of risk, and requires a willingness to trust in others. Change also requires a sustained investment to ensure that the change results in a positive outcome. Shifting to a value-driven focus requires changing the roles somewhat of several major tiers of your organization. You will need to lay out expectations clearly to allay fears that this might result in a power shift away from those tiers. You do not want your executives thinking "A year from now only half of us will be here." The kinds of change required here should not disempower anyone: instead, the changes should result in better cooperation between those tiers and better enablement of their functions. Change should result in growth and a stronger position for all. Both IT *and* the business will find themselves more empowered, not less. In short, if the fear can is eliminated, then it will not be a zero-sum game.

Before trying to implement these changes, the CEO should:

- Be prepared to change how things are done in "non-IT" parts of the business in response to issues raised by the CIO/E.
- Be prepared to make changes to the budget process and the initiative prioritization process.
- Be prepared to provide a compelling partnership model that requires everyone to be successful for anyone to be successful. Only then will each part of the business work its hardest to help all others succeed in implementing the change.
- Be prepared to explain to your board why there will be some costs associated with the changes, but that eventually these should be paid for by increased capabilities, increased overall agility, and eventually offset to some degree by increased efficiency and predictability across all initiatives.
- Be prepared to explain how the changes will benefit *all aspects* of operation over time, how each element of the business will play a vital role in the change, and how their individual and joint contributions will be recognized.

In terms of changes, the CEO will need to do the things listed in Table 5, more or less in that order of completion:

162

Table 5: Changes that must be driven by the CEO.

Change	Reference
Define the CIO/E role and what it entails.	Chapter 6
Help the CIO/E to develop an operating model for the CIO/E unit.	Chapter 6, 10
Help the CIO/E and operating units to reach a consensus on how to measure business value.	Chapter 7
Develop a roadmap and migration timetable.	NA
Provide for oversight.	Chapter 5, page 91 ff.
Provide a funding mechanism.	Chapter 6, page 119 ff.
Establish a mandate.	Chapter 6, page 116 ff.
Begin to migrate responsibilities for capability development to operating units, in accordance with the roadmap.	Chapter 6, page 116 ff.

The need for these changes has already been discussed in the sections referenced in the table. In sections that follow I will examine the impact that each of these changes will have on your organization, how you can help bring them about, and how to ensure success.

Redefine the CIO Unit As a Capability Unit

In Chapter 6 I define the CIO/E role at length, including the following seven key aspects of the role:

1. It is not limited to or defined by what is "IT".
2. It is measured according to its holistic success at an enterprise level, not an itemized project level.
3. Its focus and purpose is to elevate the capabilities of the organization.
4. Its mission is to ensure that all important enterprise concerns are identified and addressed.
5. Its methodology is to *incorporate the concerns directly into* business processes, rather than appending them.
6. Its methodology is to enable, not to do, so that those it elevates are left truly elevated and not dependent on the CIO/E.
7. Its methodology is to *leverage* subject matter experts (SMEs), by learning their concerns and helping other parts of the business to learn and incorporate those concerns as well, rather than always calling on the SMEs.

These methodologies and value propositions must be explained to the rest of the organization so that they know what to expect. Few people really have a clear idea of what a CIO does or should do: fewer will grasp quickly the intended role of an "Enterprise CIO".

Redefining the CIO's organization will induce some culture shock. Many (most perhaps) in IT do not understand that they need to be more business focused today than they were ten years ago. Some will not be able to make the adjustment, and you must identify those people and allow them to leave gracefully. Do not invest effort trying to convince them: invest your time with those who grasp the concept and who are comfortable with it. Hold several offsites with executive management running through the ramifications for the organization and its operations, and identify the issues that must be resolved: there will be many; but be true to the core ideas, or the entire proposition will be at risk. The seven elements listed above are quite interdependent. For example, if one does not leverage SMEs properly (element seven), then there is little hope of being able to elevate the capabilities of operating units (element three). As another example, if the CIO/E is burdened with IT infrastructure, the organization will still tend to think of the role as a technology role and not a business-focused role.

Establish Expectations For Skills Of The CIO/E

If you plan to make your CIO a CIO/E but keep the old title, then rewrite the job description for the CIO so that it specifies the skills needed for the new role. The job description should list things such as communication, developing a mentor-focused organization, managing investments, and managing internal partnerships – all with a strong focus on automated and people-centric capabilities. A CIO/E job is not a technology job. It is a change management job on steroids – and with business-focused accountability. A job description for the position might look something like the following:

Job Description: Enterprise CIO

Responsibilities:

- Report to the CEO.
- Accountable for risk management and value management.
- Work closely with operating units and the COO to devise strategies for change management and business success.
- Work closely with the CTO and COO to help move technology from the lab into operations.
- Manage enterprise architects.
- Manage IT system development resources, and provide those resources to operating units as needed.

Skills required:

- Highly effective leader.
- Strong executive level operational experience in a dynamic organization with a large IT component.
- Strong knowledge of the business of our company.
- Some experience managing IT functions for a large organization.
- Experience in financial management practices and value-centric financial analysis.

The second bullet point, regarding accountability for risk management and value management, has been discussed before in this book (see the section Empowering the CIO/E on page 116), but seeing it in a job description provides concreteness. What it means is that the CIO/E is accountable for the organization's success at managing its risks and its value propositions together. This is not a position of merely measurement and tabulating controls. This is a change management position, and perhaps the most dynamic and strategic position in the organization. Getting operating units to actually change how they work is what we are talking about. It is not a position on the sidelines: it is front-and-center.

As everyone knows, accountability with no authority is a recipe for failure. The CIO/E position has authority: it has the certification stick. Also, the COO must be jointly accountable for the CIO/E's success. It is a team effort.

Help the CIO/E to Establish an Operating Model For How The CIO/E Unit Will Work With Other Parts Of the Business

Once the CIO/E unit is a funded unit, it will compete with other units for resources. The perception of a zero-sum resource game must be undercut by fostering partnerships and non-zero-sum joint ventures between the CIO/E unit and other operational units. In the early stages the CEO and COO must assist the CIO/E to make this happen and to create a climate of cooperation and partnership. The culture that is established early will determine how future relationships proceed, so early success is extremely important.

> **Do not give the responsibility of internal compliance auditing or assessment to the CIO/E unit.**

Toward that end, the CIO/E unit must have the trust of other units. For this reason you should not give the responsibility of internal auditing or assessment to the CIO/E unit. To do so would be to place the CIO/E unit in an adversarial role. Further, spend a lot of time focusing on what the value proposition is for the CIO/E unit from the perspective of the business units that it mentors: the value proposition must entail both a carrot and a stick. The carrot should be (a) to help those business units to make strong cases for change initiatives, and (b) to help them to achieve certification. The stick should be that certification is required.

It might seem natural that the CIO/E unit would provide an assessment function. After all, this is kind of what certification is, which we have talked about. But the difference is in how the certification function is performed. When the CIO/E unit certifies an operating unit, it does so by mentoring that unit until it can be certified. No "failure grade" is every given: only a passing grade. No detailed deficiency report should be written. The CIO/E unit should be a partner of any operating unit that it certifies, but accountable to the organization as a whole.

So who oversees the CIO/E unit to make sure that they are not certifying every operating unit blindly? For this purpose there needs to be a separate assessment function in the organization, to accredit the certification process in a sense and to spot check actual processes to make sure that the certifications are legitimate. This provides for oversight of the CIO/E unit's effectiveness. More on that below.

The mentoring role and certification role are not a conflict of interest. However, this is why the CIO/E unit must have its own funding and be accountable to the organization, so that it does not feel pressure to be lax with certification.

In a true partnership both side contribute resources and effort, and both share in the risk and rewards. This should be true of the CIO/E function and its partnerships with other operational units. Every joint effort should have a business plan that relates to business goals and measures success in terms of the strategic concerns of the organization. These measures should plug into a higher-level performance plan for the purpose of rollup for strategic performance reporting.

A Primary Role of Subject Matter Experts Should Be to Assist the Mentors

In the section beginning on page 67 I explain the concept of a mentor as a stand-in for a subject matter expert (SME) for conveying specialist knowledge to those who must design and implement new capabilities. For this to work, SMEs must budget an adequate portion of their time for working with the mentors sufficiently so that the mentors can accurately represent the concerns and knowledge of the SMEs.

The more knowledge that can be transferred to your mentor unit, the more they will be able to spread that knowledge, freeing up the valuable time of your organization's most knowledgeable expert staff. People in lines of business and finance with deep operational knowledge are accustomed to being accosted by IT and others who want to tap that knowledge. Over time they tend to set limits on their willingness to provide this type of assistance, which they view as a form of side work. These experts are also typically overburdened with departmental work, and have limited time to help others anyway.

A capability team can reduce the time that experts spend helping others. An important goal of the capability mentor team should be to learn what concerns the SMEs have and be able to serve as their proxy for the purpose of initiative planning. This leverages the knowledge of the SMEs and frees them up. The time that experts spend with capability mentors is therefore worthwhile for those experts because it will reduce the time that they later have to spend with a larger number of different IT teams trying to integrate capabilities and plan new ones.

Operations experts should be acknowledged for their critical role in helping capability mentors to be successful. They should be true business partners.

The experts need to understand this value equation and be willing to spend the time that it takes to turn the capability mentors into true proxies for the purpose of initiative planning. These experts should be expected to cooperate fully with the capability mentors, and should be acknowledged for their critical role in doing so. In short, helping the capability mentors should be "on their scorecard" – and on their boss's scorecard – or whatever means is used to provide incentives for them to help the capability mentoring group be successful. Experts and their supervisors should share in the success and rewards of projects on which they assist mentors.

Experts should not "bill to" the capability mentor team, any more than they should bill to initiatives that are planning new capabilities. It should be part of their job function to help with this type of planning.

> # Each successive use of blueprints should be tracked as a joint success for the capability unit and the expert groups who helped to develop the blueprints.

Encourage the capability groups to involve the experts when the former define repeatable blueprints for success. This makes the experts partners in the repeatability of each success, and will increase their interest in helping to implement blueprints by helping projects that are using them. In short, the repeatable blueprints published by the capability unit should also bear the name of the experts who contributed, and each successive use of those blueprints should be tracked as a joint success for the capability unit and the expert groups who helped them to develop the blueprints. This "success contribution traceability" is fairly important and is somewhat problematic in that typical success metrics only focus on recent activities. However, it can be achieved informally if the capability team makes a point to faithfully acknowledge in slide decks and documents who the contributors to templates were whenever they are subsequently used.

Help the CIO/E To Crack the "Business Value Measurement Nut"

In the section Why Today's IT Architect Is So Ineffective (page 150) I discussed the problem that IT architects are ineffective because they cannot justify their recommendations in business terms. Enabling them to do this requires mandating that business units collect and provide this kind of information, and requires that they work with the CIO/E unit to develop a common set of metrics for expressing those intangibles such as risk, complexity, and non-transparency that have a high probability of leading to future costs but are hard to quantify in today's dollar terms. There must be consensus about the validity of these metrics and about how they are arrived at, or they will be useless, and this consensus must be established from the top down. As CEO, you are in a position to make this cross-organizational consensus happen, starting from the highest level.

Comparing intangibles with tangibles requires a common set of metrics for expressing those intangibles such as risk, complexity, and non-transparency

You also must make it clear to your CIO/E that you expect every initiative to be justified in concrete business value or risk terms using the agreed upon metrics, and that these business cases should roll up into strategic models. You should make it clear that you expect there to be continuity over time with regard to these "business cases". Finally, you should make it clear that any business architecture mandates or IT architecture mandates should be justified in business terms.

This will have the effect of empowering the various architects in your organization. Once they learn to speak in true business terms they will communicate better with others in the company, will earn respect, and will be able to make their cases more effectively. True and meaningful tradeoffs can then be made with regard to IT policies. In the end, the business should be able to violate any policy – but it should do so with full knowledge of what the ramifications will be.

In the section Measure Future Value At Risk in chapter 7 I present a methodology for treating capabilities as risk reduction elements that roll up into larger-grained business plans. You must mandate a methodology for linking business value to initiative plan elements. Otherwise, your departments will flounder whenever they have to make decisions that would unwind prior decisions – and nowadays this is the norm.

DILBERT: © Scott Adams / Dist. by United Feature Syndicate, Inc.

Unify Capital Planning and Business Planning

One of the greatest mistakes made by organizations – especially government organizations – is to separate capital investment planning and business process planning. For example, it is common practice for US Government agencies to prepare capital investment plans for large IT purchases, and these plans are completely divorced from the business processes that they enable or embody.

The result of this is that IT planning takes place independently form business process planning. An artificial division is created between IT and the business as a result, and attempts to bring these together are frustrated by this capital planning wall.

It makes no sense to invest in an IT system independently of investment in changing business processes. Therefore, this wall must be broken. Investment planning should account for the creation of all of the components of a business process: knowledgeable people, authoritative artifacts, and technology.

Develop a Roadmap

Even though the CIO/E must have certification clout from the outset, you should start small by setting a trial scope for the implementation of the mandate. This can be done by establishing dates for compliance, with the date for each operating unit chosen based on an estimated timeline of when the CIO/E's function and the operating unit will have had time to address their unique issues.

The first operational processes that you should require to be certified by the CIO/E should be those that are most friendly to the goal, and that are in a good position to help the CIO/E to establish a working process of capability piloting and subsequent evangelism of the lessons learned. When the CIO/E has succeeded with the help of the first operational unit, an ally will have been made and the CIO/E unit will be ready to take on a larger scope to repeat the success.

Success must be attributed to all stakeholders

It is therefore critical that the CEO or president oversee the CIO/E's first partnership with an operational unit and make sure that it succeeds, even if it must be extended in time to "get it right". Both the CIO/E and the operating unit must come out winners or the entire scheme will be at a credibility disadvantage. Further, success must be attributed to all stakeholders, or the climate of cooperation that you have worked so hard to establish will not be sustainable.

The transition roadmap – as for any capability development plan – should be expressed in terms of *capabilities achieved*, and not in terms of the completion of initiatives. For example, it should include milestones pertaining to the realization and validation of (a) the ability of each business area to conceive and plan its own IT capabilities, (b) the ability of the CIO/E unit to certify those capabilities as being compliant with all major enterprise concerns, and (c) the ability of Finance and the CIO/E to develop true integrated plans. No milestone should be marked as achieved until it has been proved in live operation. This fundamental principle must be applied at all levels of the roadmap, and must become a standard approach to defining plans and measuring progress.

The roadmap should include pilot efforts in which the CIO/E attempts to collaborate with one or a small number of departments to conceive improvements to their processes. These pilots will occur in parallel with ongoing efforts that were initiated in prior periods and that must co-exist until all legacy projects have completed and there are only projects under the new model. Further, there will continue to be new projects under the old model until the new model has been piloted sufficiently to allow it to be used more broadly.

The next chapter provides guidance for a prospective CIO/E in developing a roadmap.

Oversight

In the section beginning on page 91 I explain the role of independent oversight in periodically validating a statistically representative sample of the certifications granted by the capability mentoring unit. This is necessary because a capability-focused team represents a significant source of power within an organization. Not only does it have the ear of the CEO, but is in a position to certify business processes. This power is needed in order to be able to cut across organizational silos and to be able to effect change quickly and deeply. However, as with any concentration of power, there is the potential for abuse. Oversight is therefore necessary. Here I would like to expand on the oversight concept by specifying the criteria that capability mentor oversight should focus on.

Oversight of the capability mentor function should encompass the following dimensions:

1. **Objectivity**: Realization of objectives, and accurate reporting of metrics.
2. **Certification efficacy**: fairness, accuracy, completeness, and timeliness of certifications.
3. **Alignment**: Alignment with organization priorities.
4. **Promotion of self-sufficiency**: Effectiveness in mentoring and elevating departments to be self-sufficient.

Oversight is inherently a risk management function and so oversight of the capability mentoring unit should be implemented by a risk management unit that reports to the CEO. The function of this unit should be to provide independent assessment and auditing of the capability creation unit from the four perspectives listed above. This auditing must be rigorous and process-driven, and employ a high degree of transparency in terms of artifacts, interviews, and criteria.

The first criteria above serves as a check that success metrics that are reported by the capability unit are accurate. This is extremely important because the budget of the capability unit or bonuses for its staff might depend on its success. For example, if a unit reports that six of its eight sponsored projects have achieved certification and that business plan goals for those are being realized, then these facts must be checked, including the way in which success is being measured. This may require auditing of a sample of those projects.

The second criteria assesses the accuracy of the certification scores that are given by the capability unit to business processes that it has certified. For example, if the capability unit has certified a department's processes with a score indicating that compliance is acceptable, then the oversight function should treat this as suspect and seek to verify it using traditional methods of auditing and oversight. That is, the oversight function should undertake to verify the legitimacy of certifications for a sampling of departmental processes. I myself have done a great deal of this type of auditing, and I can tell you that project managers often do not realize when things on their own projects are amiss until someone from the outside comes in and looks.

Oversight of alignment is an assessment of the presence of bias in the operation of the capability unit with respect to one or more organizational concerns. For example, if the capability unit tends to pay more attention to domestic market concerns than overseas market concerns because it simply knows more about the former, then this needs to be uncovered as an unintended bias. As another example, if a particular business unit's processes always tend to get certified because that unit is very vocal and political, then this unintended bias needs to be uncovered as well. Uncovering bias should be achieved through independent assessment of a sampling of processes and comparison with the certification findings of the capability unit.

Oversight with respect to the promotion of self-sufficiency should seek to detect when departments become dependent on the capability unit and do not learn to operate on their own. The capability unit's function is to elevate the various parts of the business – not to replace them. As such, it should operate as an organization-wide mentor that steps in to help initiate and catalyze change but gradually make itself unnecessary for the skills that it has transferred. In the meantime, the capability unit should be developing new skills and looking toward how it can elevate the organization further. In this role it should liberate the departments that it helps – not make them dependent. Oversight of the capability function should verify that departments are actually learning new ways of doing business. The telltale sign should be that the metrics for success of the capability function should change continually: if success is reported based on the same projects in the same departments each year and the capability elevation metrics are the same – e.g., increased ability to develop business plans – then it means that the capability unit is operating as an outsource service provider and not a mentor.

Certification Waivers

Certification should represent a high bar and many legacy processes will fail certification. A business case analysis should reveal whether these processes should be upgraded. In the meantime, a "light-on" waiver might be necessary to allow current processes to operate. The decision to grant such a waiver and its duration should be made by the same executive committee that reviews proposals for new initiatives. The reason is that the extension of a legacy system is ultimately a business decision and the decision should be made based on the same criteria as are applied for new initiatives. There should not be a separate board for granting certification waivers.

Establish a Mandate

In the section Empowering the CIO/E (page 116) I explain that the requirement for certification of all business processes should be an executive-driven mandate. The mandate should be implemented as a corporate policy to give it durability. The policy should define the mentoring group's operating model, and it should identify the functions that the group performs (see page 120). However, these functions should be spelled out in more concrete terms.

Without a strong mandate, a CIO/E is in an impossible position. It is the old "lots of accountability but no authority" dilemma. So many companies have tried creating a "king of change management" or a "sultan of data quality" or – and this takes me back to the eighties – a "leader of computer-aided management". These positions never work if they have no clout behind them; but they also do not work if they are not grounded in the realities of lines of business, and this can only be achieved by being accountable along with the lines of business for success, profitability, and all of the strategic concerns of the enterprise.

Do not create a CIO/E position until you are ready to provide it with clout. This clout should take the form of a mandate that eventually all operational processes must be certified by the CIO/E. This is the stick that the CIO/E needs in order to get people to give him or her a chance to help them. It also lets operational units know that they are going to have to comply with corporate policies, and the CIO/E is their road to achieving signoff on that.

Define the means by which the CIO/E will participate in the organization at a strategic level, e.g., by being on the executive committee. To be effective, the CIO/E needs to have an up-to-the-minute understanding of the thinking of the organization's leadership, to be able to anticipate the concerns that have not yet been formalized. Without this, the CIO/E's plans and suggestions will be out of touch.

Start Empowering Operating Units

In the section Let's Get Right To It: Who Owns What (page 119) I make it clear that the CIO/E's function should be to twofold: (a) to help operating units to improve their own capabilities, and (2) to provide tactical resources that the operating units can borrow for that purpose. I would like to put a finer point on this.

Operating units should have their own capability development expertise. The function of the CIO/E is to help the operating units to improve their own capabilities, and then certify them: the CIO/E's function is *not* to compete with the operating units for the right to conceptualize and build systems. The goal of the CIO/E should therefore be to strive to make the operating units self-sufficient; as they become so, the CIO/E should shift focus to new kinds of capabilities and ways to increase business effectiveness and reduce risk. The CIO/E is always thinking of how to do things better, and how to enable the operating units to do things better *on their own*.

Start to give the operating units their own business architects and lead system development staff, to be distributed in permanent positions among the various departments of the unit. If a department is too small to be able to manage these kinds of staff, allow the department to outsource system development to external providers, but require them to develop their own system conceptualization capabilities, and to maintain their own process models and data models – not outsource these. The business intelligence and the ability to communicate it and maintain it are critical skills for each department. Only the lowest level or most specialized skills should be considered for outsourcing. Examples

176

of what might be outsourced include system development, based on technical specifications developed inhouse, independent testing to supplement in-house testing, and independent expert-level data security and application security analysis.

Do not permit the CIO/E unit to act as an internal outsource provider, except in the mode of offering trained and ready-to-go resources. To do so is to blur the line between the responsibilities of the operating unit and the CIO/E unit in terms of who is accountable for achieving success. As I explain in Measuring the CIO/E (page 122), the burden of success for a particular initiative must rest solely and entirely with the part of the business that will directly benefit. The CIO/E's success must be measured in terms of success across *multiple areas of the business* to advance in terms of agility, compliance, and competitiveness.

Helping the CIO to Let Go of System Development

As discussed earlier in Let's Get Right To It: Who Owns What (page 119), the CIO/E should not be directly accountable for system development. Putting system development in a separate IT function, apart from lines of business, is one of the reasons that lines of business in many companies are so clueless when it comes to IT, yet IT is now a central aspect of their operation.

Operating units must bear responsibility for defining and implementing their own capabilities, even if they outsource actual development. If they do so, they should bear managerial responsibility. That accountability should not be delegated to an IT unit, even if most of the actual resources come from an IT pool.

One ramification of this philosophy is that operating units must have a substantial capability for defining system functions. Otherwise they will not be able to write implementable requirements. They might even need to have a significant number of business-oriented software development staff. In any case, the task of documenting business functions or requirements should never be farmed out to an enterprise team or to an external vendor.

Another ramification is that operating units must have a substantial capability for managing capability development, including the development of IT systems. This is necessary in today's fast-changing world: without the ability to manage change, operating units are dependent on processes that they do not understand and yet that they have power over. That is the source of the unhealthy tension today between IT and operating units in many organizations: IT gets requirements (if they are lucky), but when they try to do the job right, the technical requirements that IT feels are necessary get shoved to the side by the business. There is no dialog due to lack of understanding.

What I recommend is that those operating units that have a substantial need for custom software should have some level of software development staff of their own so that they appreciate the challenges and learn to rely on themselves to the degree that is practical. This is true regardless of whether the software is built using enterprise resources or is outsourced. In addition, they should have a mature capability for managing the development of new business capabilities, including IT systems. Achieving this might require assistance over time.

This means that the definition and creation of software function cannot be a hands-off activity. Automated functions are key to success, and so operating units should be involved in the definition, creation, maintenance, and lifecycle of those functions.

For this to work effectively, the organization has to have effective standards and practices. This is where the mentoring organization comes in of course. Further, the standards and practices must be mature and well vetted, and evolved through usage in partnership with the operating units. Otherwise the mentoring group will be seen as an ivory tower organization that does not understand the business and the operating units will be able to get away with doing things their own way, leading to chaos.

Since the need for programming staff waxes and wanes there needs to be a resource pool of capable IT staff. That pool should be under the CIO/E. This places them in an ideal position for training and learning to do things the right way, based on enterprise priorities. The CIO/E's function therefore has two primary aspects: (a) to work with operating units in a mentoring role to elevate their capabilities, and (b) to provide trained implementation staff as needed. The CIO/E should not take on the responsibility of software development management however.

Does this mean that all of your existing IT managers will have to be migrated to other functions? No! It does not. They can breath a sigh of relief that they will no longer be responsible for delivery of working software systems, since operating units should ultimately bear this responsibility: but on the other hand the IT managers will be responsible for helping operating units to plan and pilot new systems – new integrated, operational, measurable *capabilities*. Some IT managers will become mentor managers, and others will become IT resource managers.

Don't Use the CIO/E Unit as a Tiger Team

Whenever there is an IT group working on activities that are claimed to have long-term benefit there is a tendency to eye that group whenever a crisis comes along and people are needed to respond to it. If you are serious about creating a capability-focused unit, do not use them as a resource pool for responding to short-term needs that arise.

Forming a capability mentor group takes time. In my experience it takes a year or more for such a group to find its legs and start to demonstrate value. If the group is frequently tapped to deal with crises, it will start to respond and behave as a crisis response group, because it will have learned that that is how its value is recognized.

Remember that the capability mentor group's mission is to help IT-related initiatives to demonstrate tangible value, so measure its performance in that way – not in terms of how many times it saved the organization from the latest threat. If there is an IT-related crisis, pull staff from other execution-level activities – not from long-term alignment activities such as the mentor team.

The greatest risk comes from the Finance area. Compliance-related or finance-related crises tend to vacuum up IT resources, even though they often have little to do with the mission of the organization. Further, the organization's Finance department tends to have an imbalance of power because it has immediate control over spending. The CEO must protect the mentor organization from the threat of being commandeered by crises, finance-driven or otherwise, so that it can mature into its true function.

Treat the CIO/E unit as an investment incubator. Expect a ROI, and be willing to fund. Expect measurable results according to a business plan timeframe. Work with the CIO/E to develop or approve business plans pertaining to capabilities. Establish accountability methods. Establish expectations for what will be achieved over time.

The CIO/E unit should be funded as any investment is. It is not a consulting organization, and it should not be in the business of trying to get funding from other initiatives or departments. To do so would severely compromise the effectiveness of the CIO/E unit to achieve meaningful strategic change. In other words, mentors should not "bill to" projects. Their primary function is to mentor, so they should bill to their primary function. Billing to a project is a consulting model, and mentoring is not consulting.

> # Mentors are not internal consultants: they are partners.

Mentors are first and foremost accountable to their enterprise (officer) function, and second to the initiatives that they mentor. Mentors are not internal consultants, acting at the behest of those who they mentor. Mentors have an agenda, and are measured by their success in establishing capabilities that balance enterprise concerns and objectives. As such they are partners with lines of business, not consultants to them.

Allow and encourage the CIO/E to recruit some of the best staff in the organization. Would you have a junior pilot train other would-be pilots? The Air Force uses its most senior pilots to train other pilots. To be successful, the CIO/E is going to need a *senior team*.

It is worth the disruption, because these staff will be highly leveraged. Do not force underutilized staff or orphan groups on the CIO/E. To be effective, the CIO/E's staff need to be the *most capable* in the company – not the least. They need to be highly experienced and knowledgeable of business concerns and how to manage relationships to achieve change. I have found that people who have been consultants at one point in their career tend to have developed the necessary mentoring mentality.[1]

Provide Stable Funding, But Expect Results

You should expect to provide the gradually increasing baseline funding that is necessary for ongoing operation and continuity of the CIO/E unit's staff, with the proviso that the CIO/E unit demonstrates that it can be effective. The CIO/E unit should not be the first to be cut horizontally when times are tight. To do so is to subvert the very mechanism that can help in recovery. However, slowing or postponing certain CIO/E partnership initiatives during tough times may be necessary in order to focus more on certain lines of business than others.

To maintain effectiveness, the CIO/E's organization must have a *stable, ongoing foundation*. It should not be funded in fits and starts, nor should its foundation be cannibalized when crises appear. To do so is to cripple the organization's ability to develop new capabilities and therefore its ability to change in response to crises. The CIO/E's operation is the primary mechanism for change, and therefore a critical mechanism for any kind of transformation – including a financial retrenchment transformation.

It is reasonable to expect that there should be increased efficiency and that costs will go down over time as a result of the CIO/E's efforts. The mentoring model relies on decentralization of capabilities, while providing for coordination and alignment. The result is that various departments become more self-sufficient, reuse increases, and various horizontal functions related to IT system design can be consolidated. This last point was discussed in the section Don't Create "Thin Layers" Of Process in chapter 5 and again in the section The Role of the Business Architect in chapter 7.

---

[1] By "consultant" I do not mean "contract worker". I mean true consultants whose job is to help an organization to assess a problem area, develop a strategy, achieve change, and then leave.

Alignment of Operational and Financial Control Activities

Finance is often the 800-pound gorilla when it comes to corporate priorities, especially risk-related priorities. Yet, finance depends heavily on IT. It is therefore critical that IT and finance have an effective collaborative relationship. This is a challenge because they are usually entirely separate tiers within the organization.

The Rationale For the Separation

According to a Spring 2005 CFO IT survey of 153 senior executives at companies that must or will comply with the Sarbanes-Oxley Act, 52% feel that there is not a clear boundary between what constitutes IT controls and what constitutes financial controls.[1]

Today's financial analysis and reporting processes at many large corporations can often be characterized as fully automated accounting silos ("engines") linked to lines of business through periodic database transfers and spreadsheets, with myriad special cases handled through departmental financial models, and adjustments handed in an often ad-hoc manner, resulting in near chaos when it comes time to explain how numbers were derived. This arrangement is also destined to have seemingly intractable data consistency problems due to delays in the propagation of retroactive data changes.

Given that automated systems are used at every step, from desktop systems to enterprise systems, it is no wonder that when the financial arm of the organization attempts to get control of their processes, they almost immediately discover that they are treading on IT turf. But since finance is the department that is on the hook for measuring compliance, they usually are given the driver's seat, and lay their plans in a manner that does not depend on the participation of IT. This is a formula for contention, redundancy, misunderstanding, and poor relations.

---

[1] Ref. [CFO_ITb05].

Crisis Management: The Auditor Has Spoken

One of the reasons that a financial audit is so perilous is that organizations do not normally plan for audit failure. That is, they prepare their financials, and if the auditor says that all is not in order, then a crisis is immediately generated, wreaking havoc throughout the organization as departments scramble to address the "deficiencies". This results in "blackouts" in other programs as resources are confiscated without warning to address the deficiencies identified by the auditor. Efforts to improve the way that data is handled are put on hold so that deficiencies can be papered over with data flows that end up on a shelf.

Case In Point

Is there no better way? Is it not possible to anticipate that the auditor will identify gaps? After all, that is their job. In a case that I will refer to as the US Federal Agency, I once spoke with a project lead on this very point. Her project had been frozen because an enterprise-wide security audit turned up deficiencies across the organization, and so all IT work was effectively put on hold while a crash effort to address the audit findings was mounted. In the words of the project lead (paraphrased), "People in the field are very unhappy that their applications get left behind because of these audit-driven freezes. After all, they are only trying to perform the business of the organization. No one gave any warning that an audit was underway and that a freeze might result." Her point is well taken, because executive management did know that an audit was underway, and they should have anticipated that there might be findings that would result in a freeze. If they had communicated this, then those "in the field" would have felt less left out and would have been able to create fallback plans to use their budgets for other things.

As with other aspects of assurance, it should be assumed that failure will occur from time to time. What makes an organization sound is that it plans for failure – before the failure occurs. By doing so, a crisis can be avoided.

I make this point because the capability mentor group is the most vulnerable target of resource confiscation when an audit crisis occurs. That is because (1) the capability group is not involved in operations; and (2) they have developed a great amount of business expertise and therefore have the most capability to respond to an auditor's demands.

You must protect them from this. That is not to say that they should not do their part if there is a crisis, but you must plan sufficiently to prevent a crisis. When planning what resources the capability group needs, you must estimate the chance of any crises that might occur and budget for that, in terms of dollars and resources. If your organization has had audit issues for three of the past five years, then you have good reason to maintain an audit response team that is part of the financial part of your organization. If you do not use this forethought, then you are setting up the capability group for failure.

Collaborative IT and Financial Systems Planning

There is considerable inherent distrust between IT and accounting. According to Robert Dent, chief executive of compliance tool vendor Achiever Business Solutions, "Monies that would previously have fallen under IT executives' control are diverted into these new compliance divisions with decisions about the compliance systems chosen and the platforms used falling outside existing IT policies." [1]

Therefore, if you don't help these groups to work together, they will likely have difficulty doing so. A common pattern is for collaboration to be superficial through various "touch points", but for actual high-level planning to be done independently. This situation does not work because it means that the different approaches and concerns of IT and accounting will not be addressed, and it will likely lead to a failure of one side to deliver things that the other side can actually use.

On the other hand, if it is not feasible to combine planning and project structures across these two groups, establish a governance structure that addresses the concerns of each on an ongoing basis, balancing long-term and short-term goals and assigning priority accordingly.

---

[1] From a proprietary report by Achiever Business Solutions and published on vnu.net, 10 Nov 2006.

Summary

Implementing the level of strategic change that is called for requires a mandate from the CEO, as well as that individual's participation to help see the changes through. Some of these changes involve defining the new CIO/E role and what it entails, helping the CIO/E to develop an operating model for the CIO/E unit, helping the CIO/E and the various operating units to reach a consensus on how to measure business value, helping to develop a roadmap and migration timetable, providing for independent oversight, providing a progressive and stable funding mechanism, establishing the required mandate, and gradual migration of responsibilities for capability development to operating units, in accordance with the roadmap. These changes therefore are not a hands-off affair for the CEO. The incentive is that if successful, the organization will have a significant strategic advantage over competitors in its ability to react quickly while still managing risk.

Another task for the CEO is to help the CIO/E to build a better relationship with the Finance and Risk Management functions of the organization, to ensure their alignment and eventually their integration. Finance will always be an independent function and for good reason, but it is redundant for it to develop its own risk mitigation strategies. Similary, if your organization has a Risk Management function, it does not make sense for it to develop its own strategies in isolation: rather, it should be performing an oversight function to measure whether risk is considered in all enterprise decisions: the CIO/E should ensure that Risk Management always finds that risk *is* properly addressed by all systems and business processes that are certified by the CIO/E.

10. Creating the Flow

A Call to the CIO

If you are a CIO and you would like to transform your organization into a more capability-focused and business-driven group according to the concepts presented in this book, then you will need to make a strong case for why that would benefit the organization and how you will bring it about. Further, your plan will need to have strong advocates, including eventually the CEO. To any executive these things go almost without saying, but it is important to explicitly recognize them.

Remember, the essential value proposition is that you will be creating a system for flowing capabilities throughout the organization, thereby enhancing the organization's agility while at the same time reducing risk! (Chapter 5.)

The changes required for the CIO function can be summarized by Table 6.

Table 6: Changes that must be driven by the CIO - now the CIO/E.

Change	Reference
The CIO will have to begin to **think of himself or herself as a CIO/E**.	Page 104.
The CIO will have to **help others to understand the mission** of the CIO/E unit.	Page 109.
The CIO will have to **let go of IT system development**. This change represents the largest change, and will of course entail some culture shock.	Page 116.
The CIO will have to establish a **very credible and knowledgeable core staff**.	Page 145.
The CIO will have to **consolidate the organization's IT architects**, in all their forms, and establish a mentor-focused group.	Page 148.
The CIO will have to develop a **methodology for incorporating business case analysis** into IT decisionmaking, in such a way that the value of architectural choices is explicitly represented.	Chapter 7.

Change	Reference
The CIO will have to help to define a means by which the **cause and effect on the business of IT-related decisions can be tracked over time**. The CEO will need to help make this happen, since people do not really like cause and effect to be tracked.	Page 143.
The CIO will have to establish a **certification process for business processes**.	Page 88.

The need for these kinds of changes has already been discussed in the sections referenced in the table. In the rest of this chapter I will discuss how to implement these changes.

Getting Started: Validating the Idea

This section is not just for the CIO, but is for enterprise architects as well who believe that business-value driven IT is the way to go and what to get started in that direction. Enterprise architects who are so inclined should start talking to their CIO about how this might work and assess the ultimate feasibility within their organization.

> **Enterprise architects should start talking to their CIO about how this might work.**

To help establish the idea, it is of course useful to demonstrate that it actually works and how it would work. Toward that end, a success case can be demonstrated by partnering with a business-side manager and establishing a pilot effort.

The published focus of such an effort should be to help the business to build things better, faster, and cheaper: no one can argue with that. However, for the new mentor team, the true agenda should be to prove that they can be helpful, and to establish some re-usable knowledge.

The value proposition for the business manager in this case is that the business is getting help that they are not paying for, and that the mentor group might be able to cut some red tape and help to overcome some obstacles. One such obstacle that crops up in many organizations is security certification and accreditation (C&A): I have seen cases where projects have been completed but that the systems could not be stood up for six months while a C&A effort completed. This can be a nightmare for a project manager, and the mentor group could help to iron out the C&A process early so that it works in a more timely manner. This is a big win for everybody, because the project delivery is timely and secure, and the mentor group establishes some repeatable and innovative ways to work with C&A.

The mentor group needs to be extremely sensitive to the worries of the projects that it tries to help. In the words of James Andrew, leader of Boston Consulting Group's Innovation Practice and author of Payback: Reaping the Rewards of Innovation, "If [business] is not the perspective you bring, then you won't be a part of the business organization and its conversations." [1] Evolving this credibility into an ability to help evaluate portfolio projects and measure overall business value is something that takes time.

The ingredients for success in an initial endeavor are therefore:

1. Identify a reliable business partner for a pilot.
2. Carve out a pilot that is significant but that also has a high likelihood of eventual success, and in which there is an opportunity to establish some innovative and repeatable new processes that the mentor group can use elsewhere.
3. Focus on defining and measuring success.

While participating in the project, do not shortcut your primary ideals or concepts of operation. For example, do not get swept up into the "anything to get it done" mentality. Your long-term agenda is to establish practices for accounting for holistic value in all projects, and measuring that value. While you are building credibility, you might have to achieve this as a side effect rather than a main purpose.

For example, suppose that the business manager claims that the main value of the pilot project is to achieve greater flexibility so that future products can be offered with a short IT development lead time. The IT strategy for achieving this might be to implement agile methods into the software development process; or it might be to utilize a technology that enables rapid modification of the code. However, while doing this, you should be cognizant of enterprise requirements, including security,

---

[1] Ref. [Andrew07].

reliability, and compliance. Lines of business *always* want to be more flexible: maintaining the balanced view is the mentor group's job. It is also your job to teach the business how to make the case for the flexibility that they seek, and to be credible this case should have a holistic view.

For this to work long term, the actual success of the strategy must be measurable: that is, once the work is done, there must be a system in place to measure whether the resulting system is indeed more flexible and that products can be introduced more quickly. That means that measurability must be built into the system. For example, how long does it now take to implement a feature change? And what does it cost to do so? And finally – and most importantly – what is the value of that flexibility? That is, to what degree are business opportunities realized earlier as a result? To establish that model (probably as a spreadsheet) IT needs to committed help of the business to take a stab at what those numbers might be. Business knows how to do it, because they do it routinely whenever they invest in new products or services: you just need to get them to understand that you want to do this.

The business value analysis of the pilot effort should be designed to establish understanding for holistic approaches to measure value. Use a common-sense approach where possible, or relate the analysis to common sense concepts. For example, do not rely on statistical methods unless those methods are *already used by the business in other domains within the organization*. There will be time later for introducing more sophistication. At the outset you are only trying to establish that the business can articulate business value and that you can – as part of a team – connect that value directly to IT strategies and measure the outcome as a direct cause-and-effect phenomenon. This teamwork is the model for future teams and eventually for the mentor team.

Once the collaborative model of the mentor team working with the business has been validated, it is up to the CIO to establish the new approach as the way that things will be done in the future. This is a gradual transformation of course, but the CIO now has ammunition for influencing the organization to start to use this model more broadly. The CIO must prove the idea to the rest of the organization, most likely by establishing more pilots, and gradually increasing the scope and mandate associated with the mentor group.

Starting Out as a Facilitation Group

Another entry point for a mentor group is possible when the organization has a difficult IT-related task to perform. The mentor group can "get its legs" coordinating that effort and in so doing make the job easier for LOB groups and gaining knowledge and credibility in the process. The danger is that the mentor group will degenerate into a "we'll do anything" group and lose sight of its actual mission. In the case of the US Federal Agency, a mandate existed to consolidate disparate IT operations into a small number of data centers, and a mentor group was formed (it was not called that) in order to spearhead the transition. To achieve this we had to inventory the applications that existed in the field, develop requirements for the data centers, and work with LOBs to devise migration plans. In the process we became familiar with these applications and developed the credibility to start to require changes according to an evolving enterprise architecture. Thus, we had a stick – the migration mandate – and we provided a carrot – assistance in helping LOBs deal with the required migration. This was particularly effective because we leveraged enterprise security rules to require that applications that went into the data center must abide by a security architecture, and this gave us clout when we asked to review designs.

Getting Into the Loop

One of the challenges of an enterprise group is to find out what is being planned across the organization. If you find out when funding requests are made, it is too late, because by then preliminary project plans and budgets have been made and expectations have been set. If the mentor group can be involved in the conception of a project then it can have the greatest impact on the project. One of the most important types of impact is to work with the business to conceive ways to enhance transparency, as well as ways to mitigate risk. These can be achieved by developing a business model and by developing architecture, prototyping, and testing strategies that address the main risks. But these things impact the project plan and hence the need to be involved early.

Some organizations have an online funding request system, and such a system can be used to see what upcoming funding requests exist. The mentor group should also have representation on the board that approves IT projects. Best of all, the mentor group should be out and about enough to be involved with the business when projects are conceived.

The Enterprise Group Must Have A Mandate

In order to broadly roll out a capability-focused IT organization plan, the executive leadership of your organization – in particular the CEO – must have made a firm decision to go forward with a mentor-based, capability-focused structure. The mandate must be firm and unambiguous; but don't expect it to start out with a broad scope or to have all of the necessary elements from the outset. You have to implement and prove your model first, and then you will receive the full mandate.[1] That is, you must prove that you can:

- Work smoothly and successfully with operating units, championing their ideas as well as your own.
- Stay true to your enterprise mission and not give in to pressure from operating units.
- Credibly certify business processes such that certification indicates a very high likelihood of a successful internal (or external) audit, meaning that few deficiencies or weaknesses are identified when such audits occur.
- Develop a credible and useful business case for any initiative, based on business value, opportunity, and risk, in a way that integrates these concerns and that plugs into enterprise planning models.
- Maintain a business case as situations change.
- Prove that business value is actually achieved, as capabilities are delivered.
- Recruit and develop the skills needed to do all this.
- Elevate the skill levels and capabilities of operating units so that they do not need you to maintain their own process designs.

---

[1] In today's large organizations, re-organization of IT often happens over a period that is shorter than the time required to fully prove the mentor concept. Therefore, one should make a point to prove the key elements of the mentor value proposition as soon as possible so that the group can survive today's continual re-organizations.

This is a tall order, and it will take time to communicate this mission to others and to build the capabilities to do all this and prove effectiveness. Therefore, it is important to start with a limited but well-defined scope, supported by a strong mandate over that scope. The commitment from the executive team must be firm, but expectations must be set in terms of which business partners you will work with and what will be achieved. This also means that you should not even start until you have a strong partnership established with at least one business area to serve as an "alpha partner" and prove the viability of the approach. Most likely this alpha partner will be the business partner who helped to validate the idea in the first place.

Again, it is not necessary that the first attempt be a success. However, the partnership must survive the first attempt, and the lessons learned must be joint lessons and include a plan for achieving eventual success. Success must be demonstrated eventually, and before credibility is fully spent. The ability to fine-tune the process, listen to others, and work together as a team, and be fully transparent and honest will add more credibility than if the initial project glosses over issues and tries to put a façade of success on what everyone knows is not quite so.

Partnership is the key. You must be organized as a peer of those units in order to be able to create a true partnership. There must be value for everyone in a partnership, and it is your job to establish and communicate the value propositions.

To be effective in this communication, your staff must have and retain a high level of credibility, in terms of business knowledge, technical knowledge, and effective collaboration. Staff who are inexperienced in the business will have no credibility with the business, and staff who do not have appropriate IT credentials will not have credibility with IT staff.

Have a Charter

It is a good practice to define the mentor group's mission from the outset in a charter. Early on, the mentor group will be seen by many as a resource that can be tapped for things that are not related to its mission, and the charter can be used to remind them what the group is for. The chater should identify the mentor functions presented in this book (see page 120 and page 121), and specify the scope and authority that the mentor group currently has. The charter's signatures serve as the required executive directive for the group. The charter should also specify the measures for success of the group, as discussed on page 122.

The initial charter should preferably identify the actual pilot effort(s) that will be used by the mentor group to prove its operating model. Thus, these early partners are best identified before forming the group. If the group has been created without doing this, then the charter should start out somewhat ambiguous so that there is time to get the group going and find initial business partners. Alternatively, the initial charter can provide a mandate to accomplish a particular enterprise IT goal, such as migration of a set of applications. This last approach compels business units to work with the mentor group, and so the mentor group should start by clarifying its value proposition with these groups so that it is not seen as a source of compliance or worse, a bottleneck.

Once the group is operating in a positive manner with other parts of the organization and has proven its value and effectiveness, the charter can be revised to broaden its scope and make the mentor group a permanent part of the ogranization.

In one instance that I was involved with, the mentor group (it was not called that) was defined during an off site meeting of IT and business executives and staff. This was a successful approach, but again, a mandate only lasts so long before people forget or become inpatient, and so one has about six months to establish the operating model in practice and start adding value. After that you are at risk of being "repurposed" as the inevitable crises occur and resources are scarce.

Publicize Your Mission

You will need to evangelize your mission and operating model to the operating units. The entire company will be watching your first efforts, as is always the case with any enterprise-level program, and you must explain what you are doing and what the plan is. Further, if you properly communicate your mission to others, then everyone will know that this is a large challenge, and will accept initial growing pains. If you do not properly communicate, then

194

any hiccup will be seen as yet-another-enterprise-program gone awry.

When speaking with operating units, make sure that you convey that your mission is:

1. Initially limited, but will grow over time.
2. Expected to have growing pains.
3. To share in the risk and the success of initiatives.
4. To understand and integrate all of the goals and concerns of the business, so that important things do not get left out.
5. To help operating units to establish an ongoing supportable business case for achieving their objectives.
6. To help operating units to elevate their own capabilities and become more self-sufficient as new business processes are developed.
7. To ensure that success and conformance with enterprise objectives can be measured in a meaningful and timely way.
8. To help to ensure that compliance audits will have the greatest possible chance of success.
9. To encode best practices in the form of an enterprise architecture, and to provide actionable tools such as reference designs.

Overcoming Emotional Resistance

"We don't need to be mentored. We know how to do our jobs."

Many groups within the organization might feel that they can operate just fine on their own, without the help of the CIO/E group. Barring the need for certification, this might be true, but who in your organization will be charged with instilling a spirit of innovation? Who will ensure that the various parts of the organization are current with regard to industry best practices? And most importantly, who will ensure that their processes are effective at balancing departmental goals with the enterprise's goals?

On the other hand, there will be some who quickly embrace the ideas of proactive innovation, incremental pilot-based capability development, and embedded integration of concerns espoused by the CIO/E group. Your time is best spent working with these people to establish a track record of value and consensus.

There will also be individuals who cannot rise to the challenges presented by the new approach, even if they want to. In particular, many in the IT architecture community will find it difficult to think in business value terms and will have a hard time communicating with non-technical individuals. These people are best allowed to remain within their technical realm as technical leads and technical subject matter experts, rather than forced to serve in the realm of the new business-focused enterprise architecture.

Create Strong Partnerships In Operating Units

Achieve a working business value model by actually implementing one in a pilot effort with an operating unit. Get out of the theoretical realm immediately: reach out immediately and try. This is art, not science.

Build Credibility By Starting Small and Listening

You need to plan, but don't wait while you plan. Expect to have to refine approaches, and set expectations that that will be the case. Set expectations that this is a joint effort, and everyone is expected to make mistakes but that the end result will be a good one and will be the basis for broader use.

Toward that end, you must establish a tone of cooperation that:

- Always gives credit where credit is due.
- Is receptive to innovative ideas that originate with operating units.

Your staff must know that you expect them to make these credos a priority. That will establish a foundation of trust at the ground level that will enable your team to operate effectively and collaborative with others.

The mentor group's function can ve viewed as a customer relationship management (CRM) function. The group develops relationships with other operating units; these often yield opportunities, those mature into plans, and those plans turn into efforts. In fact, in the US Federal Agency engagement that I have referred to, it was one of the leads who pointed out the close similarity to CRM, and we even used a CRM system to track our situations with the various LOB groups.

As in any customer relationship function, never say no out of hand. Always allow a business process owner to make a case for their point of view.

Frequently ask the business how you (the mentor group) are doing: are you being helpful? Listen all their points of view and concerns before you tell them that they must do something. Always argue from logic, issues, and enterprise rules - not your (the mentor group's) rules.

The mentor group should not have "rules" for the organization to follow. Standards created by the mentor group should be "frameworks" or "roadmaps" that serve to help and guide: goal is to help projects get certified, and as any "standard" is but an a-priori decision, any decision or standard can be challenged if one has a good argument.

Provide a project plan template that projects can use; this is discussed more in chapter 12 when I discuss capability development lifecycles.

Your team must be familiar with what people are doing, what they are using, and what the issues are. However, they don't need to be on every status call, effectively creating make-work. Focus on control points: the points at which your team can actually add value, and keep them out of everything else. Avoid fire drills.

Finally, you must develop an approach for prioritizing requests. This should be based on transparent criteria, such as urgency, risk, and value as defined by the organization. This is discussed more in chapter 12 when I examine the issue of portfolio balancing.

Establish an Operating Model

In the previous chapter on page 166 I explain that the CEO[1] needs to help the CIO/E to establish an operating model for the

---

[1] As explained previously in this book, when I say "the CEO" is am using shorthand for whichever executive has over-arching responsibility for

CIO/E unit. This is because the operating model reaches across many tiers of the organization and so high-level involvement is required. On page 119 I also discuss the division of roles and responsibilities of the proposed CIO/E unit with respect to Operations. Here I would like to take that a step further and define a basic operating model that brings together many elements that I have seen work and that incorporates the principles that have been discussed in this book so far.

Probably the most important thing to realize when creating an operating model is that it should not be focused on the review and maintenance of documents. *Enterprise architecture is about decisionmaking*, and *perpetuating the intent of architectural decisions*. Thus, it is really about people and their capabilities, knowledge, and ability to collaborate.[1] Documents are but one tool toward that objective. Documents are not the objective.

> # You do not need a special effort to "create an enterprise architecture".

If one takes this view, then one realizes that once an operating model is established, enterprise architecture will fall out as a side effect. Thus, you do not need a special effort to "create an enterprise architecture". If you create the right teams and the right operating model, then those teams will develop and implement an enterprise architecture in the course of their work. You will not even have to tell them to do it.

The operating model must be self-sustaining. To achieve this, there must be a significant incentive for each player in the operating model. The main players are:

- The Mentor Team (led by the CIO/E). These comprise the enterprise architects.
- The other operating units of the organization (led by other members of the executive team).
- Internal oversight mechanisms.

---

business operations, financial operations, legal concerns, marketing, and business development. In very large organizations this is usually not the CEO, but a COO who oversees these functions.

[1] Focusing on collaboration over artifacts is a key concept of Scott Ambler's Agile Modeling approach. See http://www.agilemodeling.com/.

Figure 11 illustrates an overall operating model for a CIO/E unit in terms of its interaction with other functions of the business. In this model every such interaction is incentivized by a value proposition for each party. In order to avoid cluttering the diagram the figure does not include CIO/E unit functions that are internal to its operation.

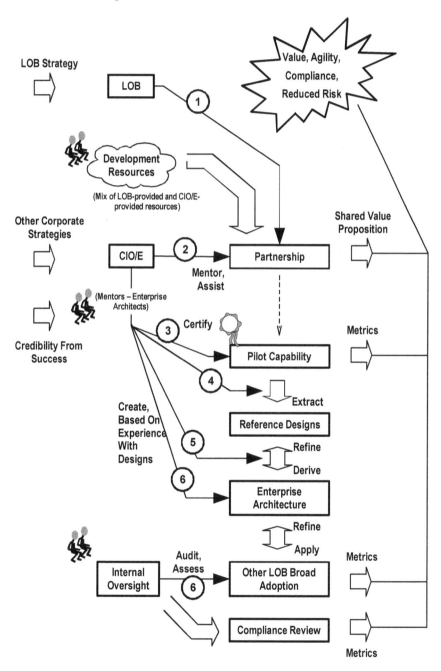

Figure 11: Overall operating model for the CIO/E unit.

The six major activities represented in the operating model diagram are described in Table 7, along with the primary actor for each activity and the value proposition that motivates that actor.

Table 7: Major activities and incentives for each participant in the operating model.

Major Activity	Actor	Incentive(s) For Actor
1: Form partnership with CIO/E. Collaborate to determine root causes of business problems, and formulate solution strategies. Commit resources toward a common objective.	LOB	▪ To spread the burden of figuring out how to comply with enterprise concerns that are not specific to the LOB. ▪ To reduce costs by using reference designs. ▪ The spread the risk of figuring out how to address difficult migration requirements.
2: Form partnership with a LOB or other unit. Mentor and assist the LOB to pilot a solution to their problem. Commit resources toward a common objective.	CIO/E	▪ The chance to create another success story. ▪ Scorecard is based on the percentage of units that comply with enterprise performance measurement and compliance criteria.
3: Certify the solution, and certify any expanded solutions that the LOB subsequently develops.	CIO/E	▪ To certify more processes as providing accurate and sufficient performance metrics and as being compliant with risk management criteria.
4: Extract reusable reference designs from the pilot work.	CIO/E	▪ To reduce the cost and time to implement new pilot projects. ▪ To enable LOBs to work independently, yet still enable the mentor team to review and certify the LOB work.
5: Refine the enterprise architecture, based on new reference designs.	CIO/E	▪ To provide a framework for deciding on technical issues that impact compliance, measurability, and risk management. ▪ To provide a framework for translating technical issues into business terms.
6: Independently assess business processes with respect to compliance with enterprise criteria.	Internal Audit	▪ To identify aspects of certified business processes that need to be improved, indicating a possible weakness in the certification process. ▪ To decrease risk with regard to mandatory external audits of all kinds.

The functions in the figure and table should be very familiar to you at this point as they have all been discussed in prior chapters. Here they are assembled into a single composite picture.

Note that enterprise architecture output of Step 6 includes a business model. That is because enterprise architecture encompasses business architecture. The components of an enterprise architecture are discussed in chapter 13.

Jump-Starting the Operating Model

With any new group that has a new kind of role, there is a risk that the group will spend so much time trying to decide how they will do what they will do, that they don't actually do anything. To avoid this form of gridlock, do not allow too much time to be spent on process definition: define activities that need to be done, and get them going.

Nevertheless, it is important to codify the process, especially in ways that establish the touch points with the rest of the organization. It is particularly effective to use the format of a "lifecycle roadmap" or "Software Development Life Cycle (SDLC) roadmap" for this purpose. That is, identify all of the things that have to occur in the lifecycle of systems, the points at which you need to interact in order to perform the mentor function, and identify those points in an un-ambiguous way by defining the interaction activities. For example, if it is important to design business performance measurement into any new business capability, then you might identify a "business metric identification" activity, and identify the mentor group's role and participation with respect to this activity. This way, once project managers are comfortable that you are a help and not a hindrance, they will start to incorporate items from your roadmap into their plans.

One challenge that you will likely have is that few people on the early team will have broad knowledge of the organization's business processes and systems. You should definitely have at least one person on the initial team who does, but you will be very lucky if you have more than one. The problem then is that a group that is not familiar with the business and its systems – no matter how smart or experienced it is in the industry – will not have the ability to make judements involving enterprise architecture, and that ability is critical to your success.

One solution to this problem is to embark on an explicit crash effort to analyze the organizations processes. This can be for the purpose of some existing business need, such as consolidation or data warehouse analysis, but your actual agenda is to get your team up to speed. Another approach is to keep a low profile with regard to enterprise architecture issues and focus on improving processes that project teams often have trouble with, such as C&A, compliance, etc., but always within your operating model. If you take the crash analysis path, make sure that your team gets what it needs in one pass, and that the team members who contact the customers are experienced at consulting and relationship management.

Value Proposition of Mentor Group Elaborated

In Table 7, the first activity is for a LOB to form a partnership with the CIO/E, and the incentive is listed as (paraphrasing) "to spread the burden..., reduce cost..., and spread the risk...." Let's look at this incentive a little more closely. Table 8 summarizes the value propositions that the mentor group provides as seen by the various other parts of the business.

Table 8: Mentor group value proposition summary.

1. **Training**: Provide training, so that operating units understand the enterprise perspective and its policies.
2. **Mentoring**: Provide mentoring, so that operating units learn how to implement enterprise policies and become self-sufficient and do not rely on the mentor group.
3. **Analysis**: Help operating units with gap analysis, alternative analysis, business case development, and the application of enterprise architecture.
4. **Piloting**: Help operating units to define and implement pilot projects to implement new approaches to control, metrics, and business value realization.
5. **Project control and metric definition**: Define controls and touch points for initiative and project risk management and value management. These manifest through a software development lifecycle (SDLC) or capability development lifecycle (CDLC).
6. **Operating control and metric definition**: Help to define controls for business process risk management and value management. These manifest as business performance metrics.
7. **Judgment**: Provide judgment with regard to which controls require focus for each project or business process.
8. **Architecture**: Develop and maintain enterprise architecture and blueprints.
9. **Cerficiation**: Provide visible acknowledgment to executive management that the business process addresses enterprise concerns; and provide assistance in increasing the chance that an internal audit will produce a positive report.

Training, mentoring, assistance with analysis, with the definition of controls and success metrics, and with judgment calls all help to reduce risk for operating units as well as to spread the burden of these and reduce cost. Table 7 however is more specific in that it calls out particular activities to be performed by the mentor group. These activities have all been disussed previously and so this table is a summary. Below I will discuss some of these to provide additional clarification.

Piloting

It is important that the mentor group approach its involvement in any project in a manner that allows it to gradually withdraw, leaving the mentor group with only a mentoring and certification role. For example, if the mentor group takes on the development of *some portion* of a pilot system, the ownership of those portions should be gradually transitioned to the business during the course of the project. The mentor group's role is to help to vet approaches and share risk, and once the various approaches have been vetted the transition of ownership should begin. In no circumstances should the mentor group take on the permanent ownership of a business system, or be responsible for the development of an entire pilot system.

Mentoring

I have talked alot about the mentor role, but here I want to focus on a few aspects that provide obvious short term value for project sponsors and business process owners. One of the perils of system implementation in large organizations today is the requirements for certification and accreditation (C&A). This is usually security-related, but it can pertain to other concerns as well. C&A is increasingly required for enterprise systems and even departmental systems. The problem is, it is usually a long process that occurs in series with respect to system deployement, thereby introducing a long lead time between when a system is accepted by the users and when it can actually be deployed for production use. Further, the C&A process is usually mysterious to most people outside the C&A realm, and it is a black box with little transparency into progress until the task is complete.

An effective mentor organization can offer application builders the chance to reduce the C&A cycle time, through two strategies: (1) to embed C&A into the SDLC, and (2) to provide a trustworthy application operation environment that is "pre-certified" in as many respects as possible. That is, by providing a secure environment that uses a fixed set of pre-certified application components (a "stack"), of known certified versions, the application builder only needs to worry about what is unique about the application.

In order to address this, the mentor group should work with the data centers of the organization and the C&A team to create a baseline application stack and environment and certifiy that environment. A list of data center requirements to consider for this purpose is provided in Table 9. The mentor group should also work with the C&A team to perform various aspects of C&A testing and analysis at various points within the SDLC, as part of stakeholder testing: the C&A team is but one stakeholder, and they should be represented at a requirements level and at each step in the SDLC. The mentor group should work to refine a set of reusable application designs and patterns that are testable from a C&A perspective. These should become part of the enterprise architecture.

Table 9: Data center requirements areas that facilitate application manageability.

Standard Application Components

- **Standard Databases, Directories, and Repositories**

  The data center may provide and support certain versions and releases of a fixed set of database product. This support may also include account creation and schema creation.

- **Standard Server Apps**

  The data center may provide and support certain versions and releases of a fixed set of application middleware product. This support may also include account creation, schema creation, and cluster configuration.

- **Standard App Appliances**

  The data center may provide and support a fixed set of appliance products, such as SSL accelerators, application protocol filters ("application protection proxies"), load balancers, and hardware clusters.

- **Standard Client Apps**

The data center may provide and support certain versions and releases of a fixed set of client-side application product.

- **Virtual Private Network**

  The data center may provide and support a fixed set of customized virtual private network (tunneling) configurations and features.

Standard Service Categories, Levels, and Environments

- **Standard (Default) Configuration Parameters by Type of environment**

  The data center may have "default" configurations and service levels for each of the following kinds of environment:

  - ➢ Dev (often on desktop machines), Dev Server
  - ➢ Integration Test, Application Inter-operability Test, Performance and Reliability Test
  - ➢ Staging
  - ➢ Production (Tier 1, 2, 3, and 4)

- **Standard Operational Service Tier Levels**

  A "tier level" is a standard category that defines the level of criticality of the application for the Forest Service. Each tier level defines a set of default minimum service level requirements and validation requirements. The following levels are typical.

  - ➢ Level 1: Mission critical. (Assigned by IRB.)
  - ➢ Level 2: Non-critical but important to the FS as a whole. (Assigned by IRB.)
  - ➢ Level 3: Important to a major FS business unit. (Assigned by a region or business unit.)
  - ➢ Level 4: Everything else.

- **Support and Operation Service Level Requirements**

  A data center may provide application support. An application support operation may provide service defined by the following parameters.

  - ➢ On-call schedule (e.g., 24x7, 16x6, 12x5, etc.).
  - ➢ Incident response time (e.g., real-time as in 911, ten minutes, 24 hours, etc.).
  - ➢ Issue resolution time and priority (e.g., real-time, 24 hours, two days, two months, etc.).
  - ➢ Escalation rules (e.g., CIO after 24 hours, Chief after 48 hours).
  - ➢ Turnaround time when provisioning a system or an environment (e.g., 24 hours during "fire season", one week, one month).

- **Environment Configuration Parameters**

  Provisioned environments may require any of the following parameters to be customized may include the following. The last five are often handled by the application team.

  - ➢ Hardware firmware versions (usually the latest for each type of equipment and OS).

- ➢ Operating system, version, and patch level.
- ➢ Standard app versions.
- ➢ No. of CPUs
- ➢ Real Memory
- ➢ NIC allocation and configuration
- ➢ Routing Bandwidth Allocation, for front end and back end
- ➢ File system allocation (initial and max) or quota
- ➢ Standard apps, mounts, and profiles.
- ➢ RAID level for Network Storage and SAN
- ➢ Standard App Configuration (e.g., configuration of WebMethods, Apache, or OAS).
- ➢ Routing configuration, to communicate among application components, with other applications, other environments, and with Internet.
- ➢ VPN with other environments or "clouds".
- ➢ IP6 capability.
- ➢ 32-bit or 64-bit.
- ➢ Hardware, OS, and software clustering.
- ➢ Vertically scalable or commodity CPU and storage
- ➢ Database replication.
- ➢ OS thread pool size
- ➢ No. of sockets and file descriptors
- ➢ Virtual Memory
- ➢ OS security configuration
- ➢ Remote application management and monitoring.

Standard Services

The data center should provide the following standard services at a minimum.

- **Environment provisioning and provisioning progress tracking.**

- **System and network operation.**

- **Network and OS level intrusion detection and response.**

- **Web-based request tracking and incident tracking.**

- **Setup and configuration of accounts, schema, and other parameters needed by developers to use their new environments.**

Optional Services

The data center may provide any of the following additional services (beyond those already mentioned).

- **Software Configuration Management**

- **Environment Configuration Management**

- **Management of Migration from Dev to Prod**

- **Rollback to Prior Release**

- **Application Level Monitoring**

- **Incident Management**

- **Customized issue management**
- **Release management**
- **Integrated Intrusion Response**
- **Backup and restoration of data and of environment configurations.**
- **Disaster Recovery**
- **Load Simulation**
- **Test Case Management**
- **User account and PKI provisioning**
- **Application distribution to remote locations.**

Judgment

The item labeled "Judgment" in Table 7 is noteworthy because it does not carry a particular deliverable or activity, but rather its purpose is to help business managers decide where to invest the most effort when their budgets are limited – as they always are. One cannot always implement all of the controls that are called for if one takes a canonical and textbook approach to risk management or business performance measurement, but rather one has to make decisions about what will really matter. This form of judgment is a realm in which the mentor group can help. For example, if enterprise policies call for the creation of controls for every kind of risk, which of these should be implemented thoroughly and which should be implemented in a cursory manner? Since the specialty of the mentor group is balancing enterprise concerns, it should be able to help to make these judgment calls.

In chapter 12 I discuss Software Development Lifecycles (SDLC) and what I refer to as a "Capability Development Lifecycle" (CDLC), and the activities above will be placed in the context of a methodology and process.

Portfolio Board Membership

Most organizations have a review board that reviews the IT project portfolio on a recurring or on-demand basis and approves requests for funding. This type of board usually contains representation from the various lines of business as well as IT, governance, risk management, and financial control disciplines. Such portfolio review boards often also have the authority to adjust project strategies or focus in various ways. If the organization also has an architecture review board, then the architecture review board will likely meet in advance of the portfolio review board in order to provide its recommendation from an architecture perspective. Without question, the mentor organization should have a representative on the portfolio review board, to ensure that issues related to enterprise alignment can be addressed.

If the organization has a mentor group as described in this book, then there is no need for a separate architecture review board. In fact, the mentor's certification function serves that purpose. The certification process can incorporate a "board" concept in its implementation, but a more lightweight approach is preferable. For example, the mentor group should have worked with the business to ensure that any project proposal already contains the ingredients needed for certification. A separate review process would therefore be redundant and too late. Instead, the review should merely be a final check. If the review is the first time that the architects see the design, then it is definitely too late.

Working With the Enterprise

You can expect that it will take awhile for a new mentor group to become aware of the various business processes and systems across the enterprise, but this awareness is crucial, because it enables the group to have a true enterprise perspective. This is why it is important to start small with a tractable problem, to gradually build knowledge within the group over time, and it is also important to seed the group with individuals who have long duration experience within the organization and strong networks across the business. As the group becomes familiar with the various systems used by the many business units, it can start to identify opportunities for integration and consolidation as well as ways to make systems more effective and improve operation. Increasing enterprise effectiveness and alignment should be the primary focus and driver, rather than on creating "architecture documents".

On the other hand, there may already exist an mandate to execute an enterprise-wide IT strategy of some kind, such as migration to a new set of platforms or migration to a new data center. In such cases the business case has already been made, for better or worse,[1] and an enterprise group such as a mentor group is an obvious choice to be tapped to help with such an activity. This can provide the group with a short-term mission and mandate.

A mandate of this type can be a powerful mechanism for implementing change and enabling a mentor group, since that group can help to plan the process and define the requirements for the new environments, as well as devise reference designs.

One of the deciisons that needs to be made on a case by case basis for any migration is whether an application should be improved, retired, or consolidated with another application. In the process, a decision needs to be made of whether the application should serve a local region or serve the entire enterprise. Even regional applications should use enterprise reference designs if possible, and the mentor group can help to make this happen.

Working With a Business Analysis Group

Many organizations have a business process engineering group that is dissociated from enterprise architecture. The thinking is that business process engineering devises change, and then appeals to IT (through enterprise architecture) to plan how to implement that change.

This approach is a relic of the mentality that business and IT should be separated. However, the approach might actually make sense in an organization that is not heavily focused on automation, in which most business processes do not have a heavy IT component. In any case, a strong collaborative relationship between the mentor group and the business engineering group is absolutely necessary. With this separation, the business engineering group essentially comprises the "business-focused

---

[1] Consolidation mandates are often made to save costs. However, I have seen cases in which the analysis was based purely on a narrow life cycle cost model and did not consider overall mission effectiveness. This is a natural outcome if IT is treated as a cost center.

half" of the mentor group's mission, and the mentor group is the enterprise architecture half. Since these are inseparable as described in this book at length, these groups must work closely as a single team.

For example, continual dialog between these two groups about new projects is necessary. No major decision should be made and no concept vetted without the participation of both, if there is any chance that there is an automation component. In the end, the business engineering group must have a grasp of IT's plans and concerns, and vice versa, and one group will merely have more of a focus on automation than the other. With the right teamwork approach, this can be effective, as I have seen it work.

Working With Lines Of Business

First Contact

When word gets out about what your mentor group does, LOB groups will come to you for help in getting their projects started or to solve problems that they are having. When a LOB comes to you for help, start by reading their artifacts. Take a positive attitude and be supportive. Be extremely responsive: try to get back to them promptly and attend their status meetings. Above all, do not get in the way from the outset by adding additional "enterprise" requiremens. After all, they came to you to ask for help, not to ask for more obstacles. Instead, ask them about their priorities and concerns, and show that you understand these. Once you have obtained their trust you can then start to have a meaningful dialog that considers LOB priorities as well as enterprise priorities.

If a LOB proposal or project plan does not address some enterprise concerns, consider whether those things can be addressed at a future time so that the project's current budget and schedule can be maintained. If the enterpise features can be added in a later release then most of the time the LOB group will be happy to plan for it, since they will have an opportunity to request funding for those additional features.

Try to involve other LOB groups beyond those you are working with directly at the moment. For example, a pilot effort with an

LOB group should include asking various other LOB groups how they solve the problems that would be addressed by the pilot, and collaboratively coming up with an architecture for the pilot. This is valuable even if the pilot does not directly involve most of those LOBs because it allows them to have a stake in the success of the pilot and gets them thinking about how they will implement the approach when the pilot is transitioned into a broader effort.

The Business Liaison Function

If IT has a buisness liaison function, that function should transition from being a "I will build what you need" approach to a "I will help you to define what you need, help you to plan it so that it is successful, provide critical resources (via the CIO's Resource Management function), and get certified to operate" approach. Essentially, the business liaison for the mentor group is the main point of contact.

If you view the mentor group as a program, then the businss liaison function is essentially a lead mentor with responsibility for a particular part of the organization. This person should be responsible for the mentor group's relationship with certain parts of the business. This person's performance measurement should be based on their contribution to the overall performance of the mentor group, *not on the performance of their own business relationship area*. Doing the latter creates a silo that is antithetical to the enterprise-wide mission of the mentor group.

Appropriate metrics for the business liaison should include the same metrics used for the mentor group as a whole, such as alignment and expected value creation over a future planning horizon, but pro-rated according to estimated contribution of initiatives underway in their respective business relationship area. This is effectively a scorecard approach.

For example, if the mentor group calculates that the organization as a whole improved its expected value position over the prior position by X amount, and activities that were undertaken in business area A are responsible for 10% of that increase, then – assuming that the mentor group has been fully engaged with that business area – the menor group liaison for that business area can legitimately claim a role in that success. The intent is to provide an incentive for each mentor liaison (indeed each mentor) to think in terms of the overall organization, and not just their own area.

If You Do Not Agree With the LOB

It will occasionally be the case that a favored project of a LOB is something that you do not agree with. Such a situation is a delicate one, because the mentor's role is to be supportive, but at the same time to ensure enterprise alignment. Certainly you do not want to be seen as working against the LOB – publicly or otherwise.

The best approach is full transparency. Make clear what your objectives and criteria are, and have frank and sincere discussions with the LOB on those terms. Leave it up to the LOB to prove to you that it can meet those criteria. If in the end a mere difference of opinion remains, escalate the issue to the lowest level board or executive committee that can arbitrate the decision rather than using your (the mentor's) role as certification authority to force your point of view.

Common LOB Concerns

Whe it comes to IT, market-focused lines of business (LOBs) are usually concerned with getting their projects funded, provisioned, executed, and deployed. If there are compliance requirements then they are concerned with addressing those as well. They do not usually think in terms of enterprise priorities, since the natural focus of a line of business is it particular product or service. If IT is to have credibility with the LOB so that it can influence it with respect to enterprise priorities, it needs to have an understanding of the LOB's broader concerns and activities.

More generally, the primary concerns of market-focused lines of business often include the following:

- Day-to-day operations: keeping the lights on, fulfilling orders, etc.
- Business unit performance and expectations.
- Meeting the demands of accounting and enterprise financial performance reporting.
- Working with other parts of the business on which the unit depends, including IT.

- Working with other parts of the business that depend on the unit.
- Obtaining required resources.
- Making effective use of resources.
- Planning improvements to business capabilities, including efficiency improvements and new products and services.

Business capabilities that are relevant to a line of business therefore revolve around addressing these concerns.

In addition, there are at least twelve generic core capabilities that tend to be valuable across all major functions within an organization. These are listed in Table 10.

Table 10: Generic core capabilities that tend to be valuable for all major functions within an organization.

Data Management
1. Workflow.
2. Information publishing, identification, and management.
3. Publishing and access to information about information: so-called "meta data". This tends to be used most heavily by those who have to build new capabilities.
4. Identification and management of business rules.
5. Establishment of provisioning and service-level agreements between departments.
6. Role-based access control.
Performance Management
7. Business performance analysis and reporting, including data quality.
8. Business modeling, valuation, and impact analysis for each type of business concern.
9. Identification, tracking, and root cause analysis of issues and problems.
10. Identification, tracking, and mitigation of risk.
Planning
11. Initiative management.
12. Resource management.

Data Management

Items 1 through 6 in Table 10 roughly fall under the category of "data management". These capabilities tend to be managed in an ad-hoc manner, with each business function responsible for its

213

own approach to managing information and coordinating the flow of information.

Organizations that have tried to remedy this have had mixed success, perhaps they found it hard to figure out at a tactical level where to spend their effort. For example, Xerox invested a great deal in IT-driven data modeling and adminstration efforts over a 20 year period, and in the words of the director of information management, "we got nowhere." [1] It seems that a big-bang approach to solving the data management problem does not work: value must be demonstrated in increments to ensure that the infrastructure that is created is what is really needed. For example, it is better to build a small meta data management system *the right way* and demonstrate success with that, rather than architect a large, complex plan for all operating units to adopt new data management processes. The latter is bound to be a high risk endeavor with an indeterminate endpoint, and you will find that there are not enough architectural skills to go around for an effort of that scale.

Understanding Your Business Function

Items 7 through 10 have to do with business performance modeling, root cause analysis, and risk mitigation, and the approaches used tend to be home-grown in each area of business function because the specific techniques are generally specific to each function. These all fall under the umbrella of "understanding your business function" – i.e., modeling and performance measurement of business processes.

In chapter 7 I explain at length the importance of employing business models for planning new capabilities. Some mechanisms for modeling business value have already been presented and will be elaborated on later in this book. The point I want to make here is that modeling of performance is a critical element for structuring a partnership between the CIO/E unit and a LOB. The reason is that it provides a clear focus for determining success. Joint success is necessary to demonstrate the value provided by the partnership. Without clear success criteria, all one

---

[1] Ref. [Daven99].

214

can say is that the money was spent and some systems were built – the rest is open to interpretation.

Organizations that use balanced scorecards for performance measurement should adapt well to approaches for tangible performance metrics. The scorecard criteria should be balanced according to the relative contribution of each success metric in the model.

Planning and Resource Management

Items 11 and 12 tend to be somewhat standardized within most organizations. However, these management functions are usually driven by goals that are defined in terms of milestones and budgets, and so the management capabilities tend to revolve around milestone tracking and expense tracking. The result is that one can never tell where one really is, except in those terms. Initiative management capabilities need to be focused on the ongoing measurement of business value metrics, and resource management needs to focus on both (a) the development of the knowledge portion of buainsess capabilities, and (b) provisioning skills based on their ultimate business value – which is generally highest for those skills that are leveraged, such as capabilitiy mentors. The first step toward achieving these things is requiring that initiatives design and produce credible measures of true progress, based on business strategies and business value, as opposed to task completion.

When developing generic cross-cutting capabilities as in Table 10 one should not attempt to use an approach of gap analysis followed by a big-bang approach of devleoping and rolling out those capabilities. I have helped to define cross-cutting capabilities in large organizations, and what I have seen is that if one tries to develop them a-priori, users do not understand what they are for, and efforts are largely wasted. It is better to develop such capabilities incrementally and have a mentor-focused group that can mentally tie them together to ensure an integrated view and identify generic blueprints for these capabilities.

215

Working With IT Operations

IT Operations is commonly a very powerful function, certainly the most powerful group in IT. This is for obvious reasons: they own the equipment; or at least, they keep the lights on. They also have the credibility of "having done it" when it comes to provisioning and installing things.

Operations has a problem though. They are usually given things to run they they had no say in the design of. For this reason, they tend to operate as an independent entity.

Operations is a critical stakeholder in the lifecycle of any business capability involving automation. These are the people who run the systems and server-based software applications. They are also the people who are the first responders to system failures, and are commonly the ones who install new applications. If their needs are not accounted for, the application might end up being unmanageable, and the system operators will resort to restarting the application without warning whenever there is any kind of problem.

To address this problem, Operations should be included in the set of stakeholders when planning and designing a new application. Their concerns generally fall into these categories:

1. **Installation**: What is the procedure for installing a new application? What are the system requirements? What are the potential conflicts with other systems? What types of testing should be run after installation to verify that the installation was successful?
2. **Monitoring**: What aspects of the application should be monitored to verify that it operating normally?
3. **Routine maintenance**: What are the routine procedures required for keeping the application healthy?
4. **Response**: What should Operations do if they notice through monitoring (or other means) that the system has a problem?
5. **Logging**: What kinds of logging are performed by the application, and what kinds of system-level logging should be enabled?

(Note that all of these areas are included in a comprehensive list of requirements areas presented in chapter 12.)

To address installation, someone from the "systems" or Operations group should work with the development team to create a design for deployment, often referred to as a "deployment diagram" or "system architecture". (The assumption here is that the Operations group has system engineers and system architects within its ranks.)

Monitoring is something that application development teams almost always omit, regrettably, and as a result operators are left with monitoring the most basic things such as whether the application has enough memory. Ideally, monitorability should be anticipated as a set of system requirements and features, for which the operator is the user. A standard dashboard should be designed for.

Routine maintenance includes things such as purging certain directories after a period of time has passed, monitoring disk usage, and so on.

Response is very important to operators. When something goes wrong, operators want a procedure to follow. They want application designers to anticipate every scenario and spell out exactly what to do.

Logging is usually built into applications and standard components, and it is not uncommon that there are multiple logs in many different places. Operators need to know what to do with these, whether to preserve them if the system is restarted, and whether additional logging at an infrastructure level is needed.

Working With Support

It is important to differentiate between Operations and Support. The role of Support is to address problems discovered by the users of the system. When something goes wrong, users do not call the Operators: they call Support. Support maintains a log of such reports ("incidents"), and analyzes them to determine what the underlying issue is. Support then assigns issues to Operations or Maintenance, depending on the nature of the problem. Maintenance or Support might assign an issue to the team working on the next release.

The Support function needs to be defined at an organization level; but it also needs to be carefully planned as part of any initiative and project, in terms of activities, roles, expectations (SLAs), and facilities.

Working With Contracting (Procurement)

If some portion of a project will be executed by an external vendor or partner, it is essential to work with the Contracting department in your organization to make sure that provisions are included in the contract that address _how_ the work will be done, and not only that it will be done.

There are many approaches to dealing with contractors, and I am not going to delve into that in this book. I strongly urge readers to consider the work of Mary Poppendieck and her discussion of software development contracts in her books [Poppendieck03] and [Poppendieck06]. However, I will address the issue of methodological touch points with vendors, to ensure that what the vendor produces will fit into your enviornment, not just in terms of functionality, but in terms of business value measurement, reliability, security, maintainability, and every other enterprise concern that you would want addressed for one of your in-house built systems.

The Contracting department of most companies and government agencies is set up as a cost control and delivery assurance mechanism – not as an overall risk management entity. It is common that issues such as the "ilities" mentioned above are not in the purview of Contracting, and so if those need to be addressed, they must be expressed as system requirements. Further, since many of the concerns we have discussed in this book must be addressed at a process level, it is necessary to change one's view from a final delivery control mindset to a process control and relationship management mindset.

For example, how will you ensure that the delivered system will be maintainable? The traditional approach is to specify the delivery of certain kinds of documentation. However, everyone who has built software solutions knows that documentation does not do much for maintainability if the documentation does not document the right things. If you leave documentation quality inspection until system delivery, it will be hard to correct deficiencies at that time, and then you have the problem of verifying that as-built matches as-designed. Instead, it is far more effective to require that documentation of the design be delivered on a ongoing basis throughout the development of the system, so that it can be critiqued and understood along the way.

I know of one instance in which a system was delivered and the system was found to be not quite what was expected, and so the vendor was told that they would not be used for further work, after which the vendor refused to provide the source code, test cases, or any access to the list of outstanding bugs for the system. That made it very hard to turn the system over to a new vendor or take charge of it. The problem was that, incredibly, the contract did not address the matter of delivery of these elements!

Ideally, a vendor contract should include the same controls that are present for in-house development. These controls are discussed later in the context of software development lifecycles (SDLCs) in chapter 12. The standard contract template should therefore embed these controls: things such as incremental delivery of design artifacts, delivery of test cases and issue lists, and an incremental acceptance process in which early builds are demonstrated, not just in terms of functionality but also in terms of non-functional requirements.

If you think of the vendor as merely an extended branch of your own team, then this approach will be almost automatic, but it must also be included in the contract because, after all, the contract is the cornerstone of your working relationship.

Working With Finance

In chapter 9 on page 182 I explain why IT and Finance are almost always entirely separate entities that need to work together and be better aligned. Now I would like to provide an overview of the concerns of Finance and propose some requirements for integrating Finance better into capability planning.

Later in chapter 12 I will examine the different approaches commonly used by Finance and by IT with respect to achieving control, and how to reconcile and integrate these.

The term "Finance" is used in different ways in different types of organization. Generally it encompasses all forms of financial analysis, accounting, and reporting, including prior period business performance as reported to shareholders (generally reporting using established accounting methods), projected performance as reported to board members (reported in whatever manner is most effective), tax reporting, and any other forms of reporting that are required for the organization's jurisdictions of business.

The primary concerns of Finance typically include the following:

- Getting access to correct, consistent, meaningful, and trustworthy data.
- Understanding the history, nature, intent, and value of business transactions and events.
- Understanding the value of assets.
- Compliance with the latest accounting standards.
- Meeting the requirements of auditors and regulators for performance reporting.
- Methods for assessing and projecting business performance.
- Compliance of the overall organization with the latest tax rules in each applicable jurisdiction.
- Compliance of the overall organization with securities laws and regulations.
- Meeting reporting deadlines.
- Retention of data, and being able to reproduce and explain historical financial results.

Business capabilities that are relevant to Finance therefore revolve around addressing these concerns.

One could argue that performance projections should be generated by the lines of business themselves, and indeed they generally are. However, such projections should be consistent across the organization, and the Finance department usually is the actor that owns the final reports in order to ensure this consistency.

For this to work Finance needs to be in-tune with measures for alignment with the organization's strategies in all areas. If the organization is asking the various operating units to measure their success in business value terms, and in terms of progress against the organization's straetegies, and if Finance is aggregating these reports, then Finance needs to understand them and know how to roll them up. This philosophy is very much in sync with the view of Finance as a driver of business performance rather than as merely a passive accounting function.

Regardless of where the work gets done, or the debate about the role of Finance, Finance clearly needs to be interpreting more than just dollars. Otherwise it will not be able to understand the purpose of investments in agility or risk mitigation, and will not be able to assess performance in a way that is useful to a board that looks at such issues.

Finance therefore needs to have staff who understand the business, and who understand the value of IT architecture strategies. A good case can be made for training business and IT staff in finance and migrating them there. I have seen this work very well, and many people in IT are in fact sufficiently interested in the business side to pursue an MBA and migrate on their own initiative, especially when the business of the organization itself is related to finance – since that is then where the opportunity is.

Finance tends to want to "work backwards" from reported data, to understand the sources of that data and to mitigate risk. Operations tends to want to work "forward" by focusing on processes and sources of errors. The two perspectives need to converge however. In the end, people who maintain the models and designs of business processes need to be the ones who create and maintain those models, and so if Finance creates its own models they will soon be out of date. The solution is to mandate that operating units create and maintain up-to-date complete process models for their own processes, with high risk data elements identified, according to a set of requirements defined by Finance. As already discussed earlier in this book (see page 57), do not call in outside firms to create these models.

Working With Security

The Information Security group in most organizations is tremendously overworked, and tends to have a somewhat adversarial stance with regard to application owners and the business. This is not their fault: it is the result of how security if viewed in most organization by management, that is, as an add-on that that is accountable but that has limited control over how the business actually works. It is also a result of the fact that people in information security generally do not have a system development background, and so as a profession they have less understanding of how systems are built; and conversely, people in software development tend to have very limited knowledge of information security, giving them an inadequate appreciation of security issues. Thus, the blame is shared all around.

As a result, security in most organizations is wofefully inadequate. Organizations live with this risk because they do not know a way out of the situation that is affordable. Most organizations have a series of "risk maanagement" practices around security, that encompass thier system operations, some scanning of applications, and auditing of applications – often under the umbrella of "certification and accreditation" (C&A). These practices are important, but are not fully effective given the way that they are usually implemented. The key to application-level security then is to make the C&A process "real" rather than a paper exercise, and make sure that it addresses how systems are built, and not just how they are deployed. Further, it must be integrated with the system development process in a practical and cost-effective way, rather than a burdensome, bureaucratic way: otherwise, it will make the cost and time of developing new business capabilities prohibitive.

The basic complaint that development teams tend to have with C&A processses is that they need to be shortened. In the words of a project manager with whom I have worked on this issue, "C&A reviews need to be more frequent and more lightweight." [1]

The responpse from the C&A tends to be that this request does not reflect how C&A works; but on pressing the issue I have found that C&A processes are in fact amenable to being iterative. The key is to have project development teams account for security requirements as an integral aspect of their design. That is, security (or the C&A group) needs to be a stakeholder from the beginning, when requirements are accumulated. C&A usually has a list of things they are concerned about, which are typically identified as "controls", and the application development team can and should

---

[1] Attributed to Laura Smyrl., USDA Forest Service.

account for these in the design of the system. If that is done, and if the C&A group is provided with early designs for these controls (even partial designs), then the C&A group can become familiar with them, provide early feedback, and then when the system if finally delivered the C&A process remains as merely a final check.

Further, much of the C&A process is actually not a very technical process. The really technical aspect of security is designing a system to be secure. In the view of C&A, this means designing in the controls. In any case, that is architecture and design work, and that is technical. The review of these designs is technical as well; but the bookkeeping of the C&A process, which accounts for much of the effort, is not technical, yet it is complicated and a mystery to application groups that are new to it. The mentor group is therefore in a good position to add value by becoming familiar with the process and helping application groups to figure it out so that they do not have to rely on the over-burdened C&A group for guidance.

Working With Marketing

In most organizations the term "marketing" refers to the three functions of market research, market-facing promotion of the organization, and sales. The reason for this aggregation is the close relationship between them.

The primary concerns of marketing often include:

- The performance of marketing: (a) How well are market-focused promotional investments paying off? And (b) How effective is the organization's market research in identifying future opportunities?
- How to link marketing objectives with sales data and the customer relationship?
- The customer relationship.
- Understanding the customer and the sales environment.
- Sales performance.
- The ability of the organization to introduce new products and services.
- Ways to creatively leverage partnerships.
- Competitive analysis.
- Sales force management.

- Business models for products and services.
- Understanding the organization's strengths and ways to leverage it.

A true capability focused team should be very interested in working closely with marketing. This can mean marketing for a particular line of business, or it can be strategic marketing, or both. In any case, in order for system planners to be able to create valid tradeoff analyses for the systems that they create, they must be aware of these issues. In particular, marketing should share these things:

1. Share performance goals.
2. Share business case analysis.
3. Share agility goals.
4. Share market environment assumptions.
5. Share generalalities of partnership vision.
6. Share information about who is considered to be a competitor, and what their strengths and weaknesses are.
7. Share the vision for market reach.

Performance goals are important because IT shares these same goals: IT merely provides the systems needed to achieve the goals. If IT is to balance agility versus time to market, under a constrained budget, it must know what the business performance goals are. This is not a single number of course, but is actually a discussion between IT and the business to achieve an understanding of the tradeoffs between the value of immediate market performance versus future performance and cost (i.e., how agiltiy factors in). Further, the results of this discussion must not remain in the heads of a few executives, but must be shared in a *tangible way* with staff – otherwise the information will not be actionable to staff.

Environmental assumptions include factors that might impact how capabilities are executed. Things such as the sensitivity of certain customers to certain issues. The way that a product is marketed differs from region to region, and the way that it is delivered might need to differ as well.

Information about potential future partnerships is critical. I have seen situations in which IT spent a great deal of time and energy developing a system only to have it made irrelevant because the board decided to merge with another entity that had an incompatible system. High level financial decisions such as this have a large impact on IT infrastructure, and these issues can no longer be treated as separate. Of course, sometimes partnership or merger discussions need to be kept confidential, but nevertheless IT can be given a heads up that certain types of changes might occur, and asked what the impact would be.

Knowleege of competitors if important when conceptualizing capabilities because one must be ahead of one's competitors in some way when introducing a new capaibility. Leaving these concerns to "the business" is a mistake, because the business relies on IT (capability development) to provide some level of vision. That vision must not be narrowly focused on technology or cost: it must be business-focused and market-focused.

Working With Human Resources

In the section Make Business Case Development One Of The Core Capabilities Of The Capability Mentor Group (page 133) I discussed the dilemma that IT professionals need to have more training with regard to financial analysis and business planning. Indeed perhaps the greatest challenge for the plan presented in this book regards finding people and training them. The current state of preparation in IT is dismal. Recently I had breakfast with the CEO of a well-known security services company and he lamented exactly that, and said that their main strategy involved growing the skills that they could not obtain in the market. He was not referring only to security skills, but to IT skills in general. He has in place an active partnership with a local area university, to recruit and train staff, and to ensure that they have the fundamentals that are really needed. In an earlier book of mine, I put it thus: [1]

- The average programmer is woefully untrained in basic principles related to reliability and security.
- The tools available to programmers are woefully inadequate to expect that the average programmer can produce reliable and secure applications.

---

[1]   Ref. [Berg2006], Preface.

- Organizations that procure applications are woefully unaware of this state of affairs, and take far too much for granted with regard to security and reliability.
- As we have seen, despite this situation we need to expect even more from our senior IT staff: we need them to have business knowledge and financial analysis accumen.

The situation is not hopeless. It means that we need to place a higher bar for who we consider to be an "architect", and it means that organizations must take it upon themselves to work with academia to fine-tune academic programs and set expectations for who they will hire. It also means that organizations must realize that they will not be able to recruit all of the skills they need: they will have to develop them; and since staff are more mobile today, they will have to provide sufficient incentives for staff to remain once they are trained.

The primary concerns of a Human Resources (HR) department often include:

- What skills are needed by departments, and when.
- Understanding and categorizing those skills.
- The budgets or pay grades that are available for obtainng those skills.
- Resources for advertising for opportunities.
- Partnerships with sources such as universities.

It is a great challenge for HR to understand the skills that are needed. We are now saying that their job must become even harder, since more skills are expected. The skills problem therefore must be addressed at a senior executive level, to help HR understand what the goal is and establish a program that is broad enough to be effective over the long term.

Leverage Your New Technology Group

Most organizations have a group that specializes in trying out new IT technologies to see if they should be utilized or incorporated into the organization's IT systems or infrastructure. Such groups are often referred to as "new technology" groups, or "technology service" groups, and they are often placed (or one might say "misplaced") under a CTO, and sometimes (more appropriately) under a CIO.

I am not referring to an R&D group. In a commercial setting, an R&D group identifies and develops technology for incorporation into products and services that are marketed by the organization or that are otherwise leveraged to build market-facing competitive advantage. In a non-profit or government setting, an R&D group develops technologies to further the mission of the organization.

In contrast, I am referring to a group that looks for technologies that can make existing business functions more efficient. The line between this function and R&D is a hazy one, since any operational improvement can be considered to be a competitive advantage. However, the distinction is that while an R&D group is very focused externally, a technology services group is focused internally.

Case In Point

Such groups are often the envy of technical staff in other parts of the organization, because the former get to "play" with new things and try them out, without the burden of delivering value according to a schedule. For this reason, these groups do not always add significant value to the organization. When that is the case it is a shame however, because these groups often have a great deal of technical expertise. Their liability is that they have little business expertise. That is, they do not know how to make a business case for their wares. Further, they often operate very autonomously, developing ideas on their own without involving the business. In one case I am familiar with, a technology services group spent a year comparing various business process modeling systems, only to then find that the one that they recommended could not store its data in IBM's DB2® product – the database of choice for that organization. If the BPM systems had been actually used as part of the pilot project with a line of business, this deficiency would have been discovered. Instead, the technology services group had the embarrassment of concluding their study and recommending a tool that did not work as expected.

A technology services group represents a vast potential that you can tap for technical expertise. To work with such a group you must provide them with what they usually do not have: business acumen. A team composed of technical staff from the technical services group and business-savvy staff from the mentoring group is well suited as a mentoring core of a pilot effort with a line of business. That is the right model. Doing things independently and then trying to align them in phases is the wrong model.

One thing about technical people: They are accustomed to being recognized for their ideas and their artifacts. It is far more important to them that their name goes on something that has their ideas, than getting recognition for leadership. Thus, these people are a natural fit for working with members of a pilot team to extract best practices and developing blueprints. Start to recognize them for their success in crating reusable blueprints and for successfully installing their work into lines of business. They thrive on this kind of recognition.

Use the mentor group to drive the process, because mentoring skills are critical to success.

Capabilities Required

The generic core capabilities listed in Table 10 (page 213) provide a foundation for higher-level capabilities, much the way that a higher layer of software relies on the existence of lower layers in order to function. These higher-level capabilities and their relationship to the core capabilities are depicted in Figure 12.

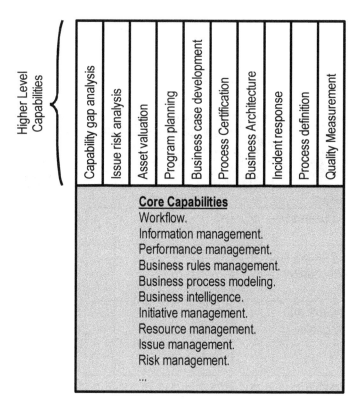

Figure 12: Core capabilities provide a baseline set of capabilities for creating higher-level task-specific capabilities.

The capabilities defined in Figure 12 are required to perform the activities of *some actor* for each of the six major activities in the CIO/E operating model (Table 7, page 200). Table 11 lists these activities.

Some of the activities in Table 11 take different forms depending on the level or domain at which they are applied. For example, detail-level activity 1 ("Establish business goals") can be performed at a department level or an enterprise level, or any level inbetween, and the specific processes for establishing goals might be somewhat different in those different cases yet the underlying nature of the activity is the same. Similarly, the process of establishing business goals is likely different for Marketing compared to Finance, but again the underlying nature of the activity is the same.[1]

Table 11: Detail-level activities for each major activity in the CIO/E unit operating model as listed in Table 7.

#	Detail-Level Activity	Required for CIO/E Operating Model Major Activities						Output(s)
		1	2	3	4	5	6	
Make Things Better								
1.	Establish business goals.	✓	✓					Documented goals.
2.	Determine cause and effect relationships.	✓	✓					Root cause identification. Documented issues.
3.	Measure gaps with respect to goals.	✓	✓					Documented issues or gaps with respect to goals or risk management.
4.	Define business value scales.	✓	✓					Consensus on a yardstick for business value.
5.	Define risk mitigation value scales.	✓	✓					Consensus on yardstick for risks.
6.	Assess value of assets.	✓	✓					Better understanding of assets.
7.	Assess value of opportunities.	✓	✓					Understanding of opportunities.
8.	Assess risk.	✓	✓	✓				Consensus on actual risk.
9.	Acquire SME knowledge.	✓	✓					Human knowledge.
10.	Establish partnership to close a gap.	✓	✓					Credibility to expand mentor program.

---

[1] Later in this book in the section Create the Right Kind Of Enterprise Data Model on page 418 I discuss ways to model things that are conceptually similar but distinct in their usage or implementation.

#	Detail-Level Activity	Required for CIO/E Operating Model Major Activities						Output(s)
		1	2	3	4	5	6	
11.	Plan a program or initiative to close a gap.	✓	✓					Documented strategies for addressing gaps. Remediation plans. Mitigation plans. Transition plans.
12.	Develop a program-level or initiative-level business case.	✓	✓					Business case.
13.	Provide resources.	✓	✓					Faster progress.
14.	Plan and execute a pilot project.	✓	✓					Reusable project level designs. Reusable business process controls. Reusable transition plans. Reusable human knowledge.
15.	Plan and execute a non-pilot project.							Project level designs. Business process controls. Transition plans.
16.	Certify a business process.			✓				Trusted business capabilities.
17.	Mentor LOB staff.		✓					LOB process staff who are self-sustaining.
18.	Assess staff.							Inventory of skills.
19.	Certify staff.							Staff with reusable skills.
20.	Recruit new staff.							Staff with generic skills.
21.	Develop and refine reference designs.				✓			Reference designs.
22.	Develop and refine enterprise architecture.					✓		Enterprise architecture.

#	Detail-Level Activity	Required for CIO/E Operating Model Major Activities						Output(s)
		1	2	3	4	5	6	
Oversight and Independent Reporting								
23.	Oversee business process performance.						✓	Knowledge of effectiveness of capability system.
24.	Account for business events.							Accounting ledgers.
Daily Operations: Keep the lights on								
25.	Monitor a business process.							Knowledge of actual performance.
26.	Contain loss.							Log entries.
27.	Determine immediate cause of an incident.							Incident report.
28.	Remedy the symptom or loss caused by an incident.							Continued operation.
29.	Mitigate loss due to an incident.							Minimiztion of loss.
30.	Reconcile data discrepancies.							Future problems avoided.
31.	Maintain business process definition.	✓						Future agility preserved.
32.	Maintain business process knowledge.	✓						Future agility preserved.

There are many activities in Table 11 that are noteworthy. These are:

Actvities #4-8: These pertain to converting intangible concepts of value into tangible concepts that can be actually measured in some way. This activity requires the *joint participation of both the business and the CIO/E* to have a meeting of the minds about how to quantify risk, opportunity, and the tradeoffs between the two. The best way to achieve this is to try it in the context of a particular pilot first, and then attempt to generalize it into a methodology that can be broadly adopted across the organization. The next chapter discusses the creation of business value scales in more detail.

Actvity #9 (Acquire SME knowledge): This speaks to the point raised in chapter 4 that to be agile, an organization must find an effective way to leverage subject matter experts (SMEs). By transferring SME knowledge to mentors, the SME knowledge is spread among people who are trained to help and train others.

Actvity #10-14: These pertain to an operating unit partnering with the CIO/E to jointly tackle a problem, from planning through execution. Item 14 in particular also has an output described as "human knowledge". This is to emphasize the extremely important outcome of mentors partnering with LOB groups to achieve a common goal: knowledge is transferred in both directions, thereby leveraging the source of that knowledge.

Actvity #15 (Plan and execute a non-pilot project): Once a LOB has learned what it needs to from the CIO/E's mentors and can build business processes that are measurable, manageable, transparent, and business-value driven, there is no need to partner with the CIO/E to enhance those capabilities or build new ones. This frees the mentors to work with other LOBs to pilot similar or entirely new capabilities, and to devise ways to deal with emerging concerns. However, the CIO/E must certify any business process (#16), regardless of whether the CIO/E's resources and mentors are involved in its development.

Actvity #16 (Certify a business process): All business processes should be certified according to requirements devised by the CIO/E unit. These requirements represent a natural balance between the incentive to get processes certified expeditiously and the need to be able to show well under independent internal audits (#23).

Actvity #18-19: These have to do with the assessment and certification (where appropriate) of staff. All managers and leads must assess their staff on a routine basis. Certification of staff is something that the CIO/E must do to ensure that the CIO/E mentor and general resource staff are qualified in the many areas that they are expected to be proficient. This is critical because many of these areas are not understood by the industry to be important (see page 145), and so the organization must set its own bar.

Activity #21-22: These have to do with the development and refinement of reference designs and architectures. Rather than being a top-down process, developing enterprise architecture and reference designs is best done as a bottom-up and top-down iterative process whereby first attempts are refined over time through trial usage in pilot efforts and in broader usage contexts. It is illogical to "wait until the architecture is complete" to begin using it, because it is never complete, and should be a living set of concepts and decisions.

Activity #24 (Account for business events): This is a placeholder for the complex activities associated with financial and others kinds of accounting in all its forms for the purpose of reporting to shareholders, auditors, and government agencies. The primary responsibility of LOB units is to provide intelligible business events that can be interpreted as accounting events. Thus, the view from a LOB is actually very simple conceptually: provide these events. Unfortunately, historically interfaces to accounting have been data centric rather than event centric and so those interfaces are often extremely complex and brittle.

Activity #25 (Monitor a business process): This has to do with the routine operational monitoring and measurement of business processes. As explained elsewhere in this book, such monitoring must be designed into processes, rather than added after the fact, in order to be effective and in terms of business value as defined by activities 4-5.

Activity #26-29: These pertain to incident response, in all its forms, from security-related incidents to business transaction failures to operational data errors.

Activity #30 (Reconcile data discrepancies): This pertains to the detection and investigation of discrepancies that surface when operational or accounting tallies or entries do not agree with what they are expected to be. This activity is predominant in accounting because accounting is in the position of reading and tallying operational data.

Activity #31 (Maintain business process definition): This pertains to the responsibility that every business function must have to maintain their own business process models. This responsibility should not be delegated to an IT group.

234

Activity #32 (Maintain business process knowledge): This refers to the responsibility that every business function must have to maintain ongoing knowledge of how their non-legacy processes work, including their automated processes. When this activity ceases for a process, that process then becomes legacy by definition.

Build Your Team

One thing you should not do is spend all of your time going from meeting to meeting, while your mentor staff toil at their project, not knowing who you are talking to and what you are communicating. If you bring on the right people, these will be highly capable evangelist people themselves – some of them perhaps more capable in that role than yourself. You should split your attention equally between them and the operating units, and leverage your mentor staff to help get the message out and to solicit regular feedback and provide updates. That is true leadership. Doing so will train them in the art of speaking to other senior managers in your organization and will help to build the scalability that your team is going to need after you succeed.

To achieve success you need a broad set of deep capabilities on your team. You need "the best and the brightest" that the organization has to offer. Yes, this is a cliché, but in this case it really does apply. These should be people who would otherwise be enterprise architects, technical managers, or senior consultants – and all of whom have an inclination to understand business. Do not hesitate to ask for them, and be prepared to pay them appropriately, to budget for them, and to challenge them. Think of it this way: would you expect a junior pilot to train other pilots? – no, you would have one of your best pilots do that job.

You also need for your staff to be natural-born or experienced mentors and facilitators, who have people skills and who seek to enable others and do not seek to become indispensable or use information for power. This is the nature of the culture that you will have to create.

Your staff will need to be architects: business architects, technical architects, data architects, security architects, compliance architects, and everything inbetween – including people with degrees in business. In fact, while you should recognize that the skills of each individual are unique and not treat them as commodities, you should not separate them by specialty. Expect them all to learn from each other and to eventually be substitutable. Expect them also to thoroughly learn about the business and not remain compartmentalized mentally in the world of IT. If you divide them into teams, make each team self-sufficient.

Your architects will have to have a blend of theoretical and hands-on inclination. Since you will be involved in a great deal of pilot work, there will be a lot of hands on opportunities for building demonstration or proof-of-concept versions of new capabilities. Yet, for these early systems to be scalable and be fit for reuse, they need to be designed correctly and have the necessary grounding in theory and best practices.

While it is easy nowadays to find commodity-level IT staff, it is a tall order to find even a handfull of highly capable IT staff who have a strong business focus and who have a track record in terms of good judgment and the ability to collaborate and communicate. Finding the right staff will be one of your greatest challenges. To address this you need to be prepared to recruit from within, and to establish an apprentice-like program to grow the diverse skills that are needed.

It was explained earlier in Empowering the CIO/E (page 116) that a CIO/E unit should not be a software development shop, but that in addition to business architecture mentors, it should be a home for software development level IT resources. This provides a means of training programming staff "the right way" so that their work will reflect enterprise practices. You should expect to eventually promote some of these staff to be mentors. Therefore, you should also seek some of the best and the brightest – although less experienced – for this pool. While you will be "renting out" the resources in this pool to projects in various operating units, you should hold these staff accountable for adhering to enterprise practices.

You also want to be known for providing high capability resources. A recent quote from a program manager says it particularly well: "In the original estimates, we assumed a development team with moderate experience, but now have the core team established and can assume a high level of experience. Changing this single parameter in our cost model resulted in a significant reduction in the development costs." [1] – and enhancing cost-effectiveness for the enterprise is one of your purposes.

Staff Size and Budget

Your mentor staff will have many kinds of activities underway, including:

1. Defining mentor group processes and methodologies.
2. Participating in other initiatives to improve processes.
3. Communication and advocacy.
4. Working with projects to adjust plans.
5. Working with projects to provide design-level advice in aspects related to enterprise concerns (compliance, testability, manageability, etc.).
6. Refining reusable artifacts and maintaining reuse repositories.

As the organization gets underway its focus will be slanted toward 1, 2, and 3. However, over time its focus should shift to be dominated by 4, 5, and 6. An early staff of five or six should be sufficient to launch a mentor group and define its core leadership. As work with pilots and projects ramps up it will be necessary to initially have one person for every 3 projects that require active involvement. Long term, one person should be able to handle more projects as the operating model is established and work becomes more routine.

As an example, if one assumes that at any time there are 100 projects underway in the organization, it will likely be the case that only a fraction of thee are in a planning stage – say 20 – and that half of these are "cookie cutter" cases that do not require active involvement by the mentor team. That leaves 10 projects that require active involvement, leading to a resource requirement of 3-4 mentors to handle this load, with a core team of an additional set (say five) to handle activities 1-3 above, for an overall total of 8-9 mentors.

If one assumes for discussion that the average project is comprised of ten people (a very gross assumption, but useful for

---

[1] Larry Bowser, US Forest Service, March 2008.

the purpose here), the mentor staff requirements translate into a staff budget that represents about 1% of the overall IT budget. For a group that can potentially have a large impact on the overall effectiveness of IT, this is a small cost, but as overhead it is a visible cost and so that is why it is necessary from the beginning to measure the business value that results.

Employ Certification For Staff

You should put in place a staff certification program from the outset and grow that program as a repository for the kinds of knowledge and skills that your staff need to have. As the program solidifies it should be opened to the operating units to help train their staff.

Certification of staff is unrelated to certification of business processes. Certification of staff is a means of ensuring that staff understand what skills they need and that management can efficiently determine who has those skills. Certification of business processes is a means of ensuring that enterprise processes meet enterprise objectives in a balanced manner.

Certification of staff should require renewal and refreshment since the requirements will change over time as it is expanded and as the sets of risks to the organization change.

Be cautious when using staff certification programs from external sources. Too often these focus on technology rather than the skills of judgment and awareness of issues; and too often they are narrowly focused and do not address important concerns such as reliability. Your own certification program should encompass all of the concerns of your organization, and should be designed to test awareness of issues as well as judgment.

There are some camps in the programming community that are opposed to certification on philosophical grounds. The feeling in this camp is that certification leads to stratification and a culture in which only those who are certified are allowed to contribute ideas. This is certainly something to watch for. However, the certification required here is that which everyone in the mentoring organization should be expected to achieve eventually, and so there should be no stratification. The point is to encourage – to demand – that staff attain the skills that are needed. And it is not a

238

small thing to demand, because the gap is large, very large: once you start to analyze what skills are actually needed and assess the skills that people actually have, you will be amazed and wonder how it is that things have gone so far afield. To do this you must dismiss what the industry norms are, and start fresh with the basic principles of what it takes to develop reliable, scalable, maintainable, manageable, and transactionally sound enterprise business processes and systems.

Here is a summary of some of the generic industry-based skills that are needed:

1. Transaction processing.
2. Distributed systems design.
3. Software and system reliability engineering.
4. Application security.
5. Financial analysis of IT systems, from an ROI perspective.
6. Consulting and mentoring skills.
7. Systems analysis.
8. Business process analysis and design.
9. Project planning.
10. Estimation.
11. Software engineering methodologies.
12. Data analysis.
13. Object oriented analysis.
14. Relational database design.
15. Operating system fundamentals.
16. Current "trend" technologies, such as Web services and contemporary languages.

Most IT architects today focus their attention almost exclusively on items 11-16. Yet, *items 11-16 are arguably the least important for an IT architect*. Certainly one should be familiar with the technology of the day: programmers will not trust you if you do not know the latest gizmos that they use, but knowing the ins and outs of these gizmos is what a tech lead is for. Architects need to have judgment about design decisions that are independent of technology and that have business-level significance.

Items 1-10 are extremely important skills for someone who makes major architectural decisions that impact the business, and who must work with members of the operating units in the organization to help them to understand the IT perspective (see item 6). The ability to model business processes, data, and systems (see items 7, 8, 12, 13), to understand integration issues (see items 1 and 2), to build reliable and secure systems (items 3 and 4), and to understand how to communicate the impact of various technical strategies on future business agility and risk (item 5) are all extremely critical skills.

Items 1 and 2 are noteworthy because they are strictly technical skills, yet I have found these skills to be sorely lacking in most IT professionals. In most organizations today, data is commonly replicated across many different systems. I address this problem on page 90. The result is that system designers are designing, *in effect*, distributed databases. Yet, these systems are commonly designed as if they were each standalone systems, with completely inadequate provisions for keeping replicated data in sync. Further, the current technologies *do not address this need at all*: the need to integrate heterogeneous data stores. In short, programmers commonly do not have the skills or tools to properly design distributed systems with replicated data, and it shows in the tremendous data quality problems that exist in most organizations.

> # Most IT architects today focus their attention almost exclusively on technology. Yet, *technology issues are arguably the least important for an IT architect.*

And that is not all. The senior mentors must have a broad knowledge of the business. Otherwise they will only be able to operate in a technical sphere, and that is wholly inadequate. Further, over time they must develop frameworks and methodological processes that encode operating models and blueprints to ensure consistency and to ensure that processes are self-sustaining. Creating these takes work, but that is not the point I am discussing here: the point here is that as those elements are created, the mentors must be well-versed in them.

All of these elements are the required skills of the mentors. It is a large set of very sophisticated knowledge. Now you can see why you cannot put junior people in the role of the mentor. These people will be the most versatile and skilled agents of change in the organization.

How To Bring It About

The first step is to create an expectation that a lot is expected of the mentor team members, and that these people are not merely "IT architects" or existing staff reshuffled. I am not even going to mention compensation, because that will take care of itself: as these staff acquire more skills they will become more valuable, and they will eventually be paid according to their value. However, you must recognize that the industry does not have an existing category for this type of worker, and so your HR department will not be able to find industry comparables.

But back to certification. The best approach is to work with a local university and explain your expectations for what you need in your staff. As I mentioned in the section beginning on page 225, a colleague of mine who runs a very respected security consulting firm has done this because he feels that schools are not producing what he needs, so he has reached out and told them what he needs and set up a program with their help.

The International Association of Software Architects (IASA)[1] has begun to establish a broad range of certifications for IT architects (including virtually every aspect of IT architecture). These certifications address the kinds of issues raised in this book, and I have helped to devise some of the curricula. This certification body is also a valuable professional organization that IT architects can leverage to become more aware of what is expected of them today.

You should also ask your own staff what they feel is required to make certification meaningful. However, be wary of turning over control to consensus, because in general most practitioners in the IT community do not know what they don't know and need to know. It is a sad truth, but it is the truth. Instead, select a small committee of staff who have specialties in the various elements listed above, and put them in charge of the certification requirements. Do not let the requirements get diverted to transient industry waves such as technology stacks, governance frameworks, or anything that has a buzzword. Certification should be about

---

[1] See http://www.iasahome.org

fundamentals, and things that are timeless and that apply across all technologies and all frameworks.

Doggedly Model Business Value

Even if your team is incomplete, you can begin to reach out to operating units in a useful way. You can immediately start by trying to create a model of business value with respect to the various concerns that you are charged with integrating. You will need such a model to enable executives to *trade off various strategies*, including short-term and long-term strategies. For example, if two initiatives are competing for resources, and one initiative has long-term value and the other has short-term value, the one that will usually win is the one that can express its value in the most concrete terms.

> An intiative business model should include *strategies* and *tradeoffs*, in either qualitative or quantitative terms.

Creating a model right away has these benefits:

- It forces you to truly understand the business.
- It forces you to involve operational units in a common cause.
- It establishes you as a focal point for converging the organization's various concerns.
- It establishes the backbone of the mentoring process: optimizing concerns.

In the process of creating such a model, you will have to deal with issues such as what kinds of business metrics can be realistically created, and what needs to be rolled up to assess overall importance – i.e., what is currently missing from the picture that executives get. Understanding these things will establish the role that your team should eventually play.

A model will help to prioritize projects. It will help you recommend which projects to invest in and in which order, and it will help to document the impact of decisions in a durable and intelligent form.

Organizational Impact

One of the major value propositions of your team should be on quantifying business value for all of those hard-to-quantify but nevertheless important aspects of capability development, such as the expected long-term cost of unmitigated risk, opportunity costs or value, and the values of the organization's architectural standards.

To give teeth to this, all projects should eventually integrate business value modeling into their planning, from the outset, as proposed in chapter 7. Your organization should be charged with *establishing the form and content* of such models, with the participation and consensus of the operating units. However, it may take some time to get to this point.

Business value for an organization is an end-to-end proposition. Yet, projects are often justified based on departmental needs. The only way to tame the dragon of locally-focused initiatives is to model and assess their impact on the organization and then decide. Without a working model, you are subject to the cry of need from each department and any alternatives that you articulate will only have subjective weight.

Measure Only What Matters

Once you have a methodology established for defining and modeling business value, you can define operational metrics for measuring it. This is actually an iterative process: the model should be expressed in terms that are measurable, or it is of little use. Getting the metrics right is hard but is essential. Some organizations have found that they only use a small percentage of their measurements[1]: identify those and focus on making them meaningful.

To achieve this you will need to ensure that measurability is considered *from the outset* in *every capability design* and that it is

---

[1] See for example [Nortel2001]. From that article, "Management examined which [budget] numbers it utilized and found that only eight line items [of more than 100 line item details] were critical to evaluating the success of the organization."

243

included in the critical requirements for *each business process*. As discussed toward the end of chapter 5, enterprise reference designs should facilitate this by embedding measurement as a core feature.

IT systems should support measurement by producing data on things such as data quality, timeliness, error rates, availability, responsiveness to customer requests, product return rates, and so on. This often requires complex correlation of events, and this is best designed in from the beginning rather than trying to achieve it afterwards through complex database queries.

You might say that measurement is elementary but in fact few IT systems are built with capability measurement from the outset: it is usually added later and with much difficulty after there are problems that make it an issue. Yet without it, you will not be able to prove that your Capability team is effective.

Shift the focus to capability creation. As discussed in chapter 7, there is too much focus in the IT industry on a task-based view of projects, in which progress is measured based on which tasks have been completed.

Frequency of reporting and thoroughness of reporting are not indicators of effectiveness either. Furthermore, the reporting approach to business is antiquated and needs to be replaced with a dashboard approach in which the business is measured continuously and processes – including strategic processes – are event-driven. Only event-driven processes can ever hope to address the need for an every-decreasing business cycle. Only event driven processes explicitly define their interdependencies and thereby can adapt easily when things change.

Strive To Eliminate Subjective Reporting Of Status

In chapter 7 I discuss the problems associated with subject status reporting. Measurement of progress is often presented in "dashboards" that summarize status for managers. Too often dashboards are hand-crafted and do not represent a true view of what is going on. Dashboards should therefore be based on objective – not subjective – criteria.

Dashboards should not be separate artifacts created just for management. Integrate the status tracking mechanisms used by your staff into your dashboard in a manner that allows you to flag items of interest.

> # Dashboards should not be separate artifacts created just for management.

If you want to have current information, then you need to do this unless you expect your staff to stay late into the night creating artifacts just for you – artifacts that will likely gloss over much important information.

Long range plans or "visions" should are often vague and success is subjective. Visions should be based on objective capability criteria – not processes, architectures, or organization structures. A vision that is not specific in terms of capabilities is of limited value because it is too open to interpretation.

You (the CIO/E) will need a strong advocate in the executive committee (besides yourself) to help institutionalize these changes of philosophy. You will need a strong collaborative relationship with operating units in order to develop metrics that have consensus, since both you and the operating units will be measured by those metrics.

Success Metrics

In chapter 7 I give the example, that completion of a project should not be determined when "we built and stood up the ABC system". Rather, it should be something like, "we created a capability to do XYZ and proved that it is effective". If you can measure that a capability is effective, then you can probably operationalize that measurement and continue to use it.

Success metrics are operational metrics that are embedded in or added onto operational processes. Success metrics measure the effectiveness of processes in terms of the various goals and concerns of the organization or department. Success metrics measure the effectiveness of the capabilities that have been built.

> # Alignment should be transparent (demonstrable).

Success should include certification that the resulting capabilities are aligned in a balanced (optimized) manner with all business goals, strategies, and concerns – not just with risk and not just with business opportunities.

Further, alignment should be *transparent*: one should be able to easily demonstrate that alignment through metrics and through easy identification of the business rules and processes that ensure alignment. This enable the organization to show this alignment to auditors, and it also allows the organization to maintain control of its alignment and keep it current as considerations change.

Apart from alignment certification, capabilities should be tested to demonstrate actual goals have been met, e.g., that data quality has improved by the anticipated amount or that product defect rates are reduced as expected. The resulting success metrics should be inputs to the business model for the initiative.

> # The ability to produce success metrics should be built into every system.

A ramification of this is that the ability to produce success metrics should be built into the system. In other words, you must tell your architects to design all of your business systems to incorporate operational effectiveness monitoring.

If you try to add this after the fact you will have a hard time, because measuring effectiveness usually requires correlating events from end to end in a complex system, and that ability needs to be embedded within the design. Further, metrics should extend to all business concerns – not just to the primary business driver.

For example, suppose that a new system is intended to provide a back office processing function that enables the handling of new kinds of products, and also suppose that enterprise concerns include security-related risk reduction and reduction of risks and costs associated with data quality. The success of the new system *in value terms* should be assessed based on: (1) the value of new products that are actually handled; (2) the overall reduction in security-related risk, and (3) the overall reduction of data quality related risks and costs. In order to measure any of these and associate the improvements with the new system, the new system must incorporate measurements at various points. Further, some measures might not show indications until they manifest downstream in other systems, and therefore it must be possible to routinely correlate those downstream events with their actual causes. Data quality problems in particular often are not detectable until later when it might be hard to determine which processing system the data has passed through.

The point is that measurement is not trivial, and it needs to be designed in, or it is very difficult to build in the necessary information that is needed to correlate failures. If a system is built "quick and dirty" without measurement, then one cannot determine if strategies (which are an investment) for ensuring good data quality or good security were successful, and so the value of those strategies cannot be proven.

When telling your architects what you want to measure, do not hesitate to be demanding. Look at the criteria against which you will be judged, and specify those. If you are accountable for risk, then demand that risk be modeled and actually measured. If you are accountable for cost, then demand that cost be monitored in near real time. If you are accountable for agility, then demand that agility be modeled and measured – it *can* be done, but it required planning and must be anticipated.

Summary

In order to be effective, the CIO/E must have a mandate to eventually certify all business processes. However, this mandate should start small in terms of its scope, and build on success to establish its viability and credibility as well as to refine the methods used.

The CIO/E will need to publicize the new mission of his or her team, seeking to win partners and identify opportunities for win-win pilot initiatives, and not invest too much time trying to win over skeptics.

A list of activities required to implement the CIO/E operating model is presented, along with a list of capabilities required to perform those activities.

The issue of staff certification is discussed, along with the skills required to perform the mentor function.

The CIO/E is encouraged to focus first on establishing success stories with respect to the measurement of tangible business value, and using these cases to refine the methodology. To be credible and realistic, business value must be an end-to-end measurement that considers the broad impact on the organization and the full lifecycle of systems.

The approach to business value measurement should impact the way that progress dashboards are constructed. Subjective measures should be gradually replaced by tangible measures that focus on value rather than milestones or tasks.

11. Modeling Business Value

Getting a Handle on the Intangibles of IT

In chapter 7 I argue that business value modeling and measurement must be a core capability of IT in order for IT to be able to articulate its concerns to the business. In this chapter I provide concepts and techniques for accomplishing this.

The failure to establish a common vocabulary and conceptual model for the business value of IT concerns, in a manner that has sincere participation and acceptance across both IT and the various business units, is a major root cause of the poor communication and disconnectedness that exists between business and IT in most large organizations. Yes, modeling the business value of IT concerns is hard, but it *must be achieved* if there is to be any hope of integrating IT planning with business planning. The implication is that IT leadership staff at all levels need to be versed in more than technology: they need to understand basic economic analysis. This book will not try to provide a complete treatment of the economic analysis of IT projects or issues, but I will describe some innovative ways of applying standard techniques, as well as some recently developed techniques, to model some of the hardest yet most important aspects of IT value.

Measuring the Value Of Architecture Choices

IT architects do not communicate well with managers in lines of business. They might have a good relationship, but if an architect is asked about the concerns that they deal with, they will mention things such as "technical risk", "coupling", "encapsulation", "reusability", the need to "refactor", and "transactional integrity". These terms mean little to people in business; yet these terms mean a great deal to IT architects and they are extremely important concepts that have a significant impact on business agility and lifecycle cost. Why then is the communication between architects and business people so difficult?

> ## IT architects are not trained to relate architecture concepts to tangible business value.

The problem is that IT architects are not trained to relate their concepts to tangible business value. For example, "coupling" refers to the amount of interdependence between components. This impacts business agility because a high degree of interdependence (coupling) generally means that changing either component is costly and difficult. Yet, architects do not have standard practices for expressing coupling in terms of lifecycle cost or agility.

This situation is the fault of our educational system. IT architects need to provide a link between technology and business, and as such they should be versed not only in how to express decisions in technical terms but how to express them in business terms as well. Architects need to have a repertoire of templates for modeling the business value of the technical concerns that they know are important.

Despite the fact that this is seldom practiced, it is very possible to do this. Later we will see how to model the value of agility by comparing possible future scenarios. (See page 283.) Coupling impacts agility and so it can be modeled in the same way. Technical risk can be modeled as negative opportunity.[1] (See Modeling Risk on page 257.) Refactoring refers to the simplification and internal reorganization of a component in order to enhance its reusability and maintainability, and so the value of refactoring derives from increased agility, a higher level of reuse, and lower lifecycle cost. Other architectural principles can be modeled using similar techniques. Thus, we see that the excuse

---

[1] In this book, and in most literature in the security community, a threat is something bad that can happen, and risk represents the potential loss due to that threat. There are other definitions of risk and threat though. E.g., the Project Management Institute PMBOK methodology inverts these definitions.

that architects do not normally model business value does not hold water. They could, and they should – if they knew how. Since they are not trained to do so, you will need to team them with staff or consultants who have experience modeling business *value* and challenge them to create models of their architecture principles.

Business value is very different from cost.

It is important to realize that business value is very different from cost. There is a great deal of literature that provides techniques for cost estimation in IT projects. Cost only impacts value when the value derives from reduced cost. Other kinds of value such as increased agility cannot be measured using cost-based techniques.

Value should be expressed in terms of goals. At the highest level, this is usually shareholder value, but can be other things. At intermediate and lower levels it can be objectives having to do with operational efficiency, revenue, data quality, or other success criteria. Thus, increased agility can translate into the ability to introduce more products as the need arises; this value need not be expressed in dollars, but can be expressed in terms of the months to introduce a new product. If that has meaning to the business and rolls up to shareholder value in the corporate plan, then there is no need to express the value in dollar terms in a departmental plan.

The Components of Business Value

When measuring business value one must establish a planning horizon. That is, value needs to be maximized over a particular timeframe. As discussed earlier in chapter 7, the time frame makes a large difference. For example, actions that accept long-term risks might be optimal if the time frame in question is one year, but other actions that manage those risks better might be optimal if the planning time frame is five years.

Organizations often have multiple planning horizons, such as short-term budget cycle planning and longer-term roadmap planning. Longer-term objectives and opportunities should be offset by longer-term risks and lifecycle costs. Shorter-term objectives and opportunities should be rolled up into longer-term objectives to make sure that shorter-term tactics do not compromise longer-term objectives.

The overall business planning horizon should be long enough to span the lifecycle of major systems. In Making Technology Investments Profitable, Jack Keen and Bonnie Digrius say pointedly, "Benefits come true when management monitors every step of the way, from project funding through system retirement."[1]

This is quite a bit longer than the span over which most organizations plan – in fast-paced organizations roadmaps are often no more than three years out at best. However, one does not need to actually *plan* over that period: one merely needs to account for costs and business impact effects that manifest over that period.

The expected value of a business capability over a planning horizon is composed of:

1. The expected income from the foreseen opportunities that the new capability will enable, *minus*
2. The expected investment, *minus*
3. The expected lifecycle cost, *plus*
4. The expected value of *unforeseen* future opportunities that the new system will enable the organization to capture.

These terms should all be adjusted to account for the passage of time, using a "net present value" (NPV) formula, but I am not even going to account for that, because as it turns out, adjustment for time tends to be a small affect compared to other factors in IT decisions, and I do not want to distract from the core concepts here by presenting complicated formulas.[2]

The first two items in the list above are straightforward: the opportunity and the investment. There are the two main aspects to any standard business plan. However, the standard type of analysis has a deep flaw: it is deterministic. That is, it assumes that the

---

[1] Ref. [Keen03], page 159.

[2] For those who wish to do a more precise calculation, it is almost trivial to define the sources of value as a time series, dividing each term by a discount rate, using a standard NPV approach. However, the discount rate used should represent the value of money, and not attempt to account for risk.

outcome is certain. A deterministic approach is fine for many investment situations in which risk is treated separately for each investment. However, in a large organization in which investments in many activities occur continuously and all impact each other on an ongoing basis over time, the business model must incorporate the inherently non-deterministic nature of investment into the core value model.

Consider Figure 13. (Note that the vertical and horizontal value scales are different.) When a new capability is contemplated it does not yet exist. Since there is a chance (often a large chance) that the capability will not be completed and deployed, and even if it is deployed, might not live up to expectations. Thus, at the outset of planning the expected value of the future capability is substantially less than its potential. It is not zero however, since if it were there would be no point in even starting the effort.

As work on a capability proceeds, the chance of ultimate success normally increases. It may actually decrease if troubles arise that indicate that the capability might not be feasible. In some cases, new information (such as development failures) might cause the chance of success to drop below the point at which investment is worthwhile. Regardless, the expected market value is the product of the probability of ultimate success and the estimated maximum market potential. This is shown by the curve in the figure.

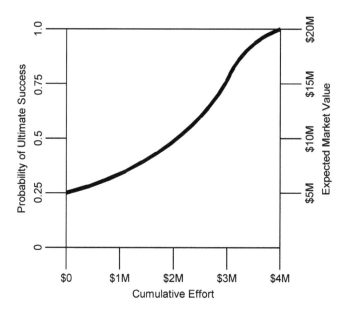

Figure 13: Expected market value approaches its maximum as work proceeds and the probability of successful completion reaches 1.

It is noteworthy that the curve in the figure takes on kind of an S-shape, characterized by a gradual – almost horizontal path – followed by a steep climb, and then a gradual approach to a probability of 1.0. The initial gradual ascent represents the period during which "show stopper" concerns are addressed. These are often technical challenges which are best dealt with by early proof-of-concept efforts.

In an IT project one usually does not consider what happens in the marketplace after deployment: that is considered to be the problem of the business side. However, to model the value of a capability realistically, one should account for all risks, including market failure. If that is not possible, then IT has no choice but to assume the market potential to be that which is articulated by the business.

Now consider the last item of the four above, the value of unforeseen future opportunities. This item represents the business value of business agility. Agility is the ability to respond to new opportunities as they occur. The specific opportunities are unforeseen – otherwise one could plan for them and one would not need to respond to them as they occur. Thus, having agility means having an ability to react in ways that one cannot predict. To preserve agility one must invest in preserving agility, because it takes effort and forethought to preserve agility. Apart from the cost though, the expected *value* of agility is not related to its cost: its value is the value of the opportunities that can normally be expected to come along.

The third item above, the expected lifecycle cost, is often treated as the cost of the expenditures that go into building and maintaining a system. The true costs go way beyond that though. If one is to use lifecycle cost to estimate the impact of changes to a system, then one must estimate a true lifecycle cost that accounts for all of the indirect impacts, including impact on the *cost of reacting to future opportunities*. In other words, we must account for the cost of foregone agility. We must also account for the expected cost of failures that occur due to risks coming true as a result of inadequate investment in risk management. These components are the cost part of the equation, in contrast to the opportunity value discussed in the previous paragraph. Any business plan must account for opportunity value and investment cost. In the sections follow I will break these components down further.

Accounting For the Value of Agility: Making the Case for Agility

Chapter 7 explained how business agility relates to many IT architecture principles, and makes the point that when one applies these principles, one must articulate their value in business terms. Here I want to explore an approach for doing that. Later in this chapter I will revisit this topic and actually work through an example.

If you expect your IT staff to preserve business agility, then you must be willing to measure the long-term impact of a series of actions that individually do not significantly impact agility but in the aggregate destroy it. This means that initiatives must anticipate the impact of any deviations from the intended architecture, and that problems that occur later must be traceable to the decision-makers who caused those problems by allowing rules to be relaxed in the interest of expediency. This is a tall order, but it will occur naturally once the organization starts to plan based on business value models, as those plans and measurements will accrue over time.

> **If you expect to preserve business agility, then you must be willing to measure and trace the long-term impact of a series of actions.**

Business-focused architects (which all architects should be) should be able to produce a *quantitative* estimate of the impact on expected lifecycle cost (item 3 above) of any major design decision. Thus, when there is a call to compromise the architecture of a system, an architect should be able to estimate what the business impact will be in terms of increased lifecycle cost.

Item 4 in the list of business value components is the value of agility: the value of being able to react to change and capture new, *unexpected opportunities that were not planned for.* Measuring the value of agility is much harder to conquer. However, it is perhaps the most important value of all. It is impossible to know the value of opportunities that have not yet shown themselves, yet this is what agility is for: to be positioned to seize such opportunities. Therefore, they must have value, and you must put some kind of metric on them if you are to be able to trade off agility with short-term cost savings.

Note that while one cannot predict actual future events, it is often possible to anticipate *classes* of future events and estimate their relative

> **While one cannot predict actual future events, it is often possible to anticipate *classes* of future events.**

probability, based on prior history. For example, while one cannot predict that a security failure will occur – with all of its associated costs in lost customer confidence – one can nevertheless anticipate that certain classes of failure will occur, and project their likelihood over time given past history combined with industry statistics and knowledge of the organization's level of precautions. Similarly, while one cannot predict that the organization will decide to introduce a particular kind of new product within the next two years, one can look back at the history of the organization to see how often it has historically introduced new products, and use this as a benchmark for what is likely to occur in the future.

The method known as *Real Options Analysis* (ROA) is an analytical approach to addressing uncertainty and can be used to measure the value of agility. The real options method is explained more later, but a simpler approach that is usually adequate for our purposes is presented in the sections that follow.

It is not always necessary to estimate the quantitative value of agility: one often only needs to qualitatively estimate the relative agility afforded by various choices – and recognize when agility will be whittled away as a result of a particular choice. However, when making a business case that *trades off agility for other concerns,* such as cost, immediate opportunities, and risk, *one must assign a value to future agility:* otherwise, there is no basis for comparing various strategies that each produce a different mix of these attributes. The value metric, and the methodology for producing it, must have consensus across IT and the organization's other operating units. Otherwise it will not be trusted.

History can be a guide to the value of agility. For example, if your organization is a product company, and one looks at product plans from five years earlier, one can ask introspective questions such as, *Were there any times when we were not able to react as quickly as we would have liked, and what would have been the value of being able to react quickly?* Asking these kinds of questions can be used to establish a benchmark for the prior value of agility, and be a basis for reaching consensus on an educated guess for its future value.

Consensus is important, because estimating the value of agility is at best educated guesswork, but if such a measure is to be part of a business model that is used to by IT in proposals that compare the relative values of architecture features in IT plans, then the measure needs to have the credibility that only a consensus-based process can produce.

Modeling Risks: Making the Case for Risk Mitigation

In chapter 7 I present a way of measuring the business value of system features based on their contribution to reducing the risk of realizing a future business capability. In this section I want to discuss risk in general, including exogenous risks that require mitigation to some degree.

Risk is often addressed in initiative proposals by simply describing the risks. While this type of intangible approach at least provides for the identification of risks so that attention can be paid to them, it does not enable tradeoff analysis with respect to opportunity. After all, risks are sometimes worthwhile if the opportunity is great. Further, different organizations have different levels of risk tolerance, depending on the expected longevity of the organization and planning horizon of the organization – i.e., how impatient its investors are.

For many kinds of risk a mere identification of risk is appropriate, but for IT the risk of reliability-related failure and the risk of security-related failure need to be compared; otherwise one might spend too much on one and too little on another. Further, these need to be compared with other sources of risk so that tradeoffs can be made intelligently. More importantly, the tradeoffs need to be explicit so that the tradeoff criteria can be reapplied and adjusted if necessary as the situation evolves and as new proposals crop up.

The real question with risk management is how much to spend on mitigation, and is the expense such that the opportunity is not a good investment? One therefore needs to create a framework for determining the optimal amount to spend on mitigation for various levels of opportunity. Such a framework makes investment in risk management transparent just as other kinds of investment are.

A risk mitigation model also enables one to provide a credible estimate for the level of risk that the organization has and the investment required to attain it. This type of information would be strong supporting evidence in any type of audit situation. Rather than telling an auditor, "we are doing all we can to reduce our risk", one can say, "our risk will be X based on our investment in mitigation, according to our model that links that investment to the level of risk".

Creating such a framework is relatively straightforward. I have done it for reliability risk mitigation and for security risk mitigation. A detailed treatment is beyond the scope of this book, but I will provide a sketch. The basic approach is to model risk as a detractor from the *expected return* on an opportunity. The impact on the risk for various expenditures on mitigation must be plotted and a maximum found for the opportunity's expected value. That is, the expected value must subtract the cost of mitigation as well as the expected losses due to some risks coming true and optimized over the various possible levels of mitigation. Once the optimum is found it can be adjusted manually based on how risk-averse the organization is.

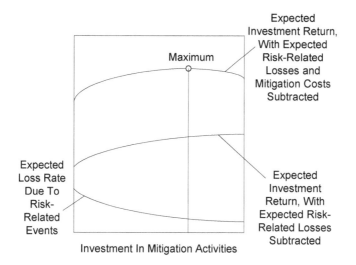

Expected
Investment Return,
With Expected
Risk-Related
Losses and
Mitigation Costs
Subtracted

Maximum

Expected
Loss Rate
Due To
Risk-
Related
Events

Expected
Investment
Return, With
Expected Risk-
Related Losses
Subtracted

Investment In Mitigation Activities

Figure 14: Plotting expected return of an investment opportunity with risk and mitigation included.

Figure 14 illustrates this technique. This figure provides a risk tradeoff analysis for a particular investment opportunity. In this figure the lowest curve plots the expected loss incurred as a result of risks coming true according to their expected rate of occurrence for various levels of expenditure toward the mitigation of those risks (including the zero level, which represents the inherent or baseline risk). The middle curve plots the expected return of the opportunity with the expected losses subtracted. The uppermost curve (offset to appear above the others for readability) also plots the expected return but subtracts both the expected losses and the cost of mitigation, providing a total picture of the investment. If the total amount of investment available is a fixed budgeted amount, then the uppermost curve must incorporate the fact that investment in mitigation subtracts from investment in the opportunity itself – i.e., safety costs money. In any case, the point of maximum on this curve indicates the point at which *the expected value of the total investment is maximized* as a function of spending on risk mitigation. If an organization is risk-averse, then the risk represented by the point of maximum might still be too high, and the organization may choose to reduce risk to a predetermined level or apply a weight that is an inverse function of risk.

The process of calculating these curves is pretty straightforward economic analysis and the basic process is illustrated in Figure 15.

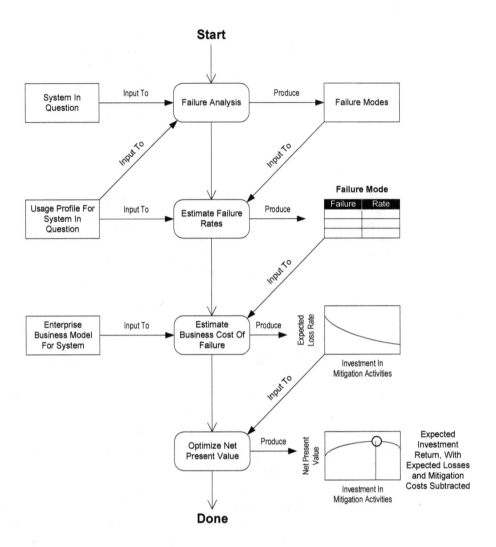

Figure 15: Combining failure mode analysis with value optimization to determine the required level of risk mitigation.

The challenge here is that risk must be quantified as an expected shareholder value[1] loss rate over time. In the figure, this is

---

[1] There are many approaches to estimating shareholder value. The intention here is to use an approach that is aligned with the intentions of the shareholders: if the intention is to liquidate the firm after a short-term rise in value (oil drilling ventures are often done this way), then value should be based on the liquidation value. If the intention is to hold shares for a protracted period and the firm is a public company, then value should be based on factors that affect the traded price of the company such as residual income from investments, reputation, debt ratio, and so on.

represented by the "Estimate Business Cost Of Failure" step. In doing so one must consider the various failure modes – the ways in which failure can occur – and their *tangible* impact on the business, including loss of brand value, loss of future business, and even losses due to litigation when risks occasionally come true.

Evaluate Strategies, Not Isolated Decisions

Traditional gap analysis presumes the existence of a definition of a future state, and evaluating a decision amounts to computing the ROI of that decision compared to a competing decision.

The dilemma is that, as has been pointed out earlier, one never arrives at the future state: the future is almost always different than the way you predict it will be. Therefore, what credibility does gap analysis have? And further, what legitimacy does the ROI analysis have if the future is so indeterminate?

A cornerstone concept of newer financial methodologies such as Real Options Analysis is that it makes no sense to compute ROI based on a particular future state: rather, one should assume a probabilistic distribution of future states. For example, rather than assuming that the actual market demand for a product will be some number X, project the expected distribution of the demand, with a mean and a standard distribution on the probability density. Thus, one might say that the expected demand will be X, with a standard deviation of 0.3 X.

With such uncertainty, it also does not make sense to predict that one will have certain choices to make in the future, and so a single decision today will be followed by choices that are unknown, all of which will impact the return resulting from the choice made today. In other words, projecting a return on today's decision is somewhat foolhearty, because events might occur that cause the organization to change direction and revise today's decision.

Instead, it makes sense to evaluate the return from a particular *strategy*, rather than a particular decision. Consider a situation in which IT wishes to compute the return from building flexibility into a new business system. IT might compute the return from that decision to be R, based on the assumption that that flexibility will actually be utilized in the future. However, it is likely that the future will bring more decisions, and those decisions might involve tradeoffs of flexibility versus expediency. What then is the return, over some period, of consistently choosing the more flexible choice, each time a decision of that kind presents itself?

That is, if one always chooses the more flexible path, will a series of decisions of that kind pay off eventually? That strategy of choosing flexibility has certain ROI characteristics, and to evaluate them one must model the generic choice of choosing flexibility, and evaluate what would happen as the scenario plays out again and again over time.

This approach is much more effective for modeling the value of many kinds of IT strategies, because many IT strategies have to do with preserving flexibility or maintainability, and the value of such a choice only accrues over time and over the course of many decisions. This approach is illustrated later in this chapter.

One aspect of modeling the value of a strategy is that the expected value of the business should accrue continuously. That is because if one pursues a strategy that has long-term tangible value, then at any point the expectation of realizing the long term value increases, and so the business systems for realizing that value are valued higher. It is as if you have planted a seed, and grown a fruit tree half way to the point of bearing fruit, and so the tree has market value ("economic value") because it *will* bear fruit, even though it is not yet bearing fruit, and as you nurture that tree and continue to invest in it, its expected value increases continuously.

Be Careful Not to Double-Count Benefits

Management, and portfolio boards in particular, often want to know the expected business benefit from each element of a plan, or each portfolio line item. Unfortunately, items are often inter-linked.

This is another reason why it is important to express the value of strategies, and not particular decisions. Interdependence of value is a good thing: it is a sign that efforts are inter-linked and working together. It means though, that a single element of a plan cannot claim the value of the plan. For example, assume that a new strategy involves creating a data management group, and to create that group, it is assumed that a data governance process will be established, and that the value of the better data quality that will result is $10M per year. When asked the value of the data management group, there is a tendency to say "$10M per year", and when asked the value of the data governance process, there is also a tendency to say "$10M per year". Management will then be confused and add these numbers and get $20M per year.

To be clear, rather than creating a large table of dependencies, it is better to express the *strategy* of data management, which requires subordinate investments in data governance, among other things, and give this strategy a value. When asked about individual elements of the plan, they do not have independent value, so do not give them one. If management says that you can only have some of the plan's elements but not all, due to funding constraints, then you have failed to give management the right choices. If the plan's elements are interdependent, the it is your job to present options that include a scaled down version of the plan, perhaps one that unfolds more slowly, but that still has the elements that it needs to succeed.

An Example

Let's look at a simple example to clarify all of this. Again, this book is not intended to be a text on economic analysis of IT projects, but the techniques presented here are only now finding their way into mainstream practices for IT, and so a short example is in order.

In this example the cost of money over time is omitted. This is a huge simplification because the cost of money is extremely relevant in a real analysis, but it is not relevant to the novel techniques that I am trying to explain.

Consider a situation in which an opportunity presents itself to implement and market a new service. The market opportunity is estimated to be at least $12, but the degree to which that can be realized depends on the level of investment, as shown in Table 12. The table does not include the downside: risks and the potential costs that they represent.

Table 12: Market opportunity realization as a function of investment in marketing.

Investment In Marketing	Expected Opportunity Value (Revenue – Direct Costs), Assuming No Failures
$1M	$6M
$2M	$11M
$3M	$14M
$4M	$15M
$10	$18M

From a risk perspective, the possible failures that are anticipated include: (a) some sales are returned due to defects; (b) financial injuries attributable to the service. These risks are summarized in Table 13.

Table 13: Failure modes, i.e., risks, and their expected long-term average cost.

Failure Type Name	Nature of Losses	Expected Cost To Enterprise Per Incident
A	Restitution to affected consumer customers.	$0.1M
B	Loss of reputation and future business. Potential loss of some commercial customers. Legal costs.	$50M

To reduce these risks, the following mitigation strategies considered: (1) a range of quality control measures; and (2) a range of intervention measures designed to avert financial injury to the consumer in most cases. If these strategies are implemented, the consequent expected rate of occurrence of each type of risk is summarized in Table 14. The mitigation strategies are assumed to be independent. If they were not, then Table 14 would need to list a set of technically viable scenarios that represent mixtures of investment in each mitigation strategy.

The total capital budget for the project is $10M, and so the investment in marketing and mitigation must be balanced and hopefully optimized.

Table 14: Expected failure rates for each risk type, for a given investment in mitigation strategies.

Failure Type	Mitigation Investment	Expected Failure Rate Over Planning Horizon	Incident Cost
A	$0	50 incidents	$.1Mx50=$5M
A	$1M	5 incidents	$0.5M
A	$2M	3 incidents	$0.3M
A	$10M	~0.01 incidents	$1K
B	$0	2 incidents	$100M
B	$1.5M	0.1 incidents	$5M
B	$2.1M	0.01 incidents	$0.5M
B	$10M	~.0001 incidents	$5K

Analysis

If we plot on a graph the expected revenue versus investment in marketing, and the expected losses as a function of investment in mitigation, we get the graphs shown in Figure 16.

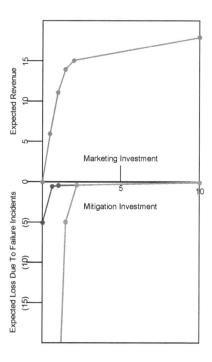

Figure 16: Revenue and losses as functions of investment in marketing and risk mitigation, respectively.

Clearly risk mitigation is important in this case: in the extreme scenario of no investment in mitigation, the potential loss to the company, due to lost future business across all product and service lines, runs way down off the graph, overwhelming any revenue from the sales of the new service. On the other hand, it would not make sense to invest the entire project budget in mitigation, since then there would be no point in investing! Clearly, investment in marketing and mitigation represent a zero-sum game, with an optimal mix of investment in marketing and mitigation somewhere in the middle.

It is worth noting that in most (but not all) organizations the decision on the mix of IT investment choices is made in a fairly ad-hoc manner: technical staff might be asked to present a couple of mitigation scenarios, or in many cases they are expected to figure this out on their own and submit a budget for development with appropriate mitigation implied. The problem with this approach is that in many cases the tradeoffs are not straightforward, and the business needs to be involved in deciding that tradeoff. To do this they need to know the business value of the various mitigation strategies, expressed in terms that they can understand, either in terms of dollars, or in terms of a risk scale that they understand and can related to priorities and ultimately dollars or enterprise value.

Finding the optimum mix of investments is of course an optimization problem and the most practical approach is often to simply define different scenarios and compare them. We are trying to maximize the present value of:

Revenue – Direct Costs – Incident Costs – Mitigation A Costs
    – Mitigation B Costs

where each term is an expected value, since we can only estimate each. Comparing scenarios is actually more practical in most cases, because usually mitigation strategies are interdependent. This is especially true in the security realm, where a particular strategy might serve to mitigate more than one type of risk. Thus, we end up with a table of investment mixes and their expected costs and revenue, and plotting the formula above results in a graph something like Figure 14.

266

Analyses Of Risk And Opportunity Should Be Integrated

In chapter 4 I refer to a poll taken by the Northern Virginia Java User's Group (NovaJUG) to assess how widespread risk management practices are in Java software projects (see page 49). One of the more astute members of the NovaJUG responded to the survey with an anecdote about how he has practiced risk management in prior projects. According to him,

> *"...we would come up with a risk, write it down, then rank on a scale of 1-10 the impact it would have on the project and a likelihood it would happen. We would multiply these together, rank them all, and make sure we had some kind of mitigation strategy (to prevent it from happening), or plan B, if it did happen."*

In other words, he used an approach that modeled risk according to the product of the probability of failure and the cost of failure, and then used this result to rank (prioritize) efforts to devise and implement mitigation strategies.

This is indeed a viable approach to modeling risk for the purpose of ranking. One sometimes only needs to rank risk to determine where next to invest effort in mitigation. However, this approach is inadequate if one must trade off the business value of mitigation against the business value of adding additional features.

For this reason it is important that risk and business value models are integrated. The drivers for accounting-related risk mitigation are often auditor-related but they should nevertheless not be dealt with independently. That said, organizations often need to have a focused risk mitigation effort in order to get through an auditor-related crisis, since auditors might not appreciate that accounting accuracy is not the company's only concern. Therefore, achieving integration between risk and value management are a great challenge. On the other hand, auditors are primarily concerns with accuracy, and accuracy is the friend of both risk and value management.

This means that risk management needs to work with the business and explain the framework to auditors. Transparency is key. Further, risk and value both need to be incorporated into architectural analysis in order to make the architectural analysis "real". If this is done, it will be clear that accuracy is a way to achieve business goals related to both risk and value, since accuracy leads to better measurement and therefore better business choices.

Triage First

When planning a risk management strategy, the best approach is to start with a two-pronged approach that includes "triage" of existing known sources of risk, and develop in parallel a business value-driven maturity framework that incorporates both risk and business value into planning. Maturity considerations are discussed further on page 289.

I have used the triage approach many times to relieve a crisis. A crisis presents an opportunity to explain root causes when attention is on an issue. For example, in the case of the Guru-Run Technology Provider, it was a crisis that precipitated my involvement in addressing reliability problems with the system, and while the root causes were clearly systemic, it was critical to maintain the confidence that the customer had in the contractor and get the system into a state in which it was recovering automatically from failure and not losing transactions.

One should leverage the attention that a crisis brings to establish expectations and consensus about the business value model for a long-term strategy that addresses the root causes. Once the immediate concerns are alleviated through the triage interest will fade, but the business value model can be used for future proposals and it will be understood. Risk triage solutions are not durable and do not enable agility, maintainability, or transparency, and so the business value model for elevating maturity must focus on those aspects. We did this for the Guru-Run Technology Provider, and I recently followed up with this project and learned that the system ended up being re-written from scratch using an entirely different set of technologies and with much more attention to reliability from the outset.

Features That Have No Independent Business Value

New features can always be developed for automated systems. However, as explained in the section Forget The "End State": Design A Capability For Evolving The Current State In The Right Direction (page 82), automated systems are not by themselves business capabilities, and a *business capability* cannot be claimed to have been created until it is demonstrable. This is because the IT components of a capability are merely the automation aspects of a capability and by themselves are useless. One could therefore make an argument that the only IT features that have independent tangible business value all by themselves are those that can be immediately deployed with no user training.

In the section Measure Future Value At Risk (page 137) I explained how one can decouple the values of interrelated features of a system and relate them to the overall value of a business capability. The justification for adding a feature that has no independent business value is to invest in the opportunity to build toward a future capability. I will refer to such features with no independent value as *precursor features* because they are precursors to the completion of a complete capability that has tangible business value. (In Figure 8 on page 141, feature set A represents a precursor features with respect to the business capability.) Having "tangible business value" means that the business value is represented in some manner in a model that has the consensus of executives.

> ## A business capability cannot be claimed to have been implemented until it is operational.

Precursor features represent partial progress toward a business capability. The progress is real, but it has no usefulness to the business. Progress on such features are analogous to the progress that one makes when one tears down barriers that stand in the way of a goal. The barriers are not themselves part of the goal, but removing them is nevertheless progress.

Unlike a precursor feature, a business capability cannot be claimed to have been developed until it is operational. That is, the business processes – human and automated – that implement the capability must be up to speed and running. The hardest part of creating a

269

new capability is the last "five percent" – which can turn out to be 50% – and a good part of that last percent is the work involved in elevating the skills and understanding of the staff and building a shared understanding of how things will work at all levels. Setting the bar of what constitutes a true capability therefore must include these cross-the-finish-line efforts to ensure that metrics for progress are not misleading.

Estimating the Value Of Precursor Features

Precursor features have no independent business value, but demonstration of progress can be in terms of a technical test suite that includes certification for compliance with all enterprise concerns. For features that have actual end-user functionality, the demonstration should be both in terms of a test suite and also in terms of end-user acceptance.

> # Precursor tasks that have no independent business value nevertheless increase the *expected value* of the end state.

Any future capability is tentative and represents risk in terms of the following factors:

1. The successful completion of the capability; and
2. The validity and success of the value proposition of the capability, which is merely theoretical until the capability is put into use. I.e., do forecasts of upcoming opportunities pan out?[1]

Precursor features or tasks are an investment in a planned future capability. Once completed, such features or tasks represent increased progress toward the planned capability but do not represent capabilities themselves. As such, they represent value because this progress has value. The value of this progress derives from the following elements:

1. Reduced risk in realizing the opportunity, and
2. Reduced remaining investment is less for completing a capability.

---

[1] This is sometimes referred to as the "option value of investment".

Risk is reduced because the feature represents successfully completed work toward the intended capability. The completion of this work eliminates the risk that the work might not be completed or that it might not work – that is why capabilities cannot be considered to be complete until they are demonstrable. The second element, reduced remaining investment, results from the fact that the work required to complete the capability has been reduced as a result of the completion of the feature. Thus, the value of the feature does not derive from the effort put into it: rather, it derives from the fact that the business case calculated after the feature has been completed is better than the business case calculated before the feature was completed.

The reduced risk (element 1 above) should directly increase the *expected value* of the planned future capability that the feature is an element of. Since any future capability is tentative and represents risk in terms of the successful completion of the capability, any progress toward completing the capability represents reduced risk and therefore increases the expected value of the capability. This is a purely probabilistic effect.[1]

The reduced remaining investment (element 2 above) means that the investment required to complete the capability is now less since the feature has been completed and tested. This progress results in a new, improved business case from this point onward: one should calculate the work required to complete the capability, and compare that work with the work that had been estimated before the feature was developed. The change represents the reduction in planned investment, given that the feature has been successfully developed.

You might wonder, what about the actual effort that was put into developing the feature?[2] Unfortunately, that is not relevant to calculating the *value* of the feature. The feature might have been implemented in a very efficient and timely way, and that efficiency has value because it reduces the cost of capability development. However, the cost of the feature needs to be accounted for in terms of the actual investment in the capability. *It is not part of the*

---

[1] For more discussion of this type of analysis, see [McAfeePr06], §4.3.3, Investment Under Uncertainty.

[2] The amount already invested is often referred to as the "sunk cost" – that is, the amount that has already been sunk into the project.

feature's value. Rather, it is what is known as a "sunk" cost – money spent and gone forever.

Let's briefly consider a simple example. Suppose that a capability will require several features, and before a feature is developed, the project manager estimates that the work required to complete the full *capability* is ten person-weeks. Work on the first feature is begun, and the feature is completed in one person-week. The project manager then estimates that the work required to complete the capability with the new feature incorporated will be seven person-weeks. Thus, the project has moved ahead by three person-weeks as a result of the new feature; yet, only one person-week was invested. The fact that one person week was invested has no bearing on how much time or effort remains in the project: all that matters is what will be required to complete the project, irrespective of how much effort has already been invested – wisely or otherwise. The work put into the feature is an investment, not a value.

To summarize, the value received after adding a precursor feature is therefore:

1. The increase in the expected value of the opportunity (due to reduced risk of completion), *plus*
2. The reduction in the remaining investment as a result of the existence of the added feature.

The threats that exist include (1) that the value proposition is miscalculated; and that (2) the project might not complete as planned.

The expected value E(V) of a capability is the expected value of the opportunity (O), adjusted for the risk (R) of failing to realize the opportunity, minus the investment cost. (One can also add to R other risks or possible costs that are of concern.) The risk of failing to realize the opportunity is primarily impacted by the risk of failing to complete the project successfully. This, it essentially represents the development risk, in terms of the potential lost opportunity.

In mathematical terms,[1]

$$E(V) \quad = \quad E(O) - E(R) - E(C)$$

Let's then consider a situation in which we are building a capability, a feature at a time, and we wish to calculate the value of a particular feature. At iteration 1 the expected value of the system (incomplete capability) is:

$$E(V1) \quad = E(O) - E(R1) - E(C1)$$

and at iteration, after another feature has been completed, two its value is

$$E(V2) \quad = E(O) - E(R2) - E(C2)$$

The change in value as a result of the addition of the single feature is the difference between these:[2]

$$\Delta E(V) \quad = E(O) - E(R2) - E(C2) - [E(O) - E(R1) - E(C1)]$$

$$= -\Delta E(R) - \Delta E(C)$$

where

$\Delta E(R)$ is the change in the expected risk in completing the capability. The change period is over the time that it takes to develop the feature. Since this change should be negative (corresponding to a decrease in risk), $-\Delta E(R)$ should be positive.

$\Delta E(C)$ is the change in the expected cost to complete and deploy the capability once the feature has been completed and integrated. Since this change should be negative (corresponding to a decrease in risk), $-\Delta E(C)$ should also be positive.

---

[1] Cost of money considerations – i.e., present value adjustments – are not included here for simplicity.

[2] We are assuming that the estimate of the business opportunity value does not change.

Both terms on the right should be positive, resulting in a net positive value for the new feature.

This situation is illustrated in Figure 17, which is based on Figure 13. In Figure 17 I have added the estimates given by IT for completion of a project at the start of the project and at the end of each of three periods of work. For example, at the start of the project IT estimated a cost of completion of $3 million (considerably less than the actual final cost of $4 million). At the end of period 3 the cost of completion from that point was estimated to be 0.9 million. (The cost-to-complete estimates made at various points during the project are shown as a thin gray line, and these points apply only to the monetary scale on the right side of the graph.)

Since in this example the actual cost did not track the projected cost, the value proposition for the project changed over time. This is shown by the thick gray line, which plots the expected business value (the expected market value minus the cost of completion). Progress from one work period to the next is simply the change in the height of the thick gray curve.

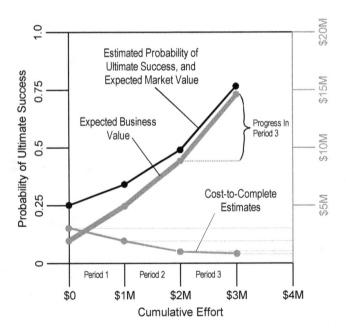

Figure 17: Expected business value changes throughout a project, and progress should be measured by the change in expected business value.

274

This approach provides a powerful instrument for projects that utilize agile development methods. In such projects, customers are allowed – encouraged – to reconsider requirements throughout a project. In that way the risk of building the "wrong system" is reduced. However, that risk is somewhat offset by the risk of constantly changing the system and getting nowhere – at great cost. A value-based analysis will show you clearly when you are spinning your wheels, because when earlier work is changed or discarded, your progress is slowed. Thus, instead of focusing only on cost and budget, one also looks at how close you are to creating real value.

It is important to note that progress is completely independent of the amount of money spent on work already done. Money spent this way is a sunk cost: it is irretrievable. Money spent on capital assets can often be retrieved, and that must be accounted for, but I will ignore that to keep things simple here.

It is also important to note that progress is not equivalent to a running ROI. An ROI can only be calculated once a capability is in operation and generating returns. An ROI calculation is a retrospective calculation, that is a function of the total amount of money spent. One could calculate a running projected ROI as a system is built, but that would be a different calculation. (See if you can derive the formula.)

Of course, in a real analysis, the time value of money should be accounted for by using time-discounted present values instead of fixed values, but I have ignored that to keep things simple and make my points. It is an important consideration however, because some kind of internal rate of return should be used to assess whether a project's value continues to justify that it continue: as the expected value fluctuates, it should be compared with the expected total investment over the time period. These detailed refinements are beyond the scope of this book, and indeed they are usually not significant for the time scales and large uncertainties that IT deals with, but I think you get the point.

There is one way in which it impacts work though: it is important to eliminate show-stopper obstacles early in a project, because doing so increases the slope of the risk curve early. In this way, project managers have more information early about whether to continue a project. In the aggregate over many projects, they must be able to decide which to continue and which to not, and getting onto the steep part of the risk curve early provides them with this information before making a large investment. Thus, from a *portfolio management perspective*, one should endeavor move forward (sooner) in time any tasks that will increase the probability of eventual success. This is common sense to a large degree, and it is consistent with the analysis here.

The question arises as to how one should estimate the probability of success. It might seem that this is a highly subjective measure, but it is important that your own subjectivity be removed from this calculation. The challenge – as with projecting costs – is to be as honest as possible. This is best achieved by compiling statistics on similar efforts within the organization and a set of criteria for predicting future success likelihood – i.e., a model. You can also ask "experts" to make educated guesses, as long as you calibrate those in some way against actual data (perhaps anecdotal) or an independent source. This is not rocket science: we are talking about a spreadsheet of estimates.

Another way of looking at project progress is based on the original estimated cost of features. Going back to our formulas, if we isolate our analysis to only the work done on a feature and ignore work done on other features, then our estimate for completion should be our original estimate with the estimated cost of the feature subtracted out:

$$E(C2) \quad = E(C1) - C_{f,est}$$

$C_{f,est}$ is the prior estimate for completing the feature.

We can substitute this in our equation as follows:

$$\Delta E(V) \quad = O - E(R2) - E(C2) - (O - E(R1) - E(C1))$$

$$= - E(R2) - (E(C1) - C_{f,est}) + E(R1) + E(C1)$$

$$= - E(R2) + C_{f,est} + E(R1)$$

$$= - \Delta E(R) + C_{f,est}$$

In other words, once a feature has been completed and integrated, its value to you is equal to the reduction in risk plus the original cost estimate for the feature.

If the feature is completed *exactly on-budget*, then the original cost estimate was accurate, and then – and only then – can actual cost be used in lieu of estimated cost as a component of the measure of a feature's value.

Adjusting For Concurrent Progress On Other Features

In real software systems it is usually more complicated than this. In particular, it is usually the case that some features cannot be tested unless other features are also built and in a testable state. Inter-dependence of features is illustrated in Figure 8 on page 141.

This fact of life complicates value measurement because it means that feature values are not independent. To deal with this, one can refrain from attempting to estimate the individual value of such closely related features and instead estimate the value of the entire set of features that must be built and tested together. The entire feature set then has a value, but the value of each feature in the set has an undeterminable value. One should not attempt to measure the value of such granular features anyway: time would be better spent on helping the team to actually build the features and verify them.

Liquidation Value

It might occur to you that if precursor features have no independent business value, then why is it that one often can sell the code of an incomplete system? I myself have seen this done. When an incomplete, non-operational system is sold, it is *liquidated*.

When one buys a system or some of its components in a liquidation sale, the value that one receives depends on the intended application of those components. The components obtained reduce the risk and cost of building the business capability that the buyer envisions. Therefore, when I say that a precursor feature has no *independent* business value, what I mean is that it has no operational value by itself. That does not mean that it does not have market value (economic value), and that value is based on the extent to which it reduces the risk and cost of completing a capability that the buyer needs.

It follows then that the liquidity of a feature has a lot to do with its value. That is, if a feature's code can be sold independently, then its value can be estimated fairly accurately, based on what people are willing to pay. Features with minimal operational business value tend to be fairly non-liquid and sell for a low price – if at all – while those with clear independent business value tend to be saleable and therefore (by definition) liquid. The price and liquidity difference reflect the difference in risk with respect to the actual value of the feature. Thus, one can view the distinction between a demonstrable capability (a completed "Minimum Marketable Feature") and a feature with no independent operational value as merely a difference of liquidity.

Modeling the Value of Continuity: Making the Case to See a Strategy Through

IT is famously beholden to organizational changes that occur outside of it or above it and that lead to sweeping changes in IT strategy – without the input of IT. Consider for example, the hiring of a new CIO, the decision to cancel a project that has just begun to bear fruit, and a merger with another company and consequent consolidation of IT activities: all of these kinds of changes usually have a massive impact on IT's ability to realize value on its prior investments, yet it usually has little say about these "strategic" decisions, even though the impact of IT affects the organization's ability to realize value.

There is an opportunity cost to abandoning strategies before they have completed. This cost is the expected value of the partially completed capabilities, minus the expected value of those partial capabilities when applied to the new strategy of the organization. That is, it is the liquidation value in the context of the new strategy.

Firms usually see unfinished investments as sunk costs and therefore irretrievable. To confuse things more, the accounting value of unfinished business capabilities is zero, because those partial capabilities are not usually assigned a market resale value, and since they are not generating revenue, they have no tangible value. Executives therefore often conclude that there is no harm in "starting over" at any point, when in fact to abandon a strategy is to discard the economic value of the partial capabilities.

Of course, this might make sense if there is reason to believe that the capabilities will not actually realize value: that is, if the expected value of the investment has dropped to the point where it is no longer a worthwhile investment, even given the work that has been accomplished.

Another factor that often confuses matters is a failure to value the investment in human knowledge. I have seem hundred million dollars projects cancelled because executives lost confidence in the cost and benefit balance of an effort that was finally starting to succeed: just as staff had got traction in delivering true capabilities, the plug was pulled because a strict analysis, at that point, of the cost and benefit showed an imbalance. However, my own assessment was that substantial value would have been delivered – a value well worth the investment – if management had placed a value on the knowledge and consensus of approach that had been developed among the hundreds of staff.

It is critical that IT have concrete arguments when trying to make the case to stay the course. Often the drivers are political and therefore very difficult to challenge. However, it is in the organization's best interests to present an honest case that assesses the value of each option, and that includes the lost opportunity costs of abandoning projects.

Another Example

Suppose a company called Gigantic E-Commerce[1] wishes to add a capability to allow business partners to market their own products through Gigantic's website. The benefit to Gigantic is that it will receive a percentage of each sale. Gigantic estimates the expected business opportunity to be $25M over three years.

In order to make this capability available to partners and customers several features must be added to Gigantic's systems and business processes.

Gigantic divides the overall capability into two distinct feature sets: (A) the Partner Interface component set; (B) the customer

---

[1] This company name is fictitious. Any similarity between this name and the name of any actual company is purely coincidental.

interface enhancements, and (C) modifications to the back-end database-related components. Each of these feature sets involves a substantial amount of work, but neither provides business value on its own: value is only realized when both features sets have been integrated and deployed as a new business capability.

Gigantic decides to use an agile, incremental development process in order to design and implement this new capability. Toward that end, Gigantic needs to develop a model for estimating a reasonable theoretical business value for each feature as it is developed. Otherwise it has no way to assess progress. Gigantic has learned that assessing progress based on which tasks have been completed does not provide sufficient incentive for teams to be inventive with respect to how they accomplish goals. Project plans must be fluid and adaptable, especially since Gigantic expects to work with prospective partners who might request for modifications to the features as they are being built. Therefore, a value-centric planning approach is critical to assessing progress toward the end goal.

Gigantic decides to first implement feature sets A and B, and then use these to solicit detailed feedback from customer service and from partners. This feedback will perhaps be used to fine-tune the feature sets. During this period work will proceed in parallel with feature set C, but feature set C will likely not complete until after feature sets A and B have been completed.

At the beginning of work, Gigantic estimates that feature set A will require about $1M to complete, and feature set B will require about $2M to complete. These are shown in the "Prior Expected Cost To Complete Feature" column in Table 15.

Gigantic also knows based on past experience that these efforts sometimes go nowhere, either because objectives change or because of technology problems. It therefore estimates that there is a 10% chance that feature set A will not succeed, causing the entire initiative to fail and eliminating the business opportunity. This 10% translates into a $2.5M risk for the opportunity, as well $1M for work on the feature set which will have been wasted. In fact, all prior work on the capability would have been wasted, but that risk will cancel out since we are estimating incremental risk for each feature.

A similar analysis for feature set B leads Gigantic to conclude that there is a 10% risk for feature set B, translating into another $2.5M plus $2M in costs. These risks are shown in the column "Prior Expected Risk To Complete Capability" in Table 15.

Gigantic then completes work on features sets A and B, with work proceeding along on feature set C. Gigantic is fortunate that partners have provided feedback indicating that no changes are needed to these feature sets, and so the work on them is considered to be completed. Gigantic's progress can be summarized by the column "Value Of Feature" in Table 15: the risk associated with each feature has been eliminated because they have been completed successfully, and the value of each feature set can be estimated by summing the risk that has been mitigated and the prior expected cost. The total value of feature sets A and B are shown in the last column and are seen to be $11M, and this value results from the reduction in risk to the opportunity as well as the value of the work done.

The actual build costs can be used to compute a theoretical ROI for each feature, based on the feature values. The build cost should include the cost to integrate and fully test the feature set.

Table 15: Example of estimation of theoretical feature value

Features Completed This Past Cycle	Prior Expected Risk To Complete Capability	Prior Expected Cost To Complete Feature	Actual Build Cost Of Feature	Value Of Feature
Feature Set A	3.5M	1M	.8M	4.5M
Feature Set B	4.5M	2M	2.4M	6.5M
Combined Feature Sets	8M	3M	3.2M	11M

It is important to understand that these feature values are only theoretical. In reality, a feature has no value by itself: only capabilities have value – by my definitions. A feature should not be treated as a tangible asset, because it is unproven. Capabilities are tangible assets: they have measurable business value. A feature is by itself an unrealized investment. If you need to estimate a liquidation value for the feature, as is the case when a company sells the IP assets for a product that has not been completed, the feature should be packaged and proven sufficiently to establish a tangible value for it.

The values calculated here for features are only for the purpose of tracking incremental progress in a manner that is as realistic as possible.

Relationship To Earned Value

The Earned Value Management System[1] (EVMS) is mandated for many US Federal Government agencies, according to US Office of Management and Budget (OMB) policy – the same entity that oversees the Federal Enterprise Architecture (FEA) standards. The National Institutes of Standards and Technologies (NIST) provides a EVMS standard that can be purchased online.

EVMS relies heavily on the ability to define objective metrics for assessing progress. However, EVMS determines value based on the planned cost. In essence, the value of a component is determined by the prior estimated cost of work required to meet certain measurable milestones such as demonstrating that components have passed their acceptance tests. This is a poor way to measure value, because it cost bears little relationship to business value, especially if one is trying to measure the value of features that do not have their own independent business value. In fact, very often the most expensive components are those that add the least business value. Instead, one must take account of the risk to the value of the ultimate planned business capability. Only then can one say that effort is valued in accordance with expected business value. EVMS is more about holding contractors on large projects to the plan rather than about measuring actual value, and that is why EVMS is used for large government projects. The business sector requires more focus on actual value, and the ability to modify the plan midstream is much more important than holding a vendor to a plan.

---

[1] EVMS is defined by ANSI standard ANSI/EIA-748-A-1998 (R2002). A tutorial can be found at https://acc.dau.mil/evm.

Relationship To Total Value of Ownership

In recent years the concept of Total Value of Ownership (TVO) has taken root.[1] The TVO idea is designed to contrast with the concept of Total Cost of Ownership (TCO) which focuses on the complete lifecycle cost of IT systems (or any systems for that matter). Since a failure to realize value can be seen as an economic cost, the shortcomings with TCO are more in how TCO has been applied than in the concept itself. Thus, TVO does not really add anything new except for a renewed emphasis on business value.

TVO is new enough that one cannot say much about how it has been implemented, but early reports seem to focus on the impact of IT systems on revenue. This is an important element, but one also needs to consider the impact of decisions on risk, and the impact that risk mitigation has on expected value.

Comparing Alternative Implementation Strategies

IT decisions often involve alternatives that boil down to "build it the 'right' way" or "build it the cheapest way". The most sensible choice depends on the balanced business impact over the timeframes that are of concern. However, the business impact of IT improvements can often be boiled down to lifecycle cost – assuming that one truly includes the full lifecycle for the IT system within the organization and the impact (perhaps many years later) on other initiatives during that timeframe. In other words, one should consider the impact on future agility and evaluate the importance of that with respect to other more immediate concerns.

To do this analysis one must define the alternatives, and then one must consider the various hypothetical future scenarios that can be expected to evolve and how costs and agility would be affected. As a simple example, consider an organization that has two systems called A and B, as shown in Figure 18.

---

[1] Ref. [Luftman05].

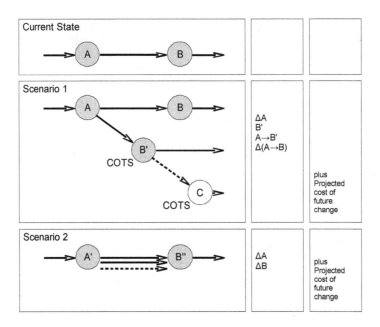

Figure 18: Example of computing lifecycle cost for alternatives.

In this example, a business unit in the organization would like to add a "commercial off-the-shelf" (COTS) system B' as shown in scenario 1. The COTS system would allow them to handle a new class of business, thereby tapping a new market. This represents a substantial opportunity for the organization in many tangible and intangible ways.

The technology-savvy members of the organization point out that the logical function of the COTS system is the same as the existing system B. The difference is that the COTS system incorporates some business rules that the existing System B does not. However they acknowledge that it would take awhile to enhance B to incorporate those new business rules, and that buying the COTS system might be a shorter path to market.

The dilemma is that adding the COTS system complicates the architecture of the enterprise: the organization would then have two systems that do similar things, and each with a very different architecture and methods of maintenance and integration. Further, if new rules must be added to B in the future, it is likely that those same rules will have to be added somehow to the COTS system, perhaps by asking the vendor of the system to add them or by adding a pre-processing or post-processing system in front of or after the COTS system. The technology-savvy folks are very concerned about the prospect of growing complexity.

The business side does not understand these arguments, because "complex" does not mean anything in business terms. So what if it is complex? Isn't everything complex anyway? The tech-savvy folks respond, "but complex means greater lifecycle cost." The business folks respond to that by saying, "Show me: otherwise I cannot evaluate that in terms that I understand; and further, give me an alternative, since not going after the new business is not an option."

The tech-savvy folks then have two tasks before them: (1) to devise a reasonable alternative, and to (2) show that the alternative is superior when one includes the combined impact of future business and total future lifecycle cost impact, *including the expected impact on the ability to capitalize on future business opportunities* (for example future ideas for new products or partnerships) that have yet to reveal themselves but that will surely come along.

This is a tall order, but the tech-savvy folks work in a very progressive capability-focused organization that has developed techniques for modeling these things, and they are respected by the business for that reason; so they devise scenario 2 as shown in Figure 18. Further, they hypothesize that once either scenario has been put in place, that there will be a new, as-yet unforeseen business opportunity, and that the impact for scenario 1 will be to require yet another COTS system C to be installed in parallel to the earlier one (B'). The impact for scenario 2, which assumes a strategy of enhancing System B, will be to enhance B again, as shown.

Thus, in Figure 18 the dotted lines represent hypothetical unforeseen business needs, and the way that the need is addressed in scenario 1 is different from the way that it is addressed in scenario 2 because each scenario assumes a different strategy: scenario 1 assumes a strategy of adding specialized systems, whereas scenario 2 assumes a strategy of extending and refactoring existing systems. These scenarios can be compared in general cost terms. **The hypothetical future scenario with the lower cost indicates the more agile strategy, since cost translates into effort**. The value of the enhanced agility can be taken to be the anticipated value of the hypothetical future opportunity, reduced by the cost and risk of realizing it. As we know, increased agility means reduced risk, time to respond, and cost for capitalizing on new opportunities.

This is a very simple example – a trivial one at that. Real business computing environments usually have a multitude of interconnected systems, and the interconnections represent enormous investments; more interconnections in the future represent even more investment and disentangling those interconnections can be an effort that escalates geometrically with the number of interconnections. To truly compare future scenarios one must define a model scenario that is representative of the systems and kinds of interconnections that are in place. This process is not too different from the practice of threat analysis employed in the security profession. The situation there is that instead of threats, we want to identify possible future events and outcomes.

If one is ambitious, one can even build a simulation model of these outcomes, estimate the probabilities of various events, and then run the simulation to see how the events combine over time to yield various overall outcomes. The frequencies of these simulated outcomes are in effect probabilities, and these probabilities can be used to estimate the expected value of alternative strategies today, since the choice of strategy will influence the outcome. This sophisticated approach is used routinely by the investment community. For enterprise architecture analysis, it is usually sufficient to merely identify the relevant future events, such as new product introduction and market changes, and project future technical outcomes by hand.

Relationship To Real Options Analysis

The Real Options Analysis (ROA) financial valuation methodology, mentioned briefly previously, is a class of analytical methods for comparing alternatives that have uncertain outcomes.[1] The ROA approach applies investment present value

---

[1] For general information on the Real Options methodology, see [DixPin94] and [Copeland03].

principles in a probabilistic context.[1] The fact that IT investments can be modified over time is taken into account, generally by allowing for a set of "options" such as (a) abandoning the original investment, (b) increasing the rate of investment, and (c) deferring a decision until events indicate which course of action is better.

ROA originates from the concept of extending the techniques of financial option analysis to other domain. These techniques are based on the famous Black-Scholes model and formula. Financial options are purchasable contracts that allow the buyer to either buy (a "call" option) or sell (a "put" option) a financial instrument for a pre-agreed price (the "strike" price) at some point in the future. However, when applying the option purchase analogy to IT, it is as if one had a financial option for which the stike price is uncertain and the option price is uncertain, since with IT investments one does not know with certainty either the eventual tangible value that will be realized from the investment, nor does one know the investment cost with certainty until the project has completed. These uncertainties make the strict application of options analysis somewhat limited, and in practice more general approaches are needed that account for the many uncertainties. However, the very idea of treating investment as a probabilistic endeavor was a breakthrough in thinking.

As of this writing the ROA approach is not yet widely used in IT, but it is used extensively in businesses that have very large capital investment decisions such as the oil drilling, biotechnology, and telecommunications. However, some have attempted to apply it to IT [2], and its use is definitely on the rise.

One of the challenges in applying a Real Options approach is that one must estimate the opportunity value of various courses of action: that is, one must estimate the probabilities of future outcomes and their up-side and downside values. This is the problem that we ran into above when trying to put a number on the value of unforeseen future opportunities. Thus, that is the

---

[1] To an economist this statement may sound contradictory, since Real Options Analysis (ROA) is viewed as a generalized method of which Net Present Value (NPV) is a special case; however, the phrasing here is meant to introduce the concept to readers who do not have a background in financial analysis.

[2] Ref. [Kazman01].

central challenge. In some circumstances it is worthwhile to utilize stochastic simulation of future events to see which general outcomes are the most likely. This approach is widely used in the securities industry to project the value of different investments given that interest rates and other indicators might follow various paths of varying likelihood; but in the end it is still an *educated* guess. In the next section I discuss stochastic analysis and its applicability to IT strategy value analysis in more detail.

Within the context of a software development initiative, some of the options include continuing or canceling projects, as well as intervening in projects to improve (hopefully) their progress. In the context of a single project, options include how to implement the software: that is, architectural decisions. These decisions impact the future capabilities, agility, and cost structure of the organization. Therefore, future events are important determinants of whether the choices made turn out to be good ones. The kind of scenario analysis described in the prior section is a useful tool for considering what the possibilities might be. In order to evaluate the expected risk and opportunity values of these possible future outcomes for a given architectural choice, one must determine probabilities for these outcomes. This is the essence of Real Options Analysis. Statistical simulation, known as "stochastic analysis", is a tool that is used in many industries for this kind of problem, but as a starting point one at least needs to define the future scenarios. As the organization becomes more experienced in applying this kind of analysis with IT projects, it can start to consider simulation and the more advanced methods used for ROA.

> **The future cost of abandoning work is not merely the lost investment: it includes the costs of *disentangling* what was built.**

When it comes to IT it is important to consider that when one chooses an option to build an expedient solution that violates an architecture, *the future cost of abandoning that decision is not merely the lost investment: it must include the costs of disentangling what was built.* For systems that have been in use for awhile and which have been interconnected to other systems, this cost can be very substantial. See the discussion in the section beginning on page 405. Thus, the cost of abandoning a project may extend beyond the sunk costs and lost opportunity value.

Another important lesson from Real Options Analysis is that there is inherent value in the flexibility to postpone a decision. That is, one can increase one's chance of success by postponing certain decisions (e.g., whether to abandon a project), and this value is tangible. The rationale is that if one waits to decide, one will have more information available and therefore make a better decision. The flip side is that there is a cost also in postponing certain decisions, in particular if work is proceeding in a direction that might be the wrong direction. Modeling these competing risks is the challenge.

Stochastic Analysis

Stochastic analysis is becoming more prevalent as a tool for estimating the business value of decisions and strategies. The basic approach is simple: try to conceive of everything relevant that might happen that will impact your business plan and strategy, and model those events as event trees; then estimate probability distributions for the events, and simulate the scenario a large number of times. The distribution of outcomes that result from the simulation are then used as the basis for computing the value of the strategy. You can repeat this process for various alternative strategies, and then compare the outcome distributions that result.

The event modeling portion of this approach is somewhat analogous to security threat modeling. In threat modeling you try to envision every way that someone might attack a system, and estimate the approaches that are most likely to succeed. Threat modeling tends to stop there, because the purpose of threat modeling is to identify weaknesses and then fix them. However, in some cases it is not possible to fix a weakness right away, and so it is necessary to evaluate the risk posed by the weakness, and the cost-benefit of mitigating the risk. Simulation can be used to model that, if one assumes a probability distribution for the success of an attack, for a given mitigation strategy.

Let's consider an example. Figure 19 illustrates a simple event model for security risk mitigation.

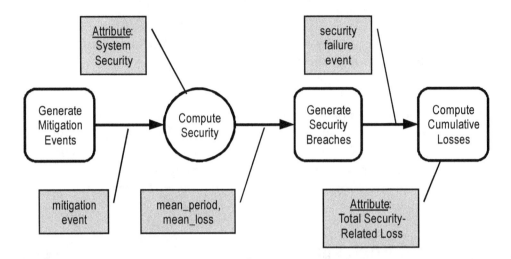

Figure 19: A simple event model for security risk mitigation.

The purpose of the model in Figure 19 is to identify the things that can happen in the lifecycle of a system, for which there is known to be a security risk. It is assumed that the organization wishes to evaluate the return from different levels of investment in risk mitigation, such as better firewalls, more analysis of application code, etc.

The first rounded box, "Generate Mitigation Events", represents the deployment of practices that reduce security risk. For example, if the organization deploys a new application-level firewall, this might greatly reduce the risk of an entire class of threats. Such a deployment would be an event in the model. The "Generate Mitigation Events" box produces such events according to a distribution over time, and each event carries with it parameters that characterize the impact on overall security.

The bubble "Compute Security" is merely a function that reads the mitigation events and calculates the net security level for the organization, according to some scale. This security level is then input to the box "Generate Security Breaches", which uses the security level as a parameter in its distribution of events that it generates. Each of the events generated by the "Generate Security Breaches" box represents an actual security failure, such as a successful hack, or a loss of data due to theft.

290

The events produced by the "Generate Security Breaches" box are received by the "Compute Cumulative Losses" box, which tallies all of the security failures that occur, along with the value of loss, to produce a total loss over a simulated period of time. This total loss can be compared with the size of investment in the mitigations. Further, by tweaking the parameters of the "Generate Mitigation Events" box, one can compare various mitigation strategies, such as whether investing in firewalls is better than investing in application threat analysis. Of course, the old adage "garbage in, garbage out" applies, and the model is no better than the assumptions embedded in each box; but at least the assumptions are explicit and can be examined and discussed, and the results compared with experience, until confidence in the model is achieved.

There is also the complexity of selecting probability distributions for the event generators (the rounded boxes). The distributions can often be estimated based on historical information. For example, if one needs to estimate the magnitude of impact on security as a result of using a certain type of mitigation, there are industry numbers for the effectiveness of different kinds of security, and the organization's historical rate of security attacks can be used to create a weighted expression for the projected impact. A great deal of judgment is required here, and one should not expect to get it right the first time. It is as with marketing: one must make educated guesses, and businesses are well-accustomed to that type of uncertainty.

It also turns out that the exact shape of a probability distribution seldom matters much in the final results: if it does, this might be a red flag that the model has some important edge conditions in it. In any case, the most general distribution for this purpose is the gamma distribution, which can be used to model a variety of stochastic event processes. In this book I am not going to go into the details of distributions: most simulation tools provide such distributions out of the box and provide guidance on selecting them.

The example shown here is extremely simple to illustrate the technique – too simple in fact to make the case that this technique is worthwhile. In fact, stochastic modeling is extremely powerful and is worthwhile in many IT decision-making situations. It provides the ability to explicitly model the interactions among decisions and the holistic impact on value creation (as well as cost), while integrating both risk and opportunity. Further, once the model has been created, it provides a basis for discussion, in terms of the model parameters and interactions. Over time, through trial and error, a consensus can be developed about the validity of the model.

Stochastic modeling can also be used for generating input to portfolio analysis. In the paper [Bhadra06], dependencies between IT portfolio investments are represented by a statistical correlation value. Correlation values (as "correlation coefficients", or as "co-variance") can be determined by simulating scenarios in which inter-related projects proceed with varying levels of investment. The correlation coefficients can then be used in an overall enterprise portfolio model. This is beyond the scope of this book, but I mention it to show the relationship to portfolio analysis.

The *Expressway*™ Simulator

There are commercial simulation tools available that can be used to create stochastic models. However, they are not generally targeted at IT architects, and so the modeling paradigm tends to be mis-matched to what architects expect. For example, architects like to work in terms of structural models, and are accustomed to programming concepts. In contrast, most of the financial modeling tools available are based on a spreadsheet paradigm, which is generally less familiar to architects. Further, the most popular tools are proprietary.

In order to address these problems, I created a tool called *Expressway*™, which can be downloaded for free from this book's website. While there is a commercial version (which is necessary to fund development of the free version!), the free version is fully usable: it merely lacks many of the features that are useful for collaboration and long-term work across an enterprise.

This is not a book about *Expressway*™, so I am not going to provide a tutorial here about the tool, but there is ample documentation on the website. Further, *Expressway*™ has pre-defined generic (and customizable) implementations of all of the architectural value models described in this book.

More Value Models

So far in this book I have provided guidance for how to model the value of things such as work on incomplete projects, risk mitigation efforts, anticipated business opportunities, flexibility in terms of its contribution to business agility, and others.

IT architects worry about many things that have strong business relevance, but that are commonly expressed in IT terminology that is meaningless to business. These include things such as decoupling, component roles, constraints about what components are allowed to do, constraints regarding communication among components, decentralization versus consolidation, generality of function versus specialization, and refactoring. (The *Expressway*^{TM} tool has generic business value models for all of these.)

There are also some technical issues which business is familiar with, because these issues have bubbled up to the business level and are easily understood: these include data quality, and the ability to make better decisions because of more transparency with regard to business rules and correlations within data – this has to do with "business intelligence", and it hinges on the ability to correlate data, which often must be built into applications because cause-and-effect correlations are impossible if they are not captured proactively.

IT is in the position of either (a) keeping its decisions about these issues to itself, or (b) explaining these decisions to business. Common practice is to do the former, except that the decisions often have a large impact: e.g., a decision about whether to consolidate applications across geographically distributed operations to save money, at the expense of the operational flexibility that those geographic sites are accustomed to. Which is the better choice? If one does a cost analysis, consolidation will always win; but what it the business cost? What is the value of the lost opportunity to be more flexible, and to be able to respond more quickly to changing business needs? To answer this, IT must help to figure out the value components, because many of them have to do with how IT systems are planned and operated: that is, IT value is not just about *what* to do, but *how* to do it.

Let's take "decoupling" as an example. Decoupling is the buzzword that one hears the most often when it comes to justifying decisions to generalize components. What does it really mean, and what is its actual value?

Decoupling is typically justified as a path to being able to reuse components and to untangle behavior. It is an expression of the degree of separation of concerns between two components. It has implications for reusability, reliability, testability, and maintainability. Therefore, its benefits should be expressed in terms of these things.

On the other hand, there is a cost associated with decoupling components, in terms of performance, effort, and complexity. The impact on complexity can be positive or negative: if two components are highly inter-twined, maintenance might be difficult because the tangle is confusing; but if too much separation is created by defining more types of components than are really needed, complexity can go up as well. The right balance is determined by judgment.

That judgment needs to be applied to estimate the impact on business processes pertaining to future development, maintenance, and testing. One should also assess the likelihood of actual reuse: it does no good to make a component reusable if it will not actually be reused.

Discussions with business should be in terms of these tangible qualities: costs of maintenance, savings from reuse, increased availability due to better reliability, and so on. Business should not be left out of these tradeoffs.

Many of these kinds of decisions are made at multiple levels. For example, one might be considering refactoring a single object class, or an entire system interface. Business does not need to be involved in the low-level decisions, but they should be involved in the strategies by which these decisions are made: does the *system* need to promote reuse? Does the *system* need to be highly reliable? Does the *system* need to be built to be maintainable? Once decided, based on a value projection, IT can execute these preferences, and attempt to live up to the projections.

The Value of Better Decisions and Data

It is difficult to justify the value of better decision-making ability. Access to higher quality information and to better models improves decision-making. The value of this depends on the decisions that remain to be made.

Over time, there will be an impact that is hard to predict, because after all, you don't know what you don't know. Therefore, the value of better decision-making capabilities is best justified by trying it on a small scale first. A pilot project to try new decision-making capabilities, through better data quality, better data analysis, and better predictive models is often the way to go. If this is not possible, one can look at other parts of the organization where better decision-making capabilities were established and assess what the impact was. If this kind of comparison is not possible, management might need to accept (or reject) the projected benefit based on instinct.

Value and Risk Management Practice Frameworks

As we have seen, risk is merely negative opportunity, and so risk mitigation is an investment in reducing the expected value of a negative opportunity. This allows us to model risk as any other opportunity and to use investment analysis to compare it with other uses of resources. Further, any business opportunity – positive or negative – is but one of any organization's many concerns that must be balanced to maximize shareholder value or other goals over a planning horizon.

In other words, every single action by an organization should theoretically be evaluated in the context of a unified model that integrates opportunity with risk, and balances those investments with other investments that are made by the firm.

This sounds logical, but of course it is cumbersome and infeasible to treat every action as an investment. For some actions it is just not worth the trouble. To make the distinction I will refer to "practice-level" actions as those activities that normally fall below the level of planning in question, and for which an analytical value analysis is not worthwhile.

For example, if one is planning a program for introducing a new product line, the plan might include a series of initiatives in different parts of the organization. In such a plan, details about the operation of those initiatives are below the radar screen and would be considered to be "practice-level". However, to those planning the initiatives, such details are very pertinent, and would be considered to be plan-level. On the other hand, some things are so granular that they are inherently practice-level. For example, the manner in which software is deployed should be treated as practice-level unless the deployment is for a strategic system and is unique in some way.

So why does this distinction matter? The reason is that it is inflexible and cost-prohibitive to perform a cost-benefit analysis for small decisions, and yet guidance or rules of thumb are necessary so that good decisions can still be made by less experienced staff. For example, suppose one has to deploy a software system, and one must choose what methods to use, depending on the value at risk represented by the system. Many organizations use categories for different levels of risk, such as "Tier 1", "Tier 2", and so on. The idea is that a "Tier 1" system is high risk or mission-critical, and therefore it should be deployed and operated in a very well-controlled manner. In that case, a "Tier 1" system would have an associated procedure for deployment that is very comprehensive and well-defined, whereas a "Tier 2" system would have a less comprehensive procedure. That is, the *practices* to be used for deploying a "Tier 1" system would be different – more strict – than those for a "Tier 2" system.

The question then is how does one select the right types of practice-level actions? What should the criteria be for selecting, for example, the right amount of software testing? The right types of use cases? These are all detail-level issues, but they are very important in the aggregate for the success of the organization when the practices are reused across many systems, and these low-level decisions must be based on business value.

To address this question an organization needs a set of prior decisions on all of the major practice issues, cast as a table and driven by criteria that practitioners can easily decide. For example, a set of criteria can be used to determine if a capability is "high-risk" from a security perspective, and all such high-risk systems might require a predetermined level of testing. The analysis can be done once: a model of a hypothetical high risk system can be defined, and the appropriate level of mitigation determined for each of several categories of system value based on business value analysis. This provides a benchmark for the level and types of mitigation that are required for all similar high-risk systems. The criteria for the high-risk system can then be reused to identify which other systems are high risk, and the same mitigations can be applied without having to redo the analysis.

The result is a decision table for which practices to use that can be used broadly to make quick decisions that are based on an integrated model of risk and business opportunity value. This type of table is an invaluable tool for guiding on-the-ground actions. It provides a kind of maturity framework – but in a much more flexible manner since it is sensitive to need and can be updated whenever the analysis model is updated.

To reiterate, the in-the-field usage of such a tool is then a two-step process: first use characteristics of a business process to categorize it, and then look on the decision table's list of mitigation practices for all practices that fall within those categories.

The details of how to prepare such a table is beyond the scope of this book, but it is fairly straightforward analysis that is little different than the techniques provided in this chapter. Those in the insurance and credit industries will be familiar with this type of analysis. The important point here is that value-based decision-making is possible at all scales of activity, and that at granular task levels it can be implemented via practice frameworks and decision criteria for choosing practices. Note that I do not use the term "best practice", because that term implies that one size fits all, when in fact what is "best" for one situation is not necessarily is not necessarily best. In fact, it is not about using the best practice: it is about using the *right* practice.

Risk management frameworks such as COBIT [1] provide very useful catalog of types of risk. For example, COBIT 4 defines a practice called "DS5: Ensure Systems Security". The specific practices that should be employed to implement this practice

---

[1] Ref. [COBIT4].

category should be very much more stringent for a high-risk system than for a low-risk system. Therefore, judgment or value analysis is required in applying any maturity framework.

Maturity frameworks such as CMMI [1] have the philosophy that an organization should basically "know what it is doing" by virtue of having defined its own processes. A decision-making practice table is certainly aligned with such an approach, and the use and maintenance of such a tool is consistent with the CMMI Maturity Level 5 category in which the organization is actively tuning and optimizing its processes.

Measuring the Value of Knowledge

Knowledge is something that exists only in the heads of people – at least as of this writing. Knowledge is much more than information: knowledge implies a level of conversance about a subject, and therefore it also implies an understanding of the subject. Knowledge does not need to be learned: it is the result of learning. That is, one reads information in the form of documents, views information in the form of presentations, and hears information in the form of explanations, and as a result one builds knowledge.

This is why knowledge has so much more value and potency than mere information: knowledge is ready for action. The potency for action is what gives knowledge its value in business. Therefore, the value of knowledge depends on the potential for action: knowledge is only actionable in business if it pertains to opportunities for value creation or risk reduction.

> **The business value of knowledge is the value of the opportunity that it represents for action.**

The business value of knowledge is the value of the opportunity that it represents for action. Rather than try to measure the value of knowledge based on the cost of acquiring it, we should measure the value of knowledge based on the opportunities that it represents. However, we must account for the fact that knowledge

---

[1] Ref. [CMMI].

is usually not sufficient to perform a task: one usually needs other resources, and so the value of the knowledge is not independent of those resources. The value of that knowledge can therefore be estimated in a manner similar to the way in which we have measured the value of features that have no independent business value (see the section beginning on page 269). That is, the value of the knowledge is the *amount by which it increases the expected value of what the knowledge can be used to accomplish.*

Another aspect of knowledge is that its integrity changes over time. Over time people generally lose detailed information. However, they can also develop a more mature and holistic understanding of a subject if they have remained involved in the subject in some manner and have therefore learned more about related subjects so that they can make mental connections that foster a broader understanding. Thus, over time, knowledge can be maintained and honed, it can be matured, or it can be lost. Which happens depends on the activities of the person in the time since the knowledge was acquired.

It would probably not be effective to try to model the loss or maintenance of knowledge, at least for our purposes here. To do so would be to create a very complex and theoretical model that would need to be calibrated and that would be subject to inaccuracy in individual cases. It is better to take a more practical approach of using subjective evaluation. Specifically, if one asks, "How effective will person A be at task Y the day after they complete related task X?" then we have a basis for assessing the impact of allowing person A to experience a period of delay between tasks during which they work on something unrelated. For example, if a year goes by and then the person turns to task Y, will they require a ramp-up time to refresh their knowledge? Similarly, what is the ramp-up time for someone who is new to the task, even if they have generic knowledge about the subject domain of the task?

These are important and relevant questions that managers ask themselves all the time, but we need to assign value to knowledge so that it is accounted for as an asset that is accumulated as a side effect of projects. In fact, such knowledge is not a side effect, but a direct result of efforts by mentors to instill knowledge in the minds of those who they mentor.

I recommend tracking knowledge as an asset. That is what it is, and if we do not keep track of where it exists and what value it has, we will not properly manage it. Knowledge of systems or processes represents an important component of the capabilities provided by those systems or processes. It should be inventories just as we inventory our business processes and our systems. That is, it is a kind of "meta" data – data about data, processes, or their elements – that one should track and associate with each individual in one's staff. Important attributes of that meta data include the nature of the knowledge and how current or robust it is. Once we track this, we are in a position to monitor it and ensure that it remains at a level that is needed to maintain business processes.

To evaluate a knowledge asset, one must assume the theater of action for the knowledge: how will the knowledge be used? Will it be used to operate an existing business process? To maintain a business system? To enable future changes to an existing business system? To enable entirely new but related business opportunities? To mitigate risk with regard to existing processes or systems? This means that the value of knowledge to us is not constant: it changes as opportunities presented to us change.

For each opportunity scenario in which the knowledge might be used, one can evaluate the amount by which the possession of the knowledge increases the expected value of an investment in pursuing the opportunity. This applies whether the opportunity is an opportunity to increase revenue or an opportunity to mitigate risk and therefore reduce expected loss.

Consider for example a situation in which a project to create a new business system completes and the team is disbanded. The members of that team bear knowledge about the business opportunities associated with the project. As they go their separate ways, they retain that knowledge for a period. If an opportunity appears to add new capabilities to the business system, one can assemble an entirely new team consisting of generic skills, or one can attempt to obtain the original team. It is obvious that the original team will have a shorter learning curve and therefore reduce the cost of completing the effort. However, what is often not considered is that the original team might reduce the risk of failure. Therefore, their presence increases the expected value of the investment. The chance of failure adjusts the expected return.

That value is higher for if the original team is used. The difference represents the unique value of that team.

Dealing with Poorly Articulated Financial Goals and Strategies

Any business value metric must ultimately roll up to the core goals or strategies of the organization. For a profit-focused incorporated entity, this is always shareholder value. However, the time period over which value is maximized depends on the planning horizon of the organization. For a non-profit or governmental entity, business value metrics must be in terms of success with respect to the mission of the organization.

The important thing is that the measurement approach and metric have consensus and be the result of an investment of time, effort, and reputation on the part of both IT and the major operating units. Otherwise they will have no staying power when difficult decisions arise.

Consider the following example core strategies for a for-profit public corporation:

1. Introduce additional competitive products.
2. Manage market risk better.
3. Reduce financial non-compliance risk.
4. Reduce information security risk.

These strategies are undoubtedly rooted in shareholder value, but the board and executive committee has analyzed the company's situation and decided that these four strategies will maximize the expected shareholder value, taking account of the impact on shareholder value of these risks and opportunities. Therefore, for the purpose of execution planning, these four strategies are the goals that management must work toward.

The problem right off the bat is that there is no guidance in the four strategies for how to trade off each of them against the others. For example, what should one do when a decision has two choices, and one choice maximizes the chance to introduce new products, and the other greatly reduces market risk? What is the value of the new products when compared with the reduced market risk?

Rather than try to crack that nut right off the bat, it is best to start by trying to define a metric or scale for each of the four goals. For example, goal 1 can be expressed in terms of the expected value of an additional product, as shown in Table 16.

Table 16: A metric for measuring the value of the introduction of new products.

Goal	Metric
Introduce additional competitive products.	Expected value of product over ten years, adjusted for direct and indirect costs.

This metric might be hard to compute, at least initially, but it defines the measurement and thereby gives planners a starting point. Also, many organizations do compute this kind of metric routinely for their products, but what is often left out are the many indirect costs. By defining this metric for IT, IT now has a chance to identify the indirect costs and tradeoffs that they know about.

Let's consider goal 3 now. I will skip goals 2 and 4 because they are somewhat redundant in character with regard to 1 and 3. Goal 3 has to do with the risks associated with failure of a financial audit, as well as any costs associated with financial regulation compliance. This is a large cost for a public company because the rules are very complex and there is a very complicated responsibility for operations to report their business transactions, which the accounting department must then translate into official ledger entries. Note that these costs are included with the risk because a failure to pass an audit results in costs for remediation of the failure.

The value of financial compliance can be expressed as shown in Table 17.

Table 17: A metric for measuring the value of financial compliance.

Goal	Metric
Reduce financial non-compliance risk.	Expected cost of failure, adjusted by the expected cost of remediation, plus the expected cost of preparation.

But wait – on the one hand I say "the value of compliance" and then the table says "non-compliance risk". Well, this is not inconsistent, because the value of compliance is that one has avoided non-compliance, and non-compliance has an *actual* cost when it occurs, and it has an *expected cost* before it occurs that is simply the product of the actual cost and the probability of non-compliance.[1] When planning for any kind of risk mitigation investment one must take both the actual and expected costs of failure into account. This has been explained in detail earlier in this chapter.

The point of Table 17 is that it gives IT a starting point from which it can start to build a model for how business losses can occur as a result of IT system failures, assess their likelihood, and ultimately work toward computing a reasonable value for the risk of non-compliance. This provides a basis for planning appropriate-cost IT solutions that can mitigate that risk.

Once the metrics have been stated, it is important for the business and IT to work together to develop a model for computing each of these metrics. For example, Table 18 provides a possible formula for computing the metric for the value of additional products.

Table 18: A model for computing metric 1.

Goal	Metric
Introduce additional competitive products.	Expected value of product over ten years, adjusted for direct and indirect costs.

Model:
NPV(
    Expected revenue
    MINUS (Expected direct costs.)
    MINUS (Integration costs.)
    MINUS (Maintenance direct costs.)
    MINUS (Marginal cost of adding additional systems.)
    MINUS (Cost of maintaining knowledge and skills.)
)	

---

[1] Financial compliance is not an all-or-nothing event. In practice, an accounting firm will generally find issues that need to be addressed before it will sign-off that the organization is in compliance. The seriousness of these issues factor into the magnitude of the "non-compliance".

Managers in operations – including IT operations – are accustomed to computing costs, and product and marketing managers are accustomed to computing revenue and the value of opportunities. The challenge is to put these together, and that is what Table 18 attempts to do.

If you have examined Table 18, then you will probably have noticed a few items as unconventional:

- Marginal cost of adding additional systems.
- Cost of maintaining knowledge and skills.

The first of these, the cost of adding additional systems, refers to the value of agility, as explained earlier in this chapter in the section Comparing Alternative.

Explicitly including the cost of maintaining knowledge and skills puts teeth into the truth that is widely known within IT, that as systems age they become harder to maintain because people with knowledge of those systems leave, and one has a choice of either taking steps to maintain that knowledge or bearing the cost of lost flexibility and ultimately a difficult and costly reverse-engineering or replacement process. By including these effects into the model, one is forced to make these hidden but very real costs explicit.

Modeling financial non-compliance risk is similar: one merely needs to identify the direct and indirect costs. This is not rocket science: it is politics.

Investment Preferences

Organizations – or any investor for that matter – do not always pursue the course that has the highest expected return. This is because investors usually have preferences for one kind of risk over another, driven by goals besides financial return. For example, many "green" companies seek to maximize profit, but subject to the constraint that the company does well by the environment or the human condition in general.

Even organizations that operate strictly for profit are biased in their preferences for one kind of risk over another. For example, some organizations are very conservative with regard to risk, while others are not. The oil drilling industry is accustomed to extremely large risk investment, and so it has evolved to deal with that risk. Organizations also tend to pursue investments that they are familiar with or that access familiar markets in order to reduce the risks and costs associated with acquiring new skills or new markets. Finally, some organizations have a preference for short-term investments while others prefer long-term investments.

Catastrophic Loss

One must always consider the possibility of catastrophic loss, such as loss of a business license or charter, an irreversible loss of market share, or loss of facilities or access to capital. Even if the expected gain is favorable, the probability of catastrophic loss must be considered because it would mean a "game over" situation. Many business plans merely consider the failure modes and refer to these as "risks", but a better risk analysis assigns a value to risk – even if the value is a magnitude or uses a relative but agreed-upon scale such as "low", "medium", and "high".

One way that consideration of catastrophic loss can be incorporated into the approaches outlined above is that one can determine the level of mitigation that reduces the probability of all kinds of catastrophic failure to an acceptable point, and set that level of mitigation as a minimum: the optimal, as determined by the analysis explained above, must produce an investment level that is greater than the minimum; otherwise, the minimum is used.

This is a simplistic approach, and does not account for the fact that even conservative organizations (or people for that matter) will sometimes accept some possibility of catastrophic loss if the up-side is high enough. In fact, everyone does this every day, whether they want to or not, since the ever-present possibility of catastrophic loss is part of life.

Preferences Given Limited Investment Resources

Another issue is that total investment dollars are usually limited, and so one must consider how investment in mitigation might reduce funds available for investment in other opportunities. Thus, instead of maximizing the return from a particular kind of mitigation, one must attempt to maximize overall return to the organization, constrained by limited funds, taking account of the organization's preferences for risk versus opportunity and for the makeup of its investment and project portfolio, as well as preferences for one kind of risk over another.

It turns out that when one takes account of organizational preferences such as aversion to risk, then the global optimal for the organization will be the point at which the "marginal rate of substitution" (of one kind of investment over another) equals the "marginal rate of transformation" (of one investment into another). Readers who are interested in these concepts in depth are referred to [Copeland03] and [McAfeePr06]. Here I will provide a brief discussion of how these concepts affect our models.

Indifference Curves

Consider an organization that provides two services, A and B. These services may be any kind of service that decision-makers within the organization feel are desirable for the organization's constituents. For example, service A might be the production of a particular product for sale, and service B might be the production of another product for sale. However, in the discussion here it will not matter what services A and B are, and so I will simply refer to them as A and B.

The organization will, through its decision-making processes, exhibit a preference with respect to the relative value of A and B. This preference might result purely from an attempt to maximize shareholder value (for a for-profit corporation), or it might reflect other preferences, such as a desire to focus the organization's activity more in one direction than another, or both. Assume that the organization is currently producing a certain amount of A and a certain amount of B. If one were to propose decreasing the amount of service A being produced, by how much would one have to increase the amount of service B being produced in order for executives to say that the overall business value remains unchanged?

The answer to this question defines a point on a curve, known as an *indifference curve*, because the organization is indifferent to where it sits on a given curve: that is, if it is at one point on such a curve, then it is happy to move to any other point on the same curve, by definition. The position of the curve defines a level of "business value", or "preference".

If one fixes the budget for the organization, so that a fixed amount of funds are available for both A and B, then the allocation to A and B is defined by a curve also. This curve is known as the *transformation curve*, because it defines, for a given budget, how much of A and B can be produced. This curve is usually convex, but for simplicity I will treat it as a straight line: that is, I will assume that if one spends twice as much on service A, then one actually gets twice as much output from service A; and similarly for B. Also, I will refer to this curve (straight line) as a "budget line", which I feel is more intuitive. Consider Figure 20.

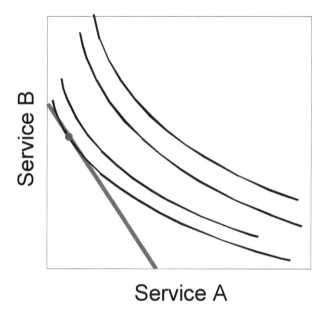

Figure 20: Indifference curves and a budget line.

Figure 20 shows a straight budget line and several indifference curves. Each curve represents a different level of perceived business value: the higher the curve, the higher the business value. The budget line shows how much of A and B can be produced for the fixed budget available to the organization. If the available budget were higher, the budget curve would be higher.

The point at which the budget line is tangent to an indifference curve is the point at which the organization reaches the highest possible indifference curve, for the given budget. Thus, this is the point at which the organization should divide funds between A and B.

Remember, an indifference curve is a curve along which the perceived business value is the same at all points, and represents tradeoffs between two services. (For three services, one has an indifference surface; for four, an indifference hyper-surface, and so on.)

A reminder of how this relates to maximization of business value: if we assume a given budget for investment, and optimize our investment strategies and portfolio, we should end up at the point of tangency indicated in Figure 20. The purpose of Figure 20 is to show graphically how the budget affects investment.

Indifference curves are of most utility when one has to balance non-financial objectives, because if the objective is simply to make the most money in a given period of time, then one need not consider preferences at all: one simply chooses the strategy that yields the greatest expected return. On the other hand, risk aversion (safety) is a kind of preference, and so indifference curves can be used to model preferences for safety versus possible gain.

When Business Value Is Not Financial

The mission of a non-profit organization or a government agency is not to make money. Therefore, for such an organization, one cannot assume that one can measure business value in terms of money saved or money earned. However, if one assumes that the organization's budget is optimal, based on the willingness of its constituents to invest, then one can assume that *the marginal value of each additional dollar spent equals the economic value (to the constituents) of that dollar*. Given this thinking, a dollar saved releases a dollar for investment in a dollar's worth of additional services, according to the mix of services that are provided by the organization. Optimality assumes that this mix represents the preferences of those who fund the organization's services: its constituents, or the taxpayers in the case of a government agency.

Mandates

A mandate from a regulatory agency, from law, policy, or any other source must be followed, and so it represents a constraint on strategy and decisions.

A mandate has no business value, because it is externally imposed, and no business value should be attributed to it. However, the actions compelled by the mandate might have business value, and the very strategy that is behind the mandate – the reason for the mandate – might have business value.

A business value analysis should therefore not place a value on an externally imposed mandate, but may assign a value to elements of a strategy or plan that implement the mandate.

Direct Cost Avoidance

A great many internal investments within organizations are made for the purpose of saving costs. For example, an investment in a new IT system might save the costs associated with the current paper process.

Direct cost avoidance such as this represents a net financial gain for the organization. As explained earlier, that gain can be re-distributed across the various services based on the organization's priorities.

Overall Mission Effectiveness

Organization governance, directives, and oversight processes are intended to ensure that projects reflect the global needs of the organization and not merely the narrow needs of particular services. If the organization has a parent organization (as all government agencies do), then overall effectiveness therefore has to do with the overall effectiveness of the organization part of the parent organization. Overall effectiveness includes areas such as fiscal responsibility, adhering to parent organization policies or regulations. Fiscal responsibility includes adhering to standards for IT, such as enterprise architecture guidelines, that are intended to promote cost effectiveness, reusability, accountability, security, and agility.

Overall mission effectiveness is optimized by finding the point at which a new budget line is tangent to an indifference curve for the organization.[1] This is illustrated in Figure 21.

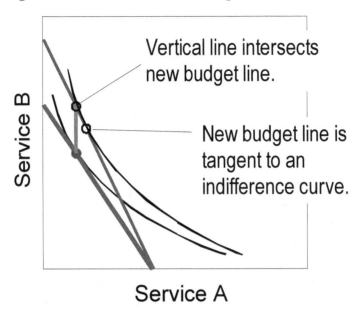

Figure 21: Command and control: When the preferences of only the organization as a whole must be accounted for.

A subtle point is that improving the efficiency of a service changes all of the indifference curves for the organization. This is not an important issue for the discussion here though. The main point is that if a service is made more efficient, management should re-evaluate the distribution of funds across all of its efforts to maximize the overall benefit to the organization. In most cases, this will result in maintaining the funding of the more efficient service, and possibly increasing it, since now more of it can be obtained for less, and so it is more cost effective.

Societal Benefit

Government agencies exist to benefit society. However, the quantitative benefit to society is different from the quantitative

---

[1] Those who are familiar with Pareto curves will note that I am assuming that the organization acts as a single decision-making entity.

benefit based on the agency's mission. The agency has a limited budget and that budget is based on priorities defined by the government's policy makers and executives. Just because an agency service activity saved a million dollars for some segment of the general public (e.g., by protecting property during a natural disaster) does not mean that the activity was worth a million dollars in the context of the agency's budget. If might have cost $100,000 to save the million dollars, so when compared to the agency's budget items the activity was worth $100,000, if one assumes that the agency's activities are balanced across the agency's priorities.

It is therefore important to not impute value to public agency activities based on the direct impact on the public or certain constituents. Internal dollars do not equal external dollars.

A Real-Life Example of Estimating Tangible Value

Case In Point

The business proposal for a $5 million project made the following intangible claims of business value:

- Improved mission effectiveness.
- Improved tracking and reporting.
- Improved auditability.
- Improved transparency of business rules.
- Reduced oversight costs.
- Improved data quality.
- Improved security.

In addition, we were interested in the possibility of benefits related to reuse and lifecycle cost, so we asked questions about those areas.

The proposed system was an advance-procurement system, and its purpose was twofold: (1) to improve the availability and quality of equipment, so that right equipment would be available when needed, and the equipment would be of the required quality; and (2) to reduce the costs associated with equipment by allowing personnel to pre-negotiate equipment leases in advance of when it was actually needed, based on competitive solicitation.

I assess tangible business value for each of these in the following ways.

Mission effectiveness. Mission effectiveness had to do with the ability to perform using the equipment procured through the advance lease agreements created with the system. The ability to perform was impacted by the availability and quality of equipment. We modeled the value of mission effectiveness by estimating the *percent improvement* in effectiveness that was expected to result from having advance lease agreements for quality equipment. This was based on the actual improvements seen through use of a prototype of the system, and the actual impact on mission effectiveness. The estimate of improved effectiveness was obtained from a credible field expert. By estimating improvement as a percent, we were later able to normalize the value of the improvement to the cost of current operations: if current operations in the area of business cost X, and effectiveness was improved by 10%, then 10% of X is free for re-distribution across the organization. Even if most (or all) of that 10% is kept by the area of business, the value to the organization is the value of having .1X more funds available for investment.

Improvements to tracking and reporting. The current system – to be replaced by the new system – was paper-based. This resulted in delays in payments on lease agreements, resulting in interest charges that had to be paid out. Thus, a decrease in turnaround of payments translated into reduced interest payments to vendors. We asked experts to estimate the decreased frequency and amounts of late payments as a result of automating the paper process, and computed as estimated reduction in interest charges. Since the current paper system processed hundreds of million of dollars of transactions per year, and payments were often late, the interest savings were substantial.

Improved auditability. For this system, financial auditability was required by law, and so we treated it is a mandate.

Improved transparency of business rules. The prototype system had little transparency with respect to the business rules encoded in it, and the business users therefore had concern over whether the rules were correct. Therefore, for the new system, a promise was made to the business users that the rules encoded in the system would be transparent and could be reviewed. The value of this was therefore treated as a mandate.

Reduced oversight costs. The current paper process was spot-audited at great cost, requiring analysts to travel on-site to review paperwork. The new system would make it possible to review data electronically from the oversight auditor's office. We estimated a savings in travel costs and time based on projections from an expert (in the oversight group) about the reduced travel and reduced time to audit data.

Improved data quality. A prior report had documented a 50% correction rate for the paper lease agreements that were in use. We extrapolated improvements obtained from the prototype system to estimate the reduced corrections required for the new system, and the cost savings that would result.

Improved security. The prototype (which handled 10% of the volume that the final system would handle) had experienced six documented security incidents in three years. One of these resulted in a severe loss of reputation because the head of a vendor association wrote a memo in the association's newsletter urging vendors not to use the prototype system. This action threatened the entire value proposition of the prototype system. By extrapolation, if the new system were no more secure, then this kind of event could be expected to happen even more frequently given the much higher volume of processing of the new system.

Reuse. The project team insisted that they expected future reuse of their system's components to be zero, even though it was built on a highly reusable SOA architecture, based on their experience with cross-departmental competition and trust. This issue was in fact an issue that was being worked at a higher level, and so it was not a surprise, even though it was a disappointment. We assumed zero benefit from future reuse.

Lifecycle cost. The project insisted that given their rural geographic location, that they could expect a high level of continuity of the team over time, and that when the system eventually went into a maintenance mode, they would be able to transition some of the developers to maintaining the system. In this way, they expected that the valuable knowledge acquired as a result of building the system would be leveraged and not discarded. We estimated that 20% of the team would remain to maintain the system, and projected a substantial reduction in maintenance cost and improved reliability and extensibility as a result.

Modeling the Interactions

All of these claims for value could simply be added, to produce a total claim for value. However, there is a more powerful way to estimate overall value: by modeling the sources of value and their interactions. That approach enables one to perform sensitivity analysis, to determine where it would pay to invest more, or which sources of value depend on sufficient investment in those areas. For the project under discussion, I developed a model, as shown in Figure 22.

314

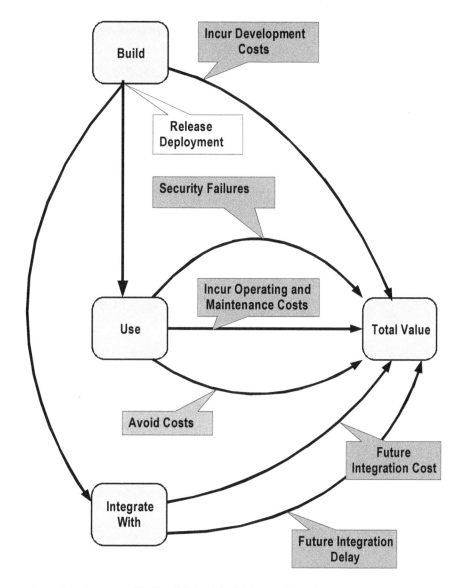

Figure 22: Cause-and-Effect Value Model for the New System.

This model contains representations of the various sources and detractors of value, and their interrelationships. For example, building the system incurs a development cost, and this is shown by the arrow leading from "Build" to "Total Value". The arrow carries a negative value whenever a development cost is incurred. Usage of the system, once deployed, is represented by the "Use" bubble, and the costs of use – operations and maintenance (O&M) costs – are represented by the straight arrow leading from "Use" to "Total Value". Again, this arrow carries a negative value whenever O&M costs are incurred. On the other hand, the lower curved arrow leading from "Use" to "Total Value" represents the business value produced by the system's function – its reason for being. The values conducted along this arrow are positive.

The bubble labeled "Integrate With" is perhaps the most interesting and subtle. It represents hypothetical future integrations with the system. Whether these future integrations will occur depends on the nature of its function, and also how easy it is to integrate with. Assuming that future integrations will occur, their cost will depend to some extent on the way in which the system is built today: that is, whether the design of the system makes integration easy or not. The upper arrow leading from "Integrate With" to "Total Value" represents the costs of future integration events as they occur: this cost will be less if the "Integrate With" bubble assumes a strategy of using an architecture that is easy to integrate with.

The lower arrow between "Integrate With" and "Total Value" represents the time-to-market cost of the time it takes to implement and deploy future integrations sooner. For example, if a future system requires integration with this system, and the architecture of this system is such that the integration can be done six months faster than if a traditional architecture were used, then the time to integrate will be six months less, and so the new system will be deployed six months sooner. Presumably there is business value in having the new system deployed sooner, and the lower arc represents this value.

In addition, the model accounts for security-related failures, that is, incidents that cost the organization in some way. Security-related failures are modeled by the arc from "Use" to "Total Value" labeled "Security Failures". The costs that travel on this arc represent the cost of each security-related incident as it occurs. These are negative sources of value. Also, these follow a distribution that has a very broad range, from minor incidents to incidents that undermine trust in the system by other organizations and partners and therefore threaten the entire system.

The model was simulated, using a variety of assumptions for the time distributions and cost distributions represented by the arcs in the model. This made it possible to see how sensitive the model was to the various assumptions, and it gave a range for the total business value to expect over time.

It turned out that the total value was very sensitive to the degree of future integrations expected and their value. The implication was that we needed to pay particular attention to projecting whether such future integrations would actually occur, and what their value might be.

The model results are also sensitive to assumptions about the magnitude of catastrophic security-related incidents. The implication was that investment in security risk mitigation to present catastrophic class incidents is highly recommended. In this way we were able to estimate the "value of security".

Summary

In order for IT architecture choices to be taken seriously by business decisionmakers, those choices must be expressed in tangible business terms.

Business value results from expected income from planned sources as well as expected income from future – and as yet unplanned – sources. Both of these must be considered in some manner, because both are impacted by architectural decisions today. Busines value is also (adversely) affected by expected investment costs and expected lifecycle costs.

Architectural decisions that provide future flexibility produce business value by increasing the expected income (or value) from as-yet unplanned sources. Thus, the value of agility is directly related to flexibility and to the expected magnitude of the unforeseen opportunities that can leverage that agility.

In order to prove the value of business agility, one must measure the enterprise-wide impact of decisions made years back. Therefore, it is important to retain business effectiveness metrics over a long period.

Risk manifests as an expected loss due to foreseen or unforeseen types of events. Investments in risk mitigation increase value because they reduce the size of the expected long-term loss.

There is an optimal point at which the marginal value of investment in risk mitigation is zero, and that is the point of maximum value with respect to risk mitigation.

Decisions about risk mitigation and investment in top-line improving activities should be compared together on a common scale.

In IT it has been especially difficult to measure the value of system features because many features do not operate independently and so they produce no direct business value of their own. Rather, their value derives from their support of other features. This is problematic because it is then difficult to estimate the value of completing the development of these features since they are so inter-dependent. This can be resolved by focusing on the increased *expected value* of the total set of features. This expected value must account for the risk of completion of the full feature set and how that risk and cost is reduced as a result of completing embedded features. The value must also accunt for the opportunity that is presented once all featuers are complete.

Very often architectural alternatives must be compared in which one alternative provides more flexibility than the other. Estimating the value of this flexibility is difficult. It can be done however by hypothesizing a future change that takes advantage of the flexibility and estimating the opportunity value of that flexibility as well as its likelihood. In this way an *expected value* of the flexibility can be estimated.

Progress in building software is actually a statistical phenomenon: it is (a) the increased chance of finishing and thereby realizing the future value of the new capability, plus (b) the reduced expected cost of completion. Project management is therefore all about probabilities, judgment, and risk management.

It is not practical to perform detailed value analysis for every IT decision. However, it is important that many kinds of decisions – such as those that affectt security or other kinds of risk – be made in a consistent manner that reflects the relative risks. Toward that end it is useful to develop a decision framework that enumerates practices and provides risk-based criteria for when to use each practice. In this way the risk and value analysis is done when the framework is created rather than each time a decision is required.

Knowledge acquired as a result of a business activity is a valuable asset, and this value must be tracked and taken into accunt when decisions are made regarding how to deploy resources. Knowledge should be tracked as an asset and should be part of the organization's meta data. The value of knowledge depends on the task, and that value is the amount by which it increases the expected value of an investment in pursuing the opportunity associated with the task.

12. Alignment Through Policies, Controls, and Enterprise Architecture

In addition to providing value-based business plans or roadmaps for realizing organization goals, planners must provide detailed guidance that staff can and must use in order to ensure consistency across the organization in how things are done, and in order to ensure that enterprise objectives are met, especially when those objectives conflict with departmental objectives. Many organizations call such guidance "policies" or "standards". Let's look at what must be included in effective guidance, and what should not be included, and how to establish an effective hierarchy of such guidance.

Focus On Human Capabilities, Not Systems Or Documents

In chapter 5 (see the section Do Not Focus On Artifacts) and elsewhere, including the previous chapter, I make the point that documents are information but they are not knowledge, and therefore one should never attempt to perpetuate knowledge merely by creating documents. To do so is folly: documents are only part of any knowledge perpetuation plan.

Unless your organization is "manned" entirely by robots, your capabilities are ultimately human capabilities. Humans leverage automation, but that automation is then subsumed by the aggregate capability that each person has. Just as a car has no capability to drive by itself, a human with a car has the capability to drive. That capability rests with the human: the human is merely enabled by the technology. The technology is not a capability in its own right unless it can operate entirely autonomously; and even if it could, it would need to be turned on, monitored, and maintained by humans, and so the aggregate capability still has humans at the top.

Need To Focus On Growing Capabilities To Match Each New Business Process

Capabilities are not generic: they vary substantially by individual, and the way in which they are integrated is the major factor in their effectiveness. Therefore, you cannot simply buy capabilities or recruit for capabilities: you must account for the vast variety that exists in real-life resources, and account for their integration as a major element.

For example, suppose you need "ten analysts and two project managers". These are generic skill sets that you can give to your HR department; but as a manager you most likely know that you will not get what you need unless the HR person is very much in tune with what those people will be doing. Further, once those people arrive, they will need to be integrated into the fabric of your environment, and only then will they become productive.

Do Not Become a "Document Factory"

Enterprise groups should not spend their time creating lots of paper. The baseline of paper that is developed up-front should be well-developed and have executive-level support, but be minimal. It should consist of a set of policies and standards. That should be it. From that point, all blueprints should be developed *as a side effect of actual work, and primarily work on pilots*: they should not be created up-front. Thus, blueprints should be tested on real projects that agree to serve as a testbed. That way they will be proven and have legitimacy.

Capability is not defined by how completely your processes are documented. It is defined by how effectively you execute your

322

processes. Rather than spending a lot of time documenting processes, spend the time teaching others to implement controls and processes correctly, and teaching them how to extract reusable templates from those.

Documents serve as a means of achieving and persisting consensus about approaches for those who are developing the processes that are being documented. Documents also serve as reference material for those who will need to learn about those processes. However, process definition documents are generally pretty useless if the authors of the documents are no longer available to mentor: that is a recipe for disaster and the *misapplication of the processes.*

> # If you have an initiative to produce documents, and the producers of those documents will move on to other efforts when they are done, STOP.

As I have said before, skills cannot be taught in a classroom. A classroom can provide a conceptual foundation, but skills must be learned by doing and can only be *taught* through mentoring in which you guide someone as they actually perform the work themselves. Workers must get to a point *at which they can execute instinctively.*

Training Your Staff In the Processes Of Blueprint Customization and Deployment

Your mentor staff need to be effective as evangelists for the reference designs – the blueprints – developed as a side effect of pilot efforts between your mentor group and operating units. For those blueprints to be used, you must be prepared to help other groups to understand and apply them. In doing so, you are not doing their job for them; rather, you are enabling them, and they will repay your efforts with support and good words about the value of your team. The organization as a whole will reap the benefits of consistency in how things are done, which will yield the dividends of agility and transparency.

323

This mentoring provides a very effective "policy rollout" mechanism.[1] However, instead of a fear-driven approach, you provide assistance and are open to feedback, which allows you to continually improve the blueprints.

If you use a workflow system in your organization, then you can use it to help to provide consistency in the way some of the blueprints are applied. In fact, the concept of blueprints encompasses repeatable work processes. For example, if you have found that it is very effective for a design review to be preceded by one-on-one informal pre-review discussions with each stakeholder, then you can encode that practice as a "work packet" that is part of the workflow, thereby adding concreteness, consistency, and repeatability to the practice.

Need a Business Process Certification Process

I have discussed the importance of certification of business processes, but I have not provided guidance for how to set that up. Here I will address that.

The goal is to establish a certification program that certifies business processes in that they represent the full breadth of enterprise concerns in a balanced way. This includes verifying that business processes adhere to the intent of enterprise blueprints, wherever available blueprints apply.

The certification process that we are talking about here is an activity of the mentor group, and the mentor team should work with each operating unit to help them attain certification.

Certification must ensure that decisions are made based on a standard business model template (a blueprint for capability business models), and that the weighting of value is based on vetted and agreed-to factors that represent the business value of intangibles such as future agility, lifecycle cost for the enterprise *as a whole*, risk, compliance, and current opportunities. In short, certification must endeavor to ensure that decisions are made based on enterprise criteria and benefits — not merely local departmental criteria and benefits.

---

[1] Ref. COBIT4, PO6.4.

Business process certification replaces the traditional approach of "architecture review boards". The problem with review boards is that they are after-the-fact, and the criteria is usually too narrow or not linked to an enterprise-wide business model. In most architecture review boards that I have sat on, one has a group of senior architects, each with a different technical ax to grind, grumbling about technical details. This is not entirely their fault: they do not have the benefit of business-focused criteria or a mandate to translate architecture into those criteria. Without that translation and without a framework for making tangible tradeoffs, review boards end up discussing the wrong things.

In chapter 5 I discuss the need for independent oversight as a check that the certification is working, and that this can take the form of internal or external audits. Certification does not guarantee that an internal or external audit will be passed, but if the process is working it provides a high likelihood.

When a business process is certified, it receives a score, indicating overall business efficacy. There should be a separate score pertaining to each major area of concern for the enterprise – including aspects that may be audited by an outside source. Giving an actual score for these aspects helps to indicate the likelihood of passing an external audit, so that a score of "50" indicates that passage of an audit with few major negative findings would be likely, but a score of "90" would indicate that passage of an audit with few important negative findings of any kind would be likely.

The core requirements for a business process certification process are that:

1. Knowledge and documentation of enterprise goals and concerns must exist, and must be _validated_ as complete.
2. Knowledge and documentation of the specific functional goals and concerns for the business process must exist – i.e., the business capability "requirements" – and must be _validated_ as complete.
3. Knowledge and documentation an operational design or "architecture" must exist that explains how all of the goals and concerns are addressed, and must be _validated_.
4. Knowledge and documentation of a business model must exist for how these goals and concerns interact, and must be _validated_.

5. Knowledge and documentation of success metrics for the model must exist, and must be *validated*. (These should be included in the architecture.)
6. The operational implementation of the business process must exist and must be *validated* to show that it conforms to the operational model.

Right off the bat you will likely notice that the items above all specify "knowledge and documentation". This is because the intent is to avoid a process whereby documented are created and handed off to the certification team for review. That indeed is the customary way that things are done in IT in non-agile environments. It is not the way things are done in agile IT environments, because those environments trust human knowledge more than documentation. However, I believe that in a large enterprise a combination is needed. I have already explained the importance of planning for the development and maintenance of knowledge rather than artifacts (see chapter 5): let's put that into practice in our certification process.

It is important that the inventory of enterprise goals and concerns include sources of hidden cost or risk such as maintainability and knowledge retention, future agility, policy and regulatory compliance, security, manageability, and so on. By "manageability" I mean the ability to operate the capability (and associated automated systems) in a smooth and controlled manner, including the ability to measure operational success, thereby implementing the metrics required by item 5 above.

It is also extremely important that these models be maintained over time, and that metric data be maintained so that years later correlations can be made with respect to value that is realized (as defined in item 4) based on strategies that were implemented (as evidenced by item 3). The inability to make these correlations in most organizations today is one of the main reasons why it is hard to justify concern for issues that are important to IT architects such as technical concerns related to maintainability, future agility, and so on. Here is the chance to create the trail of evidence. But to do it you need a credible business model linked to architectural choices, and the business model needs to be based on measurement scales and methods that the business understands and finds credible.

Item 2 is simply the set of requirements articulated by the intended users of the capability. These requirements state the scope and goals of the business process, possibly down to a very detailed level. Validation of these requirements is actually out of the scope of the enterprise certification that we are addressing here, except that it is important to the enterprise that a system's requirements are complete and correct, and therefore there should be a quality check of some kind on these requirements to satisfy enterprise certification.

Figure 23 illustrates the project duration lifecycle for item 1, the validation of knowledge and documentation of enterprise goals and concerns. As shown in the figure, I advocate an ongoing process characterized by milestones for completeness, rather than an all-or-nothing review. That is, instead of review points at which the certification team would examine artifacts and make a pronouncement, I believe in a process whereby the certifiers work with the team to help them understand what they need to do, and that the milestones be checkpoints at which the certifiers evaluate how close the project team is to the certification requirement.

I also believe that instead of review meetings, that one should focus meetings on knowledge transfer and any collaborative decision-making that is needed. For example, once the project team feels that they have a good enough understanding of the requirements to write down 75% of them in their own words, they should do so and then call a meeting with the SMEs and the other stakeholders, to explain their understanding of the primary requirements. This is in contrast to a meeting in which everyone is expected to have read a requirements document from cover to cover and comment. Rather, the team should step through the requirements, defending their articulation of the requirements, and focusing on the important issues, until there is consensus about which requirements are understood and which are not.

I am not advocating a lack of formality: formality is needed in the evaluation; but it need not be characterized by scary review events. Rather, it should be a continual process of guidance with firm criteria for success.

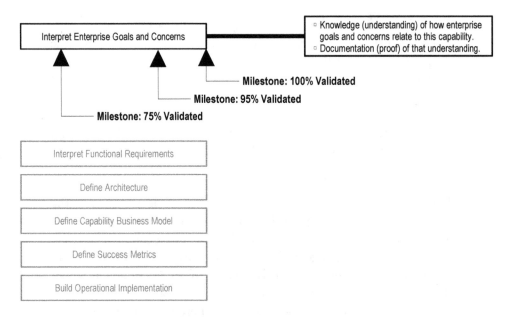

Figure 23: Validation of knowledge and documentation of enterprise goals and concerns.

Our primary goal therefore is not to evaluate a business process, but it is to help the process builders enhance the process sufficiently so that it is indeed worthy of certification, and then certification is a mere side effect.

Two other important outputs of this process are shown in the figure: (1) knowledge and understanding on the part of the process builders, and (2) documentation of that understanding. These represent a combined asset that should be maintained: the project initiative should include provisions for leveraging and maintaining this knowledge over the lifecycle of the system. Mere documents of automated systems are drastically inadequate for this purpose: what is required is that managers take steps to ensure that there is always a group of people who understand the system, at least until the system's replacement has been designed.

By this point you should gather that I advocate that certification occur in real-time with respect to the development or modification of a business capability, rather than as an after-the-fact review. After-the-fact reviews are for independent audits, not for mentor-based certification. To be most helpful, the certifiers need to be right in there, not as part of the implementation team, but as mentors and available to identify risks, design patterns, approaches, and certification requirements.

Figure 24 illustrates milestones and outputs of the process of creation of the capability's architecture. Again, certification should encompass working with the architects to understand the automated systems and human processes, and to understand how the architecture addresses the enterprise goals and concerns that are articulated in item 1. Note that there is *no reason why these processes need occur in series*: in fact, they should proceed in parallel in order to be able to provide for feedback between them.

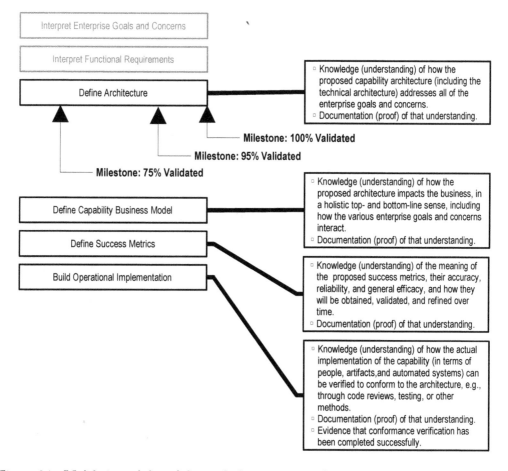

Figure 24: Validation of knowledge and documentation of operational design or "architecture".

As shown in the figure, the last item, Build Operational Implementation, should include evidence that the as-built capability matches the as-intended capability. This means that the architecture and business model must be adjusted whenever decisions change.

In order to verify that the as-built capability matches the models, one can resort to a variety of techniques. It should be up to the project team to implement these verification techniques, and for the certification team to oversee their use and evaluate their efficacy. Such techniques include the creation of test suites, the creation of design rule-based test suites, and manual reviews of code *for the purpose of proving that the code matches the design*. This last technique is a departure from the way that code reviews are traditionally practiced. Regarding the use of rule-based test suites, a colleague of mine makes extensive use of this approach in his work as a project recovery expert. The projects that he routinely saves are almost always large and complex projects involving automated systems that process petabytes (a billion megabytes) of data or tens of thousands of transactions *per second*, so the argument that this technique cannot be used in complex systems is specious; in fact, he considers it to be an invaluable tool for checking that programmers do not subvert the system's intended architecture.

Don't Follow a Rigid Framework

Some frameworks for strategic and tactical planning pre-define rigid processes for mapping strategic goals to execution plans. Such a framework has the overhead associated with learning the intricacies of the framework, and can be limiting in that it might not fit your needs. For example, the COBIT framework specifies that a CFO should merely be informed of the linkage between business goals and IT goals.[1] The assumption of one-directional communication between the business goals and IT is perhaps rooted in the assumption that business-level financial goals are not within the purview of IT initiative planning. In fact, your planning process *should* allow for the possibility that *any* strategic concern – financial or otherwise – might require two-directional communication between "the business" and IT.

---

[1] See COBIT4, Process PO1, RACI Chart.

Frameworks exist for IT architecture as well. In the next chapter I compare the TOGAF IT architecture framework[1] developed by the Open Group. As you will see, there is much benefit to be derived from learning the TOGAF framework, but I do not advocate adopting it wholesale. In my opinion it is better to use such frameworks as a source of ideas for how to improve the processes that you already have. Rather than using rigid frameworks, it is better to use a *minimalist approach* and allow for evolution from your current environment, rather than follow a rigid template and try to replace all of your current policies and governance mechanisms. It is also important to first focus on the governance-driven decision-making processes rather than the processes for creating artifacts. Good decision-making is what architecture is all about, not the creation of artifacts.

Similarly, software development frameworks such Rational Unified Process (RUP)[2] provide a valuable structure and taxonomy for things to worry about or do at various stages of your IT system lifecycle, but every project is different, and it is better to develop the capability within your staff to assess risk and be aware of your organization's concerns than to try to encode all of this into written processes.

Keep Artifacts Spartan, But Maintain A High Standard For Accuracy And Meaningfulness

Your mentors should instill the philosophy of simplicity in their "clients".

Corporate documents that are distributed outside of a department are usually highly polished, and often contain boilerplate sections that give a lengthy background on projects and departments. This kind of preface material adds little value, and creates an ethos of heavy documents. Consider replacing them with lightweight Web-based documents.

---

[1] "TOGAF" stands for The Open Group Architecture Framework. See [TOGAF].
[2] Rational Unified Process. The Rational Unified Process and RUP are trademarks of IBM.

In business processes, less is better. This is because less is simpler, and less is easier to change. The less you have to manage, the lower your costs. You should provide the best functionality that you can for your budget, but achieve that in the simplest manner possible.

Would you trust an internal business document that gets right to the point, with no lengthy background and no long list of references and change history at the beginning? With no company logo at the top? What about a corporate standards document? Do you expect such a document to have a fully developed presentation, fit for publication in a technical journal?

Perhaps you would not. But if that is the case, it is probably because you associate quality control with a finished presentation, and assume that something that has not had its presentation polished has not gone through a QA process. If you know that your organization has a highly effective QA process, you will trust a document no matter what it looks like. Thus, effort should be invested in making the organization's processes trustworthy, including the documents that those processes produce. If you achieve that, it will not matter to your employees what documents look like, because they will trust them regardless.

Fancy and lengthy documents inhibit innovation and cultivate a culture that gives credence to appearance over substance. Management should set an example by producing very spartan but well-written internal documents. Show your employees that you do not care what a document looks like as long as it uses correct and clear English, is consistently formatted and neat, is understandable by the most-novice members of its intended audience, contains exactly what it needs and no more, and above all, is accurate and well thought out. Omit the separate title page. Reduce the company logo to a very small size. Forget the boilerplate. Trim down the background section such that it discusses only the background that is relevant to the document's topic, not to the entire project or department. Skip the project history section. However, treat even small errors or inconsistencies as serious, because they destroy the trust in the document.

The Policy Hierarchy

There are three levels at which enterprise strategies must be formally articulated. Each is represented by a type of written artifact. These artifact types are:

Policies integrate enterprise objectives with enterprise concerns. Policies provide required mandates, and identify applicable standards. Policies sometimes take the form of "directives" that are issued by a memo and published within the organization's internal website or LAN.

Standards provide strategies and detail-level decisions for how to implement policies. Standards define roles and responsibilities. Standards should be written to be as concise as possible, but they are usually much more voluminous than the policies that they implement.

Blueprints provide out-of-the-box re-usable, customizable processes and designs. Blueprints implement standards and provide repeatable process templates and design templates for use by execution teams. Blueprints incorporate the baseline of decisions that reflect process policy and enterprise choices with regard to how projects should be conducted, how standard business processes should be performed, and how systems should be designed.[1]

These artifact types are depicted in Figure 25. Policies are definitive statements about how the organization should conduct its affairs. A well-written policy is unambiguous, but minimalist and to-the-point. A well-written policy also includes an explanation of what the policy intends to achieve.

Rather than outline the entire operational plan for how a policy should be implemented, a policy should refer to one or more standards that serve that function. This allows the details to be worked out independently without impacting the policy.

Blueprints are where an enterprise mentoring group comes in. Blueprints are a purposeful and important side effect of the

---

[1] Many argue that there is a distinction between "blueprints", "design templates", "design patterns", and "reference designs". I agree that these distinctions are important when discussing the details of architecture artifacts, but for the purposes of this book the distinction is not important, so I include all of these concepts under the umbrella of "blueprints".

piloting efforts that the mentoring group leads. If a pilot initiative is successful, blueprints are extracted from it that can be reused to bootstrap other initiatives and help those other initiatives to implement standards and policies without having to begin from scratch with the policy and standards documents and figure out how to design systems that meet the intent of the policies and standards. Over time, an enterprise architecture should be assembled that encodes a consistent approach for important issues such as control strategies and business agility.

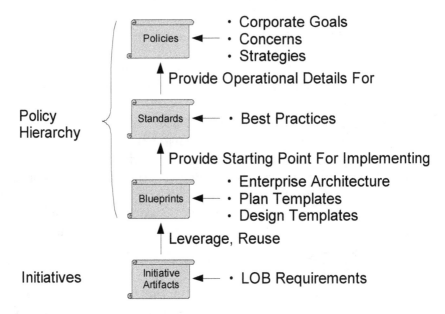

Figure 25: Hierarchy of guiding enterprise artifacts.

Policies, directives, and standards must address major enterprise architecture issues, including service-oriented architecture (SOA) governance, service level agreements (SLAs), data quality processes, and other technical issues that are important to the organization. Enterprise architecture (EA) is discussed in detail in the next chapter. Here I only want to consider how

Include In Processes the Important Step Of Process Customization And Artifact Template Definition

Plans that have been used successfully before provide a starting point for new initiatives. However, each initiative is unique. Would you use the same process for a large business-critical software project requiring 50 programmers as you would for a small one-person departmental project? Would you require the same steps and the same artifacts? Of course you would not, because the large project has very different risks and challenges than the small project, and so you would engage your limited resources in a way that maximizes your chance for success. For the small project, you would also endeavor to engage your resources in an optimal way, but the optimal mix is different, because a small project does not have the inter-personal communication difficulties that a large project has, and a departmental software application does not generally have the security, reliability, and manageability challenges that a large business-critical software application does.

When a project manager plans a project, a methodology must be chosen so that the milestones and activities can be projected. At this time, high-level choices must be made regarding how the methodology will be customized to fit the project. For example, if a test suite will be created and maintained, how comprehensive must that test suite be? The answer depends on the level of assurance that is required for the resulting software.

When the project is initiated, the methodology must be refined further. In particular, artifact templates (blueprints) should be selected based on their applicability to the project, and those templates should be customized so that they focus on the issues that are important for the project. For example, a template for a software design might include a section for listing all of the database transactions. However, if the application is not going to have a database, then this section is not even applicable.

Need a Means Of Ensuring that the Customized Process Reflects Enterprise Choices, From All Strategic Perspectives

Customizing plans requires experience and a high level of refined judgment. It is a task for an architect and manager in collaboration. The customization must not dispense with enterprise concerns. For example, when customizing a requirement template, care must be taken not to label as "not applicable" an item that is in the template in order to ensure that a legal requirement is met. For this reason it is important to include

335

in the customization process appropriate SMEs who can represent each enterprise concern. Even better, the organization's managers and architects should be trained to understand the enterprise concerns. The best way to achieve this is to have an enterprise mentoring team help the department or unit to develop a planning customization process, in collaboration with the department's architects and managers, and certify that that process appropriately accounts for enterprise concerns.

In this way, an organization can leverage its SMEs – including its executive officers – rather than having them directly involved in every decision and hoping that executives find out about all of the important decisions. Knowledge is explicitly pushed down and sideways, leading over time to a more intelligent organization.

That said, a level of control is needed, to ensure that the knowledge is applied properly on an ongoing basis, and to ensure that an appropriately credentialed authority is included in decisions that require that from a legal, regulatory, or other standpoint. Therefore, the processes defined by departments, with the help of mentors, need to include a means for identifying signoff points and decision points that require a credentialed individual. Further, the mentoring group needs to continue to monitor processes and occasionally participate in or pre-audit initiatives to verify that processes are being appropriately applied and maintained. However, auditing is an oversight function that is not part of the mentor function. Rather, the focus should be on mentoring, not grading. Pre-audit results should never be reported to executive management; rather, they should only be used as a basis for certification and refining the mentoring focus. Processes must be periodically re-certified, and certification of a department's processes does not mean that mentors cease to have an interest in the department.

Linkage To Compliance And Accountability

The need to work with accounting was discussed in chapter 10 in the section beginning on page 216. However, I did not address how controls should be approached.

The kinds of controls that are of interest to auditors are those that ensure the trustworthiness of data and that enhance the transparency of those aspects of operation that are of interest for compliance. For example, the issues that are typically of interest to auditors include:

- Integration of operation and accounting, from the perspective of consistency and source of record.
- Need-to-know based access to data and segregation of duties, and fraud prevention.
- Change control, controlled deployment, and coverage of testing and verification.
- Transparency of business rules and models.
- Oversight.
- Compliance with accepted industry methodologies, rules, or frameworks, e.g., GAAP[1] and COBIT [2].
- Use of uncontrolled systems and databases, such as spreadsheets and PC-based data.
- Sufficiency of data quality controls, and concrete understanding of the coverage and efficacy of those controls.

Fundamentally the lines of business are interested in accuracy and transparency as well, since these impact the ability to monitor and control the business. The primary difference is that while auditors are concerned mostly with actual operations, lines of business are also concerned with a forward-looking view and understanding trends; but trend analysis requires the existence of accurate and detailed information on current and past operations, which is exactly what auditors are interested in.

There is therefore considerable overlap and alignment between what kinds of controls auditors need and those that lines of business need. For this reason, the two classes of controls should be integrated, even if different measures are emphasized.

---

[1] "GAAP" stands for Generally Accepted Accounting Principles. In the United States, see the FASB website at http://www.fasb.org/, as well as FASAB at http://www.fasab.gov/ and the GASB website at http://www.gasb.org/.

[2] "COBIT" stands for Control Objectives for Information and related Technology. See [COBIT4].

Defining Attestable Interfaces

To make the problem of control tractable, it is necessary to decompose accountability along organizational boundaries. Departments that produce outputs that are used by other departments must be willing to promise an agreeable level of assurance with respect to those outputs. This usually takes the form of a service level agreement (SLA) at the interface between two departments. A service level agreement codifies quality attributes between a provider of output – usually data or a service – and a consumer of that output. This agreement is irrespective of the technical manner in which the outputs are provided or stored, e.g., whether it is organized in a shared central store or handed off from one party to another.

If an organization has confidence that its SLAs are adhered to, then it can attest to the outputs produced. Therefore, there needs to be a means of assessing the efficacy of the SLAs and whether they are actually adhered to. This assessment is not a simple matter, and usually involves a combination of ongoing measurement, tracking of problems and issues, and randomized assessment – so-called "detective controls".

Some organizations have "blanket" SLAs for their IT processes. This is a bad practice, because it allows the business to avoid the issue of defining SLAs. Further, it provides IT with "cover" in that they can say that operations are covered by an SLA and so there is no need to implement a special one. There should be a business-focused SLA between each producer (business owner) of a service and each part of the organization that uses that service.

Data Ownership and Accountability

Data is the eventual deliverable of most IT processes in a service organization. A *data steward* is accountable for the syntactic quality, timeliness, consistency, and semantic quality of data that they provide to others. A data steward is therefore accountable for:

- The semantic rules and algorithms that are used to produce data.
- The quality of their own sources.
- The quality of the interfaces that they use or provide.

338

Data quality is a nebulous concept to most people, but must be measurable and specified in concrete terms. E.g., the following metrics apply to data quality:

- Frequency of inconsistency between one source and another.
- Frequency with which data is not timely.
- Frequency with which data is incomplete.
- Frequency with which the meaning of a data item is ambiguous, or changes meaning in an unexpected way.
- Frequency with which data is found to be incorrect due to a known cause.
- Frequency with which data is found to be incorrect due to an unknown cause, requiring root cause analysis.

A SLA should define what levels of data quality are acceptable for the range of data quality characteristics that apply. For example, it may be acceptable to have erroneous data 50% of the time as long as the cause of each error is immediately discernable and 99% of the time can be handled through a standard exception process.

Certification As Gap Analysis

A certification effort will initially reveal gaps that stand in the way of certification. When push comes to shove, certification will usually give way to time-driven tangible business needs. Therefore, the mentoring group needs to develop expertise in establishing the tangible business value of each certification requirement so that realistic comparison of business priorities can be made. Do not feel complacent with regard to the durability of a certification requirement: its value must be demonstrated and continually reinforced.

The mentoring and certification group must become a powerful ally for making a business case for any effort to enhance capabilities to fill the gaps, including governance-related capabilities. As experience grows, a link should be established between governance requirements and a maturity model, in recognition of the fact that one cannot institute policies overnight. Such a model provides a framework for transition. The model, again, should establish concrete links to business value for each maturity level, rather than merely preaching the motherhood of "more maturity is better".

Crafting Agile Enterprise Policies

An enterprise policy is a decision, representing a strategy for achieving enterprise goals. Policies can be at any level, and can be vague or specific. It is usually appropriate for policies to be stated as abstractly as possible however, so that they do not constrain the organization in how the policy is implemented. Implementation is best left for standards – blueprints – when possible. It is then up to management to ensure that the implementation satisfies the intent of the policies. Also, policies have official standing: organizations are often liable based on the nature of their officer-stated policies, whereas standards are defined at a lower level in the organization and therefore have somewhat less stature legally.

It is important to retain the rationale for the policies, in the form of a policy addendum, preamble, or simply explanation in the body of the policy. This allows the policies to be reviewed periodically with an eye to whether the policies are still serving their original intentions.

Finally, policies should be aggregated and published in a well-known and easily accessible location, rather than merely via an email memo. This allows all staff to locate applicable policies when they need them.

Implement a Certification Mandate As Policy

In the section Empowering the CIO/E (page 116) I explain that the requirement for certification of all business processes should be an executive-driven mandate. The mandate should be implemented as a corporate policy to give it durability. The policy should define (or reference) the mentoring group's operating model, and it should identify the functions that the group performs, previously discussed in this book in the section The Mentor Function (page 120). However, these functions should be spelled out in more concrete terms that spell out actions as indicated in Table 19.

Table 19: Activities of the CIO/E Mentor group, correlated with CIO/E functional responsibilities.

CIO/E Function Mentor Group Activities	Capability Planning	Enterprise Architecture	Control Strategy Pilotin	Capability Mentoring	Capability Piloting	Capability Certification
Solicitation and understanding of strategic concerns.	X	X				
Creation of enterprise architecture and reusable blueprints, to serve as a baseline for use by departmental projects.		X	X		X	
Mentoring of departmental groups, to help them define their own compliant, maintainable, and flexible business processes.				X		
Monitoring and certification of departmental processes.						X
Co-Leadership of arbitration processes for resolution of difficult issues such as ownership of data and processes.						
Occasional auditing of departmental processes and initiatives, only for the purpose of assessing mentoring effectiveness.						

If you have had experience with an enterprise architecture group, you probably wonder why there is no architecture review activity. That is because architecture review is not necessary if one uses a proactive approach of co-developing architecture with those who will implement it, and then certifying the resulting design and business process. In other words, rather than a "big bang" review, I advocate an ongoing refinement process that ultimately must satisfy both the users and the mentor group.

The arbitration activity provides a means of resolving complex issues that impact organizational boundaries or responsibilities, such as who should assume ownership of a given business process or type of data, what service levels can be expected, which priorities take precedence, and who should pay for fixing problems. The intent is to provide a routine mechanism for addressing these kinds of issues: strategic impact issues of course may need to be escalated to executive management.

Arbitration should also be an opportunity to fine-tune the way in which business priorities are evaluated and compared: since I am advocating a metrics-based approach, arbitration should ideally be more about how to weight metrics than about subjective criteria. The arbitration board should be prepared to explain its decision process, and that process should utilize a consistent business value framework, and should not hesitate to refine the framework as part of its activity.

The auditing activity in the last row is for the purpose of assessment of effectiveness of the mentoring function. By assessing actual success of the business in achieving objectives in addressing enterprise concerns, the organization can determine whether the mentor group is doing its job and if its certifications really mean anything.

The effect of these policies is to create a powerful but adaptable tactical control point that is focused on enabling and elevating your organization, rather than disciplining it. These people will be the company's boots on the ground for achieving cross-departmental goals. For this to work, the mentoring group must have teeth – it cannot merely be an educational group – but with a charter to bring capabilities and processes into line with enterprise objectives.

How a Departmental Business Process Is To Be Defined, and How That Definition Should Be Overseen

It is extremely important that *departments define their own processes*, and that the mentors not do it for them. The *mentors are supposed to show departments how to define their processes*, and train them in tools, techniques, and corporate standards for doing so.

For example, the mentoring group would not define a purchasing process; rather, they would define the process that Purchasing – or any department – should use to define their own processes. Thus, Purchasing would say to the mentoring group, "What must we do in order to define our processes?" and the mentoring group would reply by explaining how they would like Purchasing to define their processes so that the approach conforms to the organization's standards and preferred practices. The mentor group might provide templates and instruction. The mentor group would also oversee the work to ensure that enterprise concerns are addressed by the processes, taking note of any failures to address enterprise concerns adequately.

Consensus on Enterprise Architecture

The mentor organization should include the rest of the business in the development of enterprise architecture and any standards that it develops or promotes. I do not believe in creating architecture by committee, but that does not mean that one should not utilize committees to discuss particular issues, to formulate plans for pilot efforts, or to discuss and approve aspects of an architecture.

It is the job of the mentor group to *accumulate* an enterprise architecture over time, as a deliberate side effect of refinement of approaches and reference designs, and also by anticipating global requirements and issues and launching efforts to find solutions to them. Thus, I am of the opinion that architecture should be issue-focused. If one takes an issue-focused approach, then committees can be very effective at developing consensus on those issues. However, for this to work, someone has to take the lead to identify and organize the issues. The mentor group is perfectly positioned to do this synthesis, and thereby orchestrate the evolution of an enterprise architecture that has everyone's buy-in because they in fact helped to create it.

As important aspects of the enterprise architecture are agreed to, they should be included in policy, either by being part of a standard, by being referenced by a standard, or by establishing a new standard or policy, depending on the issue and its importance.

Establish a Policy Requiring Certification

Establish a policy that all departmental processes are to be identified and certified by the mentoring group, and assign real dates for that requirement for each department.

This policy helps to give authority to the mentoring group, but in a manner that gives departments a chance to bring themselves up to a level where they can be rewarded for their certification accomplishment rather than reprimanded for not meeting objectives.

Certification should be granted only if a department succeeds in defining its own processes and those processes conform to enterprise guidelines as defined by the mentoring group.

Implement Minimal But Powerful End-To-End Effectiveness Measures For Mentoring Success

As discussed in chapter 5, it is more effective to invest effort into elevating capabilities than in micro-measuring a business process. Measurement efforts should focus on overall progress – i.e., actual realized value – and on how effective the mentoring team is at helping other groups to be productive and effective. From this vantage, the success of the mentor group can be assessed by:

1. How well departments realize enterprise goals and address enterprise concerns, including realized business value and reduced loss incidents or demonstrably reduced risk.
2. How well departments adhere to enterprise policies and standards, as long as the practices mandated by these policies and standards are based on balanced value and risk analysis.
3. How productive IT-related activities have become, in terms of realized business value per dollar spent.

Independent evaluation of end results is necessary. This puts everyone on the same team, and creates an incentive to work together. This point was also made in chapter 5.

As explained in chapter 6, measurement of the mentor group's effectiveness should be from an enterprise perspective, and not on a project-by-project basis. In other words, effectiveness should be rolled up to the enterprise level before it is assessed.

Adherence to policies (item 2 above) is best assessed by an independent auditor that is not associated with the enterprise mentoring group. Passing an audit creates a success for the department that is audited, and also for the mentoring group that helped them to define the processes that passed the audit. A series of successful audits indicates that the mentoring group is working effectively with the departments that they are assisting and certifying, although the primary success rests with the owner of the audited business process.

Success with respect to enterprise goals and concerns (item 1 above) is harder to measure, but it is the real success, and measuring it requires the existence of a business model and measurement for each area of the business that is required to be certified by the mentor group as of the current date.

Measuring the productivity of IT-related efforts (item 3) is the most challenging for all the reasons that it is normally hard to measure the productivity of knowledge workers. However, if one looks at the dollars spent on IT-related efforts that result in certified business processes, and compares it with the enterprise-wide business value that results from those efforts based on the associated business models, one can compute an enterprise productivity that accounts for the total cost and total value received.

The question then becomes, what is an IT-related effort? The scope of such efforts should be all effort involved in defining, implementing, and deploying a new information-related business capability; and this calculation should include efforts by non-IT staff.

Review Policies Regularly

The time to review policies is when organizational goals change for the planning horizon, when the policies are not proving to be effective (audits are failing), or when changes in the business climate put policy rationale into question. These kinds of events should be monitored on an ongoing basis, making the process agile and event-oriented rather than calendar-based.

An effective agile strategic planning methodology should map the dependencies between plan goals, plan assumptions, plan strategies and policies and their rationale, and tactical approaches to implementing those strategies and policies. Changes to any of these need to be constantly monitored, with immediate impact analysis. In this way, unexpected events such as an announcement by a competitor can be quickly assessed in terms of current business strategy, and the impact of strategy changes can be assessed just as quickly.

An agile planning structure helps also to prevent policy obsolescence. Employees often complain that policies are onerous or outdated, leading to a perception that the organization does not consider its policies to be important. Having a dynamic set of policies and basing standards and processes around them gives weight to the policies and sends the message to all employees that the policies are for real.

Reconciling Financial and IT Controls

In chapter 10 I discussed the common ground between IT and Finance, and ways for business processes to help Finance to do its job. Then in the section Alignment of Operational and Financial Control Activities in chapter 9 I discuss the need for executive leadership to temper its instinct to always give financial reporting concerns immediate priority, and suggest ways for Finance and IT to collaborate.

In this section I intend to compare the approaches often used by Finance and IT with respect to control, validation, and adjustment of data and business processes.

There is substantial tension between the finance operations world and the IT world today at lower levels of the organization. Much of this is due to lack of appreciation of the challenges and concerns of each group. Both of these groups want to operate efficiently and both want to satisfy the needs of internal and external auditors. However, there are real differences in the philosophy and approach of these two communities, and understanding these differences is important if one is to reconcile them and enable these groups to work together toward their common goals.

Comparison Of Quality Control Philosophies

One of the paramount differences in methodology used by the accounting and IT communities has to do with the way that systems are verified. The financial world verifies through reconciliation of independent computational paths. Verification is end-to-end, and focuses on numerical data. Error analysis requires progressive reconciliation of sub-calculations, and is usually planned and executed in an ad-hoc manner. Models are usually created as spreadsheets or workflows. Workflows are almost always sequential and batch in their design. Processes are often driven by calendar events, such as the end of a reporting period, or the end of a business day. This tends to promote a waterfall-like process because it is most efficient, even though it can never be real-time. Processes are often well-understood, and change only incrementally from year to year, and are supported by organizational structures and responsibilities.

In contrast, the IT world verifies through progressive verification of subsets of rules and algorithms, in a process known as "unit testing". Thus, data is not verified: functionality is. The verification often focuses on behavior rather than numbers, e.g., does the system detect an invalid input? Or can it identify or categorize a data item that is input? Models are almost never created as spreadsheets. Flow charts are often used, as are system structure diagrams and use cases. Flow charts are often transaction-oriented, indicating the potential for concurrency and focusing on the smallest possible units of work. Processes are ideally driven by receipt or completion of a processing request. Processes are often entirely new to the IT team, and are often poorly understood by the IT team. Team structure must be created from scratch and is organized around IT process lifecycle functions rather than business functionality.

In practice one needs both. The tension around these different philosophies lies in that IT analysts want to know business process rules a-priori, whereas accounting professionals generally need scenarios to work from in which they decide which rule would apply. This creates a very substantial communication barrier: IT professionals cannot come up with these scenarios, and often do not appreciate that they need to do this. Financial analysts view themselves as experts and do not expect to have to come up with scenarios to explain how they make decisions, much less lay out the rules in a top-down fashion.

One solution is to require your IT teams to have a substantial base of accounting knowledge. Another solution is to have some IT people in your accounting groups. The career migration path tends to go in the latter direction.

347

Comparison Of Quality Control Approaches

Besides a difference of philosophies, there is also a difference of approach with regard to remediation. The traditional practices of the accounting profession espouse the insertion of checks and controls at various points within a process to ensure that all is well.

This control-based approach that is often espoused by auditing firms is to address the problems on a case-by-case audit-oriented basis, and add more "controls": more reconciliation, more range checks, and more layers of approval.

In contrast, the IT approach is to step back and simplify – the term is "refactor" – the process so that it is correct by design and fewer checks are therefore even needed. Thus, the paradox is that if root causes are addressed, more trustworthy IT processes actually have *fewer* checks, not more. Thus, the number of "controls" is an extremely misleading and fallacious measure of the trustworthiness of a system. A posting to an IT newsgroup highlights the tension around this issue:

> *A traditional PMO Governance Approach can be frustrating for agile teams as they often measure the "wrong" things and look for conformance to processes that are counterproductive to the true goals of delivering business value. I.E. PMO's check for compliance activities rather than business value delivery because: a) these checks are easier to codify and conduct, b) they work from a belief that more process control equates to a better quality output.[1]*

The posting, which is very insightful, then goes on to say,

> *...the good news is that traditional PMO's want the same things as we do, successful projects, it is just that their path for getting there is different from an agile approach.*

The control-based approach has its roots in the history of financial auditing, which is based on the concept of "summative evaluation": the evaluation of a business process after the process has completed. A natural approach to remediation of failures

---

[1]   Posted by Mike Griffiths on the Agile Project Leadership Network (APLN) Yahoo group, September 13, 2006.

detected by summative evaluation is to add explicit mitigation steps – active controls – that detect and correct errors. This approach is in contrast with "formative evaluation" which evaluates in real time and impacts the process to improve it so that success is ensured. For example, any kind of mentoring or re-engineering process includes formative evaluation.[1]

The right solution is a middle ground. Simply adding more controls and layers of approval for change will create a Department Of Homeland Security-like organization (which has no fewer than 25 functions each representing a category of concern reporting to the Secretary [DHSOrgCht]). On the other hand, controls are important; but control can also be achieved by simply addressing quality. Even if quality is improved, independent checks are needed to ensure that quality is what one thinks it is. The right strategy requires collaborative work to come up with a solution on a case-by-case basis that reflect the concerns for accuracy and transparency, but that retains agility and is lightweight.

Challenge Of Different Timeframes

The financial world tends to turn according to the cycle of reporting requirements: annual and quarterly deadlines as well as end-of-day and end-of-month cutoff points. In contrast, business operations tend to be event-driven and live from moment to moment. Ironically, financial processes usually work off of business events; yet because they report aggregate results, it is often necessary to wait until all of the events for a period are known before financial processes can be run because the outcomes of later events sometimes impacts the accounting interpretation of earlier events (we can thank our lawmakers for that).

Certification of Controls

Remember that in the model espoused by this book, the CIO/E leads a capability-driver tier that acts as a change management

---

[1]   For a discussion of summative and formative evaluation and a comparison of IT evaluation approaches see. [Remenyi00], p. 27.

entity and an advocate for enterprise concerns. In this role, the mentor group is in a position to defuse some of the tension between Finance and IT, but in its place is the pressure for certification.

Since the mentor group certifies business processes, and business processes contain controls, does this mean that the mentor group must be capable of certifying financial controls?

The answer is emphatically yes. However, since the primary stakeholders for financial controls are the Finance department and each business process owner that produces source data for Finance, certification of controls cannot be the purview of the mentor group alone: certification of any financial IT control must be a combined effort between the mentor group, the business process owner of the data or process that is being controlled, and Finance.

One can be sure that Finance will not wait for the mentor group to come up with a way for these three parties to work together, so progress in this area should be worked over time, in an incremental manner. The onus is on the mentor group to propose a workable collaboration model. The incentive for the mentor group is that it is on the hook for demonstrating business value. The incentive for Finance is that it can offload the burden of maintaining control definitions. Finally, the incentive for each business area is that it can make Finance happy and get certified by the mentor group at the same time. That is, certification of a business process cannot occur unless the process is shown to meet the concerns of Finance along with all other major enterprise concerns.

Remember though that certification does not replace auditing, and that the internal auditing unit (for Finance and for all other enterprise concerns) is separate from the mentor unit. Therefore, certification does not guarantee that an internal financial audit will be passed; but if it is not passed, then the shame is shared by Finance, the operating unit, and the mentor unit. Certification only means that the mentor unit *thinks* that a business process will pass an audit, and therefore the business process is fit for operation until an internal or external audit says otherwise.

Points Of Intersection

Assuming that the financial unit is operationally independent of the CIO/E or CIO, as is typically the case unless the CFO owns IT, then it is to be expected that the financial unit will have its own standards with regard to controls and procedures. These should be aligned with the CIO/E-mandated controls and procedures and the enterprise architecture in general. This means that the CIO/E and CFO need to work closely to ensure this alignment, and that a set of policies and standards need to be co-authored by the two units, or at least that their respective standards need to be consistent and supportive of each other. In particular, the financial unit will likely require a data management standard that defines how reported data is to be managed, and the standard should be consistent with and supported by any data management standards developed by the CIO/E unit.

Another area that crosses the boundary between IT and finance is the operational capabilities needed to design, implement, and operate IT-built controls that pertain to financial data. For example, systems for managing *meta data* – that is, data about data – should be designed so that they meet the needs of both the overall corporation and of the financial unit. This is a challenge because the needs tend to be very different: finance tends to focus on data elements and have a lineage and control perspective, whereas the rest of the business tends to focus on processes that produce data and have a hierarchical perspective in terms of groups of data, the processes that produce them, and the lifecycle and change cycle of the data.

Both finance and operations tend to be interested in business events that change data, although their interpretation of the events might be very different. Business events are often omitted from enterprise models, despite their tremendous importance. A clear definition of business events can serve as a foundation for communication between IT and finance, since even though the interpretation of events may differ, the events themselves can usually be made unambiguous.

351

Organizational Impact

Planning for remediation of financial control problems must be integrated with planning for IT capabilities. The overlap between financial operations and IT is so huge that a failure to integrate these areas is a failure of strategic proportions.

Yet the primary goals of IT and finance are very different. Finance seeks to measure and reduce risk, whereas IT is historically driven by business opportunity. Integrating these functions therefore requires integrating these very different points of view.

To achieve this, the financial and IT departments must develop trust if finance is ever to rely on IT and if IT is to rely on finance: trust that can only be built incrementally through progressive steps of working together. Toward that end, these departments should plan pilot efforts that integrate their planning processes and that integrate their concerns in a balanced way.

A Model for Data Controls Taken From the Security Domain

In the field of information security, it is widely accepted that in order to demonstrate that a data element is trustworthy one must present an *assurance argument* for that data element. The assurance argument is a logical explanation of the reason why the data element should be trusted, and it usually involves the identification of the features of the systems that protect the element, as well as the pathway that the element follows during its lifecycle. The argument may be rigorous and even mathematical for a very high risk system, or it may be informal and even anecdotal for a low-risk system. However, the concept is that a data item cannot be consisted to be trustworthy unless you can present an argument for why it should be trusted. That is, the default is to not trust anything, unless it is proven worthy of trust.

The same notion can be applied to data quality, since data quality is about trust in the value of a data element. The source of mistrust is not *necessarily* malicious intent, but errors due to omission, sloppiness, or technical errors. Nevertheless, the concerns for data quality are very similar to the concerns for security.

As explained in chapter 5, active controls are controls that operate in real time while a business process operates. For active controls, the system features that implement a control are often specific checks designed to check the reasonableness of a business fact (data element). In such cases, the assurance argument is merely the set of rules regarding the range of allowed value for the business fact. In such simple cases the relationship between (a) business fact, (b) assurance argument, (c) control, and (d) the system features or procedural activities that implement the control are all one-to-one. These four elements are depicted in gray in Figure 26, which illustrates the relationships between controls and system features or quality control activities

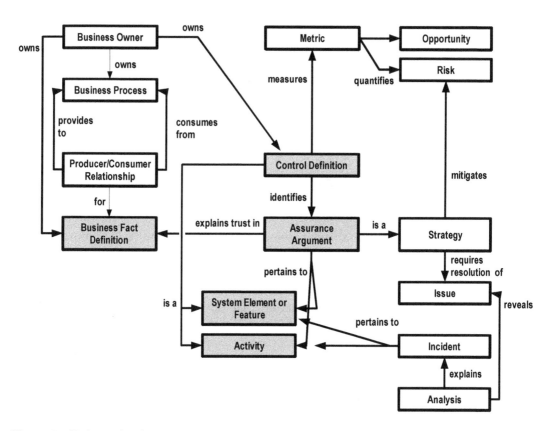

Figure 26: Relationship between controls and system features or quality control activities.

The one-to-one relationships are a degenerate case: for controls that operate earlier in the lifecycle, such as during design, testing, or deployment, the relationships are normally not one-to-one between a business fact, its assurance argument, the control(s) the protect the fact's integrity, and the system(s) that implement these control(s). Therefore, in order to be able to track which system features or operational procedures ensure the correctness of a given data element, one must examine the very design of the system and business processes and explain how these work together to ensure that the element can be trusted. In this situation, a control is less a physical thing and more a concept represented by the assurance argument that applies to a data element.

This does not mean that one cannot enumerate controls. On the contrary, one should, because only then can one be sure that each data element is trustworthy. The model that I propose is that each data element have an accompanying assurance argument, and that each such assurance argument be identified as a "control". These assurance arguments should be part of the designs of the systems that implement the data flows of the organization (this is discussed more in the next chapter). The implementation of the features that are demanded by the assurance argument then comprise the actual manifestation of the control.

Portfolio Balancing

So far I have discussed IT portfolio management in the context of the need to consider the manner of execution (see Portfolio Management is not Sufficient, page 55), and also in the context of portfolio board membership (see Portfolio Board Membership, page 207). Here I would like to revisit the first topic and delve a little deeper into the factors that inhibit the effectiveness of IT portfolio management.

The first factor is the problem of estimating the business value of a project or an IT investment. It is common practice that IT project funding requests are accompanied by a "business case" that explains the value of the proposed project, and that provides the budget requirements, the benefits, and a rough plan of action. This is often done in one page. Further, it is often the case that the numbers are literally guessed at to a large degree.

The intention here is not to belittle the guesswork that takes place, as gut-feeling guesswork can sometimes be quite accurate! The problem is that the business value is usually expressed in intangible terms, such as "will improve data quality" and "will make process X more efficient". This makes it very hard to balance the portfolio because with these intangible justifications one cannot compare one investment with another.

It is not always possible to eliminate all intangibles, and in fact it is not always worth the effort, but in cases it can be done, and if doing so enables a comparison of approaches, then it is worth it.

One should also not only address the business case from a cost perspective: One should account for the business value of freeing up capital once the benefits start to accrue. The value of the freed capital should be taken into account in the portfolio analysis, since more available funds means more projects can be funded.

Another factor that is often left out of funding requests is the nature of interaction across projects. Such interactions are often stated, such as having a footnote stating that a certain part of project requires that another project be executed concurrently. However, this says nothing about the value that will be realized if that part of the project is not performed. In other words, the portfolio board often does not have sufficient information about the business impact of the choices that are available.

It is not possible to do proper portfolio analysis if one does not have the inputs that are needed, and project managers should provide this information. Their architects should take the lead in enabling them to do this, because it is the architect's job to know what the technical tradeoffs are and how they will impact effectiveness of the system, which translates directly into business value. In short, the architect should provide a model that can be used to explore options and their respective value and cost characteristics.

Current industry practices fall short of this ideal, and so to enable this process to be fixed the mentor group should be involved in refining the portfolio process. For this to work, the mentor group needs to be involved in project planning early – before funding is requested. Therefore, it needs a forward view of what is coming. This can often be obtained through the organization's online funding request system: since it takes time to prepare a request, the mentor group can look at the requests that are being worked on and then contact the project owner. At that point the mentor group can help the project owner to prepare a proposal that properly accounts for business value and tradeoffs. If the prospective project manager is working with an architect to conceptualize the proposed solution, the mentor group can work with that architect to identify the technical components to the value proposition.

Working Groups

It is common practice for portfolio boards to create various working groups to focus on different areas, such as technical architecture, business architecture, and do on. I do not feel that these working groups are necessary. They tend to be a symptom that business benefit analysis is not being done properly, in a tangible way, with an enterprise value model behind it. Enterprise architecture analysis and business architecture analysis should be unified – that is one of the main points of this book – and so they should not be split across different working groups. Further, these should be overseen by the CIO/E's organization. By the time a proposal gets to a portfolio board, the value analysis should all have been done, from every perspective that matters, and so working groups should not be needed.

Capability Development Lifecycle

In the view presented in this book, developing automated software-based systems is not distinct from developing business capabilities that require automation. The utility of the term Software Development Life Cycle (SDLC) is therefore in question, and at a minimum is subsumed by Capability Development Life Cycle (CDLC). However, as I will explain later, there is utility in retaining a distinct SDLC concept, that is an "automated system development" aspect to a CDLC.

Organizations usually keep their SDLC self-contained and focused on actions that are specifically limited to the design, implementation, and maintenance of automated systems. The reason for this is automated systems require a high level of technical skill to create and maintain, and the technicians who perform that work traditionally are not from the lines of business and do not have a business focus. This partitioning is part of the reason for the perpetuation and institutionalization of the poor communication between business and IT.

Nevertheless, even a strictly technical SDLC needs to reflect business concerns, and this intersection is often described as "touch points" – that is, the points at which business concerns touch and therefore impact the SDLC processes. Traditional touch points include requirements, standards, and acceptance testing.

In our CDLC view of capability development the "touch points" approach needs to be replaced with a more holistic and integrated approach. Instead, the touch points are everywhere, by centering the CDLC around business value-driven decision-making.

In this book I am not going to prescribe a detailed map of a CDLC, and in fact many variations are possible, just as there exist many SDLCs. However, the following elements are necessary:

1. Business **value assessment (including risk) must be as tangible** as possible.
2. Business **value assessment must be integrated at a _design level_** – not merely at a project management or portfolio level.
3. IT **architects must be accountable for incorporating business value** into their designs.
4. Projects must be accountable for **incorporating operational business value measurement** as an implied requirement for every system: this requirement must be a standard.
5. There must be a **yardstick for measuring business value**, and this yardstick **must be co-developed with the operating units** to ensure that it is credible. Further, the yardstick development (discussion) should ongoing – not a one-shot deal – and should evolve into a methodology that accounts for the idiosyncrasies of the business. This methodology is intended for use at a project level and above, and for guiding major architectural choices.
6. There must be a **framework for quickly projecting the business value of various practices** when it is impractical to apply the full methodology. This provides

staff with "rules of thumb" to use for all of the basic situations.

7. Assessment of technical **progress must account for risk and be in terms of value** as described in earlier in chapter 11 – ie., not merely in terms of tasks completed and money spent.

8. The business value that is realized from a system must be **tracked over a long period of time** – long enough to reflect the impact of accumulated changes – and correlated with the impact of other business actions. Otherwise there is no incentive to protect the long-term value proposition of a capability as changes to connecting systems are created.

9. Architect staff must be expected to have business knowledge, financial analysis acumen, and technology acumen.

10. **Knowledge of business practices and systems must be managed as an asset**; the focus of projects must be on the development and transfer of knowledge in and among particular groups of staff rather than on creating artifacts.

11. Architect staff should **not be separated by skill specialization**. E.g., there should be no distinction between a senior "information architect" and a senior "technical architect", since at a senior level the concerns of the various disciplines overlap way too much. If you reach the level of architect – which should be a major career milestone – you should be above such specialization and be valued mostly for your *broad knowledge* and *keen judgment*.

12. The CDLC should promote the use of a **pilot approach**, whereby capabilities are created by first building them in a small way, learning from that effort, and then attempting broader deployment, all the while assessing performance of the capability in terms of enterprise value rather than localized value.

All of these elements have been discussed previously in this book, and all of them strongly impact the SDLC or CDLC at its heart: the manner in which architectural decisions are made and measured in the field. *Details such as which artifacts to create are not even important.* What is important is that *the right decision points are identified and made*, and that *decisions are traceable to business value.*

One thing is clear from this: a lot more is expected from staff than in traditional SDLC processes. Architect staff must have business knowledge and must be able to make a business case that is professional and sound and that provides an integrated view of opportunity and risk at an enterprise level. This cannot be delegated to project managers because the business case must be integral to technical decision-making. IT architects must think about business agility instead of system flexibility, and they must think about cost to the business instead of merely cost to maintain a system. To think in these terms they must have a business model in their heads. Thus, to become an "architect" now means much more than it meant before. It means that you have reached a level of maturity at which you can truly integrate technical and business concerns.

Ensuring That Decision Points are Identified

Software engineers make decisions every time they write a line of code or drag and drop a design element. It is a very difficult task to ensure that those myriad of decisions are executed such that they are consistent with the intent of enterprise strategies and standards, and also aligned with initiative and project strategies. Traceability is also important: that is, keeping a record of each decision and how it addresses requirements and enterprise concerns.

The now age-old approach to achieving this is to create very detailed design documents and having in-depth reviews that examine those and even examine the code through code reviews. These approaches have largely been discredited in a business setting because they are too slow, too costly, too inflexible, and are not even robust. Newer approaches that are collectively characterized as "agile" approaches put the emphasis back on creating business value and relying on the constant sharing of team knowledge and customer interaction to ensure that requirements are addressed. These approaches do not often provide adequate assurance however that higher-level enterprise concerns are addressed. Concerns for security, for example, often fall by the wayside. In an article that I authored with Scott Ambler we describe an adjustment to agile approaches to address such concerns.[1] Our adjustment is to rely on a competent architect to be aware of enterprise concerns and to identify risk areas that require a higher level of design and scrutiny. We describe our approach as *Agile Assurance*: practicing agile methods while applying a measured amount of care in a risk-based manner.

> **The Agile Assurance approach relies on a competent architect to be aware of enterprise concerns and to identify risk areas that require a higher level of design and scrutiny.**

The Agile Assurance approach is highly consistent with the principles outlined in this book. The concept of mentor presented here is someone who makes it their job to be aware of the entire breadth of enterprise concerns, and to interact directly with lines of business to inspire pilot projects and then to transfer their knowledge to those projects. Those pilots help the mentor architects to validate approaches that can then be extracted as reference designs for use by other projects. Such reference designs incorporate ways to address all enterprise concerns – not just immediate functional requirements.

The role of the architect is therefore critical. This is the person who is charged with risk management, through identification of critical decision points, evaluation of business value and risk, bringing in SMEs on an as-needed basis to help with complex evaluations and issues such as security and compliance, ultimately framing all decisions in business terms, and ensuring traceability for all design decisions by documenting those decisions. It is important that in this approach time is not wasted documenting other issues up front. The architect's main value to the organization is their ability to identify the important decision points so that the team can invest extra effort on those. Time should not be wasted crating detailed designs for issues that do not really matter. This "just in time" approach to risk management is what makes the process agile and cost effective and is what differentiates it from traditional approaches.

---

[1] Ref. [BerAmb2006].

By now you should be able to see why the form and content of artifacts is not critical to adhering to this approach. Once a risk area has been identified, it should be designed through carefully using whatever artifacts are appropriate and consistent with prior practices for the team. Form does not matter here: substance matters. Judgment matters, and knowledge matters. The architect matters.

Understanding Software Development Lifecycles

Before considering the elements of a CDLC up close, it is useful to first review the elements of a software development lifecycle (SDLC). The CDLC elements can the be viewed as an extension and contrasted with the more limited SDLC concept.

One source of confusion about many SDLCs is that they often identify "phases" according to generic activities such as planning, analysis, design, development, and testing. Yet, the reality is that all of these activities occur during in phase. For example, some amount of development may occur during the requirements phase if it helps to create a quick prototype to test an idea. Labeling phases according to these generic activities can therefore be confusing.

Another point of confusion is that it is often the case that some activities are re-performed several times at different levels of confidence or detail. For example, a preliminary architecture might be created during a proposal phase, and then an architecture re-created later when work starts. Thus, just because something has been done does not mean that it should not be done again or refined in another phase. In fact, most document artifacts – which are essentially quality control devices – are created at the outset and refined progressively throughout all phases. Even waterfall processes allow for this refinement, through change notices for artifacts that have been accepted.

A colleague of mine [1] addressed this confusion by defining an SDLC in which each *category* of project activities is a row in a table, and each column is a "phase" or "state", and the cells indicate the specific activities that need to be done. Further, for each activity,

---

[1] The colleague was Sean Rutledge.

the "gates" that allow the activity to be assessed and approved are identified. This approach (in extremely simplified form) is shown in Table 20.[1] In an actual table of this kind, the activities in the cells should be precisely named and defined, along with an identification of who leads and participates in their execution, and who approves them and what their criteria for completion should be.

Table 20: Progression of activities across all phases.

Activity Category	Pre-Approval	Mobilize	Rqmts/ Design	Dev	Accept Release
Project Plan	Draft High Project Level Plan	Revise Project Plan	Complete Project Plan	Maintain Project Plan	
Rqmts	Draft High Level Concept	Revise High Level Concept	Create Detailed Requirements	Maintain Detailed Requirements	
Architecture or Design	Draft High Level Architecture	Revise High Level Architecture	Refine Architecture into Design	Maintain Design	
Quality Plan	Draft High Level Quality Strategies	Revise High Level Quality Strategies	Create Detailed Quality Plan	Maintain Detailed Quality Plan. Implement Quality Plan.	
Dev Envt		Provision Dev Envt.	Configure Dev Envt.		
Test Envt		Provision Test Envt.	Configure Test Envt.		
C&A		Engage C&A Team.	Plan C&A. Design Security Controls.	Certify.	Accredit.
Release Executable Installation Script Ops Manual				Create Release. Test Release.	Execute Acceptance Tests

Remember that the phases identified along the top of the table merely identify sets of activities and do not necessarily preclude concurrent activity across phases. We can agree to use the traditional approach of naming phases according to the

---

[1] An actual table of this type that I created for an SDLC was more than ten pages, in landscape mode, legal page size.

predominant activities for that phase such as requirements, design, or implementation, recognizing that some of these might be iterative or overlapping and not actually time-based.

Misapplications of this View

One mistake the project managers often make is that they assume that a methodology can be executed as a "cookbook" or a "checklist". That is, if one merely creates all of the artifacts listed in the methodology, then you are done.

It does not work that way. Not at all. Judgment is the most important element of a project, and a great deal of judgment is needed in deciding _how_ to perform each activity. For example, in Table 20, the activity "Draft High Level Project Plan" is not something that one should merely pass to someone and say "do this". Instead, considerable thought is needed about what needs to be given the most attention in the plan, who should be consulted, and so on. Certainly a plan for adding one feature to a small Web application should look very different from a plan to create a new multi-million dollar system. They would not even have the same elements in the table of contents. The judgment about how to execute each activity is a primary value add of the mentor team: to help project managers and project architects make the judgments they need to make about _how_ to perform each activity.

Another mistake often made is that activity completion is defined in terms of whether a document has been created. However, that is not a good criteria, because it excludes any assessment of whether the document meets the need. Documents are merely proof that a person has performed certain intellectual activities. For example, a test plan is proof that a test planner has enumerated the tests that need to be done, and explained their rationale. However, one does not know if test planning is actually complete unless someone credible and impartial assesses whether it is. Further, if all of the activities are equated with documents, we have then defined a huge set of documents to be created, and that is not a very good approach to building software. It might make sense to have a small set of documents (or even website areas) that serve as the home for many of the activities in the table.

Note that many of the activities in Table 20 are "draft" activities. That is, their completion is fuzzy, and they are allowed to be incomplete, and unvalidated. Drafts are a first cut that can be examined and built upon. However, any activity that is not a draft is not complete unless there has been a test that *the knowledge has actually been created*. This is very different from merely checking that a document has been created.

Gates and Release Management

When a project manager plans a project, the manager must decide which tasks will be performed, by whom, and when. In an agile project, this is first done at a high level, and then refined progressively as more and more components are built. Nevertheless, these decisions take place; and even in an agile project, some long-range decisions must be made up front, even if they end up being fine-tuned later: the project manager must decide how configuration management will be performed, how software will be tested and released, and how stakeholders will approve of the product.

These activities – configuration management, testing, release management, and stakeholder approval – are all *control activities*. That is, they are not an end in themselves, but exist to ensure that the final product is of quality and meets expectations.

As explained in chapter 5, controls can be proactive (a-priori) or after-the-fact. It is up to the project manager to decide what kinds of controls are appropriate for the project: that is, how to implement the activities in the methodology chart of Table 20.

For example, in a project using a waterfall methodology, a quality plan – which is purely a control activity – might be implemented up front as a full-blown end-to-end detailed test plan. In contrast, an agile project might devise a set of test strategies for each major category of requirements (e.g., functional tests, performance tests, and concurrency tests), and progressively refine the tests over time: this would be in addition to unit tests that are produced in the course of development. The activity of devising and refining the quality plan therefore takes a very different form, depending on the methodology chosen.

Regardless of how the control activities are implemented, the question inevitably arises of how one determines if a control is satisfied? That is, who determines if the tests passed, or if the design review passed, or if the release candidate has been approved for release to a particular production environment? Certainly the project manager has some say, as does the project architect, and as does the end user; but in a large organization there needs to be more control over these decisions and they are an aspect of tactical governance. For this purpose many organizations require each production environment have a *configuration control board* for making release decisions, and it is also common practice that a person is appointed as a *project release manager* to oversee the various approvals and decision processes that must be made for a project. The release manager therefore is the facilitator of project-level governance, and the project's primary interface to stakeholders and to the configuration control board for production.

The rules and approvals for when a software artifact, such as a design or a module, can be released from a process (such as design) and passed to another process (such as coding) are often referred to as "gates", and it is the release manager who is charged with ensuring that the gates are adhered to. Configuration control tools are often used to help in this regard, but a person must be in charge of the process or there is the substantial risk that the process will become ad-hoc with a serious impact on quality.

It should be noted that the term "configuration management" is highly ambiguous in IT, and that it is used to mean at least two different things: (1) configuration control of artifacts, and (2) the implementation of higher level control processes such as gates, stakeholder approval, and oversight of a software environment. Both have to do with control, and are different levels of the need to ensure that the progressive development of artifacts is a controlled process.

Roles and Job Categories

When defining the activities that must occur in a software development process, one must define the roles that should be involved in performing each activity. These roles should be abstract and not identify individuals, particular groups, or parts of the organization. This allows the activity and role definitions to be tailored to different projects. For example, at the start of a project, the project manager might decide that the organization's primary data center should perform the role of hosting provider, and that the same staff will also provide the role of application operation. If these roles are well-defined, then it is clear what is expected. A list of possible roles is provided in Table 21.

Table 21: SDLC Roles and Sub-Roles.

Role	Sub-Roles
Sponsor	
End user	
Business owner and business analysts	Authorizing Official. Business Analyst. Business Owner. Business Operations Staff. Business Project Manager.
Information System Owner	
Compliance and risk management	IT Governance. Agency and Department Governance. Agency and Department CFO. CM Board. Release Manager.
Security	C&A. ISSPM. Security Operations. Privacy office.
Technology Provider or Developer	IT Project Manager. Project Architect. Technical Lead. Programmer. IT Contract Manager. Technology Vendor. System Architect or Engineer. Database Architect.
Mentor	Engagement Manager. Business Analyst. Enterprise Architect. Application Architect.
Application-level testing	Application Test Analyst. Application Tester.
Performance testing	Performance Architect. Performance Test Tool Specialist.
Hosting provider	Network Engineer. System Engineer.
Installer	Application Installer. Database Administrator.

Role	Sub-Roles
Operators	Database Administrator. Application Operator.
User support	Support Manager. Application Support Specialist.
Maintenance	Application Maintenance Technical Lead. Application Maintenance Programmer.
Training	
Contracting officer	

Now let's return to the activities defined in Table 20. Each of these activities should define which roles should perform or participate in the activity. If the project manager makes sure that each role is assigned to an actual person or group, then each activity will be covered, and people should know what they are supposed to do.

Iteration

All software development is iterative to some extent, in that a release is commonly followed by additional releases that fix bugs or that add new functionality. The principal difference between software methodologies has to do with the period between iterations, and with the degree of overlap permitted between activities of different phases. At one extreme, traditional "waterfall" methodologies have long iteration periods – often years – and do not allow any overlap in activities that belong to different phases. At the other extreme, highly "agile" methodologies employ periods between releases of only a few weeks. These releases may be production ready, or they may be only for the purpose of demonstrating functionality to the stakeholders. Regardless, they are not merely builds: they are releases with demonstrable functionality. So-called "spiral" methodologies assume that changes to requirements or design only occur during those phases of a release cycle, where highly concurrent methodologies such as eXtreme Programming (XP) allow anything to change at any time, except generally the set of requirements "stories" that are considered to define the scope of a release.

In any case, these SDLC methodologies are generally limited to software development: they do not address business process

367

change, nor do they address the important step of conceptualization of the need for a solution. These dimensions traditionally occur at a business level outside the purview of IT, and that is one of the laments of this book. Nevertheless, let's first look at a typical SDLC to establish a baseline for our understanding.

The section that follows may be largely a review for many readersand, but those who are familiar with SDLCs might want to at least skim it nevertheless because there are some points made that pertain to CDLC issues.

A Typical SDLC

Figure 27 illustrates the set of activities, deliverables, and controls that exist for most software development lifecycle methodologies. Artifacts or activities that serve to provide control on the process are indicated by triangles.

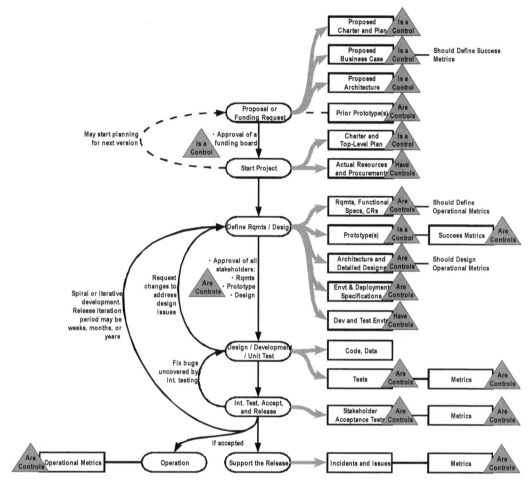

Figure 27: A typical Software Development Life Cycle (SDLC).

Proposal or Funding Request

This phase aggregates the activities associated with making the case for a capability development effort. This always begins with an idea, a need, or a mandate which sparks the effort to conceive the new capability or change an existing capability. Those who conceive the idea usually seek an executive level sponsor who evaluates the need for the project from a business strategy perspective and stands behind the project when the request for funding is made.

In the commercial world this phase commonly involves preparing a project description and request for funding that is evaluated by an IT portfolio board. In the US Federal Government arena the process is similar except that it is often more formal, such as requiring certain standard documents to be created that describe the business case, identify the proposed solution architecture according to Federal Enterprise Architecture standards, and the identification of business performance metrics. As in the commercial case, the request is considered by an IT portfolio board. If a request is approved, then it might need to be added to a larger funding request for consideration by a higher board, such as an Office of Management and Budget (OMB) board, and so approval by the organization's board might still mean that there is a considerable wait until funding is actually received.

Issues that come up during the lowest-level board review process might result in requests for more information or analysis. In both the commercial and government case, the outcome is either a funding approval or a rejection; and in the case of an approval, changes can be made to the funding level as well as the project scope and other aspects. The board is the primary control on the funding and oversight of projects, from the perspective of the overall organization. Some boards have auxiliary boards or committees for examining certain issues, such as enterprise alignment so that the primary board can focus on the portfolio from an investment perspective.

> **The business case produced by the mentor group for the review board should comprise an integrated view, accounting for not only alignment, value, and risk, but also the *value of the alignment strategies*.**

A mentor group should be represented on the IT review board, and brings with it expertise with respect to alignment as well as value. Thus, the business case produced by the mentor group for the review board should comprise an integrated view, accounting for not only alignment, value, and risk, but also the *value of the alignment strategies*. For example, if a funding request involves the development of a solution rather than the purchase of a COTS solution, the business case should consider the value of the business agility realized over the planning horizon, as well as full lifecycle cost.

The requirement for performance metrics is important and provides for tangibility. Unfortunately, performance metrics are often not implemented well because they are often focused on cost rather than opportunity or flexibility because these last two are often difficult to model or measure. That is why I spent so much time in this book on the modeling of the business value of IT flexibility and IT's ability to respond to business opportunity. If these aspects can be incorporated into the performance metrics, then a much larger and more realistic picture is achieved. The IT architects are needed in order to make this happen, because IT flexibility is deeply related to IT architecture choices. The ability to actually measure the metrics must also be anticipated during the design of IT systems and business processes, because such measurement usually involves making run-time correlations that are difficult or impossible to create later in an ad-hoc manner.

Project Initiation

Once a project actually begins, the project manager must assemble the team, define the project's activities via a revised project plan, and bootstrap all of these activities. In many organizations projects are given a formal charter that states the project's scope and objectives, the budget, key strategies and assumptions, and how success will be measured. The charter is often drafted when the project is first proposed but then modified and finalized when the project is funded based on any changes required by the review board or executive sponsors.

Key artifacts should be assembled in this phase, and project infrastructure put into place such as configuration management. Kickoff meetings are held with stakeholders. If some portion of the effort is to be outsourced, then statements of work are drafted and bids are solicited. If a large portion of the work is being outsourced, then the project might actually consist of managing the statements of work and vendor performance.

It is worth noting that "executive" departments of the US Government are required to define performance metrics for projects before those projects can be initiated. Thus, the identification of metrics is built into the mandated lifecycle process. However, such metrics often fall short in their implementation. Estimates of business value are often very subjective, and more importantly, they typically do not address

371

IT's concerns properly. For example, estimates of improved operational flexibility might be developed, but the longer-term impact on agility of IT strategies are often not addressed with regard to the future flexibility provided by building systems using a common business event model versus created yet more point-to-point solutions. In short, the strategies that IT architecture staff think about seldom are articulated in the business case.

Stakeholders

Stakeholders are often thought of as the end user. In an enterprise, this view is inadequate, as there are other stakeholders of comparable importance. These typically include:

- CSO or information security.
- Risk management and governance – who ensures that enterprise-wide risk management practices are adhered to?
- Accounting (for GAAP compliance).
- Legal.
- Operations – who will run the system?
- Support – who will respond to incidents?
- Maintenance – who will respond to requests for small enhancements and repair?
- Executive sponsor(s) – who will benefit from the system?
- Enterprise architecture – who has the high-level view of how the system fits within the environment?
- Development – who is building the system?
- Training and change management – who will have to teach others how to use the system?
- Legacy system owners or users – who will be transitioning from an older system?

If these various stakeholders are not represented in some way, then the representation is incomplete. Further, each of these stakeholders needs a way to test that the system meets their requirements.

This perspective puts a new light on "acceptance testing" which often involves only the end user. To be legitimate, acceptance testing should achieve the acceptance of all stakeholders – not just the end user or project sponsor. It may be that some of these stakeholders are not interested in a particular project, but a project should consider whether each of these should be consulted and represented in some way. These stakeholders should be represented at a requirements level, a testing level, and an acceptance level.

The mentor group should provide help in assembling the stakeholders, and facilitating the collection of requirements from these groups. The mentor group should also provide templates for acceptance testing plans, as well as guidance on how to integrate various concerns into the development process. For example, security C&A should be addressed from the outset, and the C&A group should be asked, "what could the development team do to make your job easier?" and "what could we do to make your process have a shorter turnaround time?" Most likely they will respond with requests that you use standard components, that you perform threat analysis during the design phase, that you verify that the software matches the design, and that you use the Secutiry group's recommended or required practices with regard to separation of duties, passwords, and other elements. If all these things can be addressed throughout the design and development process, then C&A will take much less time and the application can be moved into production more quickly.

Requirements Definition and Design

Most traditional SDLC methodologies distinguish between a requirements phase and a design phase. However, agile methodologies tend to combine these under the assumption that a lot of design takes place during the requirements phase and that it is difficult if not impossible to fully separate the two. This pertains to both functional ("logical") design as well as technical design. For example, if users express a requirement to have a Web-based transaction capability, then analysts will likely find that it is most effective to work up a paper-based design of the screens; and while they are doing this, project architects might start considering which platforms will provide the required level of performance and scalability. Experienced analysts and architects think about all of these dimensions while they plan requirements, rather than completely separating these decisions. The reason is that there are often tradeoffs such that requirements impact technology choices but technologies also often impact requirements, due to costs, whether a certain technology is already present in-house, and so on.

373

Even if requirements and design occur somewhat contemporaneously, these aspects should be maintained in separate artifacts because requirements and design do not map one-to-one. Rather, as explained in the next chapter, design is a series of choices made to satisfy requirements and the relationship between requirements and design decisions are many-to-many.

It is important to realize that the various artifacts produced pertaining to requirements and design exist *to serve as controls* on quality. That is, their main function is to provide assurance that all requirements are transparent and are met. Viewing artifacts as controls gives meaning to their existence, and enables one to discuss the tradeoffs in using alternative approaches. For example, if one replaces a design document with extensive tests, is the requirement for control met? In some cases it might be.

When assembling requirements and a draft design, it is critical for a large enterprise that all stakeholders are included. It is also critical that service level requirements related to data timeliness and consistency are addressed explicitly. This will be discussed more in the next chapter. Table 22 provides a list of the kinds of requirements that should be considered in an enterprise environment. The stakeholder for each type of requirement should be identified, and asked what their particular concerns are, and these concerns should be addressed in the overall business plan for the project and the business capability that will result, through mitigation strategies or design features as appropriate. It is not necessary to work through all of these concerns in detail up front, but the major concerns should be identified and addressed at a strategy level, and no important concern or requirements area should be overlooked.

During the requirements and design process, the mentor group should help to identify requirements areas with respect to enterprise concerns, and provide design templates based on prior similar projects. It should also help to identify the need for prototypes in order to manage risk.

Table 22: Types of enterprise requirements to consider.

This is intended as a checklist that can be used to query system owners to determine if there are areas that are important for a given system that have been overlooked. Not all of the elements in the checklist will be important for all systems: the intention is to have a list of all things to consider. Also, the requirements need not all be gathered up front.

Potentially Applicable Standards

> Enterprise policies and directives. For US Federal Government: agencies, agency-level or departmental directives and policies should be considered, as well as OMB-mandated policies and directives that apply. These often reference NIST standards (e.g., NIST SP 800-53: Agency SDLC). Of course, there is also the OMB Federal Enterprise Architecture requirements and reference models. Laws such as "Section 508" (Disabilities Act) and FISMA should be considered.

Business Case

- **Current Usage**

  > Are there currently users who depend on the system? How many, and how critical is the work that they use the system for?

- **Lifecycle Value**

  > Is the need for the system expressed in tangible terms? Will the system help to protect human life or property? Will the system save money over time? Will the system help to further the mission or strategies of the enterprise? Will the system help business processes to be more effective? Will the system enable flexibility that will in turn reduce anticipated future costs?

- **Lifecycle Cost**

  > Is the lifecycle cost of the system properly estimated? Is the cost of maintaining the skills needed to maintain the system accounted for? Is the cost of servicing and repairing the system accounted for, as well as the cost of responding to user calls for assistance?

- **Urgency**

  > Is there a cause for time-related urgency with respect to the implementation of the system?

- **Accountability for Data and Services**

  > Who will own the data produced by and managed by the system, and the services provided by the system? (See also "Transparency of service level requirements" and "Protection against disruption in data sources" below.)

Functionality

- **Verifiability.**

  > How completely can the system's functionality be tested? That is, what is the test "coverage"?

- **Testability.**

  > How readily (conveniently, quickly, and repeatably) can the system's functionality be tested, especially if the system is modified? For example, are most of the tests

automated?

- **Who are the intended users?**

   Is the system intended for general enterprise use, or a specialized group of users? In consideration of the application's intended user community, does the application need to be made available to the entire enterprise network, or could it be deployed such that it is available only on a sub network?

- **Usage authorization requirements (see also "Securability" below).**

   How clearly and completely are the user access roles and rules defined? Is authentication required to be inter-operable with other domains? For example, is Federal eAuthentication required?

- **Legality**

   Has an attempt been made to identify all of the applicable laws and regulations that apply to the system and its users, in the system's location of operation and in the locations of its users? Has legal counsel been consulted with respect to the system's functions and its planned regions of operation and use? Have governance boards been consulted? (See also "Accountability and transparency" below.)

- **User Provisioning and account management**

   How will users obtain access to the system? How will they obtain their password? Is single sign-on required in some manner, or should standard desktop login credentials be used? How will users be removed from access when appropriate? How will user access rights and accounts be managed, and by whom?

- **Data retention**

   Are there applicable data retention or records management requirements?

Standard Components

- **Are standard components to be used, including the following?**
  - Database server.
  - Application Server or Web Application Server.
  - Application Server Runtime Toolkit or Framework.
  - Web Server.
  - Mobile or Wireless Communications.
  - Desktop Application Software.
  - Desktop components (e.g., .NET, graphics libraries or drivers, desktop database).
  - Other.

- **Will the application be deployed via a data center, or installed manually?**

- **Is a particular version or release required? Are there any components that are not the latest or most secure supported release? Are there any components that are not a supported release, or that are soon to be unsupported?**

   Many COTS or GOTS components contain or require embedded components, such as a Web server, an application server, Java, or a database. It is important to identify these dependencies form a maintainability and security perspective.

- **Are standard data center procedures to be followed?**

- **What procedures are to be followed to maintain the various components at their most secure supported version?**

  Is ISO expected to do this? If not, who will?

- **What should be done when a component is no longer supported?**

  Are there alternatives that could be substituted for the various independent components of the system? What type of effort would be involved in making those substitutions?

- **Have existing enterprise designs been researched and considered, to allow for the possibility of reusing them in some manner?**

  Reuse is important not only to save effort, but also to ensure consistency in how things are done. This facilitates maintenance as well as consolidation where appropriate.

Service Level Requirements

- **Who will operate the system? Who will maintain the system? Who will extend the system when new requirements arise throughout its lifetime?**

- **Transparency of service level requirements: is there an SLA that identifies each type of user?**

  How completely have the kinds of requirements defined in this section been identified, documented, and *agreed upon* (via an SLA) for each of the various intended users of the system?

- **Protection against disruption in data sources?**

  Are there, or will there by, SLAs with the providers of data and services that are used by the system?

- **Risk-based attention to all of these requirements?**

  Has the risk associated with each function in the system been identified and used as a starting point for planning the diligence and attention to service level requirements for that function?

- **Required scale, and response time at scale.**

  What response time should users expect to see, at normal load and at peak load (and everywhere in-between)?

- **Usability (with respect to convenience and learning curve).**

  How easy is the system for a new user to learn to use? How efficient and comfortable is the system to use for an experienced user a routine basis?

- **Availability profile, time to recover from routine failure, protection against loss of data due to routine failure, and overall robustness.**

  What percent of the time, on average, can the system be allowed to be out of service (for maintenance, recovery, or other activity)? What is the maximum permissible contiguous time that the system can be unavailable?

  To what extent should the system protect against loss of data due to overload, the crash of a component, or other "normal" lifecycle failure events?

- **Recovery from catastrophic failure ("DR").**

  What provisions should there by to protect the system and its data against failure due to an unexpected catastrophic event, such as a hurricane, flood, fire, or terrorist attack? Given such an event, what provisions should there be to restore operation?

- **Internal data consistency.**

  To what degree can the system's data be allowed to be inconsistent, given that errors can occur due to user input mistakes and due to system processing glitches? To what degree must such inconsistencies be automatically detected?

- **Data consistency with respect to *other systems*, particularly with respect to allowed latency of change propagation?**

  Are there other systems whose data must be consistent with this system, and to what degree? Is there a time period allowed for inconsistency? Or, must consistency be designed to be absolute within the limits of the technology? If inconsistent data results due to any reason, what provisions must be made to make the data consistent or to deal with the inconsistency?

- **Data accuracy.**

  How accurate must the data be, given that users often make data entry mistakes, and given that data rounding errors and other kinds of processing errors can occasionally occur? What provisions should exist for detecting and correcting inaccurate data?

- **Accountability and transparency (recording and reporting of transactions and data).**

  Is the system required to record business events or data for the purpose of subsequent reporting (e.g., financial reporting) or forensic analysis (e.g., to provide traceability in the event of unauthorized actions)? To what extent must this type of reporting data (which is often sensitive) be protected or separated in terms of access control or physical protection to protect against subsequent deletion, modification, or viewing?

- **Securability (part of risk management).**

  In what ways must the system be secure by design so that complex configuration, procedures, or user action are not required? Should the system's data be classified according to sensitivity or role-based access?

- **Manageability (ease of administration and operation; part of LCC), monitorability (part of availability), and measurability (with respect to performance of primary and non-primary mission metrics).**

  In what ways must the system be installable so that complex configuration is not required? In what ways must it be monitorable, so that operators and users can detect abnormal events as well as assess the health of the system? In what ways must the system provide for ongoing measurement of its mission effectiveness (mission performance)? Should (and do) the latter map to project metrics for project performance?

- **Verifiability of implementation of architecture strategies and design (that implementation matches design and requirements; part of reliability and risk management as well as maintainability).**

  What evidence should be provided that the system's implementation actually matches the documented design?

- **Testability of service level requirements (part of verifiability).**

  How readily can service level requirements be tested, especially if the system is modified?

- **Maintainability (part of LCC).**

  How well is the system's design understood by those who will maintain it? Is the design sufficiently simple? Are the system's primary design decisions documented? Are the primary data structures or object models documented? Is the configuration documented? Are the non-functional and functional requirements documented? Are all of these maintained in a location that is under configuration control and that is easily accessible to those who will maintain the system? Is there a convenient means for users of the system and operators of the system to provide overall feedback to the maintenance team as well as log trouble reports?

- **Extensibility (determines business agility; related to maintainability).**

  Does the design of the system lend itself to being extended or modified over time? What aspects of the system's design are a concern with respect to future extension? For example, are there customized interfaces or business rules for particular users? Are there specialized components (e.g. COTS components, or poorly documented home-grown components) that cannot easily be extended? How will others in the organization know that this application exists, and obtain information about its use and design?

Design and Development

Just as it is difficult to fully separate the requirements and design processes, it is difficult to fully separate the design and development processes. Regardless of the methodology, a great deal of design occurs during development (programming), and some programming even occurs during design, such as when a quick prototype is created in order to work through a design issue. Many IT managers do not appreciate *how many decisions* must be made during design and development and the extent to which these must bubble back to requirements and design.

Despite the intertwined nature of design and development, the artifacts of design and development are different because current IT technologies do not lend themselves well to working at a design-only level and so again the mapping between design elements and implementation elements is not one-to-one. Of course there have been attempts to create tools to unify design and development, but the effectiveness of these tools is mixed.

The goal of design and development is to produce a working system that is maintainable and that meets the requirements, and to do so in a manner that allows for sufficient control such that risk is managed. Design artifacts help to provide this control as well as maintainability, as do tests. Along with the tests there should be a set of metrics that indicate how many tests are passing and how comprehensive the tests are (what the "coverage" is).

The processes of requirements, design, and development can iterate many times, depending on the methodology. If the design reveals a discrepancy or inconsistency in the requirements then changes to the requirements might be warranted; or, if the running software reveals a shortfall in the requirements or a flaw in the design, then either of these might need to be changed. Inevitably iteration occurs, and some processes allow for this to occur in a fluid manner while others require a great deal of traceability with change notices. In the end, what matter is how trustworthy the various artifacts are: if the code is trustworthy and complete then the system can be operated; if the documentation is trustworthy and complete then the system can be maintained.

During the development phase, the mentor group should attempt to ensure that the development team uses practices that will make it possible to verify that the implementation matches the design. That way enterprise alignment can be verified more readily, and so the mentor group's certification process can be performed more efficiently. The mentor group should also help to set up the verification processes, and introduce tools to the developers to

380

streamline this. The mentor group should also help to implement prototypes that try various design strategies, but these prototypes should be throw-away. Production code should be built by the development team, not the mentor team.

Integrated Testing, Stakeholder Acceptance, and Release

The question of "what will the testing group be testing?" turns out to be not so obvious. In many projects that I have seen code moved from development to testing and eventually to a production environment, like a car moving down an assembly line. This is not the best approach. The job of the development team is to produce a working product. The job of testing is to test it. The job of the deployment team is to deploy it. What deployment deploys should be identical to what testing tested, and therefore the only thing that should "move" is a release package: it should move from development into a configuration control system, and from there it should move to testing. Similarly, deployment should obtain the same package from the configuration control system – unchanged. This is important for many reasons that are beyond the scope of the discussion here, but suffice it to say that development builds a product – not just code, and deployment, operations, training, and end users all use that product. Thus, all aspects of the product need to be tested: the installation process itself, as well as the operations guides, should all be part of the release package and should all be tested. Further, all these elements should be defined by testable requirements.

Testing needs to be designed for, and there should be tests for every category of stakeholder. Examples of categories of tests include end-user functionality, security, performance and scalability, reliability, manageability, and maintainability. You might wonder what kinds of tests serve to verify maintainability: a review of the documentation to verify that as-built matches as-designed is one such test. Tests for reliability include those that stress the system in various ways and verify that the system continues to produce correct results and that it remains available and responsive. Tests for manageability include those that verify that the requirements of those who will operate the system have been met. Tests for security include design review and verifying that as-built matches as-designed, threat analysis, vulnerability scanning, and penetration testing.

Acceptance testing should not be only in the hands of end users. That is, acceptance is a process in which *every stakeholder* should be required to sign off. End users are not the only stakeholders. For example, if a system meets the end user's requirements but it does not meet the requirements of enterprise security, then it is not acceptable and should not be released.

Operation and Support

Once a system is accepted it can be delivered and deployed. At this point the two primary activities associated with the system are its operation and its support and maintenance. Operational metrics should measure business performance and correspond to the business performance metrics and goals called for in the capability's business plan. The support function should collect metrics with respect to system maintenance, incidents, and issues. These should be correlated with events and operational conditions so that trends and root causes can be discerned and failures predicted.

Environments and Configuration Management

Some discussion of environments and configuration management are necessary here in order to provide a foundation for a discussion of gates and control points, for allowing a release candidate to be promoted to release status.

Development Environment

Purpose: For the Development Group to create a capability to produce the products or services defined by the business plan. With respect to software, the capability consists of a release package that can be distributed, combined with a support organization and possibly training and operation organizations as well.

Testing Environment

Purpose: For the Development Group to validate the capability that they have produced. For software, this involves integration testing for the various components of the system, scalability testing, and interoperability testing to verify that the system works with the other business processes and systems that will be present in its intended operating environments. A Testing environment should be a well-controlled environment, and it should test the full release package produced by Development, as checked into a configuration management system. Scalability testing requires that the environment has the ability to support the load required by the scalability tests.

Acceptance Testing Environment

Purpose: For the various stakeholders to perform their own tests. This environment should be well-controlled, and it should be possible to "clean" the environment thoroughly before each set of tests. Further, it should be possible to install and operate test instances of other applications in this environment to test for interoperation. Testing should be performed against the release package, obtained from the configuration management system.

Staging Environment

Purpose: To install (deploy) the application and verify that the configuration is correct for the environment. For this purpose, "smoke" tests are performed. Additional tests may be performed as well, including interoperability testing. The environment must be as similar to the actual production environment as possible.

Gates, Controls, Roles, and Project Profiles

A "gate" is an important type of control, in that a gate is a checkpoint that verifies that a release meets the criteria. For example, a gate between development and testing might include criteria that the release pass all of its unit tests and that the requirements and design for the release are complete and accurate. Having passed the gate, the next step in the SDLC can accept the release and perform its work on it.

In defining an SDLC, one must decide first what the activities are (e.g. development, testing, etc.), and then one must decide who will do what. For example, programmers perform development, and testers perform testing. This is straightforward for the most part, but there are some activities that require some care in terms of defining those roles and who performs them. For example, many projects have a release manager role who ensures that the various controls are actually adhered to. A CM board may also be necessary if changes must be made to artifacts that have been formally accepted by stakeholders, especially if interoperability with other business systems might be impacted. CM boards also oversee changes to environments, most especially production environments.

Once the activities, their controls, and the various roles have been defined, it is useful to define "profiles" for projects that serve as a guide for applying the SDLC based on the project size and its various characteristics. Fore example, a project to create a Tier-1 (mission critical) business system should implement the SDLC more thoroughly than a less critical project. Profiles help to define these things ahead of time so that one does not have to make these decisions anew for each project. Ideally, most projects in the enterprise portfolio would it into one of the standard project SDLC profiles.

OTS Software

Off-The-Shelf (OTS) software is software that is obtained as a release package from an external source and installed for use. Such software generally should also be subject to an Acceptance Testing phase, unless it is already trusted or Acceptance testing has already been performed by a trusted entity. Once the required level of trust is achieved through testing and any required C&A procedures have been performed, the software can be installed to a staging environment to validate the intended deployment configuration, and then installed to the production environment.

Routine Software Updates

It is common for IT organizations to "push" updates to infrastructure products on a regular basis. These pushes include desktop software as well as server software. Such updates are extremely important, but they can be very disruptive for development teams and even for production.

Mass pushes such as this are in effect deployments without integration testing. Before a mass push, IT should do one of two things: (1) it should provide the upcoming updates to the test environment of each project, on an opt-in basis, or (2) it should rigorously test the updates itself with each major application.

Pushing updates without taking these precautionary steps creates the impression that IT is in its own world and out of touch with the application teams, and it puts the business at risk for disruption of application services.

A CDLC View Up Close

In this section I hope to provide some new insights by considering SDLC in a larger context to include the conception, development, and measurement of business capabilities. Toward that end, consider Figure 28. Note that the blocks labeled "Build Operational Implementation" and "Implement New Workflows" comprise system development and business process re-engineering activities, respectively. (Similar figures were presented in Figure 23 and Figure 24, but those figures essentially fit into the "Build Operational Capability" block in Figure 28.)

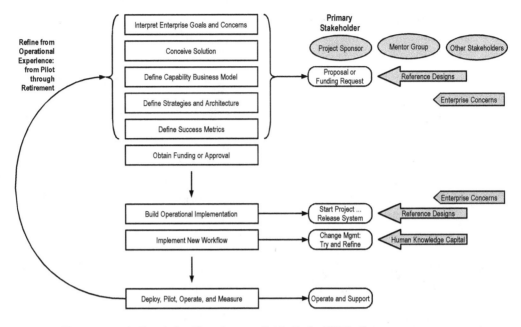

Figure 28: A Capability Development Life Cycle (CDLC)

This figure depicts broad categories of activities that should occur from the point at which a need for a new business capability is identified through the deployment and operation of that capability. (Retirement of a system is implicitly included, since retirement is merely a deployment that removes the system and modifies the business process accordingly.) Let's look at each of these categories.

Interpret Enterprise Goals and Concerns

This category of activities represents a planning function, and is the starting point. The higher level goals, mission, or strategies of the organization are considered, in the context of the current environment and challenges and issues that have presented themselves from within or from without. If the planning is being performed at the highest levels of the organization, then this function is a strategic planning function.

Conceive Solutions or Strategies

Once the environment has been assessed and higher strategies have been considered, a solution or set of go-forward strategies can be devised. The various horizontal concerns of the

386

organization should be represented in the solution, as well as the vertical part of the organization. These various stakeholders will later be contacted again to form a stakeholder board for accepting the solution when it has been implemented.

The solution should document the thinking behind it so as to provide traceability and also to make it easier to revise the solution when the situation changes. A draft project or initiative charter should be created.

Define Capability Business Model

A business model for the solution, representing a new or modified business capability, should be created. All enterprise concerns should be addressed, as well as cost, risk, and opportunity. Purely cost-focused or risk-focused models are incomplete. The mentor group should establish a strong expertise in the development of these models so that it can assist operating units in accounting for cost, risk, and opportunity in a balanced and measurable manner.

Define Execution Strategies and Architecture

As I have said before (see the section "Implications For Initiative Planning" in chapter 4), it is not enough to merely carve out an initiative and then toss it to IT to execute it: the *how* of execution is as important as the *what*. Therefore, when planning a solution one must delve into the execution process and design to some extent, and knowing how far to go is an art and is why judgment across business and technology issues is so critical in IT planning. The highest level strategies and components of a system should be defined at the outset, at least in a tentative manner, to identify and address the main risks and choices. Outstanding issues should be identified so that they can be addressed later through a prototype or further attention. The overall approach to execution should also be addressed, including how the skills will be obtained and retained throughout the lifecycle of the business capability.

Define Success Metrics

Success metrics should be identified at the outset, in a preliminary way, to set expectations about how the effectiveness of the new capability will be measured. Note that I did not say "effectiveness of project execution", as that is an aspect of project execution and should be part of the execution strategy. What I am referring to here is the set of operating metrics that the new business capability will produce throughout its lifetime and which should be used to assess whether the capability is meeting its objectives. These metrics should be related to identifiable tangible objectives in the business case.

These metrics are separate from project execution effectiveness, yet they should be integrated with project execution metrics. This is because acceptance testing should include the actual measurement of these metrics in a pre-operation environment. A "warrantee" concept can be used to make acceptance conditional on the actual success in the operational environment for some period.

The metrics should address the concerns of every stakeholder, not just the business stakeholder. For example, metrics with respect to security incidents or random penetration testing results should be addressed.

Build Operational Implementation (the "SDLC")

This is where a traditional SDLC kicks in: the point at which the required business capability has been conceived, and a system needs to be built. During the SDLC process, the system requirements need to be re-defined or made more detailed, since prior to this point they are most likely specified at a conceptual and objective-oriented level. In addition, requirements should ideally be re-articulated by the development team, to make sure that the team's interpretation of the requirements is what was intended by the business.

Any architecture defined in order to get funding needs to be re-examined and updated at this point to reflect any changes directed by the portfolio approval board or executive sponsor. Eventually the architecture must also be made much more concrete and exact. This occurs over the course of the SDLC process. Project plans that were part of the proposal package must also be updated, and procurements of resources need to be performed. If the system is to be outsourced, bids will be requested at this point. Of course, the development team must also be assembled, and stakeholders are ideally aggregated into a formal structure such as a structure such as a board or committee.

At various points during the SDLC there are assessments performed by stakeholders. It might turn out that the system is not meeting the intent of the expressed requirements; or it might turn out that the requirements are not correct. In either case, it might be necessary to escalate the issue to the business and revise the requirements and even the business case. Hopefully this will not happen too often, but this avenue needs to be accommodated.

Implement New Workflow

SDLCs generally omit the important dimension of business process design or re-design, yet most IT architects who I have met agree that business process re-design should be addressed as an integral part of the solution. Why SDLCs continue to omit this aspect therefore is somewhat curious, and perhaps is because IT is so frequently removed from business process re-design that as a group IT does not know how to codify the process. In any case, this book as addressed this need from many directions, including the value of having a mentor team work with the business to re-define business processes, to have mentor staff who are knowledgeable of the business, to encourage the operating units to originate and be accountable for new capabilities, to use the mentor group to enable operating units to conceive of capabilities that have an enterprise focus rather than only a localized focus, and to formulate the business case not only in terms of cost but also in terms of opportunity.

It turns out that the skills that are needed to plan a new business processes or workflow are very much the same skills as those that are needed to design a new system, since in both cases one must address issues of data ownership, process ownership, service levels, exception handling, and data flow. The only real difference is manifests when it comes to implementing the new system, since the components consist of groups of people.

The ways to change human processes include training, as well as prototyping and piloting the new processes. Organizational change management is also an important element of course. If the required IT systems are not yet ready when the new human processes are being tried out, then prototyping of the new processes can be performed by simulating them using manual steps to perform dry runs. For this purpose, test cases must be devised, test data created, and the expected outcomes pre-determined. A post-mortem discussion is essential and issues identified are used to fine-tune the process and possibly even to modify the requirements for systems being built.

The most crucial element is that the business owner should be responsible for documenting the new process, and must be made to understand that the process will be certified based on whether it meets all enterprise concerns, including measurability, maintainability, security, and so on. Thus, the process flows must be kept up to date, or later re-certification will fail.

Deploy, Pilot, Operate, and Measure

This set of activities begins with the standup of the new capability, including the distribution and installation of any required software release packages and the kickoff of any new human workflows using those software systems.

Installation in an enterprise environment usually includes first installing the release in a "staging" environment and performing "smoke" tests to validate the configuration. If all goes well, then the installation is performed again in the production environment.

At this time the System Operation function and the User Support function must begin, to operate the new system and to field incident reports, respectively. Operation includes starting, stopping, and managing the system according to its operation manual. This usually includes running diagnostics according to a pre-defined plan when problems occur; but Operation is not responsible for diagnosing unanticipated kinds of problems: that is what Support is for. The Support function also usually handles many routine functions having to do with user relationship management, including provisioning of accounts.

The Operation function should monitor the performance of every business system, using monitoring features designed by the application's designers. Such application-level monitoring is actually somewhat rare in the industry, as most application designs to not provide for this requirement. As a result, applications are

390

usually monitored based on gross system parameters such as process memory and file space usage; but it is much more effective to give Operations application health signals that they can monitor using their own standard monitoring tools. This way, Support only needs to be called when something unusual happens, and Operations will be able to handle most situations.

Business performance metrics as discussed above under "Define Success Metrics" should be reported directly to management via a report or online Web page. This allows for real-time, event-based response to unexpected changes in business performance. Even so, there should be a periodic review of the performance of the business capability, as part of the normal executive performance oversight and governance processes.

Example

As an example, let's consider how a Support function might be addressed from a CDLC perspective. Assume that the need for a new business capability has been identified, and that the automation component of that capability has been conceived as an IT system that needs to be acquired and integrated. During the planning of this initiative, the identifies that a Support function will be needed, and defines it as a group of people who (1) have experience handling user requests for assistance, (2) have deep technical knowledge of the data and business process; and (3) have skills for diagnosis of user-level problems with the IT system. The Support people will also need IT systems to help them to reproduce the problems that people report, to track these, and to perform analysis of the problems to identify each problem's cause.

The organization already has a User Help Center (UHC), and that center has volunteered to take on the support of the new business capability. The business asks the UHC to provide a representative for the stakeholder team, to help to define Support requirements and to define the Support processes.

The UHC already has experience, as a group, of handling user requests for assistance, so they can leverage that skill for the new business capability. They also have an incident management system that can be used to track reported problems. What they will need to develop is: (a) technical knowledge of the new capability's data and business process, and (b) features built into the new IT system to provide the diagnostic data needed to diagnose problems.

The business project manager defines several activities that need to be performed in the course of developing the new Support capability. These are:

1. Perform knowledge transfer to the Support team, to enable them to diagnose reported problems.
2. Establish a process to maintain the currency of knowledge of the Support team, as the new business process and IT system evolve through future releases.
3. Establish a process to ensure that the knowledge is maintained over time, is reusable in a cost effective manner, and does not suffer from key-person dependencies.
4. Define and implement the IT system requirements for ensuring that Support has the data that it needs to diagnose user-reported problems.
5. Incorporate the support of the new business capability into the existing UHC's problem tracking system.

Note that none of these activities list the creation of documents: whether documents are created is to be determined. Further, none of these activities identify milestones, tests that must be passed, or other concrete validation actions: such actions must be added to the plan as part of an exercise to define how each of the above activities will be implemented. The activities listed above are stated in terms of their true objective.

In order to address the first activity, knowledge transfer to the Support team, the business project manager will work with the UHC manager to define how this can best be achieved. For example, it might be decided that certain documents need to be provided to UHC, or instead it might be (better) decided that UHC will develop those documents, with assistance from the IT system development team and business analysts. Further, it might be decided that the individuals who will actually support the system be involved in the creation of those documents, thereby ensuring that the documents have the information that is needed, and also ensuring *that those individuals actually acquire the knowledge that they will need.* Whatever plan is decided upon, the project plan should have detailed activities pertaining to the execution and validation of each step. This should be true whether execution is incremental or waterfall.

For the second activity above, the intent is to ensure that as time passes, that the Support team is "in the loop" with regard to changes in the business process and the associated IT system. New releases of the IT system should be preceded by knowledge transfer activities that make the Support team aware of new features and changes, and allow them time to update their own documents that they use for support. The business project manager should work with the UHC manager to define how this will happen, and build steps into the overall business process to ensure that it does. The project plan should incorporate activities to establish these steps, as part of the business process, and validate them. For example, the project plan might define an activity to create an advance release notice process that is sent to Support at the beginning of development of a new release, to make Support aware of new features that are planned for the release. Support should be a stakeholder that approves the release, and at that time they can verify that the new features turned out as expected.

For the third activity above, the intent is to ensure that the Support team maintains its proficiency over time. It is common that key people who have the most knowledge get transferred or move on to other opportunities, and if steps have not been taken in anticipation of this, the Support function can suffer dearly. Therefore, Support should take steps to ensure that there are multiple staff who have deep knowledge of the system, and that the knowledge is maintained in a knowledgebase of some kind. Doing the latter alone is not sufficient, because as explained before, information in documents is not actionable knowledge. Therefore, the business project manager should ask Support how this continuity of knowledge will be ensured, and incorporate activities in the project plan to verify that Support does what it needs to do to live up to this commitment.

For the fourth activity above, the intent is to prevent a situation where Support is spinning its wheels, frustrated because the IT system is producing errors but Support is unable to figure out the cause or source of the problem: that is, what the _issue_ is, and whether it is an issue that is already being worked on. Unless Support figures out the general issue or cause, they cannot pass it to Maintenance, because it might be a user problem. Support must be able to discern whether the reported problem is a user problem or an internal IT system problem, or a data problem, and assign the problem to be fixed by the appropriate group. To do this, the IT system needs to provide a trace of its output that indicates the series of data changes or events that lead to the problem. In short, Support needs a "smoking gun" for each problem. This has implications for the design of the IT system: a system should be designed to be "diagnosable", just as it should be designed to be testable, to be securable, and to be maintainable. Thus, Support should have an opportunity to express requirements for what they will need to efficiently diagnose user-reported problems. These kinds of requirements should be captured by the Support team early on, and the Support process should ideally be tested to see if simulated problems can actually be diagnosed. These activities need to be incorporated into the detailed project plan.

The fifth activity above is something that is so visible that it rarely fails to be done: Support needs an incident and issue tracking system. In this example, UHC probably has one, and so they need to "stand up" the new business capability (mostly the new IT system) in their existing tracking system, so that they can start tracking problems that are reported when the new system goes live. The standing up of this system to support the new IT system should be addressed by the project plan.

Existing SDLCs and CDLCs

Large organizations that want to adopt agile processes often have a preference for the business process methodology families known as "Lean", and the "Six-Sigma" and hybrid "Lean-Six-Sigma" methodologies. This is perhaps because these approaches originate from full lifecycle cost reduction and effectiveness programs within large companies (Toyota, Motorola, General Electric, and others), and so there is a perceived conservativeness about them. In contrast, agile methods such as eXtreme Programming ("XP"), Scrum, and Crystal are proposed primarily by individuals. Further, these latter methodologies are primarily focused on software development, whereas organizations often need to plan for new capabilities that extend beyond software. As a result, these latter agile methodologies struggle to gain credibility in conservative and business-focused settings.

And for good reason. Many agile approaches do not *explicitly* address the issues that impinge on a software project that exists within a large organization, and worse, do not address important lifecycle issues such as maintainability and security. There are exceptions. For example, the Scott Ambler's Agile Unified Process (AUP) [1] extends the extremely popular Rational Unified Process (RUP), perserving the lifecycle concepts of RUP while adopting a "value-based" agile approach. AUP also addresses the issue of design and documentation, which are both important for maintainability and security, but again from an agile perspective. Also noteworthy is Ambler's Enterprise Unified Process (EUP),[2] which explicitly takes account of enterprise requirements such as maintainability and all of the other "ilities", as well as addressing the linkage to business value and even portfolio management.

More recently, Ambler and Per Kroll (both at IBM/Rational) have developed a concept of "Lean Software Development Governance", [3] which addresses the need to adopt a risk-based approach to software development, and for organizations to adopt a control-based framework in order to ensure that software projects return the maximum value. Ambler and Kroll's Lean Governance takes the approach of defining practices that achieve the effect of control but that operate in a pro-active enabling manner, as described here in Chapter 4. The practices include (1) defining risk-based milestones, (2) adapting the process to the project, (3) continuously improving processes, and (4) embedding compliance in processes, among others. These practices have all been discussed in this book. What Ambler and Kroll provide is a coherent set of arguments, backed by experience, framed in the context of software development projects. Given the significance of their prior work, these arguments deserve attention.

Lean, 6 Sigma, and Lean Six-Sigma

There is a great deal to the Lean philosophy of executing business processes, and these are highly applicable to software development. Lean processes are fundamentally about focusing on what matters, and refining processes to a high level by enabling

---

[1] Ref. [AmbAUP].
[2] Ref. [AmbEUP].
[3] Ref. [AmbKroll07].

tactical decisionmakers to have input to those processes. Six-Sigma is more about achieving perfection by relentlessly refining a process until all failure modes are handled. It is highly applicable to repeatable processes, but does not apply well to processes that involve alot of decisionmaking or that are substantially different each time they are executed. Software development falls into that category, and so Six-Sigma is not very applicable to software development except in special situations that are very "cookie cutter" in their nature.

One the other hand, there is no reason why one cannot utilize a Lean development process in order to create a Six-Sigma business process. By analogy, one can use an agile process to create software development tools that are used in waterfall projects, ironic as it may be.

Summary

Never attempt to perpetuate knowledge merely by creating documents. Rather than spending a lot of time documenting processes, spend the time teaching others to implement controls and processes correctly.

Blueprints should be developed as a side effect of piloting initiatives.

Pilot efforts should undertake to pilot metrics as well, and measure actual business value in the context of a standard value measure such as ROI, NPV, etc., for the entire enterprise.

Establish a certification program that certifies business processes in that they represent the full breadth of enterprise concerns in a balanced way.

Business process certification replaces the traditional approach of "architecture review boards".

The core requirements for a business process certification process include the validation of the business domain's knowledge and documentation of (1) enterprise concerns, (2) functional goals, (3) process architecture, (4) process business model, (5) success metrics, and (6) accurate correspondence between these and the actual implementation of business processes.

It is not necessary to adhere precisely to external industry frameworks. Such frameworks are best seen as a souce of ideas and templates.

Enterprise architecture artifacts should be minimalist but maintain a high standard for accuracy and meaningfulness.

Policies, standards, and blueprints form the foundation for enterprise architecture.

When a project manager plans a project, high-level choices must be made regarding how methodologies will be applied to the project. This is a task for an architect and manager in collaboration.

A data steward is accountable for the semantic rules and algorithms that are used to produce data, the quality of their own sources, and the quality of the interfaces that they use or provide. A SLA between a data steward and a consumer of the data steward's data should define what levels of data quality are acceptable.

Management should issue a policy that defines the mentoring group's operating model, and identifies the functions that the group performs.

The mentors should show departments how to define their own processes, and take care not to do the business process definition or system conceptualization for them.

The success of the mentor group should be assessed by (1) how well other departments collectively realize enterprise goals and address enterprise concerns, (2) how well departments adhere to enterprise policies and standards, and (3) how productive IT-related activities have become across the organization.

There are substantial real differences in the approaches to control used by the financial domain and by IT.

Eleven requirements are laid out for a Capability Development Lifecycle (CDLC).

13. Create the Right Kind Of Enterprise Architecture

The call to create an "enterprise architecture" comes from many quarters. Auditing firms view the lack of an enterprise architecture as a risk and an indication that the organization is out of control. Public sector organizations in the US and elsewhere have mandates to establish an enterprise architecture. Finally, good sense says that one should have an enterprise architecture – whatever that is!

The first step that most organizations take is often to document a "current state" architecture. This is often problematic because chaos has no high-level architecture, and so one cannot document what does not actually exist. It is like saying to a very disorganized person, "Show me your design for how you have organized everything." You will get a blank stare, and no such diagram can be created – because there is no design, not even an undocumented one.

In the section beginning on page 82 I make a case that spending too much time documenting the current state or future state is a waste of time. The effort is better spent developing a self-sustaining process for evolving the current state to something better, based on sound business-focused and issue-focused decisionmaking processes. Bits and pieces of the current state will evolve naturally out of those processes, along with the desired future state. These comprise the enterprise architecture.

In this book I am not going to define the format of the documents that comprise an enterprise architecture. That is a prescriptive technical topic and is appropriate for a different book, but I will provide some insight into how you can determine if your architects have developed a complete and actionable architecture, and I will point out some pitfalls and signs to watch for.

Fast-Tracking Current State Analysis

A very large corporation that I worked with wanted to consolidate its fragmented data for the purpose of enhancing important data quality attributes such as consistency, authoritativeness, and easing integration woes. Toward that end, it began with a strategic initiative to identify strategies for that consolidation. The company's lead architects were drafted into the effort, each committing about 15% of their time for two months. I was asked to lead and facilitate this effort.

The traditional approach would be to begin with a current state analysis, followed by a "future state" analysis, then gap analysis, and finally the development of strategies for eliminating those gaps.

Such an undertaking would have taken a year, and we had two months. Further, the gaps were already known to the collective minds of the architects who were participating in the effort. In short, they knew the answers: they just needed to organize their collective thoughts, validate those thoughts, and proceed directly to the development of strategies.

Our approach therefore was to fast-track our analysis and focus directly on the problems – the gaps – and skip the traditional documentation of the current-state. To validate our thoughts about these gaps we performed research to prove the existence, scope, and impact of each known systemic problem.

To catalyze our thinking, we established a framework for categorizing the systemic problems, as follows:

- Business events, including so-called "exception cases".
- Physical data sources, and the data transactions against those sources.
- Data source-of-record and ownership rules.
- Business-level data state and lifecycle transitions (e.g., a transaction progressing to "initiated" to "closed"), and data ownership rules pertaining to those different lifecycle states.
- Timing.
- A high-level logical data model that included relationships between data.

- Data consistency rules.
- The processes by which all of these are designed into the automated systems and human procedures, and maintained and enhanced.

In a truly agile spirit, we modeled *only enough* to be able to credibly identify and validate systemic problems. The judgment of what was enough was done along the way, in a highly tactical just-in-time manner.

One of the chief stumbling blocks that we encountered was that the most challenging issues centered around how to get from the current state of affairs to a future state in which we had addressed all of the problems. Simple data flow issues represented a quagmire, and so we separated our strategies and discussions according to migration issues and data management issues. The latter were our true goal, but the former were show-stoppers. By separating these we were able to make rapid progress in decomposing the problem.

Using this approach, we were able to develop a high-resolution model of the systemic problems pertaining to the management of the company's core data, and we produced a set of *strategies for addressing those problems* in a comprehensive and practical way, taking account of current initiatives. These strategies were used to justify funding for a remediation effort the following year.

Adopt a Problem-Focused Approach

IT architects often approach an initiative as if it were a large puzzle to be solved. A lot of effort is put into creating intricate diagrams in which everything connects and nothing is left out. Indeed, popular frameworks such as TOGAF define artifacts to be created encompassing every aspect of enterprise architecture.

Yet, as I explained earlier in this chapter, such approaches provide little real guidance. Programmers must usually re-investigate all of the issues and convince themselves that the architecture meets the requirements.

I am not saying that you should not use a framework such as TOGAF. Rather, I am saying not to use such frameworks in a top-down manner, and be selective. Develop what you need at the time, and no more. Be *problem-and-solution focused*, not artifact focused. Be incremental. Be business-driven, not technical completeness-driven.

As discussed on page 94, an architecture is merely the highest level set of decisions for a system, along with any definitions of elements needed to articulate those decisions, and no architecture element should be in an architecture unless it is there to state or support a decision. Thus, the reason for each architecture element is actually the backbone, yet it is often omitted, and this makes the architecture unintelligible to non-architects (and even many architects) who read the architecture document.

An architecture should be *organized around the problems, concerns, and goals, and strategies* that it is trying to address or implement. The architecture is a set of decisions about these, whether the decisions are represented in a graphical, tabular, or textual manner. Over time an architecture can evolve to be so complete that it starts to look like one of these top-down artifacts, but it should not start out that way.

Any design, including an architecture, should address these dimensions: (a) The problems or goals; (b) analytical concepts; (c) solution strategies; (d) rationale for each strategy; and (e) how success should be measured. The analytical concepts are devised by the architects to help explain the architecture. A common type of analytical concept is a component class: by identifying component classes and the allowed interactions between component classes, one can more easily articulate strategies for achieving objectives such as security, reuse, and agility.

The goals, rationale, and success metrics should be expressed in business terms – not merely architecture terms. Chapters 7 and 11 discussed ways to do this at length.

If these five elements are present then your architecture is likely to be a useful architecture. If they are not present, your architecture will be of limited use. And if any more than these things are present, then your architecture will be overly complex and difficult to utilize and maintain as an agile architecture.

The Importance of the Rationale

At the very beginning of this book I began with a discussion of the importance of capturing both the "what" and the "why" behind each IT decision. The "why" is the rationale: the reasoning behind each decision.

I cannot overstate the importance of including rationale in architecture. The rationale for an architectural element is the *why* for a decision. Documents that describe business processes and software almost always focus on *what* happens, but ignore the single most important ingredient of all for making the documents useful: explaining *why* things happen. If the reader of a document knows why, the reader often can anticipate the what. If why is omitted, the reader must reverse engineer to recreate the why, because true understanding is not possible without knowing why. This is because at the highest level, the why explains the business value, and without knowing the business value, you cannot understand the reasons for why things are done a certain way, and hence you do not really understand them. Only by knowing why can you put the whole picture together and have a useful grasp of function.

For this reason you should develop a culture of stressing the why. Require your process mentors to instill this important value into your staff. Convince your organization's COO, CIO, and CTO that capturing *why* is critical to the maintainability and agility of business processes, and to prevention of key-person dependencies. Make sure that "why" is a central focus on architectural blueprints. In concrete terms, architectural edicts or decisions should always be accompanied by their rationale.

Gap Analysis Must Address Critical Service Level Requirements

Gap analysis is usually performed by modeling the "current state" and the "future state" and deriving the difference between the two. Unfortunately the most important information is usually omitted from both the current state and the future state. When tactical gap analysis is performed, the current and future state are usually described using information flows, but such flows *lack the semantics required to describe the phenomena that usually cause problems.*

Therefore, meaningful gap analysis needs to account for much more than information flows.

> # Current and future state models are usually described using data flows, but data flows *fail to describe the phenomena that usually cause problems.*

For example, information flows do not model concurrency, data integrity or quality, data versions, data aggregation and consistency rules, data ownership, data entity lifecycles (e.g., the lifecycle of a business transaction), allowed state changes in data, data history, meta data, data relationships, the data views and relationship views that are of interest to different parties, and so on.

> # Information flows do not model concurrency, data integrity or quality, data versions, data aggregation and consistency rules, data ownership, data entity lifecycles (e.g., the lifecycle of a business transaction), allowed state changes in data, data history, meta data, data relationships, the data views and relationship views that are of interest to different parties, and so on.

These factors are the *sources of problems related to integration, attestability, transparency, and other issues that are often of strategic concern;* yet, traditional data modeling methods as practiced by the vast majority of data modeling practitioners *do not account for most of these important types of information.*

> # Data modeling methods as practiced by the vast majority of data modeling practitioners do not account for the very factors that are most often of strategic concern.

These information attributes are pertinent to *the usage* of data by business applications, as opposed to the meaning of the data.

Perhaps for this reason, the data modeling community has not addressed the need to account for these factors when modeling data, since the data modeling community has historically focused on data's meaning.

Core Idea: Focus On Service-Level Requirements

It is therefore no wonder that people have a hard time getting a handle on their problems, since data modeling as it is commonly practiced does not even attempt to understand application usage or development in terms of the *service levels* required by the organization. It can also be said that the application development community does not understand data modeling, since application silos built by developers are the main manifestation of data integration woes. Thus, one must architect with an integrated view, accounting for data and processes, and accounting for data integrity and other important non-functional requirements.

The Three *Technical* Reasons Why Corporate IT Loses Agility Over Time

If you agree that architecture should be problem-focused, then it is worthwhile to spend some time considering what the major architecture-related problems are within most organizations.

Ultimately every IT failure is a failure of either luck, judgment, or process. If an organization does not have and cannot obtain the resources needed to achieve success in an IT initiative, it is because someone made a bad decision, a good decision was made but the organization had an unlikely but unfortunate turn of events, or the process for decisionmaking was defective. Technical reasons are never the root cause except that some decisions are technical and therefore judgment failures occur.

However, when mid-level managers and system designers are given the task of fixing an organization's business processes, what they usually see is a host of challenges that are by that time technical in nature. The root causes may be process-related, or decision-related, or the result of bad luck; but by that time the root cause is water under the bridge and the designers see the problems as technical challenges. In a KPMG International survey 67% of the financial services executives surveyed cited the need to re-engineer business processes as the top barrier to implementing online business capabilities.[1] In other words, they found themselves painted into a corner by their process designs.

The technical challenges for redesigning business processes usually fall into the three major categories below.

Data Population Discontinuities

I first mention the concept of data populations on page 90, where I discuss the problem that data in most organizations is replicated with inadequate means of keeping it in sync. Let me clarify what I mean by a data "population". A data population is a subset of a database, based on some criteria such as geographic region, product type, etc. Thus, two different populations might share the same database tables, but each population might be processed by a different system that can handled the unique needs of that population.

Data population discontinuities occur when certain subsets of data are handled by some systems and other subsets are handled by other systems in a convoluted multi-stage pattern such that one cannot identify a small number of easily understood end-to-end flows. This situation does not normally start out this way, but is usually the result of the accumulation of expedient system-to-system interconnections over time.

Figure 29 illustrates the situation. In this figure, System A and System B each process different sets of data, for example each might handle a different type of product order. Servicing of these orders is then broken up based on *other criteria* such as the region in which a customer lives, indicated by Systems L and M. These flows are fragmented again in overlapping ways by Systems Q and R which handle another function such as financial reporting.

---

[1]   See [FinExecInt2001].

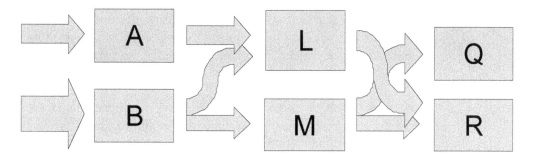

Figure 29: Data population discontinuities destroy agility.

The result is that if one asks, *which data coming out of R originated from B?* one will have a difficult time answering the question. This means that if one needed, for example, to disconnect and replace some of M's functionality, that one would need to perform a very complex analytical task to determine the many interdependencies. It would not be possible to concisely articulate the interdependence, because it is so inter-woven.

The only way to avoid this problem is to take the future loss of agility into account every time a new discontinuous interconnection is contemplated. In chapter 11 I have presented some techniques for doing this, in the section beginning on page 283. Discontinuities might be justified or they might not be, but to know one must take the full lifecycle and impact on the overall processing environment into account.

Untangling a convoluted data flow is extremely challenging. The problem is that to change anything one must change everything, because downstream systems are so dependent on obsolete decisions about what subsets of data they are expected to handle. This is not a book about architecture, so I am not going to propose a general solution to the problem, but suffice it to say that the only way out of this mess is to gradually generalize the functions that individual systems perform.

Data Representation Differences

The problem is worse if the systems in the figure are interconnected via different data representations – which is often the case because COTS systems usually provide their own proprietary formats. Having different representations means that, for example, one cannot easily simply enhance L to stand in for M as M is being replaced. Changing out any of these systems will then be almost impossible because *any change impacts all downstream systems*. Thus once again, to change anything, one must change everything – at the same time.

This high level of interdependence leads to more expedient interconnections because changing things the right way has become so difficult. Increasingly the organization finds that it cannot add new capabilities because change has become so difficult. Agility has been killed, and the organization cannot react to changes in business needs. Eventually a major overhaul becomes necessary and the organization finds that only a risky and expensive "big bang" approach will work.

Lack Of a Data Synchronization Strategy

Perhaps the most important omission from most enterprise architectures – de-facto or planned – is a set of service level criteria with respect to data synchronization. The IT community seems to have forgotten that data must be consistent and that is provided by databases, but if one employs several databases then there is no mechanism for ensuring consistency. In Figure 29 if System L runs and then System B is run followed by System M, then the data in L and M will be out of sync. For example, price catalogs might be updated inbetween the runs of A and B. As a result downstream System R will receive inconsistent data. Further, even if a database is used to aggregate all of the data, the problem will still exist since the data going into the databases is inconsistent: garbage-in, garbage-out.

The failure to deal properly with data consistency issues is one of the greatest shortfalls in architecture as it is practiced today. The impact for the business is data quality problems and the destruction of agility because planners are stymied by problems and no clear way to fix them, when the root cause is an underlying architecture that does not deal properly with the consistency issue.

IT system designers are stymied by the problems of data population discontinuities, data representation differences, and the lack of provisions for data synchronization because these problems represent a form of gridlock and intertwining that is not easy to untangle. In other words, because planners cannot come up with a clear strategy for getting out of the mess, the organization's agility is lost. Change is inhibited; new products cannot be introduced; new channels cannot be tapped; new risk mitigation strategies cannot be completed.

These three technical outcomes therefore have substantial cost to the organization in terms of lost agility, and the unit that develops business models for initiatives should take care to take these outcomes into account and watch for them, as they tend to creep in as more and more departmental solutions are slipped in.

> ## See also The Three Business Reasons Why Corporate IT Loses Agility Over Time, in the section beginning on page 143.

The organization's enterprise architecture should address these types of problems head-on. It is the job of the IT architects to interpret these technical problems in business terms, and establish credible business-focused models that translate IT agility into business agility. The technical architecture should then contain strategies for mitigating the loss of business agility based on its value compared to other concerns.

Important Enterprise Architecture Elements

Table 23 lists the elements that I have found need to be present in an enterprise architecture for the internal IT operations of most organizations. The table is divided into two parts: (1) "Things", and (2) "Decisions...". The "Things" exist to provide a vocabulary and framework for architectural analysis and ultimately choices and decisions. The "Decisions..." is the actual architecture, which boils down to a set of decisions in various forms about how to build a system or a set of systems. Decisions can take the form of choices, strategies, approaches, and generally any form that represents a stake in the ground on some issue. In addition, every decision must be supported by rationale: otherwise, there is no basis for re-examining the decision as situations change. The need for rationale is specifically called out in item 10 in the table, but it is actually needed in some way for every item under "Decisions...".

Table 23: Logical architecture elements.

Element	Description
Things	
1. Functions	A taxonomy of the generic business functions or processes performed by the various parts of the organization.
2. Components and Their Roles	A taxonomy of the kinds of components and actors in the data processing environment, and their intended roles with respect to each other and that environment.
3. Data Classifications and Models	A taxonomy of the kinds of data that must be handled by the architecture, and their interrelationships.
4. Capabilities	A taxonomy of the kinds of knowledge, skills, and abilities that are required to perform the required Functions.
5. Special Technical Considerations	A list of actual components, actors, or choices that represent constraints on the architecture.
Decisions, Choices, Approaches, and Strategies	
6. Patterns	Standard approaches or templates for solving particular recurring kinds of data processing problems. These problems usually have to do with non-functional requirements such as integration, distribution or provisioning of data, concurrency, reliability, consistency, access control, mobility, and so on.
7. Controls	A taxonomy of different kinds of controls and control design patterns, providing for measurement and alignment with respect to enterprise concerns.
8. Value Scales and Value Analysis Framework	A taxonomy of the different kinds of enterprise opportunity value and risk categories, how to quantify them, and how they relate to each other.
9. Principles	Guiding principles for system design, in support of corporate business strategies.

10. Guidance (Architecture Strategies)	Detail-level guiding principles, rules, and decisions, specific to each kind of data processing situation or issue that can be anticipated. The **rationale for each of these**, and where appropriate a model for estimating the opportunity value (or risk) of architectural choices.

At this point few of the elements in Table 23 should be new to you, as most of them have been discussed. The elements that are new when compared with what one often sees in current real-world enterprise architectures are items 5, 7, and 8:

5. Special Technical Considerations.
7. Controls.
8. Value Scales and Value Analysis Framework.

I will explain item 5 momentarily. First let me explain items 7 and 8.

Item 8, *Value Scales and Value Analysis Framework*, is probably the most difficult and non-intuitive for the now traditional IT architect. Architects are not used to thinking in terms of business value, and the transition to this way of thinking will take time. In this item the enterprise architect must document the *business model*. The techniques of chapter 11 should be used, and the lines of business should be engaged at an executive level to reach a consensus on how value can be measured, in terms of what yardsticks to use for oppotunity, risk, and any other fundamental concern that is important to the enterprise. This is where the CIO/E needs to be directly involved, as explained in prior chapters. For example, if risk is to be represented on a scale of one to three, then what do these values mean? How do they weigh against opportunity?

I have already talked at length about item 7, controls, in this book. The place that controls have in an enterprise architecture is that the core, repeatable patterns for achieving alignment must be defined. These patterns should provide for measurement in terms of business value as defined by item 8. The other design patterns in the architecture, item 6, should make reference to control patterns so that it is clear how the control patterns should be applied.

Design Patterns

In item 6, Patterns, one should only spend time documenting reusable patterns that are important for business value and risk management. Do not undertake to anticipate every kind of design pattern that might be encountered or required.

Address Failure Modes

It is not usually the practice in business software architecture that attention is paid to failure modes, except as an afterthought. However, it is important to do so. Failure modes represent some of the most important and challenging architectural issues. The failure modes are where attention really needs to be, because these are the situations that directly impact value and risk and these must be controlled. For example, in a pattern that addresses data integration, if there are edge situations in which the data integration strategy fails (often the case), then those failure scenarios should be identified and a strategy proposed for recovery – i.e., for identifying the failed transactions and how to fix them. These failure recovery strategies should be part of every enteprise pattern. This is consistent with the enterprise strategy of planning to accommodate routine failures, described on page 43. My book *High-Assurance Design* [1] covers the failure modes that are common in enterprise business applications and provides patterns for dealing with them.

> # Failure recovery strategies should be part of every enteprise pattern.

Some of the important issues that warrant special attention in most businesses are:

- Data propagation, replication, integration, consistency.
- Retroactive changes.
- Business events.

---

[1] Ref. [Berg2006].

- Recording of operational business transactions.

The first of these has to do with all of the technical issues and data ownership issues surrounding the maintenance of data as it is shared across many different users and many different systems. It is very important that fundamental patterns are identified that address these issues. Such patterns include:

- Optimistic concurrency control.
- Caching.

The Optimistic Concurrency Control Pattern

Optimistic concurrency control is a general strategy that is explained in almost every database textbook, for addressing how to recover from data becoming out of sync when it is accessed by multiple parties concurrently without locking the data. It is essentially a failure recovery pattern.

The Forward Cache Pattern

When locking is feasible, there are caching patterns that are applicable. Caching patterns exist in many forms, but one that is especially relevant to the problems that most organizations have for keeping data in sync as it is replicated are the "forward cache". In this pattern, data can be replicated to a local cache, but a strategy must exist for obtaining a lock when it must be updated.

The Read-Only Cache Pattern

In most business applications it is not feasible to create locks across systems because the systems are usually heterogenous, and so a revised caching pattern is applicable, which allows for requests of the form, "Give me the value of the data as it existed at 10:30pm." If retroactive changes to historical data are infrequent they can be performed offline or at a time when all caches of the data are disabled. Thus, cached values of the historical, time-stamped data will always be valid. One does not have to worry about changes to the data, because the historical data does not change, and when it does (infrequently), the cache will be taken down briefly and then refreshed.

For this to work, the caches must be for read-only access. That is not usually a problem though since in most cross-system business

413

applications one merely wants a local cache of data from another system. If near real-time values are requried, the cache can be refreshed in a "push" manner whenever new values are added to the source system.

Retroactive Changes

Retroactive changes to data are necessary when an error is found representing the state of the business as it existed at a prior point in time. For example, if it is discovered that an incorrect dollar amount had been entered several months back to represent a customer's payment at that time, the discrepancy must be corrected by logically modifying the earlier data. Of course, change history for this correction should be preserved, but the data must be "logically" changed. Such a change is retroactive because it updates data as of an earlier point in the business's history of transactions.

Two patterns for implementing a retroactive change are:

- Prior-Period Adjustment
- Cancel and Correct

A prior-period adjustment is when a retroactive change is made directly to historical data. This often has a ripple effect, requiring many prior business calculations to be performed again. It can also result in inconsistency if systems are not designed to be "idempotent" – that is, allowing calculations to be performed many times without adverse side effects or incorrect results. For example, if a calculation is additive, then performing it again will incorrectly add to prior values rather than computing the correct values. As a concrete example, re-performing a calculation that updates balances by adding the days transactions will erroneously apply all of those transactions a second time. While it is usually obvious that such a calculation should not be performed again, there are sometimes not-so obvious situastions such as if a business event is generated by a system and that event is generated again erroneously when the process is re-run. To avoid this, processes must be analyzed as to whether they can be safely re-run.

An alternative is to make an adjustment to current data to offset the historical error. This is known as a "cancel and correct" adjustment. For example, if a transaction from a prior month was assumed to complete but did not actually complete, then rather than going back and changing the transaction result one could enter in the current period an equivalent transaction but of a negative amount, thereby offsetting or "reversing" the bad transaction. The new transaction is a "fake" transaction that corrects the data balances. This approach has great problems because if allows erroneous data to remain in the system and that data can be mis-interpreted later. However, that cost is sometimes less than the cost of having to re-run prior calculations.

It is sometimes best to use a hybrid approach in which prior bad data is flagged but otherwise left as is. If the bad transaction is linked with the offsetting transaction, it is easier to design processes so that they can sort this type of situation out. In any case, if records are to be changed, they should never be *physically* changed, but rather logically changed by creating update records.

Business Events

Business events are changes to the state of business transactions and other events that have business significance. Most business require accurate and timely announcement and recording of business events, however few businesses actually implement a coherent system for achieving this, instead relying on a myriad of ad-hoc processes to dump historical records from transactional systems and try to piece together what happened for accounting purposes. It is no wonder that most accounting departments want to have their own systems for piecing things together, because they do not trust the actual operational business systems.

A better approach is to design operational systems so that they send messages to all interested parties whenever data changes that has business significance. This design approach has the advantage that it decouples systems significantly, and it forces the organization to incorporate the identification of busines events into its information systems design. Business events are the missing element of many enterprise data processing models.continue here.

Operational Transaction Recording

If clear and unambiguous business event messages are broadcast by operational processes, then it should be a simple matter to record those events and accumulate them to create summaries of the operational state of the business. Most businesses do indeed perform such status rollups, but this is often done in a manner that is not clear in terms of the meaning for other non-operational concerns such as accounting or other forms of reporting. Thus, these other concerns have to go back to the source data and cannot use the operational rollups for the purpose of reconciliation with accounting data.

This is a sad state of affairs because it means that the Accounting functions have a lot more work to do than they should. It also means that the business cannot get a clear picture of where it is in all respects at any point in time because its operational numbers are not precisely defined.

If business events are well-defined and are understood by all, defined by a global model just as data can be defined by a global model, then any rollups that are created based on those should be well-understood as well. Therefore, an accurate definition of business status, in a form that is auditable, unambiguous, complete, and accurate, is a natural outcome of a clear definition of business events.

Meta Data Architecture Is Still Architecture

Table 23 is intended to apply to any type of business system consisting of both human and automated components. An important category of system is those systems that manage "meta data": that is, data about data and systems. Meta data is discussed later in this chapter. The point here is that architectures for meta data capabilities require the same kinds of elements as for any other system, and should not be treated differently. It does get confusing though, because a system architecture is a kind of meta data, and so one can get into a loop of designing a capability for something that you need to design the capability. In such situations you just have to make the best and use existing systems to design the new system. This is called "bootstrapping" and people with IT training are very familiar with this kind of problem.

Later in this chapter I revisit the topic if meta data, and propose some strategies for managing it.

External Dependencies

There are some architectural elements that are critical but that are not listed in Table 23 because they are not actually part of the architecture per se. These are:

- Enterprise business strategies.
- Enterprise policies and standards.

The enterprise architecture relies on the existence of these elements, rather than creating them. Enterprise business strategies are defined by the business executives – hopefully with some appropriately business-focused participation by the CIO/E or whichever function represents IT. Enterprise policies and standards are established by every major branch of the organization, including IT, and such standards need to be aligned with architecture strategies. Standards in particular need to be co-developed to some extent with IT to ensure that this alignment is anticipated under a vision of how things are going to work to achieve various strategies and objectives. For example, standards for security are only actionable if a practical and cost-effective architecture can be devised for implementing the standards, and so it is important to work closely with enterprise architects when devising such standards and when setting the dates for when they go into effect.

Architecture Versus Top-Level Enterprise Design

Architecture is nice, but at some point executives will want to know whether decisions have been made for what to *actually do* with their systems. In other words, the architecture must be applied to the actual concrete problems and needs of the organization for *each and every business function*, and decisions need to be made for each and every business system.

At an enterprise level, architectural decisions are usually abstract rather than concrete. For example, in Table 23 item 2, Components and Their Roles, an enterprise architecture would not normally identify actual databases, data processing systems, or departments, but instead would identify classes of systems and business

417

functions such as "Data Producer", "Data Consumer", and "LOB Function". Similarly, in item 10, Guidance (Architecture Strategies), one would usually say things such as "Every business function must identify an authoritative source for its data" rather than "The Purchasing Function will use the Purchasing System as its authoritative database."

I say that an enterprise architecture usually does not specify particular systems or lines of business, *although it may*. That is a choice of the architects. The advantage of keeping concrete decisions out of the architecture where possible is to allow for flexibility: as systems change, the core architecture remains relatively stable. Some systems might be so important that they deserve to be called out, and that is the purpose of item 5 in Table 23. For example, if the business is based on its ownership of an important asset such as a proprietary network or other resource, then the architecture can hardly avoid specific mention of that. However, for other kinds of replaceable or non-strategic assets it is best to treat them generically in the architecture.

Keeping things abstract in the architecture has a disadvantage though. It means that one must then create a top-level enterprise design that applies the architecture. This separation can be confusing to executives. However, once they see the top-level design they will forget about the architecture because the top-level design will be much more meaningful to them. In the top-level design you should remove all genericity at the top level, and develop an overall business case for the design that accounts for every major design strategy, choice, or decision. This business case is your main mechanism for communication with other executive management and even with other architects and managers. The business case applies architecture item 8, Value Scales and Value Analysis Framework, to the concrete elements and decisions of the enterprise design.

Create the Right Kind Of Enterprise Data Model

Business organizations have business cultures, and technical organizations have technical cultures. The technical camp in most large organizations is usually focused either on the development of data models or object models, but usually not both. This preference of focus has a large impact on the ways in which architecture is developed. It has been my experience that data-focused teams tend to have a great deal of trouble organizing non-hierarchical information, trouble that object-focused teams seem to avoid. On the other hand, object-focused teams often fail to recognize the importance of data modeling.

For comparison, I was once involved in a six-week effort with Peter Coad to develop an enterprise *object* model for United Overseas Bank in Singapore. The effort proceeded rather smoothly, and in six weeks we had our model. In contrast, I have been involved in countless *data* modeling efforts focused around relational models and data classification schemes, and the arguments never seem to end. Without digressing into the technical sources of trouble, let me say that many data modeling or classification methodologies are handicapped because they do not easily handle situations in which data needs to be simultaneously classified in *multiple ways*. For example, if a data entity is conceptually a type of contract, but legally it is a type of financial instrument, then rather than choose between the two one might be best served to model it as both. Object oriented modeling accommodates these challenges in a very natural way.

Further, object-oriented modeling allows for a very natural way of expressing *relationships between elements*, whereas some (but not all) data-centric methodologies require the modeler to jump through hoops to model relationships and separate them from the elements that are related. There are certainly proponents of every kind of approach, and certainly one can successfully use almost any methodology if one applies it in a certain way, but I am saying that my own personal experience has been that object-oriented modeling is the most natural and efficient way to reach the goal of understanding the business data and its interrelationships for a large and complex organization.

I am not prescribing a data classification methodology here, but here is a sign to watch for: if your architecture teams or data analysts are using a data-focused methodology and do not seem to be able to agree on a single enterprise data model, perhaps it is time to try an object model approach.

One final word about enterprise data modeling: data classification and data modeling *are not rocket science*. You should not need to use a formal methodology: it is all about obtaining an understanding of data and creating simple diagrams and definitions to capture that understanding. Experience in modeling *both data and business objects* is very valuable for this task, but do not spend time dotting the i's according to some formal multi-step process. If your teams cannot create a baseline model quickly then either they do not have access to SME knowledge or they are stuck in some manner and you need to get them un-stuck.

An Example: Data Classification

Let's consider a hypothetical situation in which a large financial services organization is trying to develop an enterprise data classification scheme. The hope is that with the existence of this scheme, various initiatives can leverage a common high-level taxonomy of data which can be embellished over time with entity-level attributes. This should, in theory, foster reuse as well as a better understanding across departments of what data the organization has and what it means.

The organization has multiple lines of business (LOB), and so the needs of each must be considered when developing the enterprise-wide classification model. Unfortunately, each LOB has developed its own terminology over time to describe and represent its business data. Thus, there is the prospect of reconciling different terms for what might be the same concepts.

At first glance, it might seem that this is merely a matter of sitting down and comparing data elements and seeing which are actually the same kind of concept. Then, these could be put into categories and the end result should be the desired classification scheme. However, as the team proceeds it finds that some elements – many in fact – can be categorized in multiple ways, and often a data entity represents more than one concept. This makes it necessary to choose between two possible categories that each make perfect sense.

For example, consider the widely problematic concept of "contract". A "contract" has a very specific meaning in some circles: one can look up the definition in various dictionaries of business terms; but this does not resolve the problem that many kinds of business instrument meet the definition, yet to call them a contract is to deny their domain-specific meaning such as

420

"publicly traded security", "purchase order", or "service agreement". To categorize a traded security as a "contract" will raise the eyebrows of a Financial Services sales group: they would likely prefer that there be a top-level category for "financial instruments" and that "publicly traded securities" should be categorized under that.

Categorization of "security" as a "financial instrument" works well for the LOB that deals with publicly traded securities, but it does not help the IT department that is trying to develop generic automated services that handle all types of business obligations. To the IT group, there might be aspects of all contracts that are common for which there could be common services, such as the ability to search by obligator and obligee. Thus, IT might prefer the "Contract" category for publicly traded securities – as non-sensical as that sounds to the LOB.

Rather than choose, one can define a conceptual category called "Business Assets and Obligations" (thereby avoiding the word "contract" to appease the business) and in parallel define a LOB-specific category called "Financial Services Assets and Obligations", and put publicly traded securities under *both*. (See Figure 30.) The meaning then is that a publicly traded security is both a contract that has general meaning *and* it is a financial instrument that has specific meaning to the LOB (Financial Services). This double categorization resolves the problem and makes everybody happy, and allows for the coexistence of two distinct but connected definitions: one to capture generic meaning and the other to capture LOB-specific meaning. There can be an LOB-specific definition for each LOB that needs to define the term "Publicly Traded Security".

421

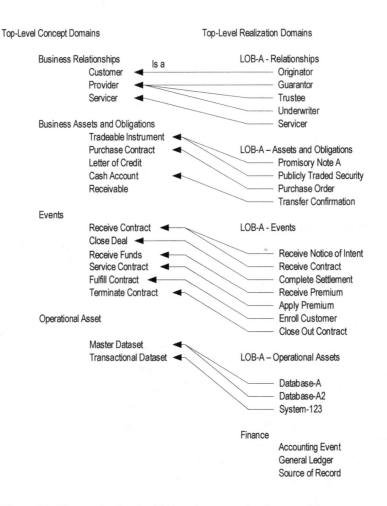

Top-Level Concept Domains   Top-Level Realization Domains

Business Relationships   Is a   LOB-A - Relationships
            Customer   Originator
            Provider   Guarantor
            Servicer   Trustee
                                                        Underwriter
Business Assets and Obligations   Servicer
            Tradeable Instrument
            Purchase Contract   LOB-A – Assets and Obligations
            Letter of Credit   Promisory Note A
            Cash Account   Publicly Traded Security
            Receivable   Purchase Order
                                                        Transfer Confirmation
Events
            Receive Contract   LOB-A - Events
            Close Deal
            Receive Funds   Receive Notice of Intent
            Service Contract   Receive Contract
            Fulfill Contract   Complete Settlement
            Terminate Contract   Receive Premium
                                                        Apply Premium
Operational Asset   Enroll Customer
                                                        Close Out Contract
            Master Dataset
            Transactional Dataset   LOB-A – Operational Assets

                                                        Database-A
                                                        Database-A2
                                                        System-123

                                            Finance
                                                        Accounting Event
                                                        General Ledger
                                                        Source of Record

Figure 30: Example of a dual-hierarchy enterprise data model.

You might think that this approach adds complexity, but actually it makes life simpler: the abstract terms on the left can be maintained by the enterprise data analysts who tend to like to generalize terms, and the very tangible terms on the right can be maintained by business-specific data analysts who are very close to how they use their own data. This division of labor decouples the analysis in a very effective way, and provides a mechanism for communication between the LOB analysts and the enterprise analysts.

Notice that in Figure 30 that some of the domain-specific terms point to more than one conceptual term. There is no problem with this: it is often the case that something performs multiple roles and therefore manifests more than one kind of concept. For example, in Figure 30 both "Receive Notice of Intent" and "Receive Contract" on the right implement the Receive Contract concept on the left. This is because a notice of intent is considered to be somewhat binding legally, although not fully binding, because once a business states its intent it begins to open itself to a degree of liability if it does not follow through with that intent. The legal interpretation of a statement of intent depends on the context, but the point here is that from a conceptual point of view – and possibly from an IT point of view – a notice of intent may serve as a type of preliminary contract with respect to a business transaction. Having a separation between the concept (on the left) and the realization of the concept (on the right) allows one to separately define these and then decide separately which business entities implement which concepts. It also allows each LOB to decide separately what this mapping is.

Relationship With TOGAF and FEAF

I have already mentioned that frameworks and formal methodologies are valuable, but one should not use them wholesale out of the box. My concerns with regard to frameworks and formal methodologies is that if one follows all of the steps and produces all of the artifacts, it is usually too late or one has spent too much money and effort on creating paper – *paper that has little real value if the individuals who created the paper are not among those who reamin to carry the work forward.*

In the private sector TOGAF (already discussed in chapter 12) has emerged as a credible framework for developing an enterprise architecture. In the US Government sector the Federal Enterprise Architecture Framework (FEAF) is mandatory for US Federal agencies. It is therefore possible that your organizaiton is or will be using one of these frameworks and you might want to know how the ideas presented here can be used to help.

The TOGAF and FEAF frameworks identify many steps in the process of developing a technical architecture, including creation of views and archtiecture "models", selection of services, and gap analysis among others. These are best seen in terms of activities rather than sequential steps. After all, each step will uncover issues and some of those issues might take more time to resolve than others, and one should not wait until all "model" issues are resolved before considering which services to compare. Again, the "agile" view of process is that you should not wait for an activity to complete before starting a dependent activity: but you may need to wait to *finish* the dependent activity until the precursor activity is *finished*.

Viewed in this way, TOGAF and FEAF provide an excellent taxonomy of activities and artifact categories. If one has the flexibility, one should view this as a pick list from which to choose where to invest effort depending on where the main problems are in your current processes. This is certainly preferable to scrapping your current processes and artifact types and forcing everyone to learn TOGAF. A client of mine tried to take the latter approach and gave up because work had to get done and there was no time to re-learn and re-do everything. One also encounters the perception that if one brings in a "TOGAF expert" that the expert can solve the organization's architecture process problems by converting the organization to TOGAF. However, those problems usually have little to do with the framework and much more to do with skill sets, poor communication between business and IT, and the quality of decision-making processes. *Changing frameworks will not address those problems.*

In the remainder of this section I will compare TOGAF with my own concepts, since the comparison with FEAF is very similar and would be redundant.

Figure 31 is excerpted from [TOGAF] and summarizes the steps in the development and implementation of an architecture using TOGAF. Not all of these steps pertain to architecture per-se: for example, step F, Migration Planning, has an architectural output in that it can impact the architecture (thorugh the creation of "Transitional Architectures"), but its primary output is a migration plan – not an architecture.

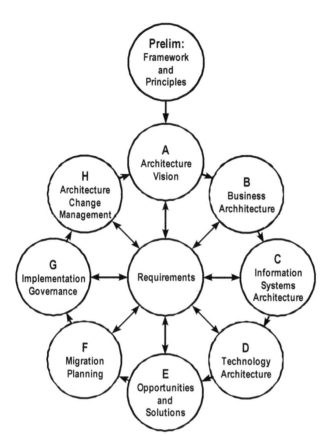

Figure 31: The TOGAF Architecture Development Cycle (ADC). (Diagram derived from TOGAF 8.1.1 with permission of The Open Group.)

The "Preliminaries" step in TOGAF is when the architects think through what has gone wrong at a systemic architecture level and articulate principles that should eventually rectify the problems if adhered to. It is kind of like saying, "If we stop allowing people to change or copy each other's data, then we will solve data synchronization problems" and then articulating a corresponding principle that states that data shall only be changed by its owner and never copied by others. Such a principle becomes an architectural principle.

The problem with such principles is that they are never absolute: there is always a reason to disobey a principle. It is therefore better to express principles as core strategies and state the rationale, so that deviations can be made intelligently, especially when principles conflict.

Technical principles should not be articulated at the outset: they should evolve. Further, the time spent to articulate them might be better spent figuring out how to measure the value of architectural choices rather than stating esoteric principles that mean little to business-side stakeholders.

Step A of TOGAF involves the statement of an architectural vision. The term "vision" is often used in business and IT but I believe that it is vague and rather meaningless: what people usually mean by a "vision" in this context is an expression of strategies that address goals and challenges, along with some concepts or assumptions that support the former. In other words, a "vision" *is an architecture* – a business architecture, or a technical architecture, depending on what kind of vision it is. Step A in the TOGAF process is therefore nothing more than establishing the handful of foundational business and technical architecture strategies that will be used to flesh out the remaining details.

The TOGAF step of creating a Business Architecture is somewhat more limited than what is described in this book as a true business architecture. I feel that a business architecture is incomplete unless it establishes a firm link between capabilities and business value, and that link is carried through to all architectural choices.

That said, TOGAF does stress the need to create a "concern matrix" that identifies how stakeholder concerns are address by the business architecture, and this is in fact all that the stakeholders want to see: they don't want to see any of the other artifacts that are identified by the TOGAF Business Architecture step. The conern matrix is "the answer" to the stakeholders, so focus on that, and do not do anything else unless it helps you to create the concern matrix (or unless you are required by contract or mandate to create other things). What you will find then is that you are focusing on business architecture strategies, and assessing their effectiveness, and that is what you should be doing. If you can do this, then it would be even better to go the final way and establish the tradeoffs between the various concerns: this amounts to quantifying their busieness value.

TOGAF emphasizes the need to create a "baseline" or "current state" of the business and technical architectures. I have already made the point in this book that investing a large effort in documenting the current state is often wasted effort, because it is not a problem-driven effort and so there is little guidance about where to focus effort, and so analysts take a top-down approach and spend forever. It is better to be more tactical. Further, effort is often spent on the wrong things, such as documenting data flows when the real problem has to do with the lack of service level agreements or a technical strategy for data synchronization. Finally, if the current systems are chaotic in their design, then there *is no architecture*: there is only a detail-level de-facto (as-built) design, and it might take a very long time to peel that apart and document it. I therefore do not encourage the creation of comprehensive as-built design baselines for old or hard-to-document systems: instead I believe in using a problem-driven approach which is focused on identifying issues and solutions.

TOGAF refers to a LOB as a "segment", and permits the development of architecture on a segment-by-segment basis, while stressing the importance of awareness of enteprise-wide architecture concerns. This is consistent with the advice given in this book. TOGAF is also not "agile" in its formulation, but can be used that way. For example, step E, Opportunities and Solutions, can be concurrent with other steps: it need not wait, and should not. Step F, Migration Planning, should not wait until after solutions are conceived, since migraiton obstacles can make solutions non-viable, or at least change their value proposition. However, it is important to separate the discussions of the *desired* future state from migration issues.

Step G, Implementation Governance, should be thought of from the outset, and should be built into the business model (step B) for how systems will be maintained, who will own them, who will own data, how issues will be resolved, how service level agreements will be established, and how the architecture will evolve.

TOGAF utilizes (borrowed from ANSI/IEEE 1471-2000) an extremely valuable concept with regard to how architecture can be differentiated based on the audience: the Viewpoint. A viewpoint is a perspective for the benefit of a specific category of stakeholder. For example, an end user might wish to examine the architecture to grasp how the system is being constructed. A security expert might need to examine the architecture from a security perspective, and a programmer from another perspective. I have not addressed what design artifacts actually *look like* in this book as this is not a "prescriptive" book, but the viewpoint concept is a very useful one.

Table 24 repeats the architecture elements from Table 23 and identifies which TOGAF step should produce or impact those elements, and which TOGAF-defined Viewpoints (aka Views) may be useful for representing each architecture element. All elements are impacted by step F, Migration Planning, because architecture must consider migration from a feasibility and value standpoint: the most value should be realized soonest when possible.

Table 24: Architecture elements produced in TOGAF ADC steps.

Element	TOGAF Steps	TOGAF Viewpoints
Things		
1. Functions	B: Business Architecture	Business Function View.
2. Components and Their Roles	D: Technical Architecture	Applications Interoperability View.
3. Data Classifications and Models	C: Information Systems Architecture	Business Information View. Logical Data View.
4. Capabilities	B: Business Architecture D: Technical Architecture	People View. Workflow View. Usability View.
5. Special Technical Considerations	D: Technical Architecture	(Any view.)
Decisions, Choices, Approaches, and Strategies		
6. Patterns	D: Technical Architecture	(Any view.)
7. Controls	B: Business Architecture D: Technical Architecture	Business Performance View.
8. Value Scales and Value Analysis Framework	B: Business Architecture	Business Strategy and Goals View. Business Objectives View. Cost View. Business Performance View.
9. Principles	D: Technical Architecture, Prelim	

10. Guidance (Architecture Strategies)	D: Technical Architecture	Business Events View. Business Services View. Business Processes View. Enterprise Security View. Enterprise Manageability View. Enterprise Quality of Service View. Enterprise Mobility View.

Each of the views in the third column of Table 24 is a kind of mini-architecture, designed to represent the overall architecture from a particular perspective, and addressing a particular set of concerns. As such, each view should represent the entire system (e.g., enterprise or segment), but address only the concerns and issues that are relevant to the view. In doing to, a view should provide the strategies for addressing each concern, as well as whatever concepts or taxonomies are useful for expressing those strategies.

It is my opinion that TOGAF puts a little too much focus on process rather than value. *If you solve the value problem, process will evolve naturally.* The core problem in IT departments today is that they are removed from the value creation equation of the business. If this problem is solved, then IT processes would become largely self-correcting, regardless which framework is used.

Architecture Should Be Simple and Understandable To Non-Technical Readers

Architecture blueprints are less useful if they are so complex that by the time one reads them and achieves a true understanding, one could have reached that point without them by doing the research on one's own. The reality is that most technical architects have very detail-oriented minds and have a natural tendency to create complex, intricate technical artifacts, as if they were creating Renaissance Era works of art.

To be maximally useful, architecture should be understandable at a basic level to all those who might have an interest in understanding it, including business architects, requirements analysts, and

429

technical managers. Further, it should be possible to find in one place how each enterprise policy or standard is addressed. The writing and illustrations should be to-the-point, minimalist but clear, and with a minimum of boiler-plate type material.

Achieving this is truly a skill and an art. But that is why it is so important to critically assess who you promote to the architect level. That role requires excellent communication skills to be effective. It also means that it might take time to build this kind of expertise. Consider utilizing an outside firm that can serve as the mentors for your mentors. Agile methodology firms have a lot of expertise in infusing knowledge of how to work in a lean but effective manner.

Invest in tools that unify design and implementation, thereby embedding design into the implementation process.

Communication is greatly enhanced if your IT design processes focus on the conceptual design issues and choices of business capabilities rather than on their technical implementation. Business process design tools shift the focus forward to the higher, more meaningful business process level. Why should you care about the implementation? Unfortunately, sometimes one must care, but that is what your architects are for. When addressing business policies and standards it should be possible to speak in business terms. When designing business processes that provide for those policies and standards it should also be possible to speak in business terms. Insist that your architects learn to speak in business terms, and that they produce primary authoritative artifacts that are expressed in business terms. To achieve this you might need to invest in business process tools and require that design efforts focus at that level.

In general, I do not believe that the architecture for a business system should contain technical syntax such as Universal Modeling Language (UML). The reason is that UML looks very complicated to lay people[1]. Unlike a building drawing, which a lay person can

---

[1] A side observation is that virtually all of the UML diagrams that I have seem embedded in IT architecture documents use fonts that are too small to read clearly. If you do include such diagrams, make sure that they are readable!

understand intuitively because it has to do with spatial relationships, UML drawings are abstract and will make a non-technical reader skip the drawing under the assumption that they cannot understand it.

It also turns out, in my experience, that precise syntax such as UML is not needed at an architecture level for business applications. Precise syntax is needed for the technical architecture of a microchip, but not for business systems, because for business systems the architecture is not so much a specification as it is a guideline for how to deal with certain classes of problems. There generally is no need to use extremely precise language, and *precision can be added as needed through annotations*. As I explained earlier, a problem-focused approach is more actionable and readable. Extreme precision is appropriate for detailed design artifacts that are one step removed from code. It is not suitable for representing the most important architecture-level decisions about a business system.

Avoid Fluff Diagrams

While architecture should be understandable, do not create special diagrams intended only for executives. If your primary diagrams are too complex, then – they are too complex. People in IT can instantly recognize "fluff" diagrams. They are often pyramids, or multi-dimensional cubes done up in a slide presentation tool. People in IT also generally know the unspoken truth that no one actually uses those diagrams, and that they are intended to give executives a warm and fuzzy feeling that we know what we are doing. As such, these kinds of diagrams are a snow-job. They are not real artifacts, and so they do not represent reality.

It is one thing to create a simplified version of an actual artifact. It is another to manufacture an artifact just to explain an architecture to an executive. If you are doing the latter, then the architecture that you *actually use* is missing some important elements.

Architecture Needs To Evolve

Perhaps the strongest advice I can give about an enterprise architecture is something that I have surely said before in many contexts: do not try to create it all at once. Establish it in a tentative, incremental manner that builds on success, usefulness, and consensus. Rather than launching a large effort to "create our enterprise architecture", establish a team that is responsible for it (the lead mentors), and direct them to establish first the most important elements, and then to pilot those elements by working with some select projects. This avoids the problem of waiting until the architecture is done – which it never truly will be. It also establishes what matters early on so that effort is not wasted on things that do not make any real difference. Perhaps most importantly, it allows LOB projects to have some input into the architecture, which makes it more real, more actionable, and makes those groups invested in it.

To continue the home architecture scenario from before, once the architecture has been interpreted for the buyer, the buyer has become a partner with the architect in terms of deciding on major issues such as cost, features, and materials. It is important to note that these decisions cannot all be made up front, because there are many small decisions on individual items that must be made.

The continuing nature of decision-making during the course of any project is the reason that architecture must be allowed to evolve. Architecture is not something that you should create up front and be done with. To do so is to constrain your project to unproven choices.

Provide For Effective Meta Information Management

Effective enterprise architecture is impossible without effective management of the information pertaining to the business models and system designs. As already mentioned in this book, such information about information is often referred to as "meta data" or "meta information". Loosely speaking, meta information is all non-operational information, including the business models and designs for operational systems, as well as any data models for how these relate to each other. Effective meta information management includes the ability to find such data, through a central directory as well as by automated searching and automated dissemination through a publish-subscribe and other mechanisms.

I cannot tell you how perplexed I am that the issue of meta information management is dealt with so poorly in so many organizations, given how urgent and important the issue is. Massive amounts of time are wasted by workers because they "do not know what they do not know", primarily because there is not a standard and easy-to-access place to look for things. Imagine the days before electronic calendars such as Lotus and Outlook, and how much order results from being able to coordinate schedules. Now consider that the average knowledge worker is still in the pre-electronic age with regard to information management. Yes, documents are in electronic form, but without a means to announce, coordinate, post, and collaborate on documents, workers are limping along, often frustrated, frequently in the dark, and often feel that their work will become "shelf-ware" because there is no standard means of publishing it and "getting it out there" in a place where people expect to find it.

Meta Information Management For Operations Is Not Free-Form

The phrase "meta information" has the connotation of being textual or abstract. However, meta information for production systems is often very concrete and must be accurate and up-to-date. Such meta data is the authoritative source of that information about systems.

Meta information becomes operational data to those whose job it is to measure and evolve systems. What is "meta" information to one department is "operational" information to another. Meta information is information that describes a process, system, or data. For example, to a portfolio trading group, the information that describes how their IT processes work is meta information; but to the IT group that built those IT processes, the information is actually operational data (even though they would not call it that) because it is the data that they use and manipulate in the course of their normal activities. IT process builders know exactly what kinds of information they need, and they benefit enormously from having it available in standard places so that they do not have to go looking for it – or worse, not even be aware that it exists.

There Must Be A Definitive and Widely Known Place To Begin Searching For Any Authoritative Specification

What is often the case is that some departments have web pages, and others do not; and what is published on those pages is up to the department. Some definitive information might be stored in specialized repositories, others on a LAN, and still others in collaboration databases. As a result, people do not know where to look for things. This leads to a lack of awareness of the existence of information.

A department's authoritative information should be stored in a single definitive hierarchy that is searchable and that can be cross-linked in a robust manner such that the cross links do not "break" when information is reorganized. The hierarchical organization of the information must be fluid and under the control of the producers of the information such that new levels of hierarchy can be added at will. In addition, the information access control must have a hierarchical ownership model with access control managed of the owners of each level of the hierarchy so that they can delegate ownership of and access to subcategories to other workers at will without having to involve a system administrator.

Having a centralized publishing repository makes it feasible to address the important issue of information classification. If information is scattered across many repositories, then the task of classifying data is made more complex because one must research whether overlap exists across the various repositories and which is authoritative on a case-by-case basis.

Team leads need an effective toolset for conveniently and quickly managing all of the information that they create, and for delegating the creation and management of portions of the information to others. Therefore, the information management control model must be hierarchical. Having a "knowledge administrator" for each project or team is not effective. *Everyone* needs to be a knowledge manager for the information that they or their subordinates are responsible for, and a project's architect or technical manager should be the one who defines the top-level structure for the technical aspects of the project. In a non-project environment, there should be a member of each team that is responsible for defining the top-level structure of the team's meta data.

For the organization as a whole, the mentor group should be the owner of the or organizer of the top-level structure of the organization's meta data, since they have the greatest understanding of how information is used across the organization. As such, they are in the best position to anticipate ways to enhance it.

To address these needs, a collaborative knowledgebase or content management system is needed, with flexible access controls that allow for hierarchy, delegation, and change history. The tool should be ubiquitous in that there should be no one in the organization that does not have access to it – otherwise it will be a niche tool and suffer the failure of non-ubiquity, namely that it will not be used at all because some people do not have it.

Kinds of Meta Data

I have found that the best way to address the need for an meta data or knowledge management system is to create a team of SMEs in the various parts of operations and put them in a room with an experienced object modeler. The result will be an object model of meta data that is important for both operations and maintenance. This is the kind of stuff that people usually have to hunt down, look up, and cross-correlate using time-consuming manual processes.

Meta data usually falls into the following categories:

1. Staff and groups of staff.
2. Roles in various business functions.
3. Knowledge, experience, and skills that staff have.
4. Business processes.
5. Producer-Consumer relationships.
6. Service level agreements.
7. Interface specifications.
8. Requirements for business processes and systems.
9. Policies and standards.
10. Models, requirements, and designs for processes, data, business rules, ETL, and (in progressive organizations) business events.
11. Models for risk and value.

435

12. Strategies and success metrics.
13. Controls, the assurance argument behind each control, and the system features, processes, or procedures that incarnate the control.
14. Blueprints and architectures.
15. Actual assets, including systems, databases, and data elements.
16. Incidents, issues, their analysis, and actions to address issues.
17. The relationships between all of these things.

Item 17 – the relationships between all of the elements – is critically important. It is the relationships that embody the enterprise-scale usage of the data. Without the relationships one merely has silo views. When modeling something like this, analysts and designers instinctively try to immediately identify cardinality – that is, the numerical relationships between the various elements. Cardinality is not important until you have to start designing a system for maintaining the data. If you are merely trying to understand it and create a language for communication, do not worry about cardinality. Instead, identify every relationship and describe the conceptual nature of that relationship. For example, a Group (item type 1) might *have* a Role (item type 2). The "have" relationship has meaning and needs to be captured: it is far more important than recording that there are many roles for each group or vice versa.

Most of this information can be categorized as either *assets*, *models about assets*, *people*, and *roles*. Grouping the object model elements into these categories helps to make it more meaningful.

One issue that often comes up when developing such a model is the issue of "who owns which data?" and "should some of the data be replicated?" The first question is a very important one for business owners to address. Generally, the owner of a business process should "own" (define and be accountable for) the data produced by the process. However, there are often cases in which a process owner allows the process to be used by other departments. In that case, those departments execute "sub-processes" even though they might use the IT system of another department. The business actor who executes a sub-process is the logical owner of that business sub-process, and that actor should be accountable for the data that they produce by that means.

The issue of whether data should be replicated is an important issue architecturally, but it should be left out of business process discussions. It is often framed as whether to create "alternative sources" for data. Consumers of data do not care where they get their data from or if it is replicated, as long as the data is accurate. The issue of whether to replicate is a purely technical one, and should be based on the required service levels for each consumer of data. For example, if a consumer needs real-time up-to-the-minute data that must be accurate 100% of the time, then that consumer needs to be confident that if they access an "alternative source" that the alternative source will be implemented using caching technology that ensures that changes are propagated in real time with full referential integrity. On the other hand, if a consumer does not require timely data but the data must be 100% accurate, then real-time updates to an alternative source can be avoided by allowing access to the data only at regular intervals. The point is that the solution is a technical choice, based on service level requirements. These requirements are the business issue: the issue of whether to replicate is not except that the cost and value of meeting service level "requirements" must be accounted for and the requirements must be balanced with the cost.

Summary

The retroactive documentation of current architecture state of a legacy environment for which knowledge and documentation have not been well maintained should be done in a tactical, problem-focused manner.

It is foolhearty to try to identify the architecture of a chaotic environment, since chaos has no architecture – not even an undocumented one.

Architecture – indeed any design – should include the rationale for every important decision.

Data flows fail to describe the phenomena that usually cause problems. Therefore, architecture should focus less on data flow and more on the high-level causes of problems and their solutions. These most often involve service level issues.

Three of the most common technical sources of lost agility over time are (1) data population discontinuities as data travels from system to system; (2) data representation differences as data is transferred, and (3) the lack of an explicit data synchronization strategy as data is propagated.

Ten important elements for an enterprise architecture are presented.

Seven design patterns are presented that can be applied to address service level issues.

Enterprise architecture should evolve from pilot architecture efforts and be allowed to mature through efforts that apply the architecture.

Data architecture is an aspect of enterprise architecture, and data classification is an important aspect of the former. Data classification should not be made overly complex, and should not take a long time to accomplish. Employ object-oriented concepts to help resolve ambiguities.

TOGAF is compared with the architecture elements that have been presented.

Architecture should focus on choices, decisions, and their rationale, and be accessible to non-technical readers. Specialized diagram notation should be avoided. Ambiguity within diagrams can be eliminated by annotating as needed, rather than resorting to specialized syntax that non-technical people do not know.

Do not produce diagrams that merely serve for executive communication but have no actual use for making or documenting decisions. Such diagrams merely prevent decision makers from having access to the "real diagrams".

Sixteen categories of meta data are described. The most important category of meta data is actually the set of relationships between all of the other kinds.

14. Initiative Planning

Build Self-Correction Into the Process

In chapter 4 in the section Implications For Initiative Planning, I examined common practices for planning initiatives to improve business processes and how those practices generally focus too much on defining tasks for creating technology and not enough on building knowledge and human processes or how to measure actual improvements in business process effectiveness. In this chapter I want to show how these shortfalls can be remedied.

The standard approach to business process improvement is to (1) identify weaknesses, (2) plan an initiative to remediate those weaknesses, and then (3) execute the plan. When the weaknesses are cultural, dispersed, and of many forms, a complex, top-down start-to-finish plan is destined to fail. Change must be implemented iteratively, and to a large extent planned by the departments that must undergo change.

When it comes to business initiatives, think in terms of small efforts that can be done right and done quickly, and then cloned or expanded, not large efforts that will encompass everything and that take forever to complete – if they complete. Forget about any large "Apollo Project" efforts: the cost will not justify the eventual business value. A "big bang" project to migrate every process to a new datamart will be a high-risk project that might get stuck in the planning phase, so do not even attempt it. Keep efforts small enough so that a single team can develop the skills to complete the effort with outside mentoring but not direct outside labor.

Dividing the Costs And Expected Returns Of a Pilot

There is some risk that is introduced when a department agrees to adopt a practice that is championed by the CIO/E group. That is why all such practices should be piloted. Piloted efforts should utilize a joint funding arrangement in order to reduce the risk to the department that will ultimately be accountable for implementing the new capability.

In a pilot effort the CIO/E group should actually participate in the development of the new capability. This participation should be limited to those aspects of the effort that are especially difficult from a compliance perspective. In other words, the CIO/E group should focus on the non-functional aspects that are being prototyped as part of the pilot and that are of interest to the CIO/E group as a possible model that could be standardized and used elsewhere in the organization.

> **The CIO/E's contribution to a pilot and the operating unit's contribution are financial apples and oranges.**

As with any joint effort, the investment should be shared. This should be primarily achieved through contributing CIO/E-based talents rather than contributing fungible funds from the CIO/E's budget. The CIO/E's goal with a pilot is to learn – not to fund others or persuade others by contributing dollars. The incentive should be based on the value propositions mentioned earlier.

This raises an important question: should the CIO/E's investment be considered when computing the return on the pilot effort? Another way of asking this is, should up-front costs be borne by the first project to invest?

The answer is no. The CIO/E's contribution to a pilot and the operating unit's contributing are financial apples and oranges. The operating unit desires to implement a new capability. The CIO/E unit desires to develop infrastructure, in the form of reusable patterns, templates, practices, case studies, and even code and systems. This kind of infrastructure must have its own value, and that value is not the direct responsibility of a particular line of business – but it is an indirect responsibility in that each LOB should be required to "think globally" and make its case based on enterprise impact and not merely on the narrow value to the LOB. To do otherwise is to fail to address enterprise-wide concerns, and the need to do that is the central premise of this book.

The operating unit might get somewhat of a free ride when participating in a pilot, but that does not matter. Its investment has its own ROI model that includes the reduced cost as a result of the CIO/E unit's participation. That said, there is joint risk because the pilot is, by definition, something that has not been tried before, and so it might not go as planned.

It is the job of the CIO/E unit to help other units to think in enterprise terms and to get the analysis right. When the CIO/E unit participates in a pilot, the CIO/E unit is representing the *organization* for the benefit of the *organization*, in the anticipation that the investment will pay off in the form of reusable material and an improvement to more than one part of the business. The investment for the CIO/E is therefore explicit in its purpose, and its return should be judged according to the criteria laid out in the section Implement Minimal But Powerful End-To-End Effectiveness Measures For Mentoring Success in chapter 12, paraphrased here for convenience:

1. How well departments realize *enterprise goals* and address *enterprise concerns*.
2. How well departments adhere to *enterprise* policies and standards.
3. How productive IT-related activities *across the enterprise* have become.

As a simplified example, let's consider only criteria 1. Lines 1-5 of Table 25 provides a simple example of a budget for a pilot effort undertaken by a line of business, "LOB A", and the CIO/E group with some contributions by a computing operations center for operational deployment. The *expected* ROI for the LOB is computed based only on LOB investments and enterprise business returns that are expected to result. On the other hand, the CIO/E *expected* ROI is based on the assumption of reuse of the non-functional aspects of the new capability across other areas of the enterprise.

Table 25: *Investment costs and return for a pilot; operating costs omitted for simplicity.*

	Activity	CIO/E Budget	LOB A Budget	Ops Cost Center
1.	**Mentoring**	$0.3M		
2.	**Development**	$0.1M[1]	$2M	
3.	**Deployment**		$0.1M	$0.1M
4.	**Certification**	$0.1M	$0.1M	$0.1M
5.	**Totals**	$0.5M	$2.2M	$0.12
6.	**Reduced Enterprise Risk Due To Increased Data Quality**	Expected Loss Over Ten Years = $1M/yr (was ~2M) Sigma = $0.6M/yr (was ~4M)		
7.	**Increased Enterprise Revenue**	NA	$12M/yr	
8.	**Net Gain**	$5M/yr, based on using this five times	$12M/yr	
9.	**ROI**	5/0.5/yr=10/yr	12/2.2/yr=545%/yr	
10.	**Payback Period**	0.5/5=0.1yr=1.2mo	2.2M/12M=0.18yr=2.2mo	
11.	**Certification Achieved**	NA	Yes	Yes

The reduced enterprise risk is based on the expected reduction in costs that are due to data quality problems. Remember, a risk is an expected rate of loss. The term "expected" is used here in the statistical sense of probable reduction in costs.

The net gain for the CIO/E business case is based on the expectation that the pilot will result in practices that can be reused at least five times in other areas of the business. It will take time to realize this business return.

Operating costs should be included as well, but are omitted here for simplicity. In addition, the non-reusable investments made by other areas of operations should be accounted for in the LOB ROI calculation but are omitted here for simplicity.

In this contrived example, the greatest ROI appears to result from the CIO/E effort. However, it must be remembered that the CIO/E cannot act alone: a business partner is always required. Therefore, much of this success is due to the necessary success of the LOB A effort. Further, it is not possible to scale up CIO/E

---

[1] The mentoring group participates in development here only because it is a pilot effort.

investment unless there are suitable partners within the organization. The large ROI is therefore the ROI that one would expect to see for any kind of seed effort, and it is accompanied by a large risk. The CIO/E's job is to manage this risk and select partners wisely.

Table 26 illustrates the rollup of the CIO/E numbers with the LOB numbers. The overall gain and ROI for the organization is totaled, based on the *total overall investments* and the *total overall return*.

Table 26: Rollup of LOB and Mentor Group business models.

	Activity	Expected Net Gain	Expected ROI	Est. ROI Sigma
1.	CIO/E	$5M/yr	1000%/yr	...
2.	LOB A	$12M/yr	545%/yr	...
3.	Total for Enterprise	$17M/yr	17/2.7=630%	...

The third row in this table shows the projected return for the enterprise as a whole, based on the collaborative efforts of the mentor group and other units with which it has partnered. This includes the overall impact on the enterprise of those efforts, from a holistic perspective. In this example, only the impact on data quality – and its consequent impact on enterprise lifecycle costs – is included, but in a real life case one should endeavor to account for all of the effects considered in chapter 11.

The last column in Table 26 is not filled in because this is a contrived example, and because the calculation would become too detailed for this book's purpose, but it is present to show that it should be there. This column should document the estimated standard deviation of each expected result, based on the sources of statistical variance that are present in the numbers from which each expected result is derived. This is very straightforward process, and significant knowledge of statistics is not even needed: it is the kind of "margin of error" calculation that one does for any college lab experiment. Its purpose here is to estimate the range of uncertainty in the projected numbers.

Admittedly this example is a very simple one. Further, I will admit that I have never seen an enterprise *fully* implement value-based IT business models or measurement. However, I have seen it work where tried, and I have seen an improvement in IT decision-making as a result. The maturity that this kind of discipline instills in IT architects leads to better communication and more problem-focused architecture, and that benefits the business in terms of agility and its IT effectiveness.

Non-Pilot Initiatives

The CIO/E organization should not share the cost of non-pilot efforts. The value proposition of the CIO/E's organization is to (1) help departments reach their goals more quickly and efficiently, and to (2) help them to become certified. This is sufficient incentive. In addition, if an effort warrants enterprise funding, the CIO/E's organization can help the department to make the case for that based on the need to become certified or to implement new capabilities in a manner that can be certified.

Don't Try To Solve the Problems Of Integration And Assurance On an Enterprise Scale From the Outset

I have already explained the issue that I take with existing maturity models: that they ignore the importance of the ability to react to change.

Further, there is a tendency for large organizations to approach maturity as a goal in its own right and forget that the whole point of maturity is to ensure that enterprise business value and enterprise risk are accounted for by the actions of the organization. Maturity for its own sake serves no purpose.

Finally, there is also a tendency to try to advance organizational maturity using a "big bang" approach. The assumption is that progress must be achieved on an enterprise scale, in lock-step. This does not work and results in a great deal of wasted false starts and wasted efforts. With large, intricate, all-at-once plans, artifacts do not pass through the important crucible of usage until large sets of them are done.

Many maturing models also implicitly embed the following two assumptions, which I take issue with:

That one must progress through phases. Maturity models seem to exclude an approach in which one pilots a new, *fully mature* process and then progressively deploys that process across the organization. For example, this approach seems to be excluded if *no part* of an organization can be considered to be at level "four" unless *all parts* are at level 3.

That business value is not measurable and actionable until one is at the most mature level: the optimizing level. That is the level at which one is measuring and can make globally optimizing decisions based on objective criteria. Yet, *business value measurement is often necessary in order to justify decisions that need to be made in order to reach a higher level of maturity!* This presents a catch-22. In fact, business value should *always* be addressed: therefore, one must start the process of learning to optimize right from the outset, even if the measuring and optimization is limited to particular issues or areas of operation.

In fact, to put a finer point on it, why would you want to build a new capability and not attempt to make it fully "mature" in the sense that it is optimized? Why design in a lower level of maturity? It seems to me that maturity should not be seen as an organizational quality at all: it is better seen as a departmental quality that can be rolled up to assess an organization if necessary.

> # One should start the process of learning to optimize right from the outset.

Thus, maturity models should *not be thought of as if they are a plan or path of evolution*. They are at best a checklist and a set of criteria to measure oneself by. For that purpose they provide great value, but do not constrain yourself to them.

> # Maturity models should not be thought of as if they are a plan or path of evolution.

Maturity models are extremely useful in helping to identify the gap between where a business process is and where it needs to go in terms of its ability to manage its activities and assets. However, maturity models are not the end-all and be-all that many people think they are.

When planning any initiative to elevate maturity, start with a pilot. Establish the requirement that there be a business value model from the outset, and that measurement be required at every step of the way. Identify the importance of agility, and how agility will be modeled and accounted for, and yet how control will be ensured.

When trying to plan a path to an end state, distinguish between end-state strategies and migration strategies: do not mix them. Otherwise you will find yourself in discussions that seem to go in circles. Do not try to define the end state too precisely, recognizing that it will change. The end state is important mostly as a framework for intellectually vetting strategies.

Who Will Maintain Your Systems?

If your most junior programmers and analysts cannot understand the design of one of your systems after a few hours of explanation and poking around through design documents, then your system is too complex. Most likely your least capable staff will maintain your systems, *and this has ramifications for how complex your systems should be.*

So-called legacy systems have that moniker because they are problematic from an extensibility and maintainability point of view. The fact that they use older technology is not in itself relevant. What is relevant is whether skills in the technology can be found, and whether the system's design is sufficiently transparent to allow it to be understood and maintained.

This is not a matter of having written documentation around. Written documentation almost never suffices. It is necessary to have people who have an understanding of the design, and that they are supported by written documentation so that they have a place to record modifications to the design and a starting point when explaining how the system works to others.

When a new system is planned you should explicitly plan for its maintenance, and for the transfer of knowledge over time as the job of system maintenance changes hands. The system's design should be simple enough so that it can be maintained with moderate skills, and there should always be a sufficient critical mass of people who understand the system. To allow this group to wane in size is to introduce a very large risk to the organization, in terms of lost agility.

In order to justify the expense of maintaining a working knowledge of your automated systems you must put a number on

446

the value of that knowledge. Chapter 7 provides some guidance for doing that. When planning new systems you should also take into account the lifecycle cost of maintaining the knowledge that is required to maintain the system.

One approach that many organizations have used successfully to preserve and propagate the knowledge of the developers of a system is to consolidate system development within a well-defined organizational IT development shop, and rotate all staff so that over time they develop experience with all systems. In this way, the knowledge of the systems is preserved through institutional knowledge in a managed way.

Unfortunately, this approach does not scale well and it is increasingly difficult to implement as lines of business become more dependent on automation and need to be increasingly involved in system conceptualization and business process definition. Over time we will likely see more and more decentralization of system development, and so keeping everyone who programs "in the same room" is becoming less feasible.

Avoid Hero-Led Projects

In many professions the ideal manager is someone who is hands-on and who takes personal responsibility for every task. If something needs doing and it is difficult, she jumps right in and does it, allowing the rest of the team to plow ahead on their own simpler tasks. If coordination is needed with other groups, the hands-on manager reaches out to those groups directly to make agreements that are needed to obtain resources, coordinate efforts, and negotiate delivery dates. When the team has an issue that needs resolution, the hands-on manager digs into the issue and makes a decision so that the team can immediately get back to work.

As it turns out, this style of management is enormously effective for projects. It is very "agile" in a degenerate sense in that little time is wasted in coordination, and the manager acts as a kind of senior architect, taking on the most difficult responsibilities. The manager is seen as a "guru" or "hero" who "just makes things happen". However, in the IT profession this style of management kills the organization. The reason is two-fold:

1. In IT, staff make countless business process decisions every day, and those decisions are embedded in code – making them relatively obscure.
2. A hands-on manager as described above does not mentor the team and train them in the decision processes and coordination processes that they need in order to function is the manager is not there.

Case In Point IT is very much driven by software projects, and the staff who maintain a system long term are rarely the staff who developed the system. If complex work is done by a manager hero, then no one else will understand that part of the work and it will not be maintainable after the hero leaves. In the case of the Responsive IT Department, the hero left because he was needed on new, difficult, time-critical projects. In Guru-Run Technology Provider the hero left because she moved on to new a new opportunity outside the company.

In addition, a manager who "just makes things happen" for the team behind the scenes does not train the team in the important coordination processes that are needed to function after the manager leaves.

The result is that a guru manager is very effective for the duration of a project, but tends to leave behind chaos. The cost to the organization is huge. Refer to Figure 32.

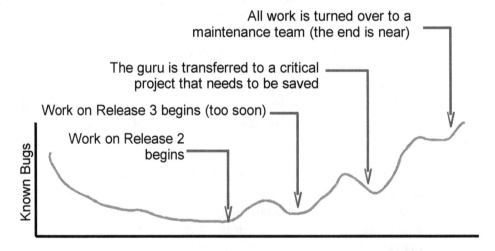

Figure 32: The lifecycle of a hero-led project.

Figure 32 illustrates some common lifecycle events and phases of hero-led projects. Early work on a project tends to go well because the hero is fully in control. The project's difficult aspects get done, and the work stays on schedule because the hero is on top of every detail and works long hours to make sure that every last detail is taken care of. The number of bugs is a one measure of progress, and it steadily decreases as shown in the figure.

At the end of the release cycle the project is delivered and the customer is very pleased. The number of known bugs increases because the customer begins to report problems found through actual usage. Work on the second release has begun so as not to allow the development team to remain idle, since fixing bugs does not require the entire team.

The customer is so pleased with the system that they start to talk about release three, even before release two has been completed. I have seen projects in which release three began in parallel even before release two was delivered. This is shown in the figure. At this point things start to get complicated even for the hero manager to keep track of, and project bugs start to exhibit some level of intractability.

Then suddenly the hero manager is transferred to another project that needs a hero to save it. The manager leaves, and the team is missing the one person who knew how everything was connected, and who had been juggling many balls to keep things on track – and sharing the details with no one. The intractable bugs and technical problems now loom and there is no one to fix them the right way, and so they are fixed in a shoddy way, which eventually leads to architectural problems and an increase in the rate at which new bugs appear as new features are added.

Much of the project team is then transferred to a new project that is considered to be critical for the organization. Work on release three is slowed and all work is turned over to a maintenance team. The caliber of the maintenance team is substantially below the original team, in terms of experience and inate capability. At this point the fate of the system is determined: it will hobble along, bug-ridden and crippled, getting worse and worse over time and inhibiting agility and defying attempts to fix it.

The situation would be very different if the project manager had focused on tam-building and process from the outset. If the hero had invested time in growing the staff and helping them to learn how to make decisions on their own, then the hero manager could have transitioned out smoothly. Since transition is normal, it is irresponsible not to plan for it.

Concrete Example: A Typical Remediation Plan

So far our discussion has been somewhat theoretical. Let's walk through a concrete example involving the functional organization of an effort to address a strategic cross-organizational weakness.

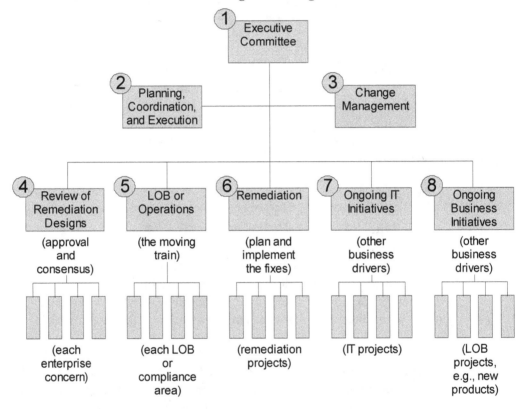

Figure 33: Typical Executive-Level Organization Structure For Addressing Strategic Weaknesses

Figure 33 represents a typical program structure for addressing a major identified cross-organizational weakness, such as inadequate controls, inadequate security, or inability to control costs. The Executive Committee (1) represents the leadership of the overall program. It typically consists of the most senior stakeholders who are accountable for the weakness. These may be officers or vice presidents, depending on the organization. The function of this committee is to oversee the program and to be accountable to the overall organization, CEO, and board for its success.

Actual program planning and execution is represented by box (2). This may be a single executive, or it may be a small team of very senior staff who are experienced at managing initiatives and who have the credibility needed to oversee a cross-organizational effort. In parallel, a Change Management function (3) provides input to help the program build processes that are maintainable so that things will not go back to "business as usual" once the program completes.

Boxes 4 through 8 represent the different functional elements of the program, in no particular order. These functions are complex because they cut across the organization, and the coordination that is required mandates a committee leadership structure in each functional box, usually combined with an management team that operates the function on a day-to-day basis.

The function of box 4 is to provide for review of new designs and concepts of operation that are devised by the program, and it is usually a committee that has representation from all of the stakeholders. The term "review" does not necessarily indicate a passive approach: the key function provided is to check coverage and correctness.

Box 5 represents the business functions that are the targets of remediation. These might be lines of business, or they might be control or reporting functions such as financial accounting or security assessment. Box 6 represents the planning and execution of efforts to enhance or create new capabilities that are needed in order to remediate the problems. It includes gap analysis. Boxes 7 and 8 represent other initiatives or programs that are underway or that are being planned for realizing other business objectives that are not directly related to the Executive Committee's program.

The basic template for this plan seems sound. However, it suffers from a serious inherent weakness: it is a one-shot deal. It is designed around the concept that you can build something and that it will then take care of itself, kind of like giving birth and then leaving the child to fend for itself. It is a "moonshot" approach, that attempts to build a rocket, launch it, and then sit back and write one's memoirs.

> ## If you solve people's problems for them, then they have not learned and you have accomplished nothing in the long run.

The primary flaw of the above approach is in the peripheral nature of the change management function (box 3). Almost as an afterthought, it sits off to the side, with nothing under it. Instead, the entire program should be focused on change management, not on building new systems.

> ## Focus primarily on change management, not on building new systems.

The counterpoint that is usually raised to this argument is that the Change Management function provides input to the Planning, Coordination, and Execution function (2). However, when push comes to shove, it is almost always the case that expediency rules, and plans end up being made to create immediate solutions instead of fixing systemic problems. After all, compliance issues must be dealt with immediately, the budget is tight, and next year's inevitable compliance failure is not factored into the cost-benefit analysis.

> ## The fact that the expected rate of future failures is seldom factored into planning causes short-term goals to trump change management goals.

On the other hand, who says that it is more expensive to fix the cause than to fix the symptom? In fact, if you enable people, they will fix their own problems if they are given suitable guidance and helped in the right ways. You can often avoid bringing in expensive outside help by establishing capability enhancement efforts.

Before considering ways to fix the program, let's drill down a little farther. Figure 34 shows a typical mid-level organization structure for implementing a remediation effort, i.e., box 6 in Figure 33.

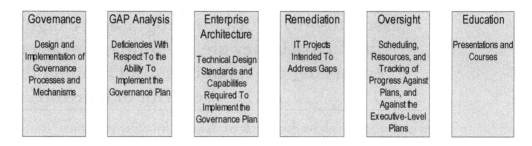

Governance	GAP Analysis	Enterprise Architecture	Remediation	Oversight	Education
Design and Implementation of Governance Processes and Mechanisms	Deficiencies With Respect To the Ability To Implement the Governance Plan	Technical Design Standards and Capabilities Required To Implement the Governance Plan	IT Projects Intended To Address Gaps	Scheduling, Resources, and Tracking of Progress Against Plans, and Against the Executive-Level Plans	Presentations and Courses

Figure 34: Typical Mid-Level Organization Structure For Implementing Strategic Remediation

In Figure 34 there are six teams, each charged with developing a "slice" of the overall set of things that need to be built in order to "remediate" the strategic weakness. The first of these is an over-arching governance process design that specifies how departments should act and interact in order to mitigate the strategic weakness. This usually takes the form of policies, procedures, definitions of responsibilities, and committees to arbitrate decisions. The primary immediate output is therefore documents that define all of this.

The second team is the GAP Analysis team. This team researches all of the ways in which the identified strategic weakness manifests throughout the business, and documents that. This documentation provides input to the Remediation team which is charged with designing software changes or new systems to address the gaps. The Enterprise Architecture team is charged with reviewing the Remediation plans and for writing technical standards in order to help ensure consistency across the various initiatives. The Oversight team tracks progress in terms of a task schedule. Finally, the Education team develops courses and other mechanisms for pushing information about the Governance standards and concepts out into the lines of business.

Again, this all seems very straightforward, but again, it is fatally flawed. The problems are analogous to those in the executive level plan. For one, education programs are highly ineffective if they are the primary means of enhancing the capabilities or changing the behavior of individuals. The best that can be hoped is that those who attend one or two classes will glean that there are new expectations of them, but they will have to live those expectations and the solution approaches in order to internalize them.

> # Classroom-only education programs are highly *ineffective* if they are the primary means of enhancing the capabilities or changing the behavior of individuals.

Secondly, gap analysis documented in long, intricate documents is not very useful. At best, it gets someone started – if it does not entirely confuse them. As explained earlier, documentation of this kind primarily serves the author, and it often omits the most important information: dependencies, relationships, and so on, which are often held in people's heads as "tribal knowledge". If the individuals who will be designing the solutions do not have access to the authors of the gap analysis, they will have to perform most of the gap analysis again under the auspices of reading the documents and designing the solution. Just as one cannot usually learn a new subject simply by reading the text and skipping the exercises, one cannot understand a long, detailed technical document unless one took part in the authoring of the document, or has direct access to the author who can act as a personal tutor.

> # Gap analysis documented in long, intricate documents is not very useful.

Case In Point

Another problem with this team structure is that the enterprise architects are siloed into specialties and expected to come up with a comprehensive architecture at the outset. The rationale is that architecture must be established before detailed solutions for the gaps can be designed. Thus, there is seriality built into the plan, and the architects are asked to foresee all technical problems. The siloing of the architects also ensures that there are not enough of them to go around. In the case of the Large Investment Product Provider a large and capable pool or enterprise-level architects were often gridlocked, each waiting for the others to make decisions, and since all of them needed to be consulted on each issue they were "meeting'd to death". Since each aspect of architecture must consider the other aspects, it would have been far better to consolidate the architects and set the expectation that they must all be knowledgeable about each other's issues. Their real asset was the experience and judgment – not their specialization. As of this writing I am told that the consolidation is being considered.

Another problem with the structure in Figure 34 is that the oversight mechanism is task-based, not results based. Therefore, if the teams find a better way to do things in the process of execution, they will be "off plan". Since this is inevitable, there is a tendency to omit important activities from plans, and to adjust reporting to gloss over or even forge those progress items that end up having little value even thought they are prominent parts of the task plan. How many of us have seen project "dashboards" that contain items that have less significance as the project evolves, but no one wants to go back and explain why they should be removed? The problems with strictly task-focused progress measurement were discussed in chapter 7.

Finally, the Remediation team is charged with building software, yet the real elements that need to change and grow are people. The software development team is again siloed and separated from the Education team, so there is a decoupling between the technical solution and the people development solution. These need to be integrated. In fact, the organization plan in the figure does not provide for integration and yet that is perhaps the greatest challenge in terms of its impact on agility and effectiveness.

> # Software development and people development should be integrated into a *capability development* system.

The organization needs to figure out how to teach its people to understand the strategic weakness and design their own solutions, with oversight to ensure consistency across the organization. That is the only way to make it sustainable, and that is not provided for at all in the team structure we have been discussing.

The Concern Matrix

Perhaps the greatest challenge to addressing a cross-organizational weakness of any kind is that the concerns of every part of the organization must be considered. That is the reason for the presence of many committee structures in Figure 33. A common arrangement is to establish committees along two axes: one axis for each enterprise concern, and another for each impacted area of business operations. This is illustrated in Figure 35.

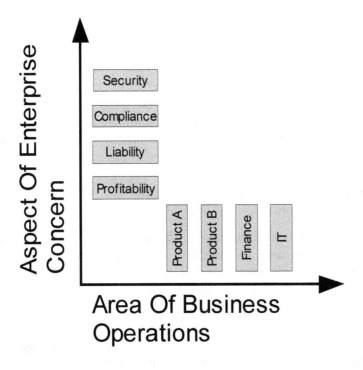

Figure 35: A Matrix Of Concerns Versus Areas Of Operation

The axes of concern are based on an analysis of what enterprise concerns are impacted by or impact the identified weakness. For example, if the weakness is that the organization does not manage its risks well, then the vertical axis must have representation for each category of risk. The horizontal axis has each organizational area of business operation that might potentially suffer from the identified weakness.

The intersections of the concerns and the areas of operation represent the points at which change must be effected, and each requires its own plan. Further, the plan must encompass functions 4 through 8 of Figure 33, and so the implication is that each of functions 4 through 8 requires a similar committee, and that all of these committees must coordinate their activities. Such committees often also contain external advisors such as security consulting firms or accounting firms.

As you can see, we are quickly getting to a point of committee overload, and the actual teams that must do the work will have a hard time figuring out who they should be interacting with. Their project managers will be able to sort some of this out for them, but there is the danger of planning gridlock. I have seen this type of gridlock happen many times. It is exacerbated when there are technical unknowns, planning unknowns, strategic goal changes, and continual waxing and waning auditor-driven upheavals. This is an agility killer.

> **Creating committees to address intersection between operational units and goal areas results in planning gridlock.**

This is not to say that this approach cannot be made to work; but to achieve success this way requires very astute management, and to achieve enduring, self-sustaining success is even harder, since the entire focus is on fixing the problems instead of fixing the causes of the problems.

Concrete Example: A Better Large Grain Transformation Plan

Assume that we have just received confirmation that our organization indeed suffers from a serious weakness that could cause it to fail. It is our objective to develop a plan to remedy that weakness. Further, we have learned that the weakness touches most parts of our organization, and so our approach must be addressed at an enterprise level.

> **If you are planning a large initiative, and it does not focus on enabling and teaching the affected operational units to invent, internalize, maintain, and extend the solution, then STOP!**

Our instinct might be to scientifically and surgically measure all occurrences of the weakness, and fix it in each place where it occurs. However, this up-front gap measurement approach does not work, as we have seen. Therefore, we will instead develop a plan that will modify our organization so that it becomes self-healing with respect to the identified weakness. That is, we will teach the operational units how to identify the weakness; and we will identify solution patterns, try them out in real situations, refine them, and teach the operational units how to design them into their own processes.

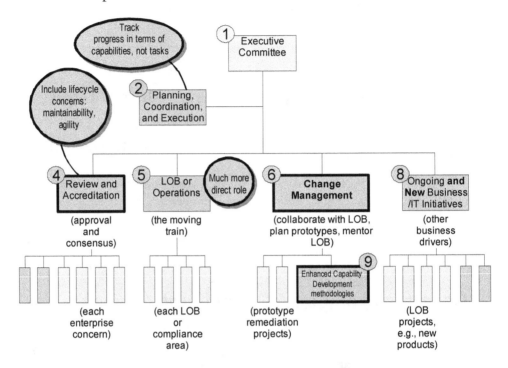

Figure 36: Improved Executive-Level Organization Structure For Addressing Strategic Weaknesses

Figure 36 shows a way to configure the program organization structure to achieve this. This is very similar structurally to Figure 33 except that the primary focus is on change management rather than on the execution of detailed remediation plans. For example, the Change Management and Remediation functions of Figure 33 have been combined (box 6 in Figure 36). Further, the role of this function is to act as the center of capability development and planning, and to work with operational units to plan pilot projects, compile lessons learned, and help operational units to plan and manage projects that build capabilities and knowledge directly within the operational units. The Change Management function is expanded in Figure 37.

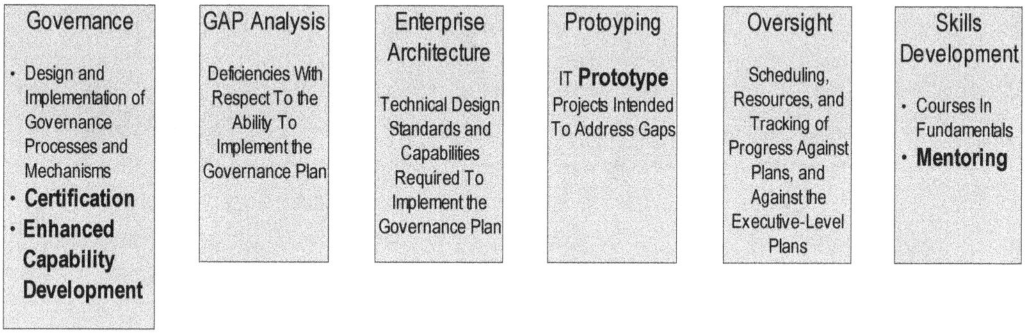

Governance	GAP Analysis	Enterprise Architecture	Protoyping	Oversight	Skills Development
• Design and Implementation of Governance Processes and Mechanisms • **Certification** • **Enhanced Capability Development**	Deficiencies With Respect To the Ability To Implement the Governance Plan	Technical Design Standards and Capabilities Required To Implement the Governance Plan	IT **Prototype** Projects Intended To Address Gaps	Scheduling, Resources, and Tracking of Progress Against Plans, and Against the Executive-Level Plans	• Courses In Fundamentals • **Mentoring**

Figure 37: Mid-Level Organization Structure For Driving Strategic Capability Changes

As a result, the operational units that are impacted play a much more direct role in their own change, under the guidance and mentoring of the change management function. These operating units are the "moving train" that must be changed in order to repair systemic organizational weaknesses.

> ## If you are planning a large initiative, and it does not begin with collaborative piloting followed by gradually increasing scope refinement, extension, and deployment, then STOP!

The Change Management function is composed primarily of people from the mentoring side of the organization. These are the CIO/E's staff, although there might be a mixture since here we are talking about an initiative structure, not a permanent structure.

We Took Steps To Ensure Consistency

One of the primary goals of managed capability development is to prevent the proliferation of departmental solutions that each do things differently and for which there is no external transparency. This issue is examined in chapter 5.

By being directly involved in the piloting of solutions, the compilation of lessons learned, and the cataloging of standard templates for solutions, the CIO/E group attempts to foster homogeneity in the way that things are done throughout the organization. This helps to economize on the hard job of figuring out how to live up to policies and standards and how to achieve the more difficult and esoteric organizational goals such as risk reduction, improved security, etc.

In our example, this is achieved through the Change Management group which reports to the CIO/E. Our Change Management group goes way beyond the role of traditional "change management" by contributing operational and architectural thought leadership, and by compiling reference designs that can be reused. These reference designs implement the spectrum of enterprise concerns in a balanced manner, thereby reducing the research that must be done by each business area when compliance with standards and policies is required.

We Provided Strategic Oversight

The strategic stakeholders in the organization must be in a position to provide oversight. For example, any plans for change must address not only the identified weakness, but also the broad concerns of the organization, such as security, liability, accountability, etc. This oversight is provided through a Review function (4), as it was in Figure 33. The difference here is that this Review function (Review and Accreditation) works closely with the Change Management function to assist in developing repeatable processes and to train Change Management teams so that the latter can usually act on the behalf of the stakeholders. As a result, the stakeholder SMEs, who have high-value expertise, are leveraged and can spend more time on their own job functions. The Change Management function can represent the SMEs most of the time, for the purpose of project planning and representation in most types of meetings and information-gathering sessions. Of course, the stakeholders are still accountable for their concerns, and they therefore must establish the appropriate checks to make sure that final results meet their expectations, but the fact that they do not have to go to every project meeting means that they actually have more time to do this.

We Included Capability Lifecycle Concerns

It is important that the stakeholders in the Review and Accreditation function include those who can assess business capability lifecycle concerns, such as manageability, maintainability, and agility. However, the mentor group should work with these

460

stakeholders to ensure that their assessment is sufficient and addresses a complete business value picture as I have discussed in this book.

Only in that way can one expect the resulting capabilities to address requirements such as the ability to be maintained effectively after programmers are transferred, or to be enhanced easily as new requirements evolve in the future. It is actually very hard to build business systems that are maintainable and that are easily changed, and someone needs to explicitly represent those interests.

We Integrated Remediation Planning Across Business and IT

Another difference between this program structure and the earlier one is that the functions of business initiatives and IT initiatives are combined (box 8). As explained in chapter 5 and elsewhere, it no longer makes sense to separate business thinking from IT thinking. Thus, Change Management does not need to deal with separate IT and business program managers when analyzing touch points with other initiatives: for each initiative there is a single planning center that encompasses integrated business and IT thinking. Achieving this requires tech-savvy business staff, and business-savvy IT staff.

We Overcame the Brick Wall Of Execution

As explained at length in chapter 4, all of this planning and organization will not amount to a hill of beans if the day-to-day activities of programmers and departmental staff are not impacted. For this reason successful change management requires that most attention is paid to how the behavior of actual workers is modified.

Box 9 in Figure 36 addresses the need to examine day-to-day processes such as software development methodologies so that they directly embed any new policies, standards, and lessons learned that result from the program. This must be done in a way that is practical, and that includes the workers in the analysis to ensure that their jobs are still doable and not mired in more checks and red tape. For example, rather than adding more checkpoints

461

to satisfy a new policy, it might be possible to elevate the skills of an individual so that they can perform two functions instead of one so that a cross-departmental checkpoint can be eliminated or reduced in frequency.

We Provided Incentives For Reaching Out In Both Directions

There must be a strong incentive for operational units to work with a change management group. The natural tendency is for departments to be self-reliant and be wary of the potential delay and perceived potential risk introduced by dealing with "mentors", even if those mentors have a lot to offer. After all, it is a natural human tendency to feel that you are safe as long as you are completely in control, and working with others dilutes that control. That is why it is important for the operational units to be firmly in the driver's seat with their initiatives, but at the same time, the Change Management function must have some clout. This is where certification comes in. The organization's executives should mandate that certain business functions be certified (perhaps eventually all functions), and that certification should be granted from one and only one source: the Change Management (mentoring) function. To achieve this, the Change Management function will need to work closely with enterprise stakeholders, and require their review and participation in signoff for certification. Certification is listed as a Governance function in Figure 37.

We Provided For Progress Measurement

One of the challenges with initiative management is achieving meaningful tracking of progress. We have already discussed the importance of tracking progress based on the creation of actual capabilities, not based on the completion of tasks. Thus, milestones should be events that represent the measurement and assessment of a new capability.

This is a fundamental change of mindset. It means that milestones are not merely the rollup of a series of tasks. Rather, milestones are truly meaningful accomplishments, analogous to passing a difficult test. Achieving a milestone might require taking the test several times.

In Figure 36 the Planning, Coordination, and Execution function (box 2) needs to demand that progress is measured in this way. Transparency should be achieved not by having accurate rollup of detailed tasks. Rather, it should be achieved by having truly meaningful assessment of new capabilities. Are departments actually achieving lowered risk? Has data quality improved? Does accounting have more reliable numbers?

> # The need to figure out how to measure capabilities might result in the establishment of measurability requirements.

The need to figure out how to measure these things might result in the establishment of measurability requirements that are factored into remediation planning. New systems and processes must be transparent in a meaningful way. It must be possible to have accurate representation of risk, of data quality, of security, or of any of the concerns that are the drivers for the improvement initiative as well as the ongoing concerns of the organization.

We Made Gap Analysis a Natural Outcome of Capability Building

If capabilities are built incrementally, and if progress is measured in terms of capabilities rather than the completion of tasks, then there is no need to perform a comprehensive detailed gap analysis at the outset in order to plan an initiative. Some level of gap assessment is needed in order to determine if weaknesses exist and to conceptualize a big picture for where you want to head, but it need not be detailed to a level. The reason is that a capability-focused remediation process incorporates capability assessment; otherwise, progress cannot be measured. Capability assessment can be developed over time and refined, and as measurement improves the project's plan can be refined. Your attention should not be on closing gaps, but on creating the processes that routinely assess and close those gaps. Initiatives should focus on establishing and refining these processes.

Summary

Change must be implemented iteratively. Think in terms of small efforts that can be done right and done quickly, and then cloned or expanded, not large efforts that will encompass everything.

Up-front costs should not be born alone by the first project to invest in new methods. Rather, the business models for the project and for the mentor group should be decoupled but linked so that they roll up into an enterprise business model. The payoff period of each decoupled model might be different, but the enterprise model that combines both is what matters.

The CIO/E organization should not share the cost of non-pilot efforts.

Both risk and opportunity should be present in any business model, or the model is incomplete.

Maturity models should not be seen as an evolutionary path, but rather as a way to assess each business process.

Most likely your least capable staff will maintain your systems, and this has ramifications for how complex your systems should be.

When a new system is planned you should explicitly plan for its maintenance, and for the transfer of knowledge over time as the job of system maintenance changes hands.

Hands-on IT managers and technical leads who do not mentor and properly train their team eventually harm the organization.

Focus primarily on change management, not on building new systems. Further, an initiative should focus on enabling and teaching the affected operational units to invent, internalize, maintain, and extend the solution.

The fact that the expected rate of future failures is seldom factored into planning causes short-term goals to trump change management goals.

An example of an initiative plan is presented and discussed.

Postscript

What the Future Portends

"Many people said to me…that the laser was 'a solution looking for a problem'." – Charles H. Townes, co-author of the first paper on the laser.

Sometimes it takes awhile for a paradigm to shift, but the basic trends of change are inexorable. The Internet bubble of the late 1990s anticipated a sea change in access to information. Things did not happen as quickly as many people predicted, but the changes that people foresaw continue.

The trend toward shorter and shorter planning timeframes is inescapable, whether we like it or not. Today's IT governance models must address this by becoming increasingly responsive.

Business is also becoming more and more non-monolithic. Companies now routinely form partnerships for particular functions. In the late nineties there were great expectations that new business models would evolve in the form of online communities or exchanges. While these goals were not quite realized there is considerable evidence that it is because the technology was not quite ready. The new version of the Internet's core technology, known as "IP6", will alleviate many of the technical difficulties in forming online communities. It will then be up to the business community to create new business models, and this will surely occur.

We can then look forward to a very interwoven business fabric, where the lines between competitors and partners are very blurred, and businesses have many synergies with other businesses while also having many points of contention and areas of competition.

In such an environment governance becomes more complex for an organization because it must consider the many competing interests of its various lines of business, their various risks, and a mixture of policies that are specific to each partnership that the business has. Tomorrow's business will become a dynamic ever-changing federated model rather than a hierarchical model, and governance will have to accommodate that change.

In a federated model, the need for nimbleness and capability-focused governance is even more urgent. It becomes harder to control the many pieces, and so more self-reliance is needed. But to ensure that the overall enterprise remains on a well-defined course, there must be a system for reconciling the competing interests of the many federations and for providing not merely polices but incentives for cooperation.

In short, the ability to manage rapid change, complexity, risk, and decentralization of function are becoming strategic capabilities and this ability needs focus and needs to be measurable and accountable. For change management to operate at a strategic level, strategic plans must be expressed in tangible terms that are meaningful and actionable for operating units. One-liners such as "introduce more products" must be replaced with business models that identify the business value of concrete success criteria.

To make matters even more challenging, the trend toward real-time business is inexorable. Batch-oriented thinking will become a competitive disadvantage. Yet, the ability to develop real-time systems on an enterprise scale – not to mention across a federation of partners – is sorely lacking in the skill sets of today's IT staff and departments. Intel predicts that in a few years our laptops will have chips that are able to do 80 different things concurrently. Today's IT and business staff are not trained to design for concurrency, at a software level or at an organization level. Today's IT staff also do not have the training they need to connect IT with business value. The skills gap is not being filled by academia: industry needs to step in through partnerships with academia and through internal training.

Capability infusion is a powerful incentive if it provides a competitive edge, and this will have to be the value proposition of the enterprise to its many departmental constituents.

References

1. AmbAA08   Agile Adoption Rate Survey: February 2008.
                 See
                 http://www.ambysoft.com/surveys/agileFebr
                 uary2008.html

2. AmbAUP   The Agile Unified Process. See
                 http://www.ambysoft.com/unifiedprocess/a
                 gileUP.html.

3. AmbEUP   The Enterprise Unified Process. See
                 http://www.enterpriseunifiedprocess.com/.

4. AmbGrShift06   The Green Shift Anti-Pattern, by Scott
                 Ambler, Dr. Dobbs Journal, July 2006.
                 Available online at
                 http://www.ddj.com/dept/architect/1916006
                 61?cid=Ambysoft

5. AmbKroll07   Best Practices for Lean Development
                 Governance (Parts I, II, and III), by Scott
                 Ambler and Per Kroll, the Rational Edge
                 (online magazine), June, July, and August
                 2007. Part III (containing links to Parts I and
                 II) can be obtained at
                 http://www.ibm.com/developerworks/ration
                 al/library/aug07/ambler_kroll/

6. AmbPS07   IT Project Success Rates Survey: August 2007.
                 See
                 http://www.ambysoft.com/surveys/success2
                 007.html.

7. Andrew07   James Andrew, leader of Boston Consulting
                 Group's Innovation Practice, in interview
                 with CIO Magazine, August 30, 2007.

8.	BenBugWal04	From Business Strategy to IT Action: Right Decisions for a Better Bottom Line, by Benson, Bugnitz, and Walton, 2004.
9.	BerAmb2006	*Agile Assurance*, by Cliff Berg and Scott Ambler, Dr. Dobbs Journal, July 2006.
10.	Berg2006	High-Assurance Design, by Cliff Berg, Addison Wesley, 2006.
11.	BergIASA2006	"The Software Architect's Skillset," by Cliff Berg, IASA Top Story, 02/15/2006.
12.	Bhadra06	Analysis of System-Wide Investments in the National Airspace System: a Portfolio Analytical Framework and an Example, by Dipasis Bhadra and Frederick Morser, the MITRE Corporation, Journal of Air Transportation, vol. 11, no. 1, 2006. (Sorenson Best Paper Award Recipient.)
13.	BuchananSoley	Aligning Enterprise Architecture And It Investments With Corporate Goals, by Richard D. Buchanan and Richard Mark Soley. (Available online at http://www.omg.org/meta-wp/)
14.	CasanaveEC	MDA for Enterprise Collaboration & Integration, presentation by Cory Casanave, Data Access Technologies. (Available online at http://www.omg.org/interop/presentations/2002/cory.pdf.)
15.	CFO_ITa05	Sarbox Surprises, by CFO Staff, CFO IT, June 22, 2005. Available online at http://www.cfo.com/article.cfm/4077444/c_4098038?f=magazine_alsoinside
16.	CFO_ITb05	Sarbox and IT: How Bad Can Things Get? CFO-IT, Summer 2005. Available online at http://www.cfo.com/article.cfm/4077489/c_4098038?f=magazine_alsoinside
17.	Chakravorti2003	The Slow Pace of Fast Change: Bringing Innovations to Market in a Connected World, by Bhaskar Chakravorti, 2003.

468

18.	Chaney03	Shredded Reputation: The Cost of Audit Failure, by Paul Chaney and Kirk Philipich, presented at the Spring 2003 Conference on Corporate Behavior and Financial Markets at the Vanderbilt Financial Markets Research Center. Available online at http://www2.owen.vanderbilt.edu/fmrc/Activity/Conference%20Presentations/ChaneyConfApril03.ppt
19.	CIODecSalSurv06	2006 SALARY AND CAREERS SURVEY, CIO Decisions, July 2006. Available online at http://searchcio.techtarget.com/magItem/0,291266,sid19_gci1191283_idx3,00.html
20.	CMMI	Capability Maturity Model® Integration. See http://www.sei.cmu.edu/cmmi/
21.	COBIT4	COBIT 4.0, IT Governance Institute. (Available online to ISACA members from http://www.isaca.org.)
22.	Cockburn1999	"Characterizing People as Non-Linear, First-Order Components in Software Development," by Alistair Cockburn, 1999. Presented at the 4th International Multi-Conference on Systems, Cybernetics and Informatics, Orlando, Florida, June, 2000. (Available online at Alistair's website, http://alistair.cockburn.us.)
23.	Cognos7Steps	Best Practices In Enterprise Planning: Seven Proven Steps To Superior Business Execution, 2003. Available from COGNOS.
24.	Cone1997	Pace Of Change: Beyond Business – The experts speak, by Edward Cone, Information Week, July 21, 1997. Available online at http://www.informationweek.com/640/40iupo2.htm
25.	Copeland03	Real Options, Revised Edition: A Practitioner's Guide, by Tom Copeland and Vladimir Antikarov, 2003.
26.	Darlin2006	Cashing In Its Chips, by Damon Darlin, The New York Times, July 9, 2006.

27. Daven99   Saving IT's Soul: Human-Centered Information Management, by Thomas Davenport, in Harvard Business Review on the Business Value of IT, 1999.

28. Denne04   Software by Numbers, by Mark Denne and Jane Cleland-Huang, 2004.

29. Devaraj02   The IT Payoff: Measuring the Business Value Of Information Technology Investments, by Sarv Devaraj and Rajiv Kohli, 2002.

30. DHSOrgCht   Department of Homeland Security Organization Chart. Available online at http://www.dhs.gov/dhspublic/interweb/ass etlibrary/DHS_OrgChart.pdf

31. DixPin94   Investment Under Uncertainty, by Avinash Dixit and Robert Pindyck, Princeton University Press, 1994.

32. eMASS   For a good unofficial overview, see the presentation at http://www.elamb.org/hacked/diacap_guide. htm. For the official source, see https://diacap.iaportal.navy.mil/.

33. FAA2005   Status of FAA's Major Acquisitions: Cost Growth and Schedule Delays Continue to Stall Air Traffic Modernization," Report No. AV-2005-061. Washington DC: Office of the Inspector General, FAA.

34. FinExecInt2001   New Economy, New Terminology, Financial Executives International, Jan./Feb. 2001. Available online at http://www2.fei.org/magazine/articles/1-2-2001_biz_briefs.cfm?

35. Fowler2003   "Who Needs an Architect?", by Martin Fowler, IEEE Software, July/August, 2003, pp. 2-4.

36.	GSmith06	Gregory Smith: Data from the top of the World, Enterprise Leadership, May 26, 2006. Available online at http://www.enterpriseleadership.org/listen/podcast-gsmith
37.	Harris06	Study: Big Decisions Best Made With Less Thought, by Richard Harris, All Things Considered, February 16, 2006. Available online at http://www.npr.org/templates/story/story.php?storyId=5220072
38.	Hein1996	EQ For Everybody: A Practical Guide To Emotional Intelligence, by Steve Hein, Aristotle Press.
39.	Hoffman2006	"From Build to Buy: Freddie Mac Makes A Huge Software Shift Freddie Mac wrestles with the cultural challenges of a huge software shift." News Story by Thomas Hoffman, COMPUTERWORLD, April 3, 2006.
40.	ITSkillsIn2010	What's Hot, What's Not: IT Skills You'll Need in 2010, by Stacy Collett, Computerworld, July 17, 2006.
41.	Kazman01	Economic Modeling of Software Architectures, by Rick Kazman, Jai Asundi, and Mark Klein, news@sei interactive, Third Quarter 2001. Available online at www.sei.cmu.edu/news-at-sei/columns/the_architect/2001/3q01/architect-3q01.pdf.
42.	Keen03	Making Technology Investments Profitable: ROI Road Map to Better Business Cases, by Jack Keen and Bonnie Digrius, 2003.
43.	Kleffel2006	Man-Machine Merger Arriving Sooner Than You Think, by Rick Kleffel, NPR. Available online at http://www.npr.org/templates/story/story.php?storyId=5576503

44.	Luftman05	Total Value Of Ownership: A New Model, by Jerry Luftman and Hunter Muller, Optimize, July 2005, Issue 22. Available online at http://www.optimizemag.com/disciplines/financial-management/showArticle.jhtml?articleID=164901577
45.	Lutchen2004	Managing IT as a Business: A Survival Guide for CEOs, by Mark Lutchen, 2004.
46.	Lutchen2005	2005 Financial Services Technical Accounting Forum, Price Waterhouse Coopers. Available online at http://www.pwc.com/images/gx/eng/fs/2005/taf_itspend.pdf
47.	May07	The Elegant Solution: Toyota's Formula for Mastering Innovation, by Matthew May, 2007.
48.	McAfeeHBR06	Mastering the Three Worlds of Information Technology, by Andrew McAfee, Harvard Business Review, November 2006.
49.	McAfeePr06	Introduction to Economic Analysis, by Preston McAfee, 2006. Available online at http://www.introecon.com/.
50.	McDonald06	David McDonald Discusses Finance's Program Management Office, Employee Communications, July 24, 2006.
51.	Meyer98	Trouble Finding Good People? Stop Trying to Hire Them, by Peter Meyer The Business & Economic Review - Fall, 1998. Available online at http://www.meyergrp.com/exec_mgmt_14.html
52.	Murphy02	Achieving Business Value From Technology: A Practical Guide For Today's Executive, by Tony Murphy, Gartner Press, 2002.
53.	Nielsen06	Jeff Nielsen, Chief Scientist, Digital Focus Inc., at a talk at FGM Inc., August 17, 2006.

54.	Nortel2001	Integrating Financial and Strategic Reporting, Corporate Executive Board, Working Council for Chief Financial Officers, March 2001, p. 6.
55.	PinsentMasons06	Publisher In £80,000 Font Raid, OUT-LAW News, 26/06/2006. Available online at http://www.out-law.com/page-7037
56.	Poppendieck03	Lean Software Development: An Agile Toolkit for Software Development Managers, by Mary and Tom Poppendieck, Addison-Wesley, 2003.
57.	Poppendieck06	Implementing Lean Software Development: From Concept to Cash, by Mary and Tom Poppendieck, Addison-Wesley, 2006.
58.	Reifer02	Making the Software Business Case: Improvements by the Numbers, by Donald Reifer, 2002.
59.	Remenyi00	The Effective Measurement and Management Of IT Costs and Benefits, by Dan Remenyi, Arthur Money, and Michael Sherwood-Smith, 2000.
60.	RichDehning06	Analysts' Forecasts and Investments in Information Technology, by Vernon Richardson, Bruce Dehning, and Glenn M. Pfeiffer, International Journal of Accounting Information Systems, September 2006.
61.	Standish06	"The end of the death march", The Guardian, June 22, 2006. Available online at http://technology.guardian.co.uk/weekly/story/0,,1802529,00.html.
62.	SullChalJha97	Software Design Decisions as Real Options, by Kevin Sullivan, Prasad Chalasani, and Somesh Jha. 1997. University of Virginia Department of Computer Science Technical Report 97-14.
63.	Swaine2006	Living with Compliance, by Michael Swaine, Dr. Dobbs Journal, June 2006. Available online at http://ddj.com/dept/architect/188700752.

64. Taub2006   Fed Governor: Sarbox Spurs Cash Jitters, by
                           Stephen Taub, CFO.com, July 18, 2006.

65. TOGAF   The Open Group Architecture Framework,
                           Version 8.1, Enterprise Edition. Available
                           from http://opengroup.org/

66. ValIT   Enterprise Value: Governance Of It
                           Investments – The Val IT Framework

67. VerizonEmail2005   Verizon's E-mail Blockade Leads To
                           Lawsuits, by John Gartner, May 11, 2005,
                           securitypipeline.com. (Available online at
                           http://www.securitypipeline.com/showArticl
                           e.jhtml?articleID=163101524). See also
                           http://www.emailblockingsettlement.com/.

68. WaltersOzzie   Ozzie, Ozzie, Ozzie: chant of change at
                           Microsoft, by Richard Waters, The Australian,
                           June 19, 2006. Available online at
                           http://www.theaustralian.news.com.au/story
                           /0,20867,19509645-36375,00.html.

69. WeillRoss04   IT Governance: How Top Performers
                           Manage IT Decision Rights for Superior
                           Results, by Peter Weill and Jeanne Ross. 2004,
                           Harvard Business School Press.

Index

B

C

D

J

K

L

M

N

O

P

R

S

W

X

www.ingramcontent.com/pod-product-compliance
Lightning Source LLC
Chambersburg PA
CBHW080133060326
40689CB00018B/3773